SURVIVING
WALL STREET

SURVIVING WALL STREET

A TALE OF **TRIUMPH, TRAGEDY** AND **TIMING**

SCOTT L. BOK

Published by John Wiley & Sons, Inc., Hoboken, New Jersey.
Published simultaneously in Canada.

For general information on our other products and services or for technical support, please contact our Customer Care Department within the United States at (800) 762-2974, outside the United States at (317) 572-3993 or fax (317) 572-4002.

Wiley also publishes its books in a variety of electronic formats. Some content that appears in print may not be available in electronic formats. For more information about Wiley products, visit our web site at www.wiley.com.

Library of Congress Control Number: 2025901815

Hardback ISBN: 9781394326693
epub ISBN: 9781394326716
ePDF ISBN: 9781394326723

Cover Design: Wiley
Cover Image: © PPAMPicture/Getty Images
Author Photo: Courtesy of the author

SKY10100161_031825

For Elliot and Jane

CONTENTS

CONTENTS

Contents

PREFACE

The pop artist Andy Warhol is famously associated with the intriguing quip that everyone gets fifteen minutes of fame. Mine came in the autumn of 2023 when I was serving as chairman, a part-time volunteer role, of the board of trustees of the University of Pennsylvania. There I became embroiled in a battle for control of that nearly 300-year-old Ivy League institution. That highly publicized contest marked the start of a period of nationwide campus unrest unlike anything since the Vietnam War protests, drawing intense scrutiny from the media, Wall Street, Congress and the courts.

Having spent a lifetime advising corporations on merger deals, dissident shareholder attacks and assorted boardroom controversies, the nature of that highly publicized contest was familiar to me. The same people–titans of the world of mergers and acquisitions (M&A), private equity and hedge funds–were involved. The same bare-knuckled tactics were utilized. And the same kind of boardroom drama played out.

The only difference was that, at Penn, the stakes were higher than in the typical fight for control of a major corporation. Among the many issues in play were free speech, academic freedom, antisemitism, DEI (diversity, equity and inclusion), "woke-ism" and the role of wealthy Wall Street patrons in the governance of nonprofit institutions.

Ultimately, what I saw at stake was nothing short of the soul of the University–and perhaps by extension the soul of all leading universities.

To understand how this spectacle came to be one must turn the clock all the way back to the beginning of my career. A time when "investment banking"–a field now so prominent that a substantial portion of each graduating class from America's elite universities applies for an entry-level position–was such a small and obscure activity that a new Wharton graduate like me had no knowledge of it. A time when "private equity"–the now familiar name for the ownership vehicle that began as an offshoot of the M&A business and today controls more than 30,000 companies globally–was, like "hedge fund" and "activist shareholder," a term yet to be defined. A time when television coverage of Wall Street stocks and corporate deals was limited to a single thirty-minute weekly show on the Public Broadcasting Network, in sharp contrast to today's full-time business news cable channels Bloomberg, CNBC and Fox Business News.

Wall Street's scale, profile, wealth and power saw explosive growth in the years that followed, with its reach ultimately extending across the entire corporate landscape and into every other aspect of American life, from politics to culture and even to sports.

But the Wall Street story is not one of unrelenting progress. Crises of various ilk are frequent, such that few firms last long in this Darwinian arena. Most firms in this domain end up either forced out of business or subsumed into a more successful competitor. The names of the departed–each of which first enjoyed an extended period of great fortune–are still familiar: Bear Stearns, Dillon Read, Drexel Burnham, E.F. Hutton, First Boston, Kidder Peabody, Lehman Brothers, Paine Webber, Salomon Brothers and Smith Barney, among many others, along with their British equivalents of Baring Brothers, Cazenove, Kleinwort Benson, Morgan Grenfell and Warburgs.

Life for those who lead these firms is even more precarious. Few Wall Street leaders get to their finish line with reputations fully intact.

The overlapping life cycles of Wall Street firms and those who run them drive the evolution, innovation and growth of this ferociously competitive industry.

Here the story of this dynamic and increasingly powerful industry is told through the tumultuous adventure tale of one firm (Greenhill, a pioneering specialist in M&A) and one man (myself, Greenhill's longtime leader), someone who came to Wall Street four decades ago as an eager but naïve new recruit–as thousands like me now do each year–and managed to grab a front-row seat for a period of epic change.

–S.L.B.

CHAPTER ONE

BEFORE THE BEGINNING

You play it the company way.[1]
— *Frank Loesser*, How to Succeed in Business
Without Really Trying

In a speech of less than one-minute told repeatedly over more than two decades at innumerable client meetings and every office holiday party, Greenhill, the man, would describe the founding of Greenhill the business in a few phrases. He wanted to spend all his time with clients rather than managing people. So he launched a new firm with only "a secretary and driver and Gayle [his wife] hanging pictures in the office." Then "people started showing up." Thereafter, as he repeated the story to *Dealmaker* magazine many years later, "We got lucky. Things just kind of happened."[2]

But there is a simplifying myth to the origin story of almost all enterprises. There is *some* truth to such stories but not the whole truth. Likewise, the story of how Robert Greenhill (the man) became Greenhill & Co. (the business) amid a spectacular albeit tumultuous period of expansion on Wall Street and developed into a global publicly traded enterprise of some renown, is more complicated and interesting. It is perhaps even instructive.

As a starting point, it is critical to recognize that the business that exists in financial capitals around the world but is universally referred to as "Wall Street", is a hypercompetitive one. Smart, extremely ambitious people are drawn to that business. There is the potential to create a sizable personal fortune, although those ambitious people routinely overestimate the probability of doing so for themselves. To maximize the money generated for participants, leverage in various forms is utilized, elevating risk. That risk is further exacerbated by the need for each firm continually to evolve to address technological innovations, changing government policies, economic cycles, fluctuating markets and new competitors.

Success in this realm is typically short-lived, and failure can be both sudden and brutal.

The combination of aggressive people who are free to withdraw their talents whenever they choose, high leverage, constant change and volatile markets explains why history is littered with stories of even the most highly regarded firms ultimately collapsing into liquidation or falling into the arms of a rival. Relative to the few dozen significant firms in this business today, many more have disappeared or been swallowed up by the survivors. In one way or another, the success of each of the survivors is born from the failure of others.

Competition within Wall Street firms is often every bit as ferocious as the competition among the rival firms. Just as in the case of star athletes, very few senior executives "go out on top." Even among those few who achieve great success, most end up later failing. Some falter when wrong-footed by a shift in markets or a cleverer competitor. Others are brushed aside by people underneath them who believe they have made a strategic mistake, not kept up with markets, aren't pushing their firm hard enough or have simply held onto their leadership post too long. And even for those whose careers do not end in quiet failure or public humiliation, there are almost inevitably harsh setbacks along the way from which they must attempt to rebound.

"There are no second acts in American lives,"[3] *Great Gatsby* author F. Scott Fitzgerald famously said. That's not completely true of Wall Street, although successful second acts are very rare indeed. It was Robert "Bob" Greenhill's attempt at a second act that led to the creation of Greenhill the firm.

His first act played out at the storied Wall Street firm Morgan Stanley, which was carved out of the esteemed J.P. Morgan bank in 1935 in response to the Depression-era Glass-Steagall Act. That law required the separation of investment banking (various activities related to stock and bond markets) from commercial banking (principally the collection of deposits and making of loans). Morgan Stanley, thus, inherited at birth a commanding position in the investment banking business – the smaller but more dynamic of the two businesses that were separated.

From the start it benefited from being a prestigious brand, yet for many years it remained a remarkably small firm. As the firm was approaching its twenty-fifth anniversary, business writer Martin Mayer noted in the revised edition of his book, *Wall Street: Men and Money,*[4] that Morgan Stanley had a single office, fewer than a dozen partners, ninety-five total employees and only $4.5 million in capital.

The firm's genteel culture was one characterized by integrity, understatement and restraint, rather than the aggressive salesmanship that would come to define Wall Street in the years that followed. Yet its distinguished heritage led it to expect, quite justifiably for many years, to repeatedly win business from America's leading corporations. Its simple mantra was the phrase J.P. Morgan's son Jack uttered not long before Morgan Stanley was created in describing his bank's strategy in Congressional testimony: "…first class business in a first-class way."[5] The belief among Morgan Stanley's partners and staff was that, if they did business in that manner, new opportunities would continue to flow to the firm, thereby solidifying its preeminent position. And indeed, it was the firm, not the individual banker, that was paramount in the Morgan Stanley ethos.

Bob Greenhill was somewhat of an outlier relative to the historic Morgan Stanley culture – one of several men who sought to drag the firm into a new era characterized by increasingly intense competition. As historian Ron Chernow put it in his weighty volume *The House of Morgan*, "Greenhill was that Morgan rarity – a partner who emerges as a distinct personality in the public mind."[6]

Bob joined Morgan Stanley straight out of Harvard Business School in 1962, having earlier graduated from Yale and served in the US Navy. He came from a modest Midwestern background and was not at all a physically imposing man. But his extraordinary energy, indomitable will and love of competition made him a memorable fellow who stood out from the crowd.

The firm of which Bob became a prominent part remained highly prestigious and discreet to the point of secretiveness, as demonstrated by the fact that even decades later (and unlike the two other firms that descended from the original banking house of J.P. Morgan), it refused to sanction a single interview with Chernow for his definitive history, nor even to answer his written inquiry as to why.[7] These characteristics helped secure for Morgan Stanley a position on Wall Street that remained far out of proportion to its size – there still being only thirty-four partners after Bob's class was promoted in 1970. At that time, the firm's perceived importance remained such that the election of new general partners merited a story in *The New York Times*. And so that July Bob and five others, including his Harvard Business School (HBS) classmate and fellow Baker scholar (signifying top 5% of the HBS class) Richard Fisher were profiled in connection with their election to the partnership.[8]

If the world of investment banking has always been a tumultuous one, then the era in which Bob made partner was no exception. What was at stake was later clarified by the ultimate fates of what Chernow identified as that era's three leading firms alongside Morgan Stanley: Kuhn Loeb, which later got swallowed up by Lehman Brothers, which in turn later collapsed into bankruptcy, and First Boston and Dillon Read, which were each later acquired by large Swiss banks and ultimately saw their once respected brands disappear.[9] The major strategic issue of that day, and for the few decades to follow, was the importance of the traditional investment banking business (which involved raising capital by executing stock and bond sales for major corporations and therefore depended on the number and quality of longstanding firm relationships with blue chip clients) versus the trading business (which required more capital, involved greater risk and was seen as less prestigious, even as it rapidly grew in parallel with increasing capital markets activity).

The rivalry between those two businesses originated from the fact that their respective participants tended to be very different sorts of people. Only rarely did an individual move over the course of their career from one business to the other. Bankers tended to think those on the "sales and trading" side of the business were less educated, not particularly hard working, generated revenue only by using copious quantities of firm capital and were prone to taking risk recklessly. In turn, traders tended to think bankers were overeducated elitists who benefited from their social connections and toiled in a business that was neither as profitable nor as scalable as trading. A banker might be scorned as "a good knife and fork man" – in other words, skilled at dining with clients but not useful for much else. Speaking of entertainment, those on the sales and trading side were more likely to bring clients to a sporting event or strip club, while bankers were more likely to bring clients to an exclusive golf club or London's Royal Opera House. Thus bankers and traders were two very different animals that did not always coexist peacefully.

Beyond the growth in the relative importance of the trading business, other changes to the historic investment banking business model were also emerging. As a young partner, Bob was put in charge of a newly formed merger advisory group, initially comprising only four people. What merger advisors would do was advise companies on what businesses to buy or sell (the threshold strategic question), when (a market timing question), how (the tactical question, often complicated by competitors seeking the same target), at what price (the valuation question) and how to finance that purchase price. But over time, the best merger advisors would come to play a role that went far beyond those technical functions. They were able to bring two negotiating parties to agreement employing the kind of "shuttle diplomacy" made famous by the American diplomat Henry Kissinger in various Middle East crises.

At the highest level, they exemplified the Yiddish word *macher*, someone who can make things happen – in other words, a dealmaker.

For many chief executives and their boards of directors, a major acquisition could be the most important decision of their career, and certainly the sale of their company would be that. Yet, while merger advice would turn into a $30 billion annual fee source for Wall Street a few decades later, at that time it was viewed as an innovation simply to charge clients fees at all for such advisory work, rather than treating that as a free service provided to enhance client relationships and thereby garner more stock and bond underwriting assignments.

Stagflation and declining stock markets meant the 1970s were generally a grim period on Wall Street, but the contested and public nature of M&A transactions drew intense press coverage. Both the advisory business and the profile of its principal combatants grew over time. Bob's colorful and aggressive personality was ideally suited to this new business, which came to thrive in the booming markets of the 1980s, when M&A became a sort of competitive sport for corporations and investors. The more that big deals happened, the more everyone was drawn into the game. As Chernow put it, "Greenhill personified the rock-'em, sock-'em style that would characterize Wall Street in the 1980s."[10]

Despite its long history of success, Morgan Stanley began to suffer from the same internal struggles that had long characterized other Wall Street firms. For one, there was a developing tug-of-war between those who wished to remain true to the old Morgan Stanley image as a conservative, client-focused, prestigious but deliberately low-profile firm, and those who felt the need to grow and compete as aggressively as possible to ensure survival and maximize profits in an evolving and increasingly competitive Wall Street. Chernow noted that, by 1983, the latter view was winning, as Morgan Stanley had become "more tense and confrontational than in the old days, full of ambitious overachievers."[11]

With several young partners including Bob jostling to lead the business, the firm followed a Wall Street custom of implementing a compromise solution intended to retain all the competing talent until the next generational change in leadership was required. In a nod to the firm's history that would have been impossible for anyone to object to, the patrician S. Parker Gilbert was named chairman in 1984. Consistent with the firm's history as an old-fashioned partnership, nobody held the title of chief executive officer (CEO).

For a firm still deeply enamored of its illustrious history, one could not imagine a person better suited to lead than Parker. His father, Seymour Parker Gilbert, was a J.P. Morgan partner, US Treasury executive and lawyer whose premature death in 1938 at only age 45 (when Parker was four) was reported in detail on the front page of *The New York Times*.[12] Parker's mother then married founding Morgan Stanley name partner Harold Stanley. And to top that off, Parker's godfather was the other founding name partner, Henry Morgan. However, an impeccable pedigree wasn't his only qualification for the chairman role. Parker had the understated style and calm demeanor of an elder statesman, even though he was only in his early fifties at the time. He did not dominate a room, nor was he someone who liked to hear himself speak. But like the proverbial E.F. Hutton made famous through memorable advertisements of the day, when he spoke, people listened. He was, therefore, in all respects the leader most likely to provide a bridge between Morgan Stanley's past and its future, all while holding together the firm's ambitious senior team.

As the private partnership prepared for its initial public offering (IPO) two years later, it continued its effort to retain all the competing talent by going out of its way to signal that, in fact, it was a four-person management committee who jointly led the firm rather than a single person. Thus, the headline of an obviously engineered *New York Times* article became "The Four Who Guide Morgan Stanley."[13] The story quoted unnamed "insiders" who said the four "operate[d] on a collegial basis, making important decisions by consensus," a claim that, if true, would have made Morgan Stanley an exception to industry norms.

Besides Parker, others in that leadership group included Bob Greenhill, now head of the powerful investment banking division (which included the merger advisory group) and his classmate Richard (Dick) Fisher, who had been named president when Parker became chairman. Fisher didn't have Parker's aristocratic background – he went to William Penn Charter School near Philadelphia on a scholarship before going to Princeton. An early bout with polio meant he used a cane much of the time. But he had Parker's diplomatic style and a polish reflective of the old Morgan Stanley. Rounding out the group of four was the cerebral Lewis Bernard, who was invariably referred to within the firm as the smartest of the group and held the dual distinction of being both the youngest person ever named partner and the first Jewish partner.

As common as uncomfortable shared management schemes are on Wall Street, so also is the short tenure of such arrangements. And so, less than 4 years post the firm's successful IPO, Parker Gilbert retired at the not-so-ripe old age of 56, thereafter devoting his energy to trusteeships with the Morgan Library and Metropolitan Museum of Art, as well as long-time leadership of the exclusive National Golf Links of America in tony

Southampton on Long Island. Dick Fisher was named chairman, Bob Greenhill president, and still there was no chief executive. The two men jointly signed the annual report and important internal memoranda, striving to create the image of a dual-headed business, consistent with the manner in which its archrival Goldman Sachs was managed in that period.

This partnership between two former classmates did not prove to be a stable one. Partly to blame was the fact that Dick hailed from the trading side of the firm, which was growing in scale and importance, while Bob came from the investment banking side, the firm's legacy business. Another factor was that Bob was always laser-focused on doing deals for clients, while Dick was more strategically minded at a time when financial services business models were evolving at great speed. Bob's focus meant he had little interest in management tasks and was often away visiting clients, while Dick was a natural manager and generally at the headquarters running what was an increasingly complex, large and rapidly growing global business.

Consistent with academic finance theory that diversification can provide a smoother stream of profits and thereby reduce risk and increase valuations, Fisher led the firm to expand geographically, scale up its trading business, increase its use of technology and acquire asset management businesses to provide further diversification. At an offsite conference held in suburban Westchester County for all firm officers (those ranked vice president and above), one of the leading bankers of that day for financial services firms presented the valuation metrics for a wide range of firms in that sector.

At the top of the heap was the huge insurer American International Group (AIG), which was seen as having tremendous scale, a highly diversified business, the most stable earnings and therefore the highest valuation metrics among the numerous financial services firms in the stock market. In presenting this analysis to its senior team the firm led by Fisher tried to reach beyond the obvious peer group to an even greater prize. Never mind that AIG would one day fall into almost full ownership by the US government to avert a feared collapse of the financial system. At that moment, it was in a position to aspire to, and thus helped propel the desire for ever-increased scale and diversity of income streams at Morgan Stanley.

By early 1993, Morgan Stanley had grown to 7,500 people broken into ten divisions, signifying the increased complexity of the business. The uneasy partnership at the top was no longer tenable, and so a *New York Times* headline in early March read, "Morgan Stanley Changing Its Leadership."[14] John Mack, a former bond salesman who had been named head of a newly formed global operating committee a year earlier, was named president, and Bob Greenhill was pushed into a "senior advisor" position, a nonmanagement role with a meaningless but frequently used Wall Street title, with which he was to focus entirely on working with clients.

Mack was a charismatic and natural leader, yet far from the prototypical Morgan Stanley senior executive of yesteryear. A former college football player at Duke who came from a Lebanese family, Mack exuded the confident swagger and intimidating power of an athlete who played a physical sport, who wasn't afraid of conflict, in fact perhaps relished it. He had maneuvered skillfully to push aside Bob, who had continued to be regularly on the road with clients and was neither interested in, nor skilled at, office politics.

The *Times* noted that the management move was "a reminder that Morgan Stanley's traditional strength as a financial adviser to large corporations ha[d] been heavily supplemented in the last two decades by its securities sales and trading." A great salesman himself, Mack was well-suited to manage a growing sales and trading business in a bull market, always pushing his team to be more aggressive to win more business.

As always, the firm tried to paper over the conflicts that were readily apparent in the management move. Bob was quoted in the *Times* story with a statement that, while it must have been difficult to say after being stripped of both title and management responsibility, was as true as any he ever spoke: "My greatest satisfaction has come from hands-on direct involvement with clients."

Bob Greenhill was well-known for his relentless focus on dealmaking and disdain for all aspects of management. But even the most junior personnel in the firm knew that he was a highly ambitious man still in his prime who would not remain at the firm long with a lame title like "senior advisor." So it was absolutely no surprise when, a few months later, Bob announced that he was leaving. Nor was it surprising that, to prevent Morgan Stanley from preempting his planned attempt to take key people with him, he waited to make his move until Fisher and Mack were both away from New York, and then refused their request to hold off on the announcement. What *was* a surprise was that he was becoming chairman and chief executive of Smith Barney, a huge retail brokerage firm owned by the conglomerate Primerica controlled by Sandy Weill, the legendary Brooklyn-born financial services dealmaker who was a longtime client and friend of Bob's.

Smith Barney employed a vast army of retail brokers focused on servicing the so-called "mass affluent." It was widely known for its advertising slogan voiced by the British American actor John Houseman: "We make our money the old-fashioned way; we *earn* it." Morgan Stanley-style investment banking was a very small part of Smith Barney's business, and Weill was anxious to change that. Thus the management task Bob took on was far greater than the one he had faced at Morgan Stanley. Moreover, the people he would be managing were largely in a business in which he had no experience.

With a mandate from Sandy Weill and a desire to prove something to Morgan Stanley and to Wall Street generally, Bob set out to build a full-service investment bank. Stories, ultimately proved accurate, quickly emerged of huge pay increases being offered as part of multiyear contracts. In the end, after trying for far more, Bob took about twenty bankers of varying levels from Morgan Stanley. Those he took were typically among the most aggressive of the firm's bankers – those more in Bob's mold than that of Dick Fisher and the old Morgan Stanley.

Notwithstanding the energy (and money) expended in launching a new competitor into the investment banking world, the new venture did not prove a success. Few had expected it would. Less than two years into the effort, a *Times* headline declared that the "Smith Barney unit [was] shaken by infighting."[15] The article explained that Bob's recruits and the legacy Smith Barney bankers had "split into warring factions." Of course, the split related to compensation, a topic that always becomes contentious when a difficult year comes, those with contractual guarantees are unharmed and longer-term employees bear the cost of a shrunken bonus pool.

The Times further reported that, because of the conflict, James (Jamie) Dimon, Sandy's youthful right-hand man and future longtime chief executive of the modern J.P. Morgan, had taken "a more hands-on role at the firm." Later, early in 1996, a year after the internal conflict had first bubbled into the public domain, Greenhill was replaced as head of Smith Barney by Dimon. As when Bob was demoted at Morgan Stanley, the various parties said what needed to be said to save face and protect reputations. Bob was quoted echoing the statement he had made at that time: "Frankly, dragging around the administrative burdens of running a large firm, I'm not made for that."[16] Sandy sounded a similar note, saying he had reluctantly concluded that Bob "could do what he does best outside the company." Meanwhile, Dimon was more circumspect, saying "time will tell" whether the investment in Bob and his team was a good one.

As time passed, the assessment of what had transpired became more candid. Later that year in a profile of Dimon, *Bloomberg* reported that "Dimon's and Weill's initial foray into investment banking proved a chaotic and costly embarrassment."[17] Still later, Weill wrote in his autobiography that "[h]iring Bob Greenhill proved more disruptive to our management process than anyone ever imagined."[18]

The year following Bob's departure, Sandy's financial services conglomerate, by then renamed for its Travelers insurance unit, made another much larger foray into investment banking, this time acquiring the major Wall Street firm Salomon Brothers for $9 billion. And in the year following that, Sandy pulled off another merger – one with banking giant Citicorp. Later that year, further demonstrating the tenuous position of those atop Wall Street firms, Jamie Dimon abruptly resigned as president of the combined business after a falling out with his career-long mentor Sandy.

In the same interview in which Greenhill's departure from Smith Barney was explained, Bob announced, without fanfare, his second attempt at a successful second act to follow his time at Morgan Stanley. *The Wall Street Journal* did not cover the story, and *The Times* and *Bloomberg* noted it only in passing that, at age 59, he would start a new investment banking boutique, Greenhill & Co., along with one young banker who had followed him from Morgan Stanley to Smith Barney. He said he hoped to recruit ten more bankers to his new firm.[19]

As Bob was later fond of reminiscing, soon enough people started showing up.

CHAPTER TWO

I WANT TO BE A PART OF IT

New York, New York!
It's a helluva town![1]
        – Betty Comden and Adolph Green, On the Town

For a few years in the late 1980s, Bob Greenhill and I both worked in Morgan Stanley's New York headquarters on Sixth Avenue. But to my recollection we never actually met, never even shared an elevator. We were a full generation apart in age, and when I transferred away from that office I was a lowly "associate" while Bob was president of the firm. By the time I returned he was gone. So the fact that, years later, we ended up partnering in his eponymous new venture was far from preordained. Indeed, the fact that I ever found my way to Wall Street at all is surprising.

Throughout my adult life countless people have assumed that I was born to privilege as the son of Harvard University's long-serving president Derek Bok. We share an unusual Dutch surname, have a common background in the legal profession, each have a connection to the city of Philadelphia and are of the right age differential for him to be my father. That Bok, whom I have never met, came from a publishing family of late nineteenth-century prominence whose titles included *Ladies Home Journal* and *The Saturday Evening Post*.[2]

My family history is considerably less illustrious. On my father's side, my grandfather Mathys Bok was a Dutch immigrant carpenter who passed through Ellis Island as a 16-year-old along with his numerous siblings in 1926, more than half a century after Derek Bok's grandfather made that same transatlantic journey. On my mother's side, my Scotch-Irish grandfather Benjamin Kennedy left Oklahoma with his young family in 1941 and headed north, having missed the Dust Bowl-era migration west a few years earlier that was chronicled in John Steinbeck's *Grapes of Wrath*. Both men settled near Grand Rapids, Michigan, then a small but prosperous town known for its many furniture makers and large population of Dutch immigrants and their descendants.

In the late 1950s my father dropped out of high school to take a job with Michigan Bell Telephone as a lineman, a blue-collar job climbing telephone poles that was immortalized first by a 1948 Norman Rockwell painting and again, a couple decades later, by the song *Wichita Lineman*, a country classic made famous by singer Glen Campbell. He would remain at what everyone then referred to simply as "the telephone company" for 35 years. And he made a similarly youthful decision, and over the six decades to follow would show even greater loyalty, regarding his marriage – meeting and marrying my mother while she was still in high school. I arrived in 1959, when she was only 18.

My upbringing – in Gerald Ford's Congressional district – was middle class, Midwestern, small town, Republican, Protestant Christian, conservative in every sense, safe and secure, but largely uneventful. To explore the larger world, I read a lot, particularly biographies of political, business and sports heroes. In 1971, my sixth-grade year, my father grabbed the opportunity to make some extra overtime pay by answering Bell Telephone's call for linemen willing to travel to New York City for several months to help deal with an overwhelming work backlog. He had done similarly many times in the past, typically going off to some Midwestern location that had suffered an ice storm or other natural disaster to help accelerate phone service restoration.

I was able to visit my dad in New York once, for a week. There I tasted my first real pizza, went to the top of the Empire State Building and saw The Rockettes perform at Radio City Music Hall, directly across Sixth Avenue from my current office location in Rockefeller Center. Notwithstanding that it was then a grimy and dangerous place hurtling toward an existential fiscal crisis, I returned home determined that I would one day live in New York.

In my senior year of high school, I pored over *Barron's* catalogue of colleges and, sight unseen, chose the Wharton School at the University of Pennsylvania. A business degree from the Ivy League school founded by the pragmatic polymath Benjamin Franklin sounded more practical than the alternatives. In the fall of my freshman year there I made my first return visit to New York City, this time on a university-sponsored bus along with my next-door neighbor from the nearly century-old dormitory known as the Quad. We bought half-price tickets at the TKTS booth in Times Square for the very last row of the highest balcony for the relatively new and widely acclaimed musical *A Chorus Line*.

While that marked the very inauspicious start to what would in years to come become a passion for theater, at that point my primary passion was writing for the daily campus newspaper. I wrote numerous stories but was ultimately passed over for the editor-in-chief role, which probably saved me from a career in journalism. More immediately, that disappointment created space in my schedule that was partly filled by my appointment as student liaison to the university's board of trustees, which four decades later I would come to chair. Academically, I focused mostly on a liberal arts degree given my interest in history and political philosophy, doing only the bare minimum needed to get the Wharton diploma that would prove to be a validating credential when I later entered the business world.

Despite my Wharton degree, I did not start out focused on a career in business. For bright children of middle-class Midwestern parents in that era, there were two professional careers to aspire to: doctor or lawyer. "Finance" did not seem like a promising alternative with the Dow Jones Industrial Average below the 1,000 threshold that it had first crossed more than a decade earlier and short-term interest rates at the previously unheard-of level of 20%. When I graduated, I did not even know the definition of "investment banker," then a small profession seemingly reserved for the offspring of well-connected families in the northeast.

Squeamish at the sight of blood, I saw the law as my path. I did well enough on the standardized admissions test to get into Penn's Law School, which I began a week after marrying an undergraduate classmate, a Jersey girl in madras shirts and tight jeans who had randomly moved in across the hall in my coed dormitory. A junior year transfer, Roxanne was straight out of Bruce Springsteen country and described herself as a "bit of a hippie," making for quite a contrast with the straitlaced Brooks Brothers wannabe from the Midwest that I was.

Working my way through law school, I initially aspired to a position at one of the prestigious old "white shoe" New York law firms. I saw myself as a litigator, not really having a sense of what a corporate lawyer actually did. Then one day, as I was starting to think about internships for the summer before my last year of law school, I received in the mail a torn-out magazine article from Jamie Dinan, a Wharton classmate from Worcester, Massachusetts, who five years earlier had accompanied me on my Manhattan bus trip. He was then working as a New York investment banking analyst and would later go on to create a highly successful hedge fund and own a piece of a championship NBA basketball team.

The article was about Marty Lipton and Joe Flom, the two leading lawyers in the field of mergers and acquisitions, commonly referred to as

"M&A." Both were leaders of relatively young, upstart, predominantly Jewish, New York law firms, benefitting from the fact that the city's older, more prestigious firms had been slow to pursue this new specialty. In the margin Jamie had scrawled, "you should work for one of these guys."

One of the visiting professors at Penn Law at that time was Harvey Pitt, previously general counsel and later chairman of the Securities and Exchange Commission (SEC). He taught a course on M&A. On the first day of class, he introduced us to the topic: "Some people question whether M&A is good for companies, whether M&A is good for the economy, whether M&A is good for society. For purposes of this course, suffice it to say that M&A is good for lawyers." It was a humorous opening line, and of course he was right.

Focusing on the two law firm choices Jamie had recommended, I chose Wachtell, Lipton, Rosen & Katz for a summer internship. I had given some thought to remaining in Philadelphia, but the Wachtell recruiting partner informed me that, "if you want to play in the NFL you have to come to New York." I wanted to play in the legal profession's version of the National Football League. And I liked the fact that Wachtell was largely focused on only one aspect of law (M&A), perennially the most profitable law firm per partner in America and modest in size. Including my entering first-year class, it would have only 66 lawyers in total, a fraction of the size of Joe Flom's firm and other leading New York firms.

The combination of small-scale, unrivaled work ethic and a focus on complex, fast-moving and high-profile projects made Wachtell seem like a very special place – a sort of nerdy version of the Navy SEALs unit. A summer characterized by working around the clock, interspersed with lavish meals at the finest restaurants in Manhattan as the firm's partners wooed my classmates and me, made it feel even more that way. Accordingly, at the end of my internship I eagerly accepted a full-time offer and declared that I would join the litigation group.

Weeks later I was back in Philadelphia for my final year of law school, which I was paying for by spending thirty hours a week at what seemed like a generous $16 per hour, writing litigation briefs at the large local firm Duane Morris & Heckscher. The lawyer I worked for was only a handful of years ahead of me but would later become longtime managing partner of what over time became a 750-lawyer firm. When I told him of my plans he advised a change of course: "I'd do corporate [in other words, M&A] rather than litigation. Then you have the option of later moving to investment banking." I had never thought of that possibility, but during my summer internship had at least started to figure out what an investment banker was. So based on that advice I quickly called back Wachtell's recruiting partner and asked if I could switch to the corporate department. The answer was an easy yes. Corporate was the essence of Wachtell Lipton and yet, strangely enough, everyone else in my entering class had chosen ancillary specialties like tax, litigation or antitrust.

I loved my time at Wachtell, working insane hours but finding it exhilarating to play a role in contentious corporate takeover battles that were routinely covered on the front page of *The Wall Street Journal*. I worked on assignments where we faced off against some of the highest profile "raiders" (or "takeover entrepreneurs," depending on your philosophical perspective) of that era: Sir James Goldsmith, Carl Icahn and T. Boone Pickens. While the latter two would have careers that extended far longer, Goldsmith in particular dazzled me with his posh British accent, flamboyant style and quick boardroom retort when told by a Wachtell partner that our client, San Francisco-based paper company Crown Zellerbach, was offering him a fair deal: "I don't want a fair deal; I want a good deal."

At one point I was assigned a stint working for a partner who had come to Wachtell from the highly prestigious and much-older Cravath, Swaine & Moore firm. He was a rarity in that he was not homegrown. This fellow had a peculiar, somewhat imperious style compared to other Wachtell partners. I could not bear working with him, and ultimately neither could his partners – I heard later that they made an extraordinary move, pushing him out of the firm for authoring a book that was seen as breaching firm confidentiality. So, in the summer of 1986, a booming time for M&A deals, I answered a headhunter's call and interviewed with Morgan Stanley and Drexel Burnham Lambert. Drexel was a pioneer in "junk bonds" (i.e. those issued by companies of riskier credit quality) and the highflier of the moment, while Morgan Stanley represented the old school Wall Street elite.

Drexel was a true innovator in financial markets, and it produced breathtaking sums of money for its partners. The annual compensation for its most prominent executive, Wharton MBA Michael Milken, was reportedly in the hundreds of millions of dollars. Not surprisingly for a firm generating that kind of money, it was known for its highly aggressive approach to business. In furtherance of that reputation, in May 1986, just as I was finishing my second year at Wachtell, Drexel M&A banker Dennis Levine was arrested on insider trading charges. Shortly thereafter, he pled guilty and agreed to cooperate with the government in uncovering other insider trading culprits. Insider trading was the cardinal sin for those who worked on Wall Street, as it involved using – essentially stealing – a client's confidential information in relation to a potential corporate deal to make highly profitable, but also highly illegal, personal investments. To a naive young man from small-town Michigan who started out wanting to be a courtroom litigator, the Levine case played out as an exciting real-life crime drama.

Later that summer I found myself working in the wee hours of a morning at one of the financial printers based downtown, as young lawyers in that day did, to finalize transaction documents. Back in the pre-email era someone had to fly to Washington and hand deliver such papers to the SEC. As dawn approached there was one last item for which we needed a sign off from the partner in charge, Ilan Reich. Ilan was a brilliant but quirky thirtysomething M&A wizard – I once walked into his office to find him gluing together dozens of the small Lucite "deal toys" that we routinely received as mementoes of completed transactions. He was creating a bizarre sort of sculpture for his office.

The junior lawyer group down at the printer called Ilan's office throughout the morning hours, only to be repeatedly told by his assistant that he was unavailable. It seemed inconceivable that Ilan would be so busy that he could not give us the critical final approval required for us to send our client's document to Washington in time for a filing deadline. We finally pressed the assistant as to whom Ilan was meeting with, seeking some clue as to what the source of the hold up was. She finally provided the names of several Wachtell litigation partners who had one thing in common: they had each worked as federal prosecutors before joining the firm.

Turned out Ilan was being grilled by his partners. He was part of Levine's network and would soon be arrested and ultimately sent to prison. Having never known anyone who was arrested for a misdemeanor, let alone sent to prison for a felony, I was flabbergasted. This whole episode thus served as an early reminder to not be too single-minded in my pursuit of Wall Street fame and fortune.

As I pondered my career options, that August I went on a weekend trip with Roxanne to the New Jersey shore near where her parents lived. On the way to Island Beach State Park we stopped to pick up Sunday's *New York Times*, as was our custom. As if to help me make my decision, the cover story of the *Sunday Times Magazine* was titled, "Leaving the Law for Wall Street; The Faster Track."[3] Much as the story validated the decision I was about to make, I worried that it would make me look like an opportunist following a hot trend rather than someone making a thoughtful career decision. I also worried that the story might flush out other talented young lawyers aspiring to be bankers, creating more competition for limited available slots.

I was able to proceed nonetheless. I chose Morgan Stanley on the advice of wise friends, and nine weeks after that magazine article was published walked into the firm's headquarters in the Exxon Building on Sixth Avenue (right across Fiftieth Street from my current office) as a new associate.

Being a rare Wharton graduate who never took a single corporate finance course, I spent my two weeks between jobs having a friend teach me how to use Lotus 1-2-3 (the primary software used for financial modeling those days) and reading cover to cover the relevant introductory textbook of that era, *Principles of Corporate Finance.*[4]

My choice of Morgan Stanley, which in an initial public offering earlier that year had transitioned from a private firm to a publicly traded company, was fortuitous. Less than four weeks after my move, the Levine insider trading case further expanded when Ivan Boesky, a prominent but controversial merger arbitrageur (i.e. he specialized in investing in corporate takeover targets), was arrested and agreed to pay a $100 million fine. The case later expanded even further to implicate others, including the head of Drexel's M&A group. This growing scandal was one in a series of events that culminated in the bankruptcy and disappearance of Drexel less than four years later.

This chain of events was my first indication that General George Patton's famous dictum borrowed from ancient Rome that "all glory is fleeting" certainly applied to Wall Street.

Although I had not even known what an investment banker was when I graduated from Wharton five years earlier, by the time I became one the profession had risen to a remarkable place of prominence in the public imagination. In my last year as a lawyer I read with great interest the lengthy *Sunday Times Magazine* excerpt from Ken Auletta's *Greed and Glory on Wall Street*[5] – the gripping tale of the power struggle at the top of Lehman Brothers. And in the early days of my investment banking career Tom Wolfe's epic novel *The Bonfire of the Vanities* and Oliver Stone's equally seminal film *Wall Street* – both cautionary tales, albeit riveting ones – found broad audiences. At the same time Michael Lewis was working on the trading floor at Salomon Brothers gathering material for *Liar's Poker*, his entertaining tale of the "Big Swinging Dicks"[6] of Wall Street trading floors.

I ended up spending ten years at Morgan Stanley. For about half of that I was based in London, and on top of my making as many as 150 flights a year across the English Channel to visit various clients Roxanne and I managed to find time for at least a weekend visit to nearly every interesting European destination while also accumulating a huge pile of playbills from the numerous West End plays and musicals we enjoyed.

From my expatriate perch in London, I watched the power struggle at the top of Morgan Stanley play out. It had been clear to me for some time that there was a war being waged between investment banking and trading – between the old Morgan Stanley and the new – between Bob Greenhill and John Mack. But even though I sat in the part of the firm overseen by Greenhill, I didn't feel like I had a dog in what was a fight between two men whom I did not really know. From across the ocean and far down the organization chart, they both seemed impressive to me; Bob for his dealmaking skills and Mack for his inspirational leadership.

While Greenhill was most at home in a CEO's office or intimate board-room setting and disliked speechmaking, Mack reveled in such opportuni-ties. I once watched him speak at a firm offsite gathering, following comments from Lord (Gordon) Richardson, the elderly and distinguished former head of the Bank of England and then sort of an honorary chair of the firm's inter-national business. As Mack finished to a raucous round of applause I enthu-siastically exclaimed to the fellow vice president next to me, "That was like watching Winston Churchill followed by Bear Bryant!", referring to the revered University of Alabama football coach of my youth.

Two years after Mack was handed Greenhill's president title Roxanne and I returned to New York with our six-week-old baby boy Elliot in tow. Months later, at the age of 36, I was promoted to managing director ("MD" for short), the corporate equivalent of the former partner title. There were vestiges of the elite old private partnership that remained in what was now a public firm, and I certainly found that appealing. The dinner to welcome new MDs was held at the legendary financier Pierpont Morgan's elegant library, now a museum in midtown Manhattan, and Roxanne and I got to sit at Mack's table.

I had come a long way from Grand Rapids.

However, things at Morgan Stanley were changing fast. While the firm was still relatively small when I joined, by the late 1980s it added around 1,000 new people annually as it aggressively pushed into new businesses. One of my mentors, a fellow reminiscent of the grumpy but wise old broker that Hal Holbrook played in Oliver Stone's movie, remarked that investment banking, once the entirety of the firm, had become "the hood ornament on the Mercedes." The large and lucrative – but riskier – trading business was the engine. In an even more colorful metaphor, he said investment banking was the hot dog stand in front of the casino. "No matter how good your hot dogs are, no matter how many hot dogs you sell, all that counts is what kind of day the boys in the casino [in other words, the trading floor] are having," he would say.

As if to underline the rapidly changing nature of the firm, in February 1997 I received an unprecedented early morning call at home summoning me to an urgent meeting of all managing directors prior to the daily opening of trading markets. Obviously something big was happening. In what *The Wall Street Journal* would call a "stunning move,"[7] Morgan Stanley was merging with Dean Witter, a much less prestigious retail-oriented Wall Street firm that competed with Smith Barney, the firm that Bob Greenhill had left Morgan Stanley to run. It had 8,500 stockbrokers, and until recently had been owned by mass-market retailer Sears Roebuck.

The combination of the two businesses would create the largest securities firm in the US. However, bigger was not necessarily better, at least from my perspective. *The New York Times* declared that the combined firm would face "the stiff challenge of integrating Morgan Stanley's aristocratic culture ... with the meat-and-potatoes environment at Dean Witter."[8] I saw it the same way. I struggled to envision myself at a firm of such scale, where what I did would feel like an insignificant role in an ancillary business.

I wanted to be part of something more significant than a hood ornament.

CHAPTER THREE

UP, UP AND AWAY

I'm flying
(Flying, flying, flying)
Look at me way up high[1]

– *Carolyn Leigh*, Peter Pan

B ob Greenhill's launch of his new firm was not deliberately planned. He was a dealmaker, not a manager, let alone an entrepreneur. He would have scoffed at the notion of a "business plan," and there was no time to develop one anyway. Long simmering tension between Bob and Jamie Dimon had boiled over, resulting in Bob's abrupt departure from Smith Barney. The notion of retirement for Bob at that point would have been inconceivable to anyone who knew him. He had too much energy and work was at the center of his life. So, what to do next?

Bob's sudden exit meant he had not been able to engineer a simultaneous move to another major organization. It's hard to imagine he would have wanted to do that anyway after two of what must have been somewhat painful big firm experiences. And given the messy outcomes at Morgan Stanley and Smith Barney one suspects that major investment banks would have been reluctant to try to fit Bob into an existing management hierarchy anyway. While a smaller firm with less need for management infrastructure might have been more appealing, the numerous so-called investment banking "boutiques" that would proliferate in years to come had not yet materialized. So it seemed natural that Bob would set up his own firm, named after himself, focused on what he loved: doing deals.

But who would join Bob in his new enterprise? The Smith Barney adventure was a brief and publicly visible failure, even if it was highly lucrative for Bob and some of his compatriots. Those at Morgan Stanley who were most loyal to Bob had followed him to Smith Barney. But under the terms of very generous separation arrangements he had agreed to with Sandy Weill, Bob was strictly prohibited, with only one exception, from bringing any of those individuals with him to his new venture. As for those who had worked with Bob but were still at Morgan Stanley, if they could not be lured away for the generous multiyear contracts Sandy had authorized Bob to offer in 1993, what were the odds they could be drawn to a small start-up operation where there were no such guarantees, particularly in a robust investment banking market in which paydays at Morgan Stanley were very attractive? Finding talent on the rest of Wall Street was a possibility, but Bob had few close relationships there given he had spent a near lifetime at one firm.

Given the recruiting challenges and the need for some critical mass of talent to win and execute large and complex M&A assignments Greenhill, the firm, got off to a relatively slow start. In its first year it received little publicity and added only one senior banker. That fellow, Bob's first partner in the new venture, was a real estate specialist from Morgan Stanley. He was not a traditional M&A banker but had previously done an administrative stint for Bob when he was running investment banking at Morgan Stanley.

Bob also attracted a couple junior bankers in their late twenties: Jeff Buckalew, a lanky, easygoing North Carolinian from Salomon Brothers who would become a favorite golfing partner for Bob; and John Liu, a soft-spoken Korean immigrant who joined from Wolfensohn, a small investment bank set up in the early 1980s by James Wolfensohn, who had left his eponymous firm a year before to head the World Bank. There were also a few junior financial analysts fresh out of college as well as a couple of executive assistants and an accountant to keep the books. This initial team was under a dozen people in total.

With little experienced talent in place Greenhill & Co. did not have a typical Wall Street client marketing effort. And given his peripatetic nature Bob did not have a stable of loyal clients upon which to rely. However, he did have a prodigious reputation. As he frequently said of those early days, his business development strategy was to "wait for the phone to ring," as it undoubtedly would for someone with his stature as a dealmaker. In his first year of business, an active period for M&A generally, the phone rang twice with major transaction assignments. One was to advise Hughes Electronics – a business once owned by the eccentric business magnate Howard Hughes – on its $3.9 billion acquisition of satellite communications firm PanAmSat. The other was to advise a special committee of the board of Genetics Institute when its majority owner, a pharmaceutical company, exercised a contractual option to acquire the remaining 40% interest in that company.

Shortly after the firm's first anniversary in February 1997, Bob attracted his first senior M&A banker to join as a partner – Tim George, a classic relationship banker who had led Morgan Stanley's client coverage group for food and beverage companies. Tim was in his mid-forties and had worked alongside Bob for such clients as global drinks business Diageo, which they had helped create by advising on the merger of the British companies Guinness and Grand Metropolitan before the combined company was renamed.

While Tim and I had not done much together, we had teamed up a year earlier on the $500 million sale of the American cracker and cookie business Keebler Foods by its British owner. On the day he resigned and left Morgan Stanley Tim stopped by my office to say goodbye, and I mentioned that I had always been intrigued by the notion of joining a boutique firm focused entirely on advising corporate clients on M&A.

Given this was back in the day when bankers were not constrained by the restrictive noncompete agreements that later became *de rigueur*, Tim started work at Greenhill the very next business day and must have immediately mentioned my parting comment to Bob. As a result the phone in my office rang early that morning. As I would learn was his custom, Bob got straight to the point: "I'd like you to have dinner with my wife, Gayle, and me tonight. Can you come out to Greenwich?"

We met for an early dinner at La Crémaillère, a French country restaurant just across the New York state line from Greenwich, where the Greenhills lived. This first brief exchange told me several things about a man I knew only by his legendary reputation. First, Bob had a powerful innate bias toward action. He was never one to make a "to-do" list. If someone suggested some step, like Tim suggesting he reach out to me, he would act immediately. Based on later experience, he was likely shouting to his assistant to get me on the phone before Tim had even finished explaining who I was. Second, his partner in business as much as in life was Gayle. She devoted herself to Bob's success at Morgan Stanley, Smith Barney and now at his new start-up firm, always ready to help entertain clients or staff. Universally well liked, her warm personality made up for Bob's often brusque, "all business" manner. Third, he started work each day early, but unless he was out of town with clients aimed to be back home in Greenwich for dinner and an early bedtime.

In innumerable recruiting discussions to come I would learn that a successful recruitment occurs only when there is a "push" and a "pull." On the surface, the "push" for me was not obvious. Despite a degree of management turmoil and the pending merger with Dean Witter, Morgan Stanley was still a highly prestigious place to work, with one of the top M&A franchises. I had successfully served in its two primary offices. Furthermore, I had recently done a stint as "operations officer," helping the M&A group head manage the day-to-day activities of that global business, typically an indication of high-future potential for a rising banker. On top of that, I had just received my annual compensation news for 1996: $2.5 million for my first year as a managing director, about double my previous best compensation level. Finally, despite a couple sizable bonuses, I had accumulated little wealth, had a wife and one-year-old son at home and knew any start-up business would be risky. There were thus many reasons to stay where I was.

On the other hand, while my compensation would seem extraordinary to future generations of junior MDs, in those heady days of an increasingly frenzied M&A market the adequacy of bonuses was routinely questioned almost regardless of their size. In my case expectations had been high given that year I had led a massive restructuring of the nearly bankrupt Irish company GPA (formerly Guinness Peat Aviation), the world's largest owner and lessor of aircraft, resulting in an innovative $4 billion debt refinancing of its fleet. That deal generated what I was told was the largest investment banking fee in Morgan Stanley history to date – more than $30 million.

More importantly, prior to the big merger announcement there had been yet another reshuffling of investment banking division leadership. Joseph Perella, a prominent senior banker brought in laterally by John Mack to fill the void Bob had left as a "name" player in the M&A game, had won out over my boss, who was then nudged aside from his M&A department leadership role. Most important of all, I was deeply troubled by the just-announced Dean Witter merger, which I feared would fundamentally alter the character of the firm and further diminish the relative importance of the area in which I worked.

As we sat down for that first meal Bob spoke few words but radiated unbridled confidence in his fledgling venture. The market environment was one of great optimism at that time, as indicated by Federal Reserve Chief Alan Greenspan's much discussed "irrational exuberance"[2] warning in relation to booming markets just two months earlier. In any event, I soon learned that Bob was always an outlier on that metric.

Over suburban New York's finest French food, I described to Bob what appealed to me: the potential for a throwback to Wall Street firms of yesteryear – a small, elite organization focused entirely on advising clients on important strategic deals. A firm with a substantial team in New York and another in London, which was a growing base for European mergers and my home until only 18 months earlier. The investment banking equivalent of my prestigious former law firm, Wachtell Lipton. Something like what Wolfensohn could have been, had Jim Wolfensohn been more focused on building an enduring institution than on public service. A successor to the old Morgan Stanley as that firm veered off toward serving small retail investors rather than major corporations.

By time dessert was on the table Gayle put her hand on my arm and said, "You're going to love working with Bob." The deal was effectively sealed at that moment.

Anyone who had worked with Bob knew he was relentless in moving swiftly to signing a deal, and some would say that he was happier than most to make whatever compromises were required to get to that point as quickly as possible. Accordingly, I received an offer letter the very next day. I promptly responded with various concerns, including requesting several amendments to the lengthy partnership operating agreement that he had worked out with his first partner just months before. In crafting my response to the detailed documents, I acted as my own lawyer, and Lincoln's famous quip that I thus had a fool for a client was probably right. Fortunately, Bob said yes to everything I asked. In any event, those initial terms would be revised several more times in the years to come. In the final contract I signed only four days after our dinner, I was promised a $12,000 monthly draw (effectively a salary), a guaranteed total cash compensation for the first year of $1.4 million and an equity ownership interest in the firm of 9.8%.

As a purchase price, or "capital contribution" to create a tax basis for my ownership stake, I wrote a check to the firm for $5,000 in what would prove the best investment I would ever make. In a sign of good things to come, it was clear throughout this brief negotiation that Bob's personal economics were not his priority. He already had plenty of money, although that would not have stopped most in his position from wanting even more. He cared far more about building a successful firm where he would have the necessary infrastructure and support to do what he enjoyed. In any event, I learned over time that he hated any kind of compensation negotiations, so he was always quick to settle. Thus in my first partial year at the firm he ended up paying me more than either my guaranteed dollar minimum or my percentage ownership interest required. And contrary to absorbing any dilution as more partners joined, my percentage ownership remained at about this same circa 10% level as we grew from the initial four partners up to twenty-three over the next several years.

Agreeing to join Greenhill was only the first step in my move. Next was resigning from Morgan Stanley, a firm that prided itself on "turning people around" and convincing them to remain onboard after an attempted resignation. What was not obvious to a young man at the time but clear in retrospect is that the threat of my departure raised issues that went far beyond my individual importance as a still relatively junior banker. The firm had just announced the huge merger with Dean Witter, and there was clearly some degree of anxiety over how the firm's "aristocratic" senior bankers would react to the surprising combination with what was seen as a much more pedestrian retail firm.

That's why my intentionally friendly three-sentence resignation letter, stating truthfully that I had "greatly enjoyed my more than 10 years" at the firm, garnered immediate attention from the firm's leadership.

Newly appointed investment banking head Joe Perella soon burst into my office. We did not yet know each other well. While he generally had a warm albeit quirky manner, his immediate reaction was emotional – shouting, arm waving and finger pointing. Taller even than my 6'2" frame, his lanky build and improbably long arms made for a disconcerting moment as I was trying to quietly pack up my belongings.

"You had better not be taking any of our people!" I assured him I had no such intention, and in fact I did not. But I did find his moralistic tone ironic given he himself had pulled off one of the biggest personnel raids in banking history. In 1988 he and M&A legend Bruce Wasserstein had led a veritable exodus from the major investment bank First Boston to form a new firm. The catalyst for that was a strategic dispute over the recurring Wall Street issue that had led to John Mack's ascendance over Bob Greenhill: the importance of investment banking versus trading.

Nobody who knew me would have thought that such an aggressive approach would turn me around. So next the firm wheeled out Dick Fisher, someone I greatly admired and who was still chairman for another few months, for a one-on-one breakfast in his private dining room. Dick had just signed up a gigantic merger to create the world's largest securities firm. As part of that deal, he would soon give up his management position and essentially retire to a part-time board of directors' role.

While Fisher clearly had a lot on his mind and was gearing up to start a new chapter of life unrelated to Morgan Stanley, he found the time for a relaxed and reflective discussion on the firm's behalf. Despite his knowing Bob for 25 years longer than I had, and without revealing a hint of the battles they must have fought, he took his usual understated, diplomatic approach, speaking ill of no one. "You and Bob are very different" was his boldest statement in response to my plans, stated with a tone that suggested he was leaving much unsaid. I was soon to learn that he was absolutely right: Bob and I were fundamentally different in nearly every respect. But on the theory that different can mean complementary, I pressed ahead.

On the last day of February 1997 I arrived for my first day in the very modest space Bob had sublet on West 52nd Street from Deutsche Bank via a former Morgan Stanley protégé who had moved to Deutsche after Bob left for Smith Barney. Including myself and Bob we would have four partners and fewer than a dozen professionals in total yet would naively feel ready to compete with century-old firms with thousands of employees and multibillion-dollar balance sheets. In our favor we had a brand name that – thanks to Bob's "rock-'em, sock-'em style" – had already been associated with large and contentious corporate mergers in the public's eye for twenty-five years, virtually the entire history of M&A as a meaningful activity. And, apart from our talent, ambition, desks and phones, we had one asset that would serve as both a means of transportation and an enduring symbol of our firm: a Citation jet aircraft.

The firm's Citation VII was not very old yet already scheduled to soon be traded in for a model X (referred to shorthand as a "Ten"), a new $16 million aircraft that was produced by Textron, one of the firm's early clients. The pilot for both aircraft was Bob himself (always along with a professional copilot, as two were required for such a jet). He had first learned to fly later in life so that he could get to and from his summer home in Nantucket more efficiently.

Fitting for Bob's hard-charging personality, the Ten was the fastest private aircraft in the world, flying at near the speed of sound. Only some military jets and the supersonic Concorde operated by British Airways and Air France were faster. But as Bob unfailingly pointed out, he could get to London from Greenwich faster than via Concorde if one factored in airport transit time. The first Ten had been delivered just months after the firm was formed, to none other than the celebrated golfer and amateur pilot Arnold Palmer, and only seven were delivered in all of 1996.[3] Our new firm got ours shortly after my arrival, financed by Bob, who took an additional preferred equity stake in the firm as compensation for providing the necessary capital infusion to pay for the plane.

The aircraft's novelty, its rarity, its speed and the fact that Bob personally piloted it were the icebreakers for nearly every client meeting. One cannot overestimate the impact that opening would have on a prospective new client in Houston, San Francisco or Basel, Switzerland. It particularly resonated with those with an engineering background as well as with a much larger group: those enamored of expensive toys. As was repeatedly evident, one thing almost all large company CEOs have in common is that they love their airplanes. And none had one as fast as our Ten. Some had larger ones, like the more luxurious Gulfstreams, but Bob dismissed those slower vehicles as mere "flying living rooms."

The special characteristics of our unique airplane helped create just the right image for our firm: high energy, fast moving, using the latest technology, of an intrepid nature and associated with success. As our new firm took off with an exuberance that was undoubtedly irrational to some degree, we had given little thought to where exactly we might be going. We were confident, however, that we had what it would take to get us there at great speed.

CHAPTER FOUR

MOVING FAST

ABC.
A–Always. B–Be. C–Closing.[1]

– David Mamet, Glengarry Glen Ross

ll substantial companies aim to develop a carefully honed brand image and a clear business strategy, and the great ones achieve that. But there is typically much trial and error before they get there. Mark Zuckerberg famously described Facebook's early strategy as "move fast and break things,"[2] essentially having a bias in favor of action and a willingness to launch numerous different initiatives to see what works, even if that means there will be some messes to clean up along the way. The "moving fast" part of that slogan certainly applied to the early days of Greenhill, and while nothing significant got broken we did try many different things, and had to do a bit of clean up, before settling on a winning strategy.

Initially, we devoted no time at all to the basic stylistic questions related to branding. Rather, we took the simplistic and somewhat cheeky approach of mimicking our shared alma mater Morgan Stanley. The typeface of our first logo and business cards was an exact replica of that on my just-retired Morgan Stanley card. Soon, however, we realized that our materials should have their own distinct look and changed to something more modern. After all, we were a start-up with a somewhat novel business model, not a decades-old institution bound by tradition.

More important than such superficial matters was that, in all our interactions with clients, the press and others, we strived to fully inherit the mantle of the historic Morgan Stanley – the small, elite, client-focused firm that it was when Bob was made partner in the early 1970s. Bob's brief interlude at Main Street brokerage firm Smith Barney did not fit the desired narrative, so it was rarely mentioned and largely erased from our pedigree. It was helpful that the four original partners of our firm were all long-time Morgan Stanley bankers, with more than seventy years of service amongst them, while the single person Bob had been allowed to take from Smith Barney had already been ushered out before I arrived. This was the first of what would be continual personnel adjustments as the firm evolved.

It was also helpful that Morgan Stanley was to some degree vacating, or at least diluting, its historic position as a leading advisor to major corporate clients. It did so first by the major expansion of its principal trading activities in the 1980s, then by a couple large acquisitions in the asset management space in the early 1990s and finally by the huge merger with retail brokerage firm Dean Witter. With respect to that merger, it was particularly helpful that the combined firm would be led by Phillip Purcell from the Dean Witter side, while Dick Fisher, the last leader whose values and style exuded the old Morgan Stanley, stepped down.

The initial pitch that Greenhill was the logical heir to Morgan Stanley's coveted M&A franchise, with some of its most experienced bankers having decamped there and perhaps more to follow, sold well to prospective clients. As a result, the firm quickly developed strong momentum in winning assignments that both generated significant revenue and provided valuable credentials for further such wins. In fact, despite that the four partners had not even been fully assembled until that year was well under way, 1997 turned out to be a remarkable year in terms of transaction advisory roles.

Our completed deals that first year reflected an eclectic collection of projects, which perfectly suited my background. While most advisors succeed as narrow specialists in a particular area, I had been a lawyer as well as a banker, worked across the US and Europe, advised on M&A as well as debt restructuring, and done deals in almost every major industry. I was a true jack-of-all-trades, master of none – what bankers call a "generalist."

We didn't need to win a large number of assignments for us to succeed. We had relatively few mouths to feed, and the fees on successful transactions could be highly lucrative. For advising on a $500 million transaction the fee to the banker on each side of the deal would typically be about 1%, or $5 million. Not bad for a role that could be performed alongside multiple other assignments by a relatively small team supporting the key senior banker over a period of months. As deals scaled up in size the fees increased, even as the fee as a percentage of deal size declined – perhaps $7 million for a billion-dollar deal and $10 million for a $2-billion-dollar deal. But success, defined as a completed transaction whether it ultimately turned out to be an advantageous one for the client or not, was critical. Only a token amount of the fee would typically be paid as an initial retainer, and usually another modest portion at the time a deal was agreed and announced. The lion's share of the fee was earned only upon completion of the transaction.

Even when we missed out on a lead advisory role, there was the possibility of a meaningful consolation prize. Increasingly, especially on large transactions, a CEO or board would want a second opinion on a transaction, particularly given growing concerns with the numerous conflicts of interest inherent in the widely diversified business model of large banks. The breadth of products and services offered by those banks meant they routinely simultaneously played conflicting roles of advisor and counterparty – most often as a lender – to the same company.

These secondary advisory roles prompted by such conflicts often involved delivering to a client's board of directors or shareholders a "fairness opinion" – a carefully drafted sort of expert opinion that the financial terms of a deal were fair relative to current market conditions. A former Wachtell Lipton colleague of mine once heaped scorn on such opinions in a Delaware court hearing, thus inspiring a comic poster with the *Peanuts* character Lucy sitting in what looked like a lemonade stand, under the banner "Fairness Opinions, 5 cents."[3] But the resulting fees (much more than nickels!) were valuable to us. And, given our narrowly focused business model and the dearth of similar competitors, we were ideally suited to win such roles. Lawyers, board members or others who had seen us in action elsewhere would frequently send such assignments our way.

Many of our earliest engagements had direct Morgan Stanley connections. In the month that the third and fourth of us arrived as partners we advised on two billion-dollar radio deals for companies controlled by the then-prominent private equity firm Hicks, Muse, Tate & Furst. Two useful connections facilitated winning the Hicks Muse business. Name partner Charles Tate had worked for Bob at Morgan Stanley earlier in his career. And Michael Levitt, one of the key people who had followed Bob from Morgan Stanley to Smith Barney, was in the process of becoming a partner at Hicks Muse. Bob's deal with Sandy Weill had prohibited him from taking Mike or others from Smith Barney, but that did not prevent those people from moving to other places where they could be useful to him.

In the first half of that year there were also two transactions announced for Compaq Computer – a small acquisition first, followed by the $4.4 billion acquisition of Tandem Computers.[4] Compaq's founder and chairman was Ben Rosen, a brainy Caltech-educated venture capitalist who had once been an equity research analyst focused on the technology sector at Morgan Stanley.

The same month as the big Compaq Computer deal announcement we advised on our first transaction in a sector where we would play a major role in years to come. That sector was our own business of investment banking, where the large banks had historically been purchasers of smaller competitors to extend geographic reach or acquire new capabilities and/or new clients. In such cases it made sense for a prospective seller to choose as its advisor a firm that lacked the scale to be one of its potential buyers. And at that moment, very few firms like ours were of small size yet had the experience and expertise to play such a role.

Our first assignment in this space was to advise the technology-focused San Francisco-based investment bank Robertson Stephens on its sale to Bank of America. Robertson was one of the so-called "four horsemen" that focused on technology IPOs when that was a modest business of little interest to the big investment banks like Morgan Stanley and Goldman Sachs. The others were San Francisco-based Montgomery Securities and Hambrecht & Quist and Baltimore-based Alex Brown. Name founder Sanford (Sandy) Robertson reached out to Bob for help when thinking of selling. There had always been significant demand for acquisition opportunities in the investment banking space, particularly in bull markets, and thus we found plenty of interest in what was known as "Robbie Stephens." It sold for $540 million.

Next came what turned out to be one of the most important assignments in our firm's history, well out of proportion to the transaction size: advising the large Dutch bank ING Group on the $600 million acquisition of boutique American investment bank Furman Selz. Like many assignments in years to come, this project grew directly out of an earlier one. ING had been a losing bidder for Robertson Stephens, so we knew it was seeking a US acquisition. Further, we came to know the ING management team during the Robertson process. In fact one of its key people in the US was married to a former Morgan Stanley colleague who had left there some time earlier to join a private equity group. Despite losing the auction the ING team obviously liked what it had seen of us across the table, so they hired us to pursue an alternative opportunity. An additional selling point was that Bob knew Furman CEO Ed Hajim well from Nantucket summers, where they were then involved in developing the new Nantucket Golf Club. While Ed did not hire our firm for the sell-side advisory role, he did guide us toward prospective buyers that he might find acceptable.

Founded in 1973, Furman was a low-profile Wall Street firm that encompassed several distinct niche businesses despite its aggregate small scale. Still, like most Wall Street firms, it had a colorful and complex history. One of its founders was a major Broadway producer who would accumulate a few dozen Tony nominations and several actual awards. And at one stage it was owned – strangely enough – by the industrial company Xerox, before regaining its independence only to be resold to our Dutch client four years later. The fact that ING was one of several suitors for this modest business provided an early lesson that business models on Wall Street come in all shapes and sizes. In the right market almost any of them can attract buyers and thus generate substantial value for their owners and key employees.

While much of the acquisition process was managed by ING's local team in the US, we had some contact with the Dutch parent company along the way, including with a fellow named Simon Borrows who was the English leader of its investment banking business. That business originated from the eighteenth-century British merchant bank Baring Brothers, which ING had acquired two years earlier. That transaction was done for only £1 plus the assumption of liabilities in the wake of a Singapore-based rogue trader episode that resulted in the sudden collapse of that venerable firm.[5]

Late in the transaction process Bob and I flew to Amsterdam, with him piloting the Ten across the Atlantic, to get approval for the deal. Over a dinner with senior management, including Borrows and James Lupton, his longtime colleague and then deputy chairman of the Barings M&A group, the discussion focused primarily on the Furman deal. To our surprise they also raised the idea of an alliance with, or acquisition of, our own tiny new firm. We were quick to reject both ideas and proclaim our preference for long-term independence. We were firm in our position, although we were flattered by the approach and intrigued with the people. As Bob and I went down the elevator that night, I told him, "those guys should come work with us."

Rounding out that first partial year, we did two more transactions for Hicks Muse, this time in the television industry. Finally, in the last days of the year, Tim George, the fellow I had followed to the firm from Morgan Stanley, announced his first deal as a Greenhill banker, advising Coca-Cola on the acquisition of the French beverage company Orangina. While this $839-million-deal announcement was exciting at the time, as doing any-thing for a company of Coke's stature was a coup for an upstart investment bank, it turned out to be one of very few deals we would see blocked by regulators over the years. Essentially, the French government ultimately concluded that this fizzy drink with its distinctive orange pulp was a stra-tegic national asset that should not be ceded to the Americans.

So ended our first partial year as a four-man partnership. As we would learn again a few years later when entering the business of making investments as principals, timing is a huge determinant of Wall Street success. And, by pure luck, we had picked a very good time to launch an M&A advisory business. There were $1.6 trillion worth of deals globally that year, up 47% from the previous year and more than five times the level when I started at Morgan Stanley eleven years earlier.[6] Globally, 1997 was the first year that there were more than 500 deals with a size of $500 million or greater, compared to only 145 the year that I had started at Morgan Stanley. We managed to play an advisory role on several of those, which provided us with $36.5 million[7] of revenue for the year and the necessary credentials to go out and win more business. After all our expenses, $27.5 million of profit was left to be divided – in appropriately unequal portions – amongst the four partners.

The year 1998 looked set to provide even more favorable market con-ditions, and an even better year for our firm as well. That year started with a bang, as we announced two deals in January. One was Nestle's acquisition of the international businesses of Borden Foods, a second brand-name consumer-sector deal won by Tim George. The other, Compaq Computer's $9.6 billion acquisition of Digital Equipment Corporation, was the firm's largest deal to date and prompted a major piece of favorable publicity that would further propel our firm forward in its early days.

In truth, our firm had received positive news coverage from the start. *Investment Dealer's Digest* covered my move with Tim to Greenhill under the heading "Bok and George Go Entrepreneurial."[8] That story noted that "[t]he Morgan Stanley/Dean Witter combination...may create opportunities for specialty boutiques." Six months later another industry publication named *Corporate Financing Week* noted that a "handful of high-profile deals" had helped us "rocket up in the M&A rankings [that] year."[9] I was quoted singing the virtues of being focused on only one business and being fully aligned with clients, rather than employing the "cross-selling" strategy that was then in fashion among the big banks. A month later *Crain's New York Business* declared we were on a "hot streak."[10] That story highlighted two additional early selling points that we used with prospective clients: that smaller firms were better able to ensure the confidentiality of transaction discussions and that firms like ours "delegate less work to [junior] associates, which means clients are dealing primarily with veteran M&A bankers." Yet all those favorable stories were in publications read primarily by our competitors, not by potential clients.

Then, in the wake of the Digital Equipment deal, *The Wall Street Journal*, the most prominent business publication and certainly one that was widely read by prospective clients, printed a front-page article titled, "How Greenhill, with Compaq, Caps Comeback."[11] The story was written by leading M&A reporter Steve Lipin, who would become a great supporter of Bob and our firm. He wrote that a booming M&A market was "a rising tide [that] lifts all boats," and noted that some of Bob's peers had left a void for him to fill by recently stepping away from the business – Felix

Rohatyn of prominent international M&A advisor Lazard had become ambassador to France, and James Wolfensohn had become head of the World Bank. In a quote from Compaq's chief financial officer, Bob's ill-fated foray with Smith Barney was compared to a bad golf shot, from which he had now recovered. In sum, the story cast Bob as a kind of deal-doing superhero, with a pioneering history in the M&A business, a love of adventure, a new Citation X jet and "a thirst for flying at a moment's notice from his homes in Maine, Nantucket, Mass., or Greenwich, Conn." For years to come the jet would be a prominent feature of nearly every profile of Greenhill, the man or the firm.

Alongside all our success on the client advisory front we pursued an eclectic strategy – if that word even applies – of trying different things. We were keeping an eye out for senior bankers to expand our small US team, and we were also planning to open in London, as Bob and I had agreed at our first dinner. But on top of those initiatives we were also collectively investing modest amounts of personal money in scattered small technology companies, in what was a skyrocketing market for such businesses.

The notion of making personal $100,000 principal investments while advising on billion-dollar client transactions seemed like a distraction to me. Adhering to my original objective of building an elite, highly focused, client-centric investment bank like I perceived those of an earlier era to be would require sorting some of this out in the future. But with plenty of client work to do and no management structure in place it was not yet worth focusing on that.

At the same time that I was worrying about the eclectic diversified activities of our little firm, the optimistic era in which we were living, combined with my own newfound entrepreneurial zeal, had led me on a personal level to similarly experiment with extracurricular activities. My boldest step into unfamiliar territory came in early 1998, amid frenzied activity at the firm, when I found time to buy the White Hart, a financially distressed, nearly two-centuries-old inn in rural northwest Connecticut's

Litchfield County. The place had once been owned by Edsel Ford of the Detroit automotive family.

Almost ten years earlier my wife Roxanne and I had acquired a modest, nondescript weekend home on a wooded three-acre lot a few miles from the inn, just off the Appalachian Trail. We were still renters in Manhattan at the time, so this $300,000 property was our first real home. We had fallen in love at first sight with the area, given its abundant deer, wild turkeys, occasional black bear sightings and coyotes howling in the night. When I first surveyed the landscape filled with farms, forests and lakes I called it "Michigan with hills." Weekends in this comparatively quiet rural arcadia would provide the perfect counterbalance to hectic weekdays in New York.

While our new home had all the usual kitchen appliances, in our early childless years there the White Hart practically served as our dining room, as even in that idyllic country setting we remained stereotypical New Yorkers unwilling and probably unable to cook for ourselves. Hence our regular visits to the White Hart. The picturesque twenty-six-room inn and tavern sat in the center of the village of Salisbury, on the green, just a few miles from the Revolutionary War-era home on fifty-six acres that we were in the process of buying. *The New York Times* would later describe the inn as a "primal slice of mythic New England...where residents, whether local EMTs or Wall Street weekenders, came for July beers and February martinis in front of the fireplace and where prep school parents from the Hotchkiss and the Salisbury Schools booked rooms."[12]

We were lured into this new venture through a local newspaper story that said the place was in financial trouble, as such seasonal establishments with aging infrastructure often are. I then reached out to the inn's owner/manager, who was half of a recently divorced couple that had bought the inn at auction and run it for several years, before the two had split and the husband returned his focus to a nearby restaurant that had been his first local venture.

I simultaneously reached out to the president of the local National Iron Bank, a small community bank in the same village that was the inn's primary lender. At first I sought to serve as unpaid debt-restructuring advisor, for no other reason than to help preserve a beloved landmark in our adopted community. But the small-town banker made it clear that what the inn really needed was a new owner, and clearly somewhat dazzled by the early high-profile success of my new firm, he invited me to step into that role. A degree of naïveté is an essential prerequisite to undertaking any entrepreneurial venture, and I had just enough of it to do as he suggested. Thus, after much negotiation with various constituencies, I ended up acquiring the inn for a token cash payment, plus the assumption of about $1 million of existing bank debt.

I had no relevant expertise whatsoever for this new role, having never even worked as a part-time busboy or waiter in a restaurant like so many high school kids tend to do. The jobs of my youth were more geared toward the outdoors – helping out on farms or running a jackhammer. I had no idea the scale of responsibility I was taking on by acquiring a business with a drafty old ramshackle building, dozens of employees, a few thousand local patrons and a proud history as the centerpiece of the village. But there was a small management team in place, and I assumed that together we would figure out how to deal with whatever problems drifted our way.

Later that year I took on another extracurricular activity alongside my busy days at Greenhill. A bit closer in content to my day job, this time I was appointed to my first corporate board of directors. A year earlier, just as I was joining Greenhill, I had taken on my first board role in the nonprofit sphere for Prep for Prep, a small but high-profile organization that Roxanne and I had already supported financially for some years. Prep searched the New York City public schools annually for high-potential fifth graders of color, many of them immigrants, put them through an extremely rigorous supplemental education program for more than a year, and then placed them on scholarship in the top private schools in New York and throughout the northeast. Wanting to be more than just another banker, I had always planned to play a role in the nonprofit sphere. Focusing on education at elite schools to help promising young people of modest backgrounds achieve their full potential resonated with me given my own history as a scholarship kid who was the grandson of an immigrant.

When Marty Lipton, my first boss and one of the driving forces behind Prep, invited me for a discussion of that program over lunch at the celebrated midtown restaurant "21" right next door to our office, I was quick to accept his offer of a board position. In fact, in my desire to please a mentor I had blurted out my acceptance before he had even finished his pitch. Marty, always dead serious and ever the thorough lawyer, promptly interrupted me to disclose the financial obligations that went with board membership – donations of $100,000 over three years plus the purchase of a table at Prep's annual benefit, the Lilac Ball. Having thereby received my first lesson in how New York's innumerable philanthropic boards worked, I confirmed my acceptance.

Joining my first for-profit board seemed like a good way to further broaden my business experience, and Dyson-Kissner-Moran Corporation (known as DKM) represented the right introductory opportunity. DKM was a private collection of industrial businesses that had been assembled by some early practitioners of the art that became known initially as leveraged buyouts and later as private equity. Rob Dyson, the chairman, primary owner and son of one of the founders of the business, raced cars on weekends at the historic Lime Rock Park racetrack, just a few miles from the White Hart. He had attended many a racing-related dinner at the inn and was enamored of the fact that I had some large-scale deal expertise but also was learning the day-to-day challenges of running a small business – "making a payroll" as he succinctly put it. With the acquisition of the White Hart and the Prep and DKM board appointments, I could see that, just as with my client work at Greenhill, one business opportunity seized can very quickly and naturally lead to another.

As I felt my way forward in these new outside activities, Greenhill likewise felt its way forward. And it was doing so without any meaningful management structure in place. Bob was the only partner with a title – "chairman." As his prior experiences had made abundantly clear, he held little interest in crafting strategy and even less in what he referred to derisively as administration. But even if there had been a traditional organizational chart designating clear leadership roles, it was far from obvious at that point precisely what the ideal business model was for Greenhill.

Not many years earlier, the investment banking segment of the financial services industry had been characterized by small, highly specialized, regional firms. Morgan Stanley itself had been a very small firm, initially focused on the US market and primarily on stock and bond underwriting for major companies, later expanding to M&A advice under Bob's leadership. When Morgan Stanley sent me to London in 1990, its offices were housed in a rabbit warren of small buildings among physician offices and retail shops in the "West End" rather than London's financial district where the dominant local firms were based or in the enormous Canary Wharf development in London's East End docklands that it would later occupy.

Other US firms had a similar approach, like First Boston and Goldman Sachs, but some had more niche strategies as well. Dillon Read, for example, was a small but prestigious American firm still focused almost entirely on advisory work. The four horsemen of the American technology sector had focused almost exclusively on investment banking for US technology companies and were the market leaders in that initially small space.

The London market had been dominated by several of what were known as the "UK merchant banks," which were focused almost exclusively on providing stock underwriting and merger advice for what they called PLCs, short for publicly listed companies, on the London Stock Exchange. Those regional financial institutions bore the names of old German and English families like Warburgs, Kleinwort Benson, Schroders,

Morgan Grenfell, Cazenove and Robert Fleming. Barings was also one of that group – its long history included a near collapse in 1890 that was a precursor to the century-later crisis that led to the ING takeover. Other markets were similarly dominated by local players – Deutsche Bank in Germany, Nomura Securities in Japan, various UK-like merchant banks in Australia, and so forth.

Over the course of my still young career there had been a massive and remarkably rapid consolidation in the industry, motivated by the same factors that had driven Morgan Stanley's evolution: globalization, growth in capital markets and trading, evolving technology and the benefits of scale. The British merchant banks had nearly all been acquired: Barings by ING as noted; Warburgs by Swiss Bank, which then merged with its national peer Union Bank of Switzerland to form UBS; Morgan Grenfell by Deutsche Bank; Kleinwort Benson by Germany's Dresdner Bank; and Schroders by Citigroup. Although the US firms had in some cases been acquirers, many of those were also gobbled up: First Boston by Credit Suisse, Dillon Read by Swiss Bank before its merger with UBS, and the four horsemen ended up owned by Bank America, J.P. Morgan and Deutsche Bank.

The enlarged acquirers moved into nearly every market in the world, squeezing out smaller local competitors with their larger product offerings and global reach. By the time our firm was launched a huge percentage of all transaction advisory fees paid globally were collected by only nine firms: Citigroup, Goldman Sachs, J.P. Morgan, Lehman Brothers, Merrill Lynch and Morgan Stanley in the US; and Credit Suisse, Deutsche Bank and UBS in Europe.

The only meaningful exceptions to this concentration of power with large financial conglomerates were Lazard and Rothschild, two firms with deep roots in Europe. Both of those very long-established firms were considerably smaller, less diversified and closer to our "pure advisory" business model. But Lazard had a long history of poor cooperation across its three main regional entities in New York, London and Paris, while Rothschild had failed to develop a US business equivalent to what it had built elsewhere around the globe.

Our firm's opportunity stemmed from the possibility that perhaps consolidation, diversification and resulting efforts to "cross-sell" numerous products, which might (or might not) be in a particular client's interests, had gone too far. Perhaps we could develop a firm that was solely focused on advising clients on important deals, of a consistent quality across key global markets, and with a collegial culture well-suited to extracting all the potential value from a team's collective relationships and skills. In small steps, that is exactly what we would seek to do.

The most important step in this process was our London expansion in mid-1998. London was a large M&A market – the world's second largest and by far the most active in Europe. It is not too much of a stereotype to say that Anglo-Americans (Americans, the British, Canadians and Australians) love to do deals. Equally important for our purposes, leading British companies were accustomed to taking advice from small, specialized firms; that is what the once numerous independent British merchant banks had been. Best of all, a large majority of those firms had recently been swallowed up by large foreign banks. So if in America we sought to be heir to the old Morgan Stanley's heritage and brand, in London we would seek to do the same vis-à-vis the historic British merchant banks.

Within months of my initial dinner with Bob I had taken the first steps forward. Based on the theory of "if we build it, they will come," and in a clear sign of our unlimited confidence in those early days, we rented office space in a new West End building near the shopping district's Regent Street, not far from my first Morgan Stanley office. From there we began the regulatory licensing process without a single local employee in place. Meanwhile I booked a room at the luxurious Victorian-era Claridge's Hotel to interview many of the leading bankers in the market, all who were well aware of our new firm and its growing momentum.

Amid those dialogues Simon Borrows, our client in the ING/Furman Selz deal, reached out to say that he and his senior colleague James Lupton – our two dinner hosts from months earlier – were planning to leave ING Barings and interested in joining us. Two of their junior colleagues, Brian Cassin and David Wyles, wanted to come with them. A large conservative Dutch bank like ING was an uncomfortable home for what was really a London-based M&A boutique, so their decision was not hard to understand.

We responded to their overture promptly and soon agreed terms with the duo, keeping it simple by providing them with the exact same economics as Tim George and myself, with Bob at a materially higher ownership level. The *Financial Times* (*FT*) reported that in London we would seek to "offer an alternative to the 'one-stop shopping' of large, integrated investment banks."[13] Lupton was quoted saying there was "a real market out there for trust-based advice," and the moniker "trust-based advisor" became a catch phrase in our London marketing efforts. We took out our first advertisement ever, in the *FT*, addressed to "our clients and friends," to announce the opening. It listed the fifteen announced deals on which the firm had advised up to that point, including three each for Compaq Computer and for affiliates of Hicks Muse.

We now had a slightly larger team, a foothold in the two largest global markets and a differentiated strategy offering independent conflict-free advice on major transactions. We also continued to benefit from an increasing number of transactions on which we could seek a role, as the number of M&A transactions globally continued to increase dramatically in 1998. Even a 1% market share in such a robust environment would result in a lucrative business for us, and of course we hoped for much more than that.

Then, suddenly, just a few months after our London expansion, the wind that had been at our back from day one turned against us.

Any observer of financial markets knows that they are prone to sharp shifts, and that those shifts are unpredictable in terms of timing and can originate from anywhere. In 1997 and into 1998 major economies were strong, stock prices were high and rising, M&A deals were readily finance-able and CEOs had every reason to confidently explore expansion oppor-tunities. All that was to the great benefit of our new firm.

Then, in the summer of 1998, a hedge fund with the generic name Long-Term Capital Management (LTCM) and the somewhat obscure strategy of using complex computer-driven models to exploit small devia-tions in the fair value of securities across different asset classes and differ-ent regional markets got into trouble.

The strategy was focused on what was referred to as "convergence"; the concept being that anomalies arise between asset values in different mar-kets, but that those values should always ultimately converge. In other words, the anomalies should logically disappear over time as traders and investors buy the underpriced security, driving up its value, and sell the overvalued security, pushing down its value. The gains this strategy could generate were modest but theoretically very low risk. And if the risks truly were very low, then such small gains could be greatly magnified by the aggressive use of leverage (i.e. debt) to take larger investment positions.

Like many funds operating under the misnomer "hedge fund," Long-Term Capital purported to deliver to its investors stable and attractive returns that were not correlated to general market movements. At first it did just that. In fact the returns were extraordinary. However, as often ulti-mately turns out to be the case, generating those high returns entailed far more risk than either the fund managers or anyone else realized until it was too late.

Among the cognoscenti Long-Term Capital was viewed, even relative to its hedge fund peers, as "the smart money." If the firm was known more broadly than similar funds among CEOs, M&A advisors and the public generally, it was due to the celebrity financiers who were involved. These included two Nobel Prize laureates, a former Federal Reserve vice chairman, professors from Harvard and legendary Wall Street bond traders from Salomon Brothers, all led by founder John Meriwether. The former head of bond trading at Salomon, Meriwether had been a principal character in *Liar's Poker*, Michael Lewis's memoir about his time as a junior employee on the Salomon trading floor. The fund had been set up in 1993 after Meriwether resigned from Salomon in the wake of a government bond trading scandal that led to that firm's rescue by none other than legendary investor Warren Buffett, who had a big investment in the firm and became chief executive for a time to clean up its reputation.

Long-Term Capital's initially remarkable returns made it the envy of Wall Street. But extraordinary returns inevitably attract increasing amounts of capital from investors wanting a piece of that action, and with more capital it becomes increasingly challenging to put all that money to work in a manner that reliably generates continuing attractive returns. There simply are not enough opportunities to do so within the realm of expertise of the fund managers. As a result, as the scale of funds under management grew the bond experts at LTCM eventually strayed far outside their core area of expertise. They got involved in areas like merger arbitrage, where one is essentially betting on stocks in relation to the outcome of pending corporate M&A deals.

When something goes wrong at such a firm, the high leverage that turbocharges returns on the upside makes for a precipitous fall on the downside. Moreover, one firm's problem can result in "contagion" affecting peer firms, as forced selling by the firm in trouble begets falling prices for the assets being sold, which begets forced selling of the same or similar assets at peer institutions, which pushes prices down further, which then forces more selling by the firm with the original problem. Everything starts to spiral downward, accelerated by the high leverage common among such firms.

In LTCM's case the something that went wrong was in Russia, a small and usually inconsequential market in financial terms. In August 1998, the government there devalued the ruble, defaulted on its domestic debt and declared a moratorium on repayment of foreign debt. This abruptly led to what later generations of traders would call a "risk off" stance, leading Wall Street firms to liquidate various risky trading positions to reduce the risk in their portfolios. LTCM was exposed to many of the affected positions. Values of various securities plummeted, and in a matter of weeks LTCM lost more than $4 billion.

Convinced of the validity of its models, LTCM held tight to the belief that if it could hang on long enough valuations would return to "logical" levels. In the meantime, LTCM scrambled to find a heavyweight investor to provide the capital needed to avoid a hasty liquidation in a falling market. Warren Buffett himself, familiar with Meriwether from his Salomon days, lobbed in a low-ball offer with a very short time fuse, which was rejected.

The crisis was resolved when, following tense negotiations involving senior government officials and the heads of the major firms with large trading operations, fourteen major financial institutions provided $3.6 billion of financing under the supervision of the Federal Reserve to avoid a fire sale of LTCM's assets that would have led to its bankruptcy.[14] Such a bankruptcy would have exposed every major trading firm to the risks inherent in huge numbers of complex securities contracts, where the transaction counterparty on which it had relied would no longer be solvent and able to make good on its financial commitments. Hence such firms had a clear collective interest in engineering some kind of soft landing for the failing fund, although each would ideally have preferred not to participate in the cost of such a rescue.

The group providing the funds included Goldman Sachs, J.P. Morgan, Morgan Stanley and most of their peers. But notably not Bear Stearns, which refused to participate despite tremendous peer pressure, yet ironically would itself be desperately seeking similar help a decade later. LTCM's management team and original investors remained convinced of the long-term soundness of their trading positions but were essentially wiped out.

This saga proved yet again the old trader dictum, allegedly first spoken by renowned British economist John Maynard Keynes, that markets can remain irrational longer than you can remain solvent.[15]

In retrospect, with knowledge of larger crises that were to come in later years, the LTCM episode seems fairly benign. But at the time it was frightening, as was obvious from collapsing financial sector stocks and further illustrated by a February 1999 *Time* magazine cover story that looked back on the crisis from a distance of several months. Titled "The Committee to Save the World,"[16] the cover photo featured Federal Reserve Chairman Alan Greenspan, Secretary of Treasury Robert Rubin and Assistant Treasury Secretary Lawrence Summers. *Time* spun a heroic tale of how this trio had stopped the Russian debt crisis from bringing down the entire global financial system. In hindsight there was more than a little hyperbole in that story, but it accurately reflected a near contemporaneous view of what was at stake.

Unlike the firms that essentially bailed out LTCM, our firm had not been at existential risk. We had no leverage, and we owned almost no assets that could fluctuate in value along with volatile financial markets. LTCM's activities were a long way from ours. We simply collected fees that related to work for well-established, strongly capitalized companies on specific deals that usually had an important strategic purpose. In terms of business model, we were much more like a fee-collecting law firm than a risk-taking financial institution like LTCM or the banks that financed it.

Despite the much lower risk inherent in our business model, however, we did not escape the LTCM crisis completely unscathed. We were indirectly impacted by the market gyrations, as a crisis in credit markets can very quickly impact the ability to finance an acquisition or merger. More importantly, the risk aversion that flows naturally from a financial crisis of any kind can rapidly spread from trading desks to executive suites, causing companies to recalculate the risks and rewards involved in taking on a new business and issuing more debt or equity to pay for it. Thus, consistent with what we would see in crises to come, many active transaction dialogues suddenly froze up as the LTCM crisis unfolded. What had looked like a strong revenue pipeline for us suddenly looked anemic at best.

While a sudden pause in corporate activity was disconcerting after eighteen months of nothing but positive surprises, we did not panic. I saw myself as unflappable, but soon learned that Bob's unwavering optimism dwarfed my own. He qualified as a veritable modern-day Stoic. He could brush aside the worst news in a matter of seconds, uttering what would become his trademark phrase in such situations: "Keep moving." And that is what we did regarding the LTCM crisis.

Fortunately, this episode was not one that would truly test our resolve or resilience. The pause in deal activity turned out to be very brief, just as it had after the epic stock market crash of 1987. Then, just as I was finishing my first year as an investment banker at Morgan Stanley, the Dow Jones Industrial Average fell 23% in a single day. This time around, in a response that would become familiar, the Federal Reserve reacted to the crisis by reducing interest rates in late September and again in October and November, thereby successfully calming markets and reinvigorating appetites for risk. The total value of all M&A deals globally in 1998 ended up rising more than 50% from the prior year's record level, and the number of deals of at least $500 million in size also hit a new record. As for our firm, we managed a small revenue increase over the prior year, generating $39 million, an impressive sum given the crisis even if we now had more partners with which to share our profits.

The Long-Term Capital episode was a test case for the question of how our firm, then still young, small and burdened with only very modest financial obligations, could handle an economic or financial crisis. Further, it provided a valuable early lesson in how such crises work. The first noteworthy observation was that almost nobody had seen the crisis coming, although the element of surprise may be essentially a truism in relation to crises, as an event that was predicted and prepared for would not likely precipitate a crisis. Yes, Alan Greenspan had warned of irrational exuberance in markets, but that was a fairly mild observation made long before the crisis actually developed.

A second observation was that the crisis had originated in a place almost nobody would have expected – Russia – before spreading more broadly. It was not a place to which most financial market participants paid much attention. My own experience with Russia was limited to a cocktail party for Russian businesspeople that Morgan Stanley hosted at its new Canary Wharf headquarters a few years after the Berlin Wall came down. The event was a memorable one given the room full of budding quasi-capitalists with ill-fitting suits and more gold teeth than I had ever seen.

A third observation was that, notwithstanding the fact that the crisis surprised almost everyone, with the benefit of just a few weeks' hindsight the harbingers of the crisis, and indeed its seeming inevitability, became obvious to all. Those omens in this case were the very notion of complex but theoretically infallible investing models, the inexplicably impressive rates of investment return generated for an extended period and the very high leverage in place, which would amplify returns similarly in both positive and negative directions.

Finally, a fourth observation was that once the crisis got momentum, many predicted something along the lines of the end of the world as we knew it, at least in a financial sense, and the press enthusiastically fanned those flames of fear. Hence the *Time* magazine cover, which was clearly intended to be taken quite literally. But as came to be said in a later crisis, "The world doesn't end that often."[17]

CHAPTER FIVE

A BUBBLE BURSTS

It's the last midnight,
So, goodbye all.
Coming at you fast, midnight–
Soon you'll see the sky fall[1]

— *Stephen Sondheim*, Into the Woods

W ith the Long-Term Capital crisis resolved, stock markets resumed their ascent and were already back in record territory by the end of the first quarter of 1999. The frenzied pace of merger and acquisition activity likewise resumed – the aggregate value of all deals globally would rise to a record $3.25 trillion that year. That was up significantly from the prior year's record level, nearly double the level of the year before that and nearly triple the level of the year before that.

Our firm's performance in 1998, producing only a token increase in revenue despite an expanded team, had been more than respectable relative to the volatile market environment. In 1999, with calmer markets and a more robust level of corporate deal activity generally, our revenue more than doubled to $86 million. While that rate of increase over the prior year was impressive, the revenue production in absolute terms was also extraordinary, given that the firm had only seven partners and a small supporting team.

Achieving that high level of revenue productivity required firing on all cylinders, and that is what our business had done. We advised our historic corporate client Compaq Computer on another transaction. We advised portfolio companies of our private equity fund client Hicks Muse on two additional transactions, including a $23.5 billion deal in the rapidly consolidating radio sector.

Personally, I advised my Irish aircraft-leasing client from my Morgan Stanley days on another in a series of transactions. I also advised a new client, International Speedway, a company controlled by the Daytona-based France family that separately owned the entire NASCAR racing circuit, on its $670 million acquisition of Penske Motorsports, which was led by racing legend Roger Penske and owned four major racetracks. In a further sign of how one opportunity seized often led to another, that assignment came to me via my DKM board of directors' position. DKM Chairman Rob Dyson knew the France family through the same weekend racing hobby that had originally connected him to me via my ownership of the White Hart inn.

On top of our financial success, later that year we benefited from a highly unusual role that resulted in token fees but served to further elevate the profile of our young firm: advising the US Justice Department on financial aspects of its landmark antitrust case against computer software giant Microsoft. This high-profile role for the Clinton Administration was a peculiar one for a firm that consisted almost entirely of free market-oriented Republicans, but somehow the Justice Department official in charge of the matter, Joel Klein, was connected to Bob, who led the project. Clearly only a truly intrepid banker would go against one of the largest and highest profile companies in the world on behalf of a government regulator. But for Bob the potential for controversy and conflict likely made the assignment even more enticing. However, in the end our firm's role was modest given that the wrangling between parties was far more legal than financial in nature. The case dragged on for years and eventually ended with a whimper rather than a bang. Nonetheless, our association with this case enhanced our brand and provided a valuable credential for other important governmental advisory roles that would later come our way.

The difference between a very good and a truly great year in 1999 flowed directly from our extremely well-timed London expansion in the middle of the previous year. European deal activity was accelerating, and London was very much the epicenter of it. During my time in London for Morgan Stanley there were only around seventy-five transactions per year with a European buyer or seller and a deal size of at least $500 million. By 1998, as we were opening the London Greenhill office, there were nearly four times as many such transactions. In 1999 there were nearly six times as many. The European deals market had thus become nearly as large as the US market and was growing just as rapidly.

While the timing of our London move was fortuitous, our choice of new partners to lead that office was equally propitious. Both Simon Borrows and James Lupton were outstanding corporate financiers in their prime. They had very different personalities but similarly strong sets of loyal clients and equally favorable reputations throughout the London market. My first impression was that they were not personally close. James seemed somewhat like Bob Greenhill – a big personality, aggressive and a bit of a showman. Simon, in contrast, seemed more like me – more reserved, less flamboyant and more analytical in his approach. In any event, in London as in New York, the differences in personalities and styles proved useful. Senior corporate executives likewise varied in both their personal style and in terms of what characteristics they looked for in a trusted advisor.

From the very start, we succeeded in our goal of creating a transatlantic firm with equivalent local expertise in each market, rather than an American firm with a subsidiary foreign branch. The subtle difference between those two business models proved meaningful both in terms of recruiting and in attracting clients. Simon and James were as authentically British as any two people could be and were able to bring their entire client base with them – there was literally nobody left at ING Barings who had the capability to keep those clients from following them to our firm. That client base was very active in what was a booming UK M&A market. In the first full year of opening our London office James advised on the first of many large transactions for Cable & Wireless, a global telecom company that traced its roots back to the nineteenth century. He also executed two transactions for the regional utility Yorkshire Water, enlisting my help for its first US acquisition.

Meanwhile, Simon advised on the $2.5 billion merger that created the leading UK newspaper company Trinity Mirror, as well as on two large transactions that ended up falling short of completion. One of those was a failed acquisition by 3i Group, an unusual – for that time – publicly traded private equity investing business. The other was a bid on behalf of drinks company Whitbread, which was rejected by regulators on antitrust grounds. Both clients, as well as London-based food and drinks conglomerate Diageo, which Bob and Tim advised from the New York office, were prominent old companies at the heart of the British business establishment. They were exactly the type of clients upon which to build an eminent reputation, which in turn would lead to even more transaction advisory opportunities.

Given the red-hot M&A market, we were busy having fun and generating copious amounts of fee revenue on both sides of the Atlantic. Almost all that money ended up in the pockets of our small group of partners. Beyond the obvious personal benefits of such financial rewards, our early success also served to solidify the working relationships among our

New York team and with our new London partners – two people of different heritage who were previously unknown to us and had only come to our attention through pure serendipity. That kind of "glue" was critical to the objective of building a global business with a strong culture and the resilience to withstand the challenges that would inevitably come.

Because there was no need to change anything about a formula that was working so well, we were disinclined to bring anyone new onboard who was not already familiar to us and seen as a "sure thing." In any event, given the conventional wisdom of the day that big banks were the best employers, most bankers were too risk averse to want to join our start-up operation. Yet those we did add played very important roles in the expansion of our business and continuation of our initial success.

In late 1999 we engaged in discussions with two prospective partners – one on each side of the Atlantic – and both ended up joining us in January 2000. The convivial Scotsman James Blyth was not, and never had been, a banker, so in some senses he was an unusual choice as our third senior colleague (initially part-time advisor, later full partner) in London. He held a board chairman role with our client Diageo, which in a later era would certainly have prevented him from affiliating with us. Earlier he had served as CEO of high street pharmacist Boots PLC, which meant he was a member of the FTSE (pronounced "footsie") club of chief executives, referring to the Financial Times Stock Exchange (FTSE) 100, an index of leading British companies comparable to similar lists compiled by Dow Jones and Standard & Poor's in the US.

In addition, a few years earlier James had been named a life peer: "Baron Blyth of Rowington." That appointment meant a great deal in the London business community and could sometimes be useful in the US as well. Better still from our American point of view, he had a disarming way of bearing that title, refusing to let anyone refer to him as "Lord." In fact it was more common within that office for Simon to refer to James Lupton as "his Lordship," reflecting James's sometimes imperious style and unwittingly foreshadowing that one day Lupton would himself become a member of the House of Lords. Although Blyth would never lead a client advisory team, nor even be based in one of our offices, he made some very valuable client introductions, added a general luster to our firm and was a pleasure to have on the team.

The other recruit that January, Robert (Bob) Niehaus, played an even more central role in our firm. Niehaus (referred to herein by surname to avoid confusion with Bob Greenhill) was just a few years older than me. He shared with Bob Greenhill (and Dick Fisher) the academically elite Baker scholar designation from Harvard Business School, and like Fisher had earlier graduated from Princeton. His career began at Morgan Stanley with a brief stint as a M&A banker before he became involved in the launch of a new private equity investment business, rising to become one of a triumvirate of young leaders in the next generation under Donald Brennan, a strong-willed and hard-drinking Irishman who had joined Morgan Stanley from the paper industry and proceeded to build an enormously lucrative business from scratch.

As so often happens on Wall Street, following Brennan's exit the succeeding generation of leaders failed to gel as a team, and Niehaus ended up negotiating terms for his departure. When I got wind of his exit, I smelled opportunity and reached out. We met for our first discussion at San Pietro, an upscale Italian restaurant in midtown Manhattan frequented by senior folks on Wall Street, including in many instances those like Niehaus who were undergoing a period of exile before taking up their next position.

Niehaus and I had little interaction while we were both at Morgan Stanley. What was then called "merchant banking" – the business of investing equity capital as a principal in private transactions – had started as an arm of the investment banking division under Bob Greenhill. At Morgan Stanley and many of its peers, this was the beginning of what became known as the private equity business, a force which would come to own a large part of the global economy. Initially the pools of capital they raised were tiny – under $50 million in the case of Morgan Stanley's first fund. But as Brennan's business blossomed into abundant profitability he carved out an important separate division within the firm.

Niehaus and I met when we found ourselves united on an unusual project not long before I resigned to join Greenhill. That project related to what was colloquially referred to as "the pig farm." Brennan's fund had made a huge investment in Premium Standard Farms, a start-up pig farming and processing business that aspired to be to pork what the corporate giant Tyson Foods was to chicken. As that business grew, Morgan Stanley not only invested more fund capital but underwrote and sold to clients some large bond issues to fund expansion. Unfortunately, it soon became clear that massive pig farms were more complicated than massive chicken farms, resulting in operational challenges and ultimately severe financial distress. Morgan Stanley thereby found itself with a major problem in both its principal investing business and its client-focused investment banking business.

Having made the mess, Brennan was not seen as trustworthy to clean it up. So Morgan Stanley President John Mack appointed one highly regarded young managing director from each of the impacted business units, Niehaus and me, to figure out a restructuring plan. On that one brief but internally high-profile assignment we found we had much in common and developed deep respect for each other's capabilities. Along the way we also each got to know Harvey Miller, the dean of the bankruptcy bar, who had several years earlier worked with Bob Greenhill on the huge bankruptcy of the major oil company Texaco and now was the key lawyer on the pig farm matter. Harvey – a tall, courtly fellow always impeccably dressed – was then a senior partner at Weil, Gotshal & Manges, the New York firm that dominated bankruptcy law and based in the General Motors building at the southeast corner of Central Park.

With Greenhill's advisory business going so well it was not obvious that getting into the investment business made sense. But at that point the client sensitivity to conflicts of interest was not as fully developed as it would become, and the business of investing private capital as a principal was seen as a natural extension of an M&A advisory business. In a sense it was simply advising one's own firm on M&A deals rather than outside clients. Hence at Morgan Stanley the two businesses were initially closely aligned, and likewise at Goldman Sachs and other major competitors. Furthermore, we were already in this business in a very small way – that was the case even prior to my joining the firm. Rather than invest token sums of personal capital in tech deals that we stumbled across while doing our "day jobs" as advisors, why not hire an expert, professionalize the effort and raise outside capital to develop a business with meaningful scale that could complement our advisory business?

It probably never would have happened had Niehaus not become available, notwithstanding the rationale for building out an investment business. In terms of intelligence, resume and style, he fit perfectly the old Morgan Stanley profile that we were seeking to replicate. Plus he was personally known to both Bob and myself. Furthermore, given the tremendous investment gains generated by his group at Morgan Stanley, he had accumulated significant personal capital to invest alongside that of outside investors, which would be critical for fund-raising purposes. He was also a natural leader, tough enough to overcome the inevitable obstacles to success. As I came to say on many occasions, the most important thing to know about Bob Niehaus, in terms of his determination, resilience and leadership skills, is that he was the eldest of twelve children. That his family was a Midwestern Catholic family filled with high achievers explained even more. An autumn weekend at my country place, walking the rural roads, dining at the White Hart and sharing our visions of what we hoped to achieve in business helped us get to know each other better and quickly solidified our plan to work together.

With the high confidence that was our firm's trademark from the start, we swiftly moved ahead with the idea of raising a private equity fund under the label Greenhill Capital Partners, or GCP for short. In seeking to tap into other people's money, it was critical to be able to demonstrate not only investment acumen but also strong financial controls. In that regard, it was helpful that Niehaus recruited Hal Rodriguez, who had served as financial controller of a packaging company that had long been one of the Morgan Stanley private equity portfolio companies Niehaus had overseen. Hal was a quiet but steady hand, capable of efficiently handling all aspects of the "back office." Shortly after he came on board, he was elevated to serve as chief financial officer of our entire firm, while continuing to handle all fund related back-office matters.

The financial rewards for managing a private equity fund can be extraordinary. Investors pay an annual management fee, typically around 1.5% of the capital they commit to the fund, which essentially covers the investment team's operating costs including base salaries. On top of that, subject to achieving a minimum-stated level of return, typically 20% of any gains on fund investments are paid to the fund managers in what is a form of profit participation called "carried interest." If the fund gains are large, the dollars of carried interest, divided among a small group of "carry" recipients on the fund's investment team, can be very significant. Further, despite much controversy and debate on this topic in Washington over the years, carried interest has traditionally been treated as lower-taxed capital gain income rather than "ordinary" income, making it even more attractive to those running a fund.

The Wall Street Journal publicized our plan by reporting our appointment of Niehaus as chairman of a proposed new fund, noting that we were part of a trend of "boutiques...reverting to the early years of investment banking by getting into merchant banking."[2] Working with Davis Polk & Wardwell, the prestigious old New York law firm that had handled legal matters for Morgan Stanley's private equity funds, we printed a prospectus for the fundraising. Niehaus would lead the fund and was the only true investment professional named in the document. With some degree of hubris we dared speak in its first paragraph of the document's executive summary of targeting an annual rate of return "of at least 30%,"[3] a highly optimistic but not then uncommon objective that similar funds would soon shy away from, as the scale of the private equity industry grew and generating such extraordinary investment returns became more difficult.

Bob Greenhill and I were also named as being involved in managing the fund, along with our rising star on the M&A team Jeff Buckalew, one of the first few junior professionals to join Bob at the firm. Among these advisory bankers, I devoted a larger portion of my time to the fund in its early years, effectively straddling that and our advisory business. Given the pace of fund-raising and investment activities, Niehaus and I walked the few steps between each other's offices numerous times a day for discussion of all kinds of topics. In conversations with outsiders he would generously refer to me as his co-chief investment officer of the fund, but equally he was my primary consigliere in developing and managing all other aspects of our business. Our growing personal relationship would prove pivotal to the further advancement of our firm.

If confidence was one trademark of our firm, speed was another. So, having made the strategic decision to enter merchant banking, we were in a big hurry to raise our first fund. Our fund-raising plan was to skip hiring the kind of "placement agent" that specialized in finding prospective investors, personally blitz over a period of several weeks our collective range of relevant contacts with requests for funding commitments, and simply take whatever money we could get. We had no idea how successful our effort would be, so we refrained from indicating a fund size on the cover of the prospectus as most do. Yet the first question almost any prospective investor will ask is, "how big a fund are you aiming to raise?" In our case we quickly developed the glib answer of "at least $80 million," which was how much our partners were collectively committing from personal funds.

I personally committed $6 million, which was more than the value of my liquid assets. I implicitly assumed that large M&A advisory fees, and related cash bonuses to me, would keep flowing in the years to come, so that I could make good on my obligation as capital commitments were called from investors in varying increments over the ensuing few years to be put to work in fund acquisitions. Given their larger personal balance sheets, Niehaus and Bob Greenhill committed a multiple of that amount, while other partners did various amounts smaller than mine.

The date on the prospectus we prepared to market the fund was March 2000, which unbeknown to us turned out to be the very month that the high-flying NASDAQ stock index peaked in what came to be known as the "dot-com" bubble, referring to the many emerging technology companies with the internet designation ".com" at the end of their corporate name. Not yet realizing that the market top had been reached, investors were flush with gains and bullish on the future. They were particularly receptive to our "new economy" pitch, focusing on businesses being transformed by emerging technologies. In sum, it was perhaps the best time in all recorded history to try to raise such a private equity fund. Thus, despite having only one experienced investment professional supported by a small advisory firm that was only four years old, we quickly found interested investors. Within several weeks we received $423 million[4] in total commitments. Although conservative investors like pension funds shy away from first-time funds like ours, we landed a long list of more entrepreneurial investors including various wealthy families like that of my friend Rob Dyson.

Our quick success in fundraising was not the only sign of a market peak. While we were marketing our new economy fund a twenty-three-year-old analyst at Salomon Smith Barney, the successor to Bob Greenhill's previous employer, issued a list of thirty-six suggestions to address the overworked status of junior bankers and, as *The New York Times* put it, "stem the flow of young employees defecting to Internet companies."[5] As one member of an earlier generation of bankers told *The Times*, "because of the supply-demand situation for talent, the inmates are trying to take over the asylum, and they're having some success." The list covered everything from a more casual dress code, to increased social events, to more money for late night meals in the office while working late. Salomon Smith Barney and other firms were quick to respond to the discontent in an effort to retain precious talent, not realizing that the bull market fueling the seemingly limitless demand for that talent was already quietly subsiding.

If amid all the market euphoria it was the easiest time in history to raise money, then one should naturally assume it was the hardest time in history to profitably invest money. Optimism, along with valuations of almost all financial assets, was running high. And, somewhat drunk on the Kool-Aid that nearly everyone was quaffing those days, we made a few early mistakes. Fortunately, they were relatively small ones, given that we initially lacked the conviction to make big bets with our own and outside investors' money when markets seemed so overheated.

We did, however, put some money to work. While Niehaus had correctly derided our firm's first principal investments – the small ones made with personal funds before he joined us – as "science projects," our first few fund investments in technology and telecommunications start-ups with trendy high-tech names like Ethentica, NerveWire and Shelflink also looked a bit like science projects. They would struggle for years to come before ultimately generating losses.

While we were feeling our way forward in the investing business, the advisory business continued to progress apace. After more than doubling in 1999, our revenue in 2000 rose a further 30% and cracked the $100 million mark for the first time. Highlights for the year included two landmark deals for Diageo, selling Pillsbury to General Mills and buying the spirits division of Seagram's. Among many other transactions, I advised my Irish aircraft-leasing client on yet another deal, and Bob handled a small transaction for Textron, maker of our flagship Citation X.

Our next move was to enter into a new business relating to a different kind of financial advice: debt restructuring. I had considerable restructuring experience from my work for Morgan Stanley in London in the early 1990s – there was little M&A to do then, given the cautious stance of companies in that recessionary period. So many of us pivoted toward providing restructuring advice to companies in financial distress. More recently, Niehaus and I had executed the infamous pig-farm restructuring together.

The timing for an expansion into restructuring advice seemed right. History showed that in every decade there were usually seven or eight years of robust M&A activity and two or three where the economy was weak, M&A activity was tepid but defaults on corporate debt obligations were high, resulting in a need for restructuring advisors. At that time the extent of the dot-com bust was not yet clear, but there were already increasing debt defaults and therefore a growing need for restructuring advice. Restructuring was a natural business for us given that large banks, our main competitors for M&A assignments, are generally incapable of advising on restructurings. The reason is that those banks have helped sell to investors the debt that is creating the problem, or at least hold some of it in their trading book, creating a conflict of interest that eliminates them, often as a matter of law, as a potential advisor. Another potential benefit of entering this business was that Niehaus and I thought the downturn might create some investment opportunities in bankrupt assets for our new fund. Having the requisite expertise in-house might help us better access them.

Debt restructuring is its own world, inhabited by very different personalities than those typically found in M&A advisory firms. Perhaps the reason for that is that both sides of an M&A deal are typically happy on the day it closes, even if usually later it becomes clear that one party got the better side of the bargain. Meanwhile, restructuring is a largely zero-sum game that, by definition, develops out of a situation where people are losing money. At the completion of a restructuring often everyone is unhappy, except for the advisors who have no capital at risk and simply collect a fee for their work.

Because neither Niehaus nor I knew the players in this very different game we reached out to Harvey Miller, the star bankruptcy lawyer who had advised Morgan Stanley alongside the two of us on the pig-farm project. He directed us to Michael Kramer, who ran the New York-based restructuring team for Houlihan Lokey Howard & Zukin, a relatively low-profile advisory firm with which I was familiar. My first boss at Morgan Stanley had left many years earlier to open Houlihan's New York office (the firm had been founded in Los Angeles way back in the 1970s). Mike, only 32, was much younger than the rest of us, had the build of an NFL lineman, and lacked the Ivy League and Morgan Stanley pedigree most of us had. But he was a savvy street fighter with relentless intensity. In other words, he was perfect for the bare-knuckled business of bankruptcies and restructurings, even if he looked to be a somewhat awkward fit for our firm.

Again the timing of our move was excellent. In announcing our recruitment of Kramer *The Wall Street Journal* noted that our "push into the corporate restructuring business [was coming] at a time when bankruptcies are soaring."[6] And we were convinced that, with the economic downturn showing no signs of abating, there would be even more opportunities to come. *The Journal* further noted that restructuring assignments were increasingly lucrative, with monthly retainer fees of $150,000–$200,000 and completion fees of $5–$10 million for a restructuring of a $1 billion company.

Typically the same kind of economic downturn that increases restructuring opportunities decreases M&A opportunities – the natural hedge created by the combination of services is precisely why it makes sense for an advisory firm to be in both businesses. Yet despite reduced deal activity we continued to find ways to keep ourselves busy with M&A transactions. At mid-year *The Daily Deal* reported in a cover story, "[b]usiness [was] booming over at Greenhill & Co.,"[7] noting that we had advised Nestlé on its $11.7 billion acquisition of Ralston Purina among many other deals that year.

When the firm's fifth anniversary passed earlier that year, it was already clear that much had been accomplished in its brief history. Our original M&A business continued to grow, we had a new private equity fund to invest at what seemed like a propitious time, and we now had a restructuring team in place that would be increasingly in demand as economic activity slowed down. We were generating impressive revenue and profit while also continuing to build a name for ourselves. Yet we remained a very small and unusual firm with increasing breadth but very little depth. I sometimes described our approach as akin to that of Noah's ark, although without even two of most kinds of "animal." We had four M&A partners in New York, along with one partner each for real estate, restructuring advice and private equity investing. Add to that three M&A partners in London and one recently recruited in Frankfurt, and we only had eleven partners in total. Still, we were able to conduct multiple businesses across two continents against much larger competitors with far more prominent brand names and infinitely greater resources.

Bob Greenhill brought to our group a recognized brand name, a wide reputation, and a charisma that flowed from his boundless energy and optimism, but each of the other ten brought something unique to the table as well. Most importantly, all had the confidence to go out as David each day and win more often than anyone could reasonably have expected against the Goliaths with which we competed.

Somehow our disparate group of partners, who were in many cases just getting to know each other, continued to function effectively with almost no formal management structure. But now with multiple businesses and multiple offices, it was clear that we needed to take a first step toward formally designating a leadership team. Bob had no interest in management himself and hated the notion of any sort of "bureaucracy," as he invariably called any aspect of management. And, given his history at Morgan Stanley and Smith Barney, he certainly did not want a rival or even a future successor waiting in the wings. Yet with so many things happening at once he agreed something had to be done. His proposed compromise solution was to create a two-person "administration committee," so called because he laughingly said, "nobody would want to be on a committee with such a name." In other words, by making management sound as mundane as possible and by giving leaders a title that seemed unimportant, he hoped to avoid the battles for control that are so common on Wall Street and had driven Bob from his two prior firms.

As I was de facto already managing most aspects of the business, I would serve on the committee along with Simon Borrows, my obvious London counterpart. This tiny committee never had a formal meeting, let alone recorded any "minutes." Given that client matters and revenue generation continued to be the primary role for both of us, that is what we each focused on. As for our management responsibilities, I essentially managed things in the New York office where the restructuring and investing businesses sat alongside the M&A team, while Simon handled the London office which was entirely focused on M&A. Apart from strategic issues relating to new businesses, new offices and potential new senior personnel, our only significant shared management task was the annual compensation process. On Wall Street that task was always time-consuming and difficult, and therefore best kept to as small a group as possible. In this and other areas, our informal and dual-headed structure seemed to work efficiently and well.

Another small step in our business maturing was our late-2000 move from the small leased space on Fifty-Second Street into the newly renovated Colgate-Palmolive building on Park Avenue, only a few blocks north of Grand Central Station and directly across from the Waldorf-Astoria Hotel, the midtown Manhattan landmark where Prep for Prep held its annual fundraising benefit. It was a prestigious and convenient location, except for the annual week in September when the United Nations came to town, filling the Waldorf with third-world dictators and other assorted dignitaries, while snarling traffic with police barricades and SUV caravans filled with gun-toting security men.

We leased 24,000-square feet of space on two floors, with the ability to add more floors over time. Bob's wife Gayle, an avid photography collector who was then becoming chair of the board of trustees for Manhattan's Institute of Contemporary Photography, found the perfect items to decorate our new and modern space. She adhered to the aircraft and adventure theme that seemed to play so well with the press and clients, displaying in our conference rooms a collection of noteworthy original aerospace-related photographs that she and Bob had acquired. The photographs included originals by Alfred Steichen that were used to create World War II recruiting posters as well as photographs relating to the Wright brothers, Amelia Earhart and the Apollo space missions.

Taking the themes of optimism, action and adventure even further, over the course of 2001 Gayle filled the rest of our office with a series of large black-and-white photographic prints of Robert Falcon Scott's 1910 expedition to Antarctica. Bob and Gayle had acquired the originals as part of their growing collection, and we had oversized prints made for the firm. These realistic but inspirational photographs of near-frozen explorers exuding grit and determination would soon encircle the floors where our bankers worked, first in New York and then later in London and other offices.

The grit and determination of contemporary New Yorkers would be tested only months later.

On the morning of September 11 I left home early for a client meeting at Davis Polk's midtown office on Lexington Avenue. I was to present some views to a large group of institutional investors who had received an unusual bid for an entire private equity fund in which they were the principal outside investors – at first glance, it had looked to me like the fund manager was trying to take advantage of his own investors, notwithstanding the fiduciary duty he owed them. Shortly after my departure from our Upper East Side apartment our beloved Jamaican nanny Claudia was to walk our son Elliot to the all-boys Allen-Stevenson School a few blocks away. He was in his second week of first grade. From there, she and our one-year-old daughter Jane would head to Central Park on what was a picture-perfect late summer morning.

My client meeting involved a large group in a conference room, plus several participants on a conference call line with their voices amplified from ceiling speakers. Shortly before 9:00 a.m., one of the men on the phone spoke up, saying his wife had just interrupted him to say that a plane had flown into the World Trade Center – an urban landmark of global renown that had been in construction at the time of my first visit to New York back in 1970. He offered no details, so we all assumed it must have been a small plane and an accident, and thus we continued with our meeting. The story of a long-ago airplane flying into the Empire State Building with limited damage was well-known, and the scale of New York's population was such that nobody rushed out to call friends or colleagues who worked in the World Trade Center to check on their status. In fact, nobody in that room seemed to know anyone who worked there – indeed, in the twelve years I had worked as a New York lawyer and banker, visiting innumerable offices of companies, law firms and financial institutions I had never set foot in either tower of the World Trade Center.

The brief meeting ended when news of a second plane came, and – still having little sense what was happening – I then walked a few blocks across midtown to DKM's Fifth Avenue office for a 9:30 a.m. board meeting, on which I sat as a principal rather than in my usual advisory role. Traffic on the streets and sidewalks was normal, but from DKM's Forty-Sixth Street location I looked down Fifth Avenue before entering the building lobby and saw smoke billowing from both towers. Yet from that distant perspective several miles away it was impossible to ascertain the magnitude of what had happened.

As I walked into DKM's office Rob Dyson greeted me by exclaiming excitedly, "a King Air crashed into the World Trade Center!" Rob frequently used private aircraft to visit his far-flung operations and was familiar with the King Air, which is among the smallest of private aircraft. Given his vantage point around five miles away, the tremendous scale of the Twin Towers had made even the Boeing 767 aircraft that crashed into them look small. Within minutes, of course, we all learned that this was a well-orchestrated and extremely effective terrorist attack. The board meeting thus never started, and DKM's directors and senior management instead sat together in a conference room, watching television in stunned silence as one tower collapsed, then the other.

Just as it is difficult for those born in the age of travel by car and plane to imagine how slow travel was prior to those innovations, so it would be difficult for later generations to comprehend how slowly information moved at the time of the September 11 attack. Facebook, the widespread use of smartphones and the constant communication with family, friends and colleagues by text and automated news alerts relating to every earthquake, plane crash, economic statistic and even sports score were to come later. Thus, distracted and confused by the rapidly unfolding events, it took some time before I even thought to call home, although I finally did so from DKM's office before heading back to the nearby Greenhill office shortly after the towers came down.

My wife Roxanne watching through the south-facing window of our thirty-seventh floor apartment living room, several miles north of the towers, literally saw the towers fall. While our Elliot was presumably safe in school, it took time to figure out where exactly his sister was. It took much longer to determine the status of our friends, neighbors and families of our children's classmates. Once I returned to my office we sent everyone home, as the subways were then closed for an indeterminate period and people would have to walk home – a very long walk for many. I joined the throngs, including some covered in dust from the site of the attack, silently walking up Park Avenue for twenty-six blocks toward my apartment. A chill ran up my spine upon hearing the roar of military jets flying over Manhattan in otherwise empty skies, there to protect us – or at least create some feeling of security – from still unknown enemies. Remarkably, and fortunately, despite more than 3,000 deaths in and around the towers, I soon came to realize that nobody I knew had been lost.

The audacity and scale of the September 11 attack was shocking and disorienting, particularly for those like me who lived in New York. A major terrorist attack on US soil had seemed unthinkable to most Americans, even though this was not even the first attempt to bring down the World Trade Center, which eight years earlier was the site of a bombing that killed seven and led to the evacuation of 50,000 people. That first bungled attempt, however, was easily brushed off as amateurish, and thus did not linger long in the consciousness of New Yorkers, let alone of Americans generally. The magnitude and success of this second attempt, felling the iconic Twin Towers and presumably killing thousands of people while much of America was watching on live television, was beyond comprehension.

While the attack was infinitely more traumatic and tragic than the Long-Term Capital failure of a few years earlier, from a purely business perspective the two events nonetheless had much in common. Both were crises that originated from an unexpected place, had not been predicted yet soon seemed easily predictable and prompted fears that much worse would follow, perhaps even the end of the world as we knew it.

Like most other Americans, Roxanne and I that night sat with our eyes glued to our television, insatiably craving news as to what happened, how many were dead, what might happen next and what it all meant for our family, our city and our country. The number of firefighters who had died – "more than we can bear," said Mayor Giuliani on television that evening when asked for a number – was particularly gut-wrenching. New Yorkers had always treasured their firefighters, commonly referred to as "New York's bravest" just as the cops were called "New York's finest," and grieved the loss of each one as we read about intermittent tragic fires over the years in the *New York Post* or *Daily News*. This time hundreds had died in a single event.

As I put six-year-old Elliot to bed that night in his room facing south towards the smoldering ruins of the Twin Towers, I asked if he wanted to say a prayer for the firemen who were lost. His words – "I hope you have a good time in heaven. I wish you could have lived longer" – were simple but profound. I could think of nothing more intelligent to say myself.

Once the kids were tucked in, conversation turned to numerous near-term and long-term questions that touched on every aspect of life. Most notably, would more terrorist strikes follow these? That seemed more than plausible, even likely, given the scale and sophistication of the attacks that day. Either way, would travel be curtailed, or simply avoided, for an extended period? Commercial air travel had already been shut down for an indeterminate period. Would people move out of New York City? Would they still be willing to live and work in tall buildings anywhere? What would be the personal, economic and market impact of potentially dramatic changes in how we all lived? Nobody knew the answers to such questions.

While those large questions swirled around in endless conversations with family, friends and colleagues, there was also the more immediate and practical question of what to do the very next morning. Elliot's school closed for the day. It had wisely kept the kids for a full day on September 11 – sending them home early to their worried parents might have seemed appropriate on first reflection, but there was no way of knowing whether all those parents were still alive. Given that the business world was largely paralyzed at least momentarily, I walked Elliot to a Central Park playground on his unexpected day off to play with his classmates and hung out with other parents chattering about what would come next.

Somewhat surprisingly, no further significant attacks followed the horrific first one, and it was soon clear that most people's fears, even the anxieties of New Yorkers, were outweighed by their desire to return to something resembling normal life. Clearly those directly affected by the attack were in a different place than that. Thousands were dead or at least missing, their pictures posted on fliers asking for help and their families overwhelmed by grief from which they would likely never fully recover. Those who survived but had worked or lived downtown were also in a different place – they had been abruptly displaced and were in some sense now homeless.

One example was our old client Lehman Brothers. It quickly made a midtown hotel its temporary headquarters for thousands of staff members given that its downtown offices had been rendered uninhabitable. Yet for those of us based even a few miles away from the carnage, there was no reason not to soon send the kids back to school, return to work and simply put one foot in front of the other. We had no loved ones to mourn, the various new security measures at airports and office buildings proved tolerable inconveniences and the economic damage from the attacks was surprisingly limited. An unexpected benefit came in the form of an outpouring of sympathy that elevated New Yorkers to an even more prominent (and far more favorable) place in the minds of Americans and others around the world. So we kept moving – just as Bruce Springsteen soon prescribed in his September 11-inspired song *My City of Ruins*[8] with the words, "[c]ome on, rise up."

Our private equity business, which was poised to benefit enormously from the sharp decline in asset valuations that began just as we were fundraising, provided a real-time perspective on how Americans were responding to these shocking events. At the time of the attack, we were on the brink of investing in a business named Heartland Payment Systems, which processed credit card transactions for small businesses across America. Heartland was a relatively new business led by a charismatic entrepreneur who possessed a rare combination of skills in both sales and technology.

Niehaus had found that opportunity through his personal connection with Heartland's chief financial officer, who was the son of the Morgan Stanley CEO who had preceded Parker Gilbert. Bob Baldwin – once described as a "classic hell-on-wheels boss"[9] – and Bob Greenhill had some unhelpful history together, but none of us knew the details. Compounding that complexity, Baldwin's son had previously been a banker at Smith Barney on the wrong side of the turf battle that developed when Bob Greenhill and his band of star recruits from Morgan Stanley showed up there. Nonetheless, Niehaus's relationship was enough to overcome that not-quite-so ancient history, and as of September 11 we were set to move ahead.

The fundamental concept underlying the Heartland investment was that the increasing use of credit cards rather than cash or checks would provide a powerful tailwind for revenue and earnings growth in that sector. Heartland's particular specialty was in restaurants, and it processed credit card transactions for thousands of small restaurants across America, including my very own White Hart inn. The favorable view of the inn's bookkeeper as to Heartland's efficient and customer-friendly approach to business was a useful element of our pre-investment due diligence review.

When the terrorist attack occurred, like most investors and companies pursuing significant opportunities, we froze. But the nature of Heartland's business provided a daily measure of credit card spending, and therefore economic activity, across America. To nobody's surprise, spending plummeted in the days after the attack, as air travel stopped and people hunkered down at home, watching their televisions and trying to come to terms with what felt like a new paradigm of life in America. Remarkably, within days we saw the credit card-spending data start to tick up steadily, signaling that Americans were resuming their lives. There was really no alternative to doing so. Hence, only weeks after the attack, we summoned the nerve to close on our $25 million investment (utilizing about 6% of our capital) to acquire a third of Heartland's equity. It would prove to be one of the great investments for our fund.

In the months that followed our Greenhill Capital Partners fund took further advantage of collapsing market valuations. In what would be the fund's most important transaction, Niehaus used his bankruptcy experience, and that of our new restructuring colleagues, to team up with another relatively new investment fund called Fortress to invest in a Florida-based owner of cell towers named Pinnacle. Most people associate the bursting of the NASDAQ market bubble with the "dot-coms" – emerging technology companies, often with outlandish business models, which lacked profits and sometimes even revenue. But the financial wreckage was in many ways more severe in the telecom sector, where heavy debt loads had been accumulated as a result of excess capital spending in that rapidly growing sector. In one of the more egregious examples, a massive accounting fraud at the high-flying but heavily debt-laden telecom company WorldCom came to light at the very moment we were evaluating Pinnacle.

Overleveraged, Pinnacle became collateral damage in the tightening of credit and collapse of valuations that ensued in the telecom space, landing it in Chapter 11 bankruptcy. But while a market in free fall is not particularly discriminating in marking down valuations and starving companies of new capital, cell towers were fundamentally a far better asset than most of the telecom and tech companies that failed in that downturn. They generated reliable and growing streams of cash flow from well-capitalized wireless telecom companies like my dad's longtime employer AT&T. Those companies all needed to extend the reach and expand the capacity of their cellular networks to meet increasing demand for mobile telecommunication. It seemed logical, even before the advent of smartphones with much broader applications, that the demand for wireless phone service was going to continue to grow long term. Accordingly, using a strategy that most private equity funds of that era would not have had the experience to employ, our fund and Fortress quietly acquired some discounted Pinnacle debt in the trading market before maneuvering to acquire the whole company as it emerged from bankruptcy.

In a third extraordinarily well-timed investment in the year following the September 11 attack, GCP took a small piece of a large deal – this time in the oil and gas pipeline business. A severe market decline that constricts the flow of debt and equity capital to overleveraged investors and corporations has an uncanny way of uncovering accounting frauds. Thus just months before the collapse of WorldCom, which indirectly facilitated our opportunistic Pinnacle investment, came the meltdown of leading energy company Enron. Enron, which until shortly before its downfall was one of the most admired companies in America, suffered a spectacular fall from grace. In Enron's heyday *Fortune* magazine had gushed that "[n]o company illustrates the transformative power of innovation more than Enron."[10] But it turned out that Enron's greatest innovation was in the realm of accounting, where its fraudulent practices ultimately came to light as markets turned downward.

The market was unforgiving in marking down valuations in the energy sector in the wake of Enron's collapse. But pipelines, like cell towers, generate strong and relatively stable cash flow as energy exploration companies pay to get their product moved from oil fields to refineries and then consumers. Pipelines are essentially toll collectors in relation to the transportation of energy. As with cell towers, at the right valuation, measured as a multiple of current and expected future annual cash flow, an investment in a pipeline can be very attractive. Our fund was too small to buy a whole pipeline, or even a significant stake in one. But we were able to get a $10 million piece of the buyout of a company that was soon consolidated into what would become America's largest pipeline company, known as Energy Transfer.

On top of this lucrative investment opportunity, Enron's collapse also led to a unique advisory assignment. I received a call asking me to advise Arthur Andersen, the theretofore highly respected global accounting firm that had been Enron's auditor. With Enron bankrupt, Andersen looked to be a proverbial "deep pocket" that plaintiff's lawyers would attack on behalf of the numerous investors who had lost money as a result of the fraud.

Andersen was hugely vulnerable. Historically it had been seen as a highly conservative firm, perhaps the most so among what was long known as the "Big 8" group of auditing firms that signed off on corporate financial statements. Its accountants once comprised a veritable army of men in white shirts, striped ties and polished black wing tips. The firm's culture over time had evolved in a more aggressive direction, in part due to the contentious spin-off of its highly profitable consulting business Andersen Consulting (renamed Accenture following the separation). Andersen's auditing partners had watched their former partners on the consulting side get rich, prompting them to ramp up their efforts to increase profitability in the historically core – but less exciting – auditing business. While the vast majority of Andersen partners were undoubtedly honest and hard-working people, the Enron story, complete with tales of illegally shredded incriminating documents, was not one to which a jury would take kindly.

My role for Andersen was a peculiar one. In February 2002, William Lerach, once labeled by *The New York Times as* "a flamboyant class-action lawyer" who had "made a personal fortune and gained the lasting hatred of corporate America by bringing more than 600 suits against companies after their stock prices dropped,"[11] was picked to lead the numerous plain-tiffs seeking compensation for their investment losses at Enron. As *The Times* noted, his "selection practically guarantee[d his] law firm the largest share of any legal fees, which could amount to hundreds of millions of dol-lars." My assignment was to calculate and convey to Lerach the maximum amount that Andersen could afford to pay without itself going bankrupt and thereby undermining its ability to make good on any settlement. We hoped that Andersen's interests would be seen as ultimately aligned with Lerach's, in the sense that he would want to extract as much money as possible without causing the firm to collapse, terminating its historically steady production of cash and thereby destroying the value of whatever settlement he had agreed.

My team and I did the requisite financial analysis and wrote a lengthy sort of quasi "opinion" as to how much cash Andersen could afford to pay without going belly up. Andersen CEO Joseph Berardino and I then flew to the West Coast to meet with Lerach and his client, the University of

California (which had held Enron stock at the time of collapse), to share the analysis. Essentially, we asked him to show some restraint – for the benefit of his client, if not for that of the company and its more than 80,000 employees. However, restraint is not something that comes easily to a plaintiff's lawyer like Lerach, who had likely heard and ignored innumerable pleas for mercy from past defendants. As weeks passed and Andersen's situation further deteriorated with both clients and partners fleeing, we went back to see Lerach. He was undoubtedly accustomed to having counterparties return to offer an increased sum to reach settlement. Given the rapidly declining state of Andersen's finances, we may have been the first to offer even less than we had put forward the first time. Lerach, however, again failed to show the slightest inclination to compromise in a way that would keep Andersen afloat.

Berardino was under excruciating stress but hell-bent on finding some solution to Andersen's dilemma that would protect the firm's partners, employees and retirees. As the situation continued to worsen, it became increasingly clear that a merger – really a sale – of the historically highly profitable firm was needed. That was not a palatable alternative for such a proud and once highly esteemed institution. But if such a deal could be engineered, there would be more funds available to pay out to claimants, some partner capital and pensions would be salvaged, many of Andersen's thousands of employees would continue to have a secure home, and a humiliating meltdown could be avoided. We thus spent a couple weeks holed up in conference rooms at the Sofitel Hotel on the west side of midtown Manhattan, meeting with delegations from the other major global accounting firms. There were varying degrees of interest in an acquisition– prior to the Enron debacle, Andersen would have been a coveted merger partner, but the complexity and uncertainty now surrounding it made reaching any sort of deal extremely challenging.

We will never know whether we would ultimately have succeeded in finding a merger solution to Andersen's problems. All talks ended when, much to our collective surprise, on March 14, 2002, came the news that the Justice Department was indicting Andersen on criminal charges in relation to the Enron fraud – charging the entire entity that employed thousands of people, not simply the few individuals who acted inappropriately. Given the role that auditors played in validating the integrity of financial statements for large public companies, an indictment, let alone a conviction, was effectively a death knell for the company. The Andersen management team and staff were devastated by the news and quickly turned their attention to finding new homes, as individuals or as part of teams. Meanwhile, Lerach got $7 billion from Enron's bankrupt estate for his claimants, and undoubtedly felt little sympathy for Enron's erstwhile auditor or its staff. To me, the unexpected Justice Department move seemed like a senseless bit of prosecutorial overreach that would disrupt the lives of thousands of innocent families, while serving no legitimate purpose beyond punishing the few people who were blameworthy.

The postscript to the Andersen episode is a fascinating one, raising questions as to who really were the "good guys" and "bad guys" in that story. The Justice Department won a conviction of Andersen the next year, by which time the firm was essentially gone, but in 2005 that conviction was overturned by the Supreme Court in what *The New York Times* called "a brief, pointed and unanimous opinion."[12] The trial court's mistake had been a fundamental one: failing to "require the necessary proof that Andersen knew its actions were wrong." Andersen's management and staff likely took some degree of psychological comfort from that higher court decision, but it came far too late to resuscitate the firm.

As for Lerach, one always wondered how leading plaintiff's lawyers like him managed to routinely secure the prime clients (like University of California in the Andersen case) and thereby win the lucrative lead attorney roles in major litigation situations. In 2008 the answer to that question was unveiled when Lerach was convicted of a long-term arrangement whereby payments, essentially bribes, had been made to people who secretly agreed to be "on call" as plaintiffs against companies whose stock prices declined.[13] *The Times* noted that, over a thirty-year period, Lerach's law firm had earned $216 million in fees, in part by illegally paying $11 million to this pool of plaintiffs in waiting.

The broad economic and market downturn made this period a particularly active time for restructuring advisors, as more and more companies followed WorldCom, Enron and others into bankruptcy. Our entry into that business therefore proved very well-timed. Then, creating the opportunity to further expand that area, Harvey Miller became available. *The Wall Street Journal* had declared Harvey, as he was universally known in the bankruptcy world, "the nation's best-known bankruptcy lawyer,"[14] and nobody would have disputed that. But law firms are often not terribly commercial operations, and Harvey was effectively being forced out of Weil, Gotshal & Manges, the leading bankruptcy firm that he had played the primary role in building. The reason for this astonishing business decision was his age, then sixty-nine.

The reality was that, notwithstanding his nominal age, Harvey remained youthful and energetic. His work was his life. He appeared to have no hobbies other than occasionally attending the opera and had never had children – his inexperience in that realm was made obvious by the look on his face when, during his visit to our country home, my two-year-old daughter Jane bounded into our library stark naked to introduce herself to Harvey and his wife Ruth. We moved swiftly to bring Harvey into the firm, triggering another round of favorable publicity and further elevating the firm's profile.

While our private equity fund and still new restructuring business were both highly active and benefiting from the market turmoil, we were also continuing to make progress on the M&A side of the firm. As a result, with our confidence in the long-term potential of our business undiminished despite the terrorist attack of a few months earlier, we made our first internal promotions of homegrown young bankers to the level of managing director. We still colloquially referred to such folks as "partner" even though we were not technically a partnership. There were four promotions in this first batch, including the early New York recruit Jeff Buckalew, a restructuring banker who had followed Mike Kramer to us from Houlihan Lokey and the two young London-based bankers who had come to us from ING Barings along with Borrows and Lupton.

Just as in professional sports, one does not build an enduring Wall Street franchise entirely by recruiting proven veterans. To borrow baseball terminology, a "farm system" is required to identify and nurture young talent with high potential. These four, soon followed by another early New York team member, John Liu, were the early products of our farm system. Each was an outstanding banker who possessed all the personal attributes we looked for in partners. Our baseball analogy does not end there, however. At the same time as these promotions, we announced the recruitment of what would turn out to be a short-lived insurance partner and accepted the resignation of the telecom-focused partner who had joined us in New York just as we were launching in London. In sum, these moves provided further evidence that our roster of senior personnel would continue to evolve as we strived to field the best possible team. Including our expanded partner group, we now had a team of just under 100 total employees across three offices.

In the end, with the benefit of restructuring work to supplement what were now reduced M&A opportunities, we managed to emerge largely unscathed from the dot-com crash, the September 11th attacks and all the economic and market carnage that followed. The decline in stock market valuations and tightening of credit – the very same factors that created extraordinary opportunities for our restructuring and investing businesses – caused M&A deal volume to fall by half in 2001, and then even further in 2002. On top of the decline in deal activity, the results of big banks were further hit by loans that went bad as well as reduced financing activity. This all served to trigger a flood of resumes to our firm.

Despite the market's painful toll on our competitors, our firm's revenue declined only slightly in 2001, before rebounding to a record of $113 million in 2002. Our partner group had grown to eighteen by then, double what it was only two years earlier. But still those relatively flat but remarkably stable revenue figures were satisfying given the difficult market environment. And our successes in that period included a number of prominent roles that served to further burnish our brand: the $5.9 billion merger of leading paper and packaging companies, Mead and Westvaco, on which I acted as lead advisor; the sale of Burger King by Diageo; the sale of Morton's Restaurant Group, our first of what would be many M&A deals for leading UK retailer Tesco; and bankruptcy-related restructurings of numerous companies including AT&T Canada and Regal Cinemas.

My personal role throughout this period of intense activity and evolving markets remained eclectic and interesting, just as I preferred. For the most part, I was an M&A banker advising corporate clients on large and complex transactions. But as our investment business grew, that also took more time. I took our second board seat behind Niehaus at Heartland and led our investment in a Texas-based insurance company called Republic. At Republic, I got another lesson in how suddenly things can go wrong in a seemingly healthy business. That company's youthful and charismatic CEO was an important part of what attracted our investment group to that acquisition. Then on our very first day of owning the business the poor fellow tragically died of a heart attack, thereby immediately and exponentially expanding the role of board members like myself, as we sought to stabilize the business and find it a new leader.

My nonprofit board role at Prep for Prep also became more time-consuming and challenging in this period, as I came to understand that charitable organizations bear many of the same market-driven risks that large corporations do. When I first joined the board, my naive assumption had been that the role of such a board member was limited to writing checks, encouraging friends to write checks and generally being a cheerleader for the organization. In this case those roles were easy given the obvious appeal of Prep's mission of using society's highest quality educational resources to accelerate the advancement of bright young people of color and thereby enhance the diversity of those in leadership positions at America's businesses, banks, law firms and educational institutions. But good times and easy money can lead to overreach in the nonprofit as well as corporate world, and in 2000 the possibilities for all types of organizations seemed limitless. Emboldened by its success in the five boroughs of New York City, Prep thus launched a significant expansion.

Backed by a grant from the charitable arm of Goldman Sachs, Prep created a sister organization that aimed to help twelve- and thirteen-year-old public-school students of color in the suburbs surrounding New York succeed in more challenging Advanced Placement courses in high school, thereby better positioning them to get into top-tier colleges. The motivation was noble, and the needs in suburbia were significant, but the challenges the new project faced were substantial. For one, suburban areas lacked the plethora of elite private high schools that Manhattan had. In the historic urban program, those well-endowed schools were our powerful allies in helping young people from disadvantaged backgrounds get ahead. More importantly, the Goldman Sachs funding was adequate only to help launch the program, not to propel it forward. I was told that foundations are often more excited to help start a new venture than to dole out funding for ongoing operations.

In a bull market where raising money from well-paid bankers and lawyers was easy that longer-term funding challenge had seemed surmountable. But now, with the sharp downturn in markets and a commensurate decline in Wall Street compensation, that fund-raising task seemed formidable. Prep thus formed a small task force of board members to figure out what to do about the program. Somehow I was tapped for that group. Being the relative newbie on the board I was perhaps the one best-positioned to dispassionately analyze the situation and state the simple truth: Prep could not afford this expansion, and the incremental cost of the new program was such that in a tough fund-raising environment even Prep's core mission in New York City might be at risk. Others quickly saw the logic underlying my conclusion, and together we decided to terminate the new program after only two classes had enrolled. Nobody likes the idea of scaling back – those in the not-for-profit world certainly don't enjoy it any more than those in large companies, but in this case doing so was the right decision for Prep.

Meanwhile, in my spare time, I was learning at the White Hart that a surprising amount of oversight and management is necessary in even the smallest of enterprises. The inn had proven a fun venue for annual summer outings for our firm's junior analysts and associates – we went biking or hiking by day, and the team would drink the bar dry after Roxanne and I went home for the night. I had acquired the inn believing I could enjoy such events while the existing management team kept me free of any meaningful responsibility or time commitment relating to day-to-day operations. But that theory blew up only weeks into my ownership when the irate father of one of our youthful restaurant servers found my New York home number and called to complain that his daughter had been harassed by the inn's male chef. He wanted to go straight to the top with his complaint, just as I would have done in similar circumstances. Soon thereafter I figured out that the inn's continuing losses were such that I needed to replace the inn manager who I had inherited in the acquisition. I even ended up getting involved in menu changes, as we tried to find the right formula to maximize revenue and minimize losses.

At the same time, back at my day job, the management task at Greenhill continued to grow. Bob always spoke of how simple our business was– that it sort of ran itself. But if the White Hart, with its several dozen employees and modest revenue generated at only one location, required intensive management time and effort, then surely a growing transatlantic business staffed by hyper-ambitious people and generating more than $100 million in annual revenue by advising on high-stakes financial transactions would require even more. With Bob having little interest in management and even denying the need for that function, the task fell largely to me. Or maybe, just as with Prep for Prep and the White Hart, I simply grabbed it.

CHAPTER SIX

REFUSING TO SELL OUT

You take one road,
You try one door,
There isn't time for any more.
One's life consists of either/or.[1]

— *Stephen Sondheim,* Follies

To sell or not to sell – sometimes that is the question.

In every prospective M&A deal involving a whole company there's a party on the sell side that must decide whether to accept a buyout offer or continue as an independent company. The attractiveness of a bid depends on the price offered and sometimes on the form of consideration (most often cash but sometimes an ownership stake in the acquiring company), as well as on whether another party might be willing to pay more than the bid on the table. In comparison, the attractiveness of remaining independent depends on the perceived future upside potential and downside risk inherent in the business as it currently exists, and on how the value implied by likely future scenarios compares to the offer price. At least that is how corporate finance textbooks view it.

In the real world, there are reasons for saying no to what financial calculations suggest is a fair offer that have little or nothing to do with money. Those reasons are often as important to the decision-making process as economic considerations. The desire to preserve what has been painstakingly built is primal. Understandably, many founders of private companies and even CEOs of public companies fiercely protect their company's independence and seek to maintain control of its destiny simply because they do not want their business to disappear within a larger enterprise or, more selfishly, do not want to give up personal control of what they see as "their" business. While private company managements may have only themselves or a single owner to whom to answer on the sale question, public company managements need the support of their public shareholders or at least the representatives thereof on the corporate board of directors. Accordingly, they must often couch their somewhat self-interested reaction to a buyout offer in more defensible terms.

Given these noneconomic factors involved in dealmaking, investment bankers look for situations where a target management or board (ideally both) is primed to sell. In determining that, bankers check, for example, how secure the target's CEO is in his position, as well as how close he is to retirement and whether a successor has been identified. For situations where neither side of a prospective deal is ready or willing to give up control, bankers often refer to the deal as a "merger" rather than "acquisition" in an attempt to downplay the transfer of control that naturally occurs upon a business combination. In cases where the two companies in question are of similar size, bankers have even developed a specific transaction structure labeled a "merger of equals," even though in practice it is rare that two companies led by inevitably strong-willed management teams can truly share control.

For firms like ours, relatively small services businesses where the only meaningful assets are people, the calculation is more complicated.

Many such businesses aspire to do nothing more than generate a good living for the people involved, enabling them to do what they enjoy doing, in a format they enjoy doing it, for as long as they wish to continue. Those with more ambition and a longer term perspective can aspire to something more: building an enduring institution that develops the scale, breadth and depth of talent, diversity of revenue sources and general resilience to outlive those who formed the business and carry on for multiple generations. A third alternative is to forego the risks and benefits of independence and take the shortcut to wealth creation by selling one's business as a work in progress to a larger company looking to expand its operations or accelerate its growth.

In my case, I came to Greenhill wanting nothing more than to make a comfortable living doing the work I enjoyed – being in the middle of large, complex and high-profile deals – in a format that I enjoyed doing it. Importantly, particularly in light of my Morgan Stanley experience, I wanted to be at a firm where what I did was the core business, if not the sole activity, of the organization and where the place's character could not be transformed overnight through a combination with a different business. That's what I had feared the Dean Witter deal would do to Morgan Stanley. As Greenhill quickly gained momentum the second alternative, building a business that was sustainable for the long term, soon began to seem like a real possibility. Clearly that was appealing. It would provide me with a full career of doing what I enjoyed doing while also providing all the psychic benefits of building and ultimately leaving behind a legacy. The third possibility, selling the firm, was not something I considered. Indeed, the potential for that sort of thing was part of why I had fled Morgan Stanley.

Regardless of my personal desires, it was clear that a lucrative M&A exit is a very real and continuing possibility in the investment banking business. That is an obvious point given that the business is populated by ambitious and financially motivated dealmakers. In relatively good times, prosperity breeds confidence, which leads to aggressive acquisition and expansion strategies. And as each deal within the sector gets announced the fear of missing out drives ever-increasing interest in deals from other industry participants. Equally, given that history is replete with stories of the disappearance of investment banks, in more difficult times firms that come to fear they are on the road to failure – a realization that can sometimes develop very suddenly – will aggressively seek a friendly acquirer as a safe port in a storm.

There are innumerable examples of M&A among investment banks in both scenarios. There was the long history of acquisitions by Sandy Weill that led to his hiring Bob Greenhill to build an investment bank to go along with what was largely a retail brokerage firm. When that failed Sandy promptly bought a major firm, Salomon Brothers, to pursue that same objective via an acquisition. There was the Morgan Stanley/Dean Witter deal that helped motivate my move to Greenhill. And given our unique position as a firm that had the expertise to advise on such transactions yet lacked the scale to play the role of acquirer, there were many other such deals on which we were asked to act as financial advisor.

The sale of the San Francisco-based technology-focused firm Robertson Stephens was the first such role, and this "mid-sized" transaction neatly illustrated both why such transactions happen and why they so often fail. From the seller's perspective, Robbie Stephens had all the risks of a narrowly focused firm – given the vagaries of the market, there can be periods of numerous public offerings of technology companies and periods of none – meaning feast or famine for the firm's owners and key people. Further, the potential to convert private partnership interests of unknown value into either cash or stock that can be sold on a stock exchange is highly attractive. Such partnership interests are typically traded within a partnership (e.g. when partners retire) at "book value," which is the net value of a company's assets calculated by standard accounting methodologies, while acquisitions and IPOs are typically done at a substantial premium to book value, based on a view of future earnings and cash flow potential. Further, income from ongoing operations is heavily taxed "ordinary" income, while proceeds of a sale are generally treated more favorably from a tax perspective as "capital gains."

From the perspective of the buyer, larger financial firms are always looking for acquisitions that will add to their capabilities. Technology sector banking was then a small yet highly specialized area – it would not be easy to simply enter that business organically. Yet that sector was seen as an area with significant growth potential, so what had historically been done by specialized small firms was becoming increasingly attractive to larger ones. Hence at the end of our sale process Bank of America, also then based in San Francisco, acquired Robertson Stephens. As is usually the case in the world of M&A, on the day of announcement both buyer and seller appeared to feel very good about the deal.

Why do such transactions so often fail? The aftermath of the Robertson deal highlighted the challenges that make a long-term successful business combination difficult, particularly in a services business without significant real assets. For one, a small entrepreneurial firm with little administrative infrastructure is very different from a large bureaucratic organization. The people who run, or even work at, the former do not easily fit into the latter. In this case a youthful West Coast firm taking risks to execute capital raises for still unproven companies in the early days of Silicon Valley was being combined with a traditional and conservative bank, which focused on taking deposits and cautiously making loans. Second, while detailed, highly negotiated terms around continuing employment of key personnel are routine in such transactions, there is no contract that can force a manager or employee to try hard or to find a way to fit into a larger management structure, or indeed to remain on board a single day longer than the contractually required period. Exacerbating both of those points is the fact that, while deal lawyers try hard to contemplate and contractually provide for every possible future scenario, nothing remains static for very long in such a dynamic industry.

In this case, less than a year after Bank of America acquired its San Francisco neighbor Robertson Stephens it did a much larger merger, with an even more conservative bank, based in North Carolina, called Nations Bank. While the Bank of America name survived that combination, the Nations Bank headquarters location, senior management team and more risk averse culture all prevailed. Complicating matters even further, Nations Bank had very recently acquired Robertson's crosstown rival Montgomery Securities. That rivalry was particularly fierce given that Sandy Robertson had broken away from Montgomery many years earlier to found Robertson Stephens. It was obvious that the two old rivals, now very unexpectedly and in a circuitous manner combined into one firm, would find it impossible to work together. So Robertson was resold soon after it was acquired, and in fact ended up enduring multiple different ownerships in the few years to come before ultimately essentially disappearing.

The ING Bank acquisition of Furman Selz highlighted similar challenges. Why was a large Dutch financial institution focused on traditional banking in Europe, and with a very limited presence in America, interested in expanding into US investment banking? If there was a strong rationale for that, why choose a small relatively unknown firm that was in truth an amalgamation of even smaller boutique businesses? There would be huge costs to overlaying a large foreign bank bureaucracy on a collection of modest US businesses, but would there be any synergies to offset those, let alone create any incremental earnings or value accretion? The fact is that this, like many M&A deals across industries, was a sort of compromise transaction. ING wanted to expand into the large and seemingly attractive US market, but it knew such a move would be a risky diversion into unfamiliar territory. So it refrained from "betting the ranch" on a more meaningful transaction, and instead spent a sum it could afford to lose. The scale of ING was such that nobody on the outside would ever even know how Furman's businesses fared. But if there were an audit even a few years later, one suspects there would have been little evidence of Furman's small businesses still thriving within ING.

A couple years later, through much of 2000, we advised on a much larger potential transaction that did not come to fruition, yet further highlighted the challenges inherent in M&A among investment banking firms. Our client Lehman Brothers made an ultimately unsuccessful attempt to acquire Donaldson, Lufkin & Jenrette, the investment banking and brokerage firm known as DLJ where my Wharton classmate Jamie Dinan had begun his career. Following the collapse of Drexel Burnham Lambert a decade earlier, DLJ had become a market leader in the lucrative business of underwriting below-investment grade (commonly referred to as "junk") bonds. Over the years, it also became a major player in merchant banking – the business of investing equity (mostly other people's money) in highly leveraged acquisition transactions. While Lehman was performing well at the time, it clearly ranked considerably behind the leading investment banking firms like Goldman Sachs and Morgan Stanley. DLJ was seen as a prize catch that could dramatically enhance its competitive position.

DLJ started out as a boutique research firm formed by three friends in 1959. It flourished in the bull market of the 1960s before successfully completing its own path-breaking IPO in 1970, at a time when nearly all Wall Street firms were private partnerships. It was later acquired by the insurance company Equitable Life before going public again in 1995. Over time, it grew into a substantial business providing a wide range of services to the middle market, with 11,000 employees at the time it was sold for a second and final time. Despite DLJ's complex thirty-year history and significant scale, it had retained its entrepreneurial management style, close knit culture and "small firm" feel.

Wall Street firms were feeling flush at that moment, not yet realizing that March 2000 marked the peak of the NASDAQ Market Index (up circa 400% in the prior five years), nor how steep the market decline from there would be (nearly 80% in the two and a half years from that peak). The large

Swiss Bank UBS had just agreed to buy the major US brokerage firm PaineWebber, and animal spirits across the industry were running high. According to *The Wall Street Journal*, several firms were interested in DLJ, perhaps in part because its stock had declined precipitously from a high in April the prior year before rebounding to some extent as possibilities of a sale of the firm became known.[2] Chase Manhattan, J.P. Morgan (which would later merge with Chase), Credit Suisse First Boston and Lehman Brothers all pursued the deal.

Bob Greenhill and I joined numerous meetings at Lehman's downtown headquarters with CEO Richard (Dick) Fuld and his executive committee to discuss its pursuit of DLJ. Fuld was highly reminiscent of Bob's old Morgan Stanley nemesis John Mack – in fact in my view he was an exaggerated version of Mack. Like Mack, he came up through the sales and trading side of the business. But he had an even more intimidating style, earning him the nickname "the gorilla," which seemed both more primitive and more accurately descriptive than the "Mack the knife" sobriquet carried by his Morgan Stanley counterpart. Neither Fuld nor others on his executive committee had any meaningful M&A experience, and he was therefore enamored of Bob's illustrious history and aggressiveness in the context of a competitive auction. Bob liked to win and wasn't afraid of making some compromises to do so.

Our meetings in Fuld's conference room were generally brief, filled with locker-room-style banter among Fuld's team and dominated by Fuld himself. There was little dissent within his executive committee, as each member jockeyed to prove he was the most willing to accept the inherent risk in what would, unlike ING's more conservative acquisition of Furman, have been a "bet the company" transaction. In our discussions Fuld and his team repeatedly referred to the enormous potential transaction as a "trade." Based on my experience, that was highly unusual and clearly indicative of a lack of understanding of the acquisition process, let alone the laborious post-merger integration that is necessary following any significant acquisition.

While our behind-the-scenes preparation for the auction process unveiled some fundamental weaknesses in Fuld and his management team that would contribute to Lehman's demise several years later, this time they were saved from what would have been a disastrous deal by an even more aggressive bidder: Credit Suisse First Boston (CSFB). CSFB was a much larger institution, and thus better positioned to fund what was ultimately an extraordinary $11.5 billion winning bid for DLJ.

The deal was CSFB's swift response to its Swiss rival UBS's very similarly sized PaineWebber acquisition, but it had two serious flaws. First, while a combination with the larger, trading-oriented Lehman would have been challenging, it was inconceivable that DLJ's unique culture could be melded into that of a stodgy Swiss bank. Within a few months *The Wall Street Journal* was writing of a "culture clash" and "exodus" of newly acquired talent to several other firms.[3] The second problem was that CSFB had acquired DLJ at the end of a long bull market, just as a steep downturn was beginning. Yet the price paid had been driven higher by the hotly contested auction process, with several ambitious bidders fighting over what was one of few sizable remaining targets in the industry.

The fact that CSFB had paid a very full price was obvious immediately. Many years later, it took a $3.8 billion accounting write-off related to the transaction, representing about a third of the purchase price.[4] Many years following, in 2022, it wrote off even more of the purchase price.[5] And not long after that, the investment banking business acquired via deals for First Boston and DLJ brought this once mighty Swiss bank to its knees, culminating in a fire sale of the whole enterprise to UBS. But even long before that tragic future played out, most contemporaries on Wall Street ranked the DLJ deal among the most poorly conceived and worst-executed transactions in the sector's history.

Around the same time as the DLJ transaction, legendary dealmaker Bruce Wasserstein was exploring the sale of his firm. Informally referred to as "Wasserella," Wasserstein Perella was in many ways simply an older and larger version of our firm. Bruce had long been a central figure in the world of deals. Widely seen as brilliant, over time he became even better known for his enormous ego, driving ambition and unabashed self-interest. He began his career as a lawyer at the prestigious New York firm of Cravath, Swaine & Moore, from which my last Wachtell Lipton boss had come, then was lured into investment banking at First Boston (before it was acquired by Credit Suisse) by Joe Perella, the man who later very briefly became my boss at Morgan Stanley. There he played a leading role in building one of the top M&A franchises. Then, in early 1988, in what was a period of record-breaking deal activity, he and Perella broke away with a large portion of their team to form an eponymous new firm.

In reporting the move *The Wall Street Journal* gushed that, in an era for mergers and acquisitions that "created stars like a Hollywood studio, no one outshone Bruce Wasserstein."[6] Much later the author William Cohan, in his definitive history of Lazard, the advisory firm where Wasserstein spent his last years, described him in more lurid terms: "arrogant, brash, boorish, and much feared...a creative and entrepreneurial genius...notoriously strong-willed and short-tempered."[7] Cohan further labeled him the "Harvey Weinstein of investment banking," well before the Oscar-winning Hollywood filmmaker Weinstein was outed as a sexual predator.

Wasserstein and Perella and the troops who followed them out of First Boston initially moved into the offices of my old law firm Wachtell Lipton. Marty Lipton undoubtedly offered the temporary space, as he did in other such situations, knowing that doing so would cement what could become a hugely valuable client relationship. From day one, the new business benefited from highly favorable publicity in an era when deals and dealmakers were closely followed by the press in a manner akin to sports stars. The new firm got off to a fabulous start amid the frenzied deal activity of the late 1980s, initially appearing high in the "league tables" ranking the various competing firms in the M&A business by the number and scale of transactions on which they advised. Only six months after the new firm's formation the Japanese securities firm Nomura paid $100 million for a 20%-equity stake in conjunction with forming a joint venture to work together on international transactions involving Japanese clients.[8]

Not long after its highly successful launch, the firm's performance and profile declined significantly amid the recession and steep downturn in M&A activity taking place in the early 1990s. Wasserella had built substantial scale right at the start, and keeping all those people busy was difficult in a less-active market. Worse, beyond suffering from the general decline in deal activity, Bruce's evolving reputation also contributed to the firm's declining fortunes. Some reputational deterioration was inevitable. The sharp stock market decline of that period meant that many deals done before the downturn came to be seen as failures, not infrequently damaging the reputations of the advisors involved. But it didn't help that over time he became known as "bid 'em up Bruce," indicating a perceived predilection for pushing clients to pay more than perhaps made sense, just so that a deal would get done and he would earn his transaction fee.

As the firm's fortunes waned key people began to leave, including Perella. He left in 1993, less than five years after he had helped found the firm, to join Morgan Stanley, where it was hoped he would fill Bob Greenhill's shoes as a brand-name senior dealmaker. Bruce's firm retained the Wasserstein Perella name – odd given that Perella himself was now at a competitor – and continued in a less visible, and less successful, manner.

Despite ensuing years of largely unimpressive performance and the departure of his co-founder, Wasserstein retained a large personal profile. As people including his co-founder left the firm, he was clever enough to increase his already large ownership position in the firm. It gave him the incentive, and a lifetime of deal-making gave him the skills, to look for a transactional solution to his continuing operating challenges. In 1997 *The Wall Street Journal* reported high-level talks regarding a merger of Wasserstein Perella and the much larger and more established Lazard firm, before that idea was shot down by senior Lazard partners.[9] Other names, including Lehman Brothers, had occasionally been linked to Wasserstein's firm in merger rumors. Then, in 2000, amid heavy deal activity within the sector, Germany's Dresdner Bank appeared as a possible acquirer.

Within the German market Dresdner was a sort of stepsibling to the powerful Deutsche Bank, but that only fed its ambition. In 1995 it had acquired the British merchant bank Kleinwort Benson, a firm that traced its roots back to the 1700s, in one of many foreign buyouts of such firms in that era. The combined investment banking businesses operated under the brand Dresdner Kleinwort but had limited potential without a meaningful presence in the US, which was by far the largest investment banking market in the world. Adding to the desire for an American presence was the fact that Dresdner Kleinwort's people were paid far below American standards and of course were unhappy about that. If a major US operation could be secured, it would be a natural next step to align pay scales for investment bankers across the Atlantic. Hence strategic and personal interests were allied in seeking a deal.

Clearly Dresdner was getting anxious, perhaps even desperate. On top of highly visible failed attempts earlier that year to merge with either of its two major German banking peers, Deutsche Bank and Commerzbank, it had been rumored as an acquirer of the large US securities firm PaineWebber. That firm was much more a retail brokerage house than an investment banking firm, but there would have been enough there to provide Dresdner Kleinwort some US investment banking presence. Then, in the summer of 2000, Swiss giant UBS bought PaineWebber, paying $12 billion in a half-cash/half-stock deal, as industry consolidation in the wake of the Morgan Stanley/Dean Witter deal continued apace. Dresdner Bank was thus zero-for-three in merger tries that year.

Meanwhile, *The Wall Street Journal* reported that it was "no secret on Wall Street that Mr. Wasserstein [was] quietly peddling his firm."[10] And even though his firm had very little similarity to the three much larger ones that Dresdner had recently failed to secure, it must have seemed like a reasonable consolation prize. Ever the brilliant tactician, Wasserstein could undoubtedly smell how anxious Dresdner was to get a deal done and would have known exactly how to use that knowledge to his benefit. Dresdner, meanwhile, had almost no familiarity with the intimidating Wasserstein beyond what it must have read in numerous newspaper stories over the years. In fact it would have known little about the US investment banking industry in general or the kind of people who inhabited it. That's why, despite no previous connection to Dresdner, our firm was brought in for a limited, late-stage role to provide tactical advice. Essentially, we were there to help deal with Bruce.

On his side, Bruce largely handled the transaction himself, with little visibility for his internal team and none for any outside advisor. He was plainly in a huge hurry, looking to take advantage of Dresdner's recent disappointments and the current frenzy for deals. At the same time, he was extremely cagey about what information he would provide to help a buyer determine an appropriate valuation.

One bit of data, however, was already public and played a significant role in the atmospherics around the deal: after a few years of relatively unexciting performance, Wasserstein's firm that year had a fifth-place ranking in the US M&A league tables. Such rankings were of disproportionate importance to large banks. They focused heavily on similar rankings for activities like debt and equity underwriting, where those generally had a reasonably close correlation to revenue generation and profitability. But M&A league tables, in contrast, could be hugely misleading and sometimes have minimal correlation to those more important metrics. In the history of M&A league tables, it is likely that no ranking was more misleading than Wasserstein's was that year.

Wasserstein's extraordinary ranking related almost entirely to a single transaction: Time Warner's $182 billion merger with America Online. The fact that this role would be seen as so meaningful was remarkable in two ways. First, the deal itself received a lukewarm initial reception, as both the strategic rationale and the extraordinary price Time Warner paid were seen as highly questionable. Indeed, soon this deal would be seen as the one that marked the end of the 1990s takeover boom and thereafter serve as a poster child for the worst M&A deals of that era.

What was even worse was what this huge deal said about Wasserstein's position as an M&A advisor. His firm played no role whatsoever in putting the deal together. In fact, it was hired by Time Warner only after the deal's announcement, after which it fought for a nominal role to get league table credit. The same was true for Goldman Sachs and Merrill Lynch, as firms scrambled to get themselves somehow associated with a landmark transaction, not yet realizing that affiliation with this particular deal would soon become somewhat of an embarrassment. The unseemly squabbling over deal credit became so intense that it led Thomson Financial, the information services firm that published the most closely followed league tables, to decide that such post-announcement roles would no longer be counted in calculating league table rankings.[11]

In regard to sharing with Dresdner actual financial information about his firm, Bruce was stubbornly guarded. Eventually, he agreed to meet alone with just Bob Greenhill and me, to share some data. There I sat in our modest conference room in sublet office space with two titans of the early M&A business, longtime competitors who clearly did not really know each other. Both were somewhat socially awkward men. Bruce was overweight, reserved and cerebral, while Bob was sinewy, focused like a laser beam and always in a hurry. Neither was skilled at gracious small talk. Bruce knew that our firm was off to a fabulous start, and that given our lean team structure we would be generating very substantial profits. He also must have known that we would be fully aware that he was in the process of making an extraordinary deal for himself at the expense of our client.

After a very brief preamble, Bruce handed over several pages of numbers. Despite a proposed price tag for the business of over $1 billion, it was quickly apparent that his firm had generated very modest, if any, real profitability in recent years. Essentially, the firm had been making just enough money in most years to compensate its people and cover other operating costs.

Before we could make a comment or ask a single question, Bruce put his spin on the data: "Bob, you've built your firm to make money. I built mine to be a platform for a larger bank to acquire." In other words, he had the chutzpah to claim that he had not even been trying to generate profit. Instead, he claimed to have been investing and reinvesting in developing a brand and team that might appear valuable to a larger bank trying to gain instant access to the lucrative American M&A market. To use a term popularized in the dot-com sector in that frothy era, his business was built to be "plug-and-play" for a large bank like Dresdner.

In the end Dresdner acquired Wasserstein's firm for $1.4 billion, approximately $625 million of which was said to end up in Bruce's pocket.[12] On top of that, Bruce had been guaranteed $25 million in annual compensation going forward.

Whether he ever intended to make the combination work from the buyer's perspective will never be known. For only three months after the deal closed, in an echo of what happened in the wake of the Robertson Stephens deal, Dresdner itself was sold to the huge German insurer Allianz for $20 billion. That unlikely transaction converted the huge equity stake Bruce had just received into cash. Then, notwithstanding that Dresdner had acquired Wasserstein Perella to gain access to the US market, Bruce promptly relocated himself to London, in what Lazard historian William Cohan later quite plausibly suggested was a move designed to avoid high New York state and city taxes on his huge capital gain.[13] Soon Bruce ended up in what *The Wall Street Journal* called "a vitriolic, public battle"[14] with his new employer, and before their first year together was over Wasserstein resigned to become head (oddly, his official title was just that: "Head") of Lazard.

Given the high-flying era in which Greenhill was launched, and given how common business combinations were in the investment banking space, it is perhaps no surprise that our firm also attracted interest from would-be acquirers. What was surprising was how quickly that interest materialized. My offer letter upon joining the firm detailed how any sale of all or part of the firm would benefit me, but I did not give much thought to that possibility. The firm was very young, with only a couple deals to its name, and the third and fourth partners (the latter being myself) were just then joining.

Yet within days of my joining the firm in early 1997 Bob Greenhill called me into his office to show me a one-page term sheet that his friend at Deutsche Bank had given him. It was a proposal to acquire a significant minority stake in our firm based on a valuation in excess of $200 million. Deutsche then had a very modest US investment banking presence and, like its European peers, was desirous of gaining a meaningful position in that large market. In retrospect, its decision a year earlier to sublease our firm space in its midtown headquarters had clearly been motivated in part by a desire to affiliate with our nascent firm and its high-profile founder. From our firm's perspective, a deal on the proposed valuation was remarkable given we had almost no track record and not much more than a dozen total employees including support staff. From my personal perspective, the proposed terms would have provided a quick and completely unexpected windfall in relation to the roughly 10%-ownership stake I had acquired only days before.

Nonetheless, I had no interest.

I had left Morgan Stanley in part because it was merging into a larger entity such that the area in which I worked would be of little importance to the combined firm. Becoming part of a large German bank seemed much worse than becoming part of an American brokerage firm like Dean Witter. Further, a partial ownership stake seemed the worst of all worlds – we would be neither a nimble independent firm nor an integrated part of a leading lending bank. I diplomatically conveyed my perspective to my new partner and boss – a man I had first met only weeks earlier – once again referencing the grand vision for our firm that we had sketched out over our first dinner.

Fortunately, while Bob was clearly flattered by the Deutsche proposal, he did not seem terribly enamored of it either. As would often be the case, Bob did not have a strong point of view on longer-term strategic matters like this; he was much more focused on whatever client deal he was working on that day. Moreover, he clearly bore scars from his rough exits from Morgan Stanley and Smith Barney, and instinctively wanted to avoid a situation where he risked again reporting to someone who might ultimately turn on him. Accordingly, we never formally responded to the Deutsche proposal, but rather simply let it die a quiet death.

Only a few months later, while our firm still consisted of just four partners and a sole office in New York, Steve Rattner, the deputy CEO of Lazard who was destined to later serve as "auto czar" in the Obama Administration during the financial crisis, reached out to Bob. Before moving to Lazard Rattner had worked at Morgan Stanley in his first investment banking job after serving as a *New York Times* reporter. He was well-connected enough in the media sector that he soon thrived in his new career, then moved to the more narrowly focused and entrepreneurial Lazard firm. Rattner's success was such that publicly visible friction soon arose between him and Lazard's top banker, the legendary Felix Rohatyn, just as it had years earlier between Rohatyn and his predecessor, the equally legendary Andre Meyer. Everyone in our industry knew this was how things had seemingly always worked at Lazard.

Overseeing the chaos was principal Lazard owner and chairman Michel David-Weill, a complex, highly sophisticated and manipulative European aristocrat who had successfully held sway over Lazard for decades. A March 1997 *Vanity Fair* article[15] exposed to the wider public the infighting within this secretive private partnership. Michel's son-in-law and supposed heir, Edouard Stern, scion of another prominent French banking family, had just resigned. Rohatyn, the man who helped save New York from bankruptcy in the 1970s, was shortly to be named ambassador to France by President Clinton. Thus, "there was a leadership vacuum at Lazard," and David-Weill was "therefore spending a great deal of time lately trying to figure out what to do next." While he had not yet made up his mind, he alluded to a compromise solution under which several existing New York partners would share power.

Before that next generation of leadership at Lazard was anointed, however, two external solutions were explored. The first was to acquire Wasserstein Perella and put Bruce Wasserstein in charge. This was an old idea, as Wasserstein and Perella had explored moving to Lazard when they were exiting First Boston years earlier. But, as previously noted, the idea of acquiring Bruce and his firm "was squelched by top Lazard partners"[16] who were all undoubtedly familiar with Wasserstein and the organizational and cultural challenges his arrival would create. The same story that reported the Wasserstein dialogue also said Bob Greenhill's name had been discussed. Indeed, it was around then that our four partners were invited to visit Lazard's offices at 30 Rockefeller Plaza, the backdrop for New York's annual Christmas tree lighting and the home to the Rainbow Room, NBC and *Saturday Night Live*.

The host was Steve Rattner, who knew Bob from his stint at Morgan Stanley and later disclosed in William Cohan's history of Lazard that the meeting was his idea.[17] A handful of other senior Lazard partners were also in the room. The meeting was awkward. The internal dissension at Lazard was well known to us and everyone else in our business. On their side, Bob's track record as a less-than-successful manager at Morgan Stanley and Smith Barney must have been equally known. Yet they had somehow concluded that combining our firms and giving Bob a senior leadership position might help solve their problems. Lazard did not have a clear view of how that would work in practice, and no specific proposal was made.

In fact, given the power David-Weill wielded over such matters, the people in that room likely had no authority to make a proposal. They were simply exploring whether the concept might be of interest.

From my perspective, a combination with Lazard would have been a personal as well as strategic disaster. But as with the Deutsche proposal a few months earlier, Bob had little interest in engaging on such matters. Again, the conversation died after just one brief meeting.

Only a few months after the awkward Lazard meeting, yet another opportunity arose. The Dutch bank ING was interested in an alliance or acquisition following the help that we provided in its acquisition of Furman Selz. Barings, the UK merchant bank ING had acquired a few years earlier, had previously benefited from ownership of the US advisory firm Dillon Read, which it had acquired in 1991, before selling it back to Dillon Read's partners after the Barings bankruptcy in 1995. As noted previously in the context of the recruitment of our initial London partners, this concept was of no interest and rejected on the spot. Fortuitously, the lack of an American partner firm to help on transatlantic deals was undoubtedly part of what drove Borrows and Lupton out of ING Barings and into Greenhill a short time later.

After those initial three approaches in our first year together, acquisition interest in our firm cooled. This was understandable; clearly history was not going to look kindly on the flurry of deals in the sector that took place just before the curtain came down on the economic and stock market boom of the 1990s. The bursting of that bubble had come suddenly, and the resulting damage to Wall Street improved the relative competitive position of our firm. Accordingly, when the inevitable healing of markets took place, it was certain that new suitors would appear.

Not too much time passed before Nomura Securities of Japan appeared in 2002. Nomura had a highly successful Japanese brokerage business but had found success elsewhere in the world elusive. Over the years it made repeated attempts to remedy that, either by recruiting teams of people or making investments such as the stake it took in Wasserstein Perella shortly after it was formed in 1988. Yet as that firm's fortunes waned so did the value of that alliance. Hence the approach to our firm, which led to Simon Borrows and myself flying to Tokyo.

One might reasonably wonder why, having turned down both American and European suitors, we even bothered to cross the Pacific to explore a sale to a Japanese firm. Yet, as noted earlier, each time a company is approached regarding a sale it has a fiduciary obligation to its owners to reflect on both the perceived future upside potential as well as the risks that lie on the existing independent path. It can then compare the value thereby implied to whatever purchase price is offered.

Clearly our firm had enjoyed an extraordinary first five years, with what was still a very small team now generating over $100 million per year in revenue. But life at the firm was not without its complexities. A business like ours needed a surprising amount of management, particularly on the personnel front given the ambitious and complex personalities that populate the whole industry. Considering our peculiar structure, with a chairman who had little interest in such matters and a so-called "two-person administration committee" that shared decision-making responsibility, all management needed to happen in a somewhat stealthy manner.

As the firm inexorably grew even a little bit larger, the management task became more challenging and less enjoyable. But also as the firm became larger it became increasingly apparent that this firm we were building was worth some "real money." The more revenue we generated (and therefore, value we created), the more questions would arise regarding the allocation of that value. Even bringing in new talent, a critical step in the firm's continued development, became more difficult, as in each case we faced the question of how much of the existing franchise value should be granted to someone who had nothing to do with creating that value.

We knew that Nomura had assigned a $500 million valuation to Wasserstein Perella when it was newly formed. What might it offer for our similar business with a considerably longer track record, not to mention the resilience to survive the Long-Term Capital crisis, the bursting of the dot com bubble, the September 11 terrorist attack and the market turmoil that accompanied each of those? We had to find out.

So off we went to Tokyo in what was my first ever trip to Japan. Simon, who flew east to Tokyo from London while I flew west from New York, met me at the Palace Hotel overlooking the Imperial gardens. There we connected with our host, Takumi Shibata, an affable, middle-aged rising star at Nomura with an easy smile and a Western manner. He would ultimately rise to deputy president and chief operating officer over the course of his career before resigning in connection with an insider trading scandal that also took down Nomura's CEO.

Our meetings were predictably stiff and formal, given the expected communication barriers, and not terribly informative as to how a combination would ever work. The visit made for an interesting cultural experience, but by the end of our day there Simon and I had already come to the right answer. Our existing independent structure had its challenges. We had already seen how unexpected events could wreak havoc in our industry, and leaving those challenges and risks behind in exchange for a large check made out to our names had its appeal. But we nonetheless confidently reaffirmed our commitment to the path we were on. Surrendering our increasingly attractive position as an independent advisor of meaningful scale and profile to become part of a large foreign brokerage firm was simply not appealing.

A year after the Tokyo trip, in the summer of 2003, we were approached by a very different kind of firm, one much more like our own: Evercore Partners. We remained disinclined to combine with any other firm but were happy to take the meeting. Learning more about a competitor firm was always interesting, and conceivably at some point an opportunity worth considering might arise. Roger Altman, the founder and head of Evercore, reached out to Bob asking for a meeting, indicating that the purpose was to explore a combination of our firms.

Altman had begun his career at Lehman Brothers before leaving for a role in the US Treasury during the Carter Administration. After briefly rejoining Lehman, he followed his former Lehman boss Pete Peterson to Blackstone, where he headed the M&A business in a new firm focused primarily on private equity investing. But with the election to the presidency of Bill Clinton, whom Altman had known since both were students at Georgetown, he returned to Washington as a Deputy Secretary of Treasury. However, only a year later he resigned in connection with the "Whitewater" scandal that became a major controversy in the Clinton Administration. Rather than return to Blackstone, which by then was even more focused on principal investing rather than advisory work, or join another established firm, he teamed up with two former colleagues to set up Evercore the same year that Greenhill was founded.

The two other founding partners at Evercore were both focused on principal investing. So, while our firm had started as an entirely advisory-focused firm, principal investing was Evercore's initial focus, alongside some advisory work led by Altman. The firm raised a $512 million fund at the time it launched, a few years before we even thought of raising our initial private equity fund.

As we were to learn in our principal investing business, timing is everything. In that regard, our timing was much better than Evercore's. Evercore ended up investing most of its fund in the late 1990s, prior to the big market correction that hammered the valuations of almost all businesses. Its highest profile investment, which oddly for someone with Altman's political background was the parent of the scandal-focused American tabloid *National Enquirer*, was made in 1999, not long before financial markets peaked. *The New York Times* noted at the time that the transaction was "not without financial risk"[18] and after struggling for years that company ultimately ended up in bankruptcy. Given such challenges on the principal investing side and some early successes on the advisory side, Evercore began to gravitate more toward the latter in the early 2000s. Later, Altman's two co-founders left the firm in a further sign of its increased focus on advisory work.

Altman, who was in many ways a peer of Bob's in the M&A business but with broad political connections as well, came alone to meet Bob and me at our Park Avenue office a few blocks south of his. It was the first time I had met him in person, although I had been on some phone calls with him and his senior Blackstone colleagues way back in the 1980s, when I was at Morgan Stanley and involved in selling Blackstone one of its first investments, a small railroad owned by US Steel. He was a genial fellow, with a politician's gift for words, in sharp contrast to Bob's more taciturn style. The meeting began somewhat awkwardly in that, as was the case with Bruce Wasserstein, the two dealmakers from the generation before mine clearly knew each other from past takeover battles but not well. Likewise, neither side knew much about the other's firm, each being relatively young and private, other than the list of M&A transactions with which each had publicly been associated.

Altman spoke first, briefly stating the rationale for exploring a combination. It was not clear whether he had brought any detailed information with him or simply wanted to test the waters for a potential deal, but I had come prepared to share a packet of papers showing our financial history. I slid my document across the conference room table, and Altman opened it to the first page, which showed in graphic form our annual revenue for the past few years. He immediately folded the cover page back onto the document, slid it back to me and said simply, "This won't work."

While he did not explain his remark in any detail, the implication was clear. While he was undoubtedly hoping for a "merger of equals" kind of transaction, our much higher revenue, which resulted from a singular early focus on M&A during a red-hot market for deals, made that impossible.

The various merger and acquisition approaches our firm received in its early years made several things clear. First, Bob liked what he was doing day to day, had little desire for substantially increased scale and even less desire for a more complex management apparatus. In fact, he preferred almost no management structure at all. On top of all that, he was no longer motivated by money, strange as that might sound in relation to a Wall Street kingpin.

For my part, I remained focused on building the independent advisory firm of breadth and depth that we had together envisioned over our first dinner. It was increasingly clear, though, that the business we were building had significant value, even at its current small size. Of course, there was some appeal to the prospect of capturing that value, particularly on days when the problems inherent in any small but growing business filled with strong personalities were evident. But so far, at least relative to all the alternate possibilities we had seen, we remained committed to staying on our current course, chasing the dream of building a significant independent advisory firm that would thrive in the long term.

CHAPTER SEVEN

A NOT SO CRAZY IDEA

Open a new window,
Open a new door,
Travel a new highway,
That's never been tried before[1]

— *Jerry Herman*, Mame

We entered 2003, the firm's eighth year in existence, with strong momentum. Despite a series of crises that led to very weak performance by our large bank competitors, our small team had managed to generate at least $100 million in revenue and abundant profitability for three consecutive years.

Despite increased headcount, revenue had been fairly flat for those three years, but flat was an accomplishment given a much-reduced level of transaction activity across world markets. Equally important, we had succeeded in developing a respected and increasingly recognized brand for trusted advice on large and complex transactions in both the US and

Europe. Further, we had raised a private equity fund and, given sharply reduced valuations for all kinds of assets, had been able to make what looked like a series of promising investments that we believed would pay off over time. Finally, we had added a restructuring advisory capability, further diversifying our revenue streams and providing a bit of a hedge against the slower M&A activity that typically coincides with recessions.

Our early success meant that we, particularly the six or seven key partners, were taking home plenty of money. We did not even have to wait for year-end bonuses like Wall Street bankers typically did, as we paid ourselves distributions of accumulated excess cash intermittently throughout each year as it piled up in the firm's bank accounts. Unlike the case with our larger competitors, there was little need to retain capital within the firm.

As the variety of approaches to buy or merge with our firm had clarified, we were at the same time building a business with significant equity value. There had been a consensus within the senior partner group in each case not to sell, but there was also increasing stress in regard to how to allocate profits fairly in a way that took into account both each partner's historic contribution to the firm's franchise value and his current contribution to that particular year's results. Twice we had completely restructured the economics of our partnership arrangements, trying to get that balance right. Dealing with how to carve up an ever-larger pie was a high-class problem, as life was pretty good for everyone at our thriving firm, but it was still a problem.

One serendipitous source of support for our evolving business model had been New York Attorney General Eliot Spitzer. Spitzer was a highly ambitious prosecutor who later rose to become governor of New York and undoubtedly aspired to even higher office until his political career ended abruptly in a sex scandal. What had piqued his interest in the big Wall Street banks was the sharp decline in stock markets beginning in the spring of 2000. Individual investors who got caught up in the frenzy of late 1990s speculation, particularly in the technology stocks listed on NASDAQ, ended up with substantial losses as the value of such stocks plummeted. A prosecutor looking to make a name for himself will invariably see a situation like that and assume someone other than the investors themselves must be to blame for those losses.

Starting in 2001 and continuing throughout 2002 and 2003, Spitzer relentlessly investigated Wall Street firms on the issue of conflicts of interest in equity research. In perhaps the most colorful example of what he uncovered, a star technology analyst at Merrill Lynch wrote in an internal email that one company Merrill was touting to investors was a "piece of shit."[2] In fact, "POS" turned out to be a well-understood abbreviation in internal Merrill emails. Spitzer's investigation took place before people came to understand the risks of casual and unguarded email correspondence, so this was not his only scurrilous discovery. As a result, in May 2002 Merrill agreed to pay a $100 million fine and change various aspects of how it conducted business. Spitzer then used that success to pursue all the large investment banks, and in early 2003 reached a so-called "global settlement" with that group involving a $1.4 billion fine and agreement on a variety of changes in business practice.[3]

Spitzer's crusade had an indirect but very positive impact on our business. While our firm was launched with the simple concept that we were experienced M&A bankers operating in a firm that concentrated exclusively on that service, over the years we increasingly focused our marketing and built our brand around the concepts of "independence" and "lack of conflicts." Spitzer had focused on one specific type of conflict of interest, relating to equity research. The concern was easy to understand: a brokerage firm had an inherent financial incentive to put a "buy" rating on a stock to curry favor with, and thereby win business from, the company that issued that stock. Investors who naively assumed that rating was a recommendation determined through an objective analytical process could thereby be misled. If they then lost money by buying that recommended stock they understandably felt aggrieved.

While Spitzer's investigation had a very specific target, his highly publicized work highlighted to our clients and to the broader public a more general problem: that the large Wall Street firms, the so-called "financial supermarkets," played a wide variety of roles. In some situations they were aligned with a client, and in other situations they were a counterparty with opposing interests to that client – in which case the very word "client" was a misnomer. Numerous examples of such conflicts of interest were relevant to our business. Sometimes the conflicts were blatant. Other times a conflict arose from the simple fact that bankers, under pressure to cross-sell their employer's many products, had a bias in favor of a particularly complex transaction that was lucrative from the advisor's perspective.

Bankers were not very good at pointing out where they were fully aligned with their client and where they were not, and their clients were not often skilled at ascertaining the differences. More fundamentally, clients historically had not fully comprehended the impact on behavior of the powerful financial incentives that Wall Street firms put in place for their employees. Simply by shining a spotlight on the broad issue of conflicts of interest, Spitzer helped us develop, refine and publicize a unique business model that resonated very favorably with corporate clients wary of bankers.

One area where conflicts had always been apparent was in M&A situations related to financial services clients. If a financial services business wanted to sell itself to a larger Wall Street firm it would not choose as an advisor a firm that might be a buyer. Likewise if it wanted to buy an asset that might also be of interest to other Wall Street firms. In either case it would be better to get advice from a firm like ours, which was neither a prospective bidder nor a competitor, and had no possible nefarious use for the confidential information to which it would undoubtedly become privy as part of the transaction process. That led to numerous prominent advisory roles for our firm.

One example was our frequent work, which I personally led, for the brokerage firm Charles Schwab, a client introduced to me by our London partner James Blyth. The gregarious Scotsman had skied with Schwab's then-CEO David Pottruck, a Wharton graduate who looked like the former wrestler that he once was, when both were clients being entertained at a large bank's outing. Over time the two became friends. Schwab was a business built almost entirely on organic growth, so nothing too exciting transpired in terms of blockbuster M&A deals on which we could assist, but over the years I advised on a couple sales of noncore assets as well as a modest-sized acquisition.

In 2003 I spent a lot of time with Schwab doing what bankers spend most of their time doing: working on potential transactions that never come to actual fruition. In this case my young colleague Rakesh Chawla, a financial services specialist who had worked at Credit Suisse First Boston and Blackstone before joining our firm earlier that year, and I were looking at the possible acquisition of any one of America's numerous publicly traded regional banks for Schwab. The notion was that Schwab would then expand the existing operation to serve its huge national client base. In the end Schwab built organically a substantial in-house bank to service its clients without starting with an acquisition on which to build. But as is often the case, our work proved worthwhile despite the lack of a short-term transactional reward. For one, the exercise served to further enhance an important client relationship. Second, as with almost any client project, even a failed effort provides a valuable learning experience.

Specifically, the Schwab assignment led to a sort of eureka moment for me in the summer of 2003 while I was vacationing at our weekend place in Connecticut. Having surveyed numerous publicly traded banks across America on behalf of Charles Schwab, it struck me that those were regional firms that lacked the national and even international brand name that our firm had, that many of them had less profit than we had, and that they very likely had much less growth potential as well. I found myself wondering if our firm could become the first of its kind to go public on the New York Stock Exchange.

Historically firms broadly similar to ours had realized whatever value they managed to create by selling their business to a larger firm. That's what Wasserstein Perella, Wolfensohn, the four horsemen of the US technology sector, all the British merchant banks and even many larger firms like Donaldson, Lufkin & Jenrette had done. Once sold, such firms essentially disappeared in most cases, with their people scattering to the four winds as soon as their employment contracts were executed in conjunction with the sale allowed.

Perhaps an IPO was an alternative way of capturing the substantial value that we believed we were creating in our firm without requiring us to cede control to a new owner. If so, over time we could gain all the financial benefits of selling our firm while continuing to do the client work we enjoyed doing, develop and grow our business, maintain our unique corporate culture and control our own destiny.

But could we actually execute a successful IPO? Such a transaction would be the first of its kind – we were a pure advisory business and a very small one to boot. A failure would be highly visible to the corporate community that we served and severely damaging to the firm's theretofore pristine reputation. Hence I resolved to craft the most "investor-friendly" IPO one could imagine, then carefully vet that idea with various experts. We needed to be highly confident in a successful outcome before first unveiling our plan to the broader public.

The first step was to develop a business plan and set of policies that would be seen as favorable to investors. Every IPO needs a rationale – investors want to know the purpose of the transaction and the planned use of proceeds from the stock sale. We would describe our primary objective as raising our firm's profile to a broader range of prospective clients. The use of proceeds from the sale of our common stock would be to invest in our private equity funds alongside the outside investors that provided those funds with investment capital. Our business would remain primarily advisory, focused on mergers, acquisitions and restructurings. But that would be supplemented by making and managing private equity investments – what Morgan Stanley, DLJ and others had historically called merchant banking. While theoretically there could be a conflict of interest between advisory and principal investing activities that flew in the face of our branding as an "independent advisor" without any conflicts of interest, our investment funds tended to pursue much smaller companies than those that were our typical advisory clients. For now, the potential for conflict seemed only theoretical and therefore tolerable.

In regard to operating costs, we would commit to targeting total employee compensation of no greater than half of our revenue, leaving the other half available to cover office rent, travel and other costs, plus provide profit and dividends for shareholders. This commitment was necessary because compensation in a professional services firm represents the ultimate conflict of interest between management and shareholders – executives and the broader team would of course always want more pay, to the detriment of shareowners. Hence the need for clear limits.

Beyond that, we would further seek to align ourselves with our new shareholders by having partners sign onerous long-term noncompete agreements that ensured they could not "take the money and run" post-IPO. Finally, we would make stock a major component of each year's compensation for all our key professionals. While we knew our people would over time sell their original shares, by issuing new stock every year as part of compensation we could ensure continued substantial equity ownership among our employee group as a whole.

I tried to flesh out all the aspects of what a public version of our heretofore private company might look like over the summer, before speaking about my idea to anyone other than my wife Roxanne and one talented and trustworthy junior banker who could help me with the necessary financial analyses and presentations. The first partner I spoke to was Bob Niehaus, who had deep experience in capital markets. He had helped many companies in which he had invested go public. Then, in late August, I flew to London to float the idea to my European counterpart, Simon Borrows. Mine was a peculiarly American idea – Simon made clear that the London market would never accept a small, relatively young company with no hard assets and no recurring revenue. But he had a good sense of the much larger and more accommodating American stock market and was supportive.

Then, on the day after Labor Day 2003, I walked into Bob Greenhill's office across the floor from my own and got right to the point. "Bob, I've got a crazy idea." He leaned forward, clearly intrigued. "I think we should try to go public." Bob paused. Ever the man of few words, he invariably responded to such ideas with unquestioning enthusiasm. "I don't think that's so crazy at all," he said, and we were off to the races.

In mid-September we held our annual partners meeting in Nantucket as usual. Our partnership no longer fit around Bob's dining room table as it had for our first years, but we had stuck with the tradition of using his summer vacation spot as the base for our annual offsite gathering. Most of our partners were golfers, and the Nantucket Golf Club, which Bob helped found in 1998, had become our new base of operations for these gatherings. Consistent with Bob's operating style, these annual off-site events were always very brief, usually comprised of a purely social dinner at his fabulous beachfront compound, a business discussion for a few hours the next morning and golf in the afternoon. Then we were promptly on our way back to the office.

At this meeting the possibility of going public, along with all the commitments that would be required from Bob and our other partners, was the primary agenda item. Not surprisingly, all were excited at the prospect of a financial windfall that would also enable us to continue in business just as we currently were.

Becoming a public company obviously requires greater formality with respect to management structure and titles. Bob clearly wanted both the chairman and CEO roles. That was fine by me, although I had the first of many conversations with him about the need to create the appropriate external impression of seamless management evolution in the manner of successful public companies. It meant we would over time need a period where he held both titles, a period where he held only the chairman title and a period where he held only an honorary "emeritus" title.

Given Bob's hands-off management style, it was important that from the start that we appoint a "president" as well, and it seemed fairly obvious to all that Simon and I, the sole two members of our boringly labeled "administration committee," should share that title, in the "co-" manner that was fairly common on Wall Street.

Rounding out our leadership team for the IPO was early employee and now partner John Liu, who would serve as a part-time chief financial officer with client M&A work remaining his day job. He had the right mix of analytical skills and even temperament to play the CFO role. Hal Rodriguez, who theretofore had performed admirably as our CFO, effectively retained that functional role in almost all respects. But he graciously gave up the official title given our view that, ours being an unusual public company, our CFO needed to be someone who was personally involved in, and therefore better able to explain to investors, the day-to-day activities of our client advisory team.

Following the Nantucket partners meeting we polished a draft investor presentation and unveiled our idea to the first person outside our firm. One of our young partners was friends with Joan Solotar, spouse of a Wachtell Lipton partner and head of equity research at Credit Suisse First Boston. Earlier in her career, she had written research reports on the major investment banks as an analyst at DLJ before CSFB acquired that firm. The DLJ experience made her familiar with smaller, more entrepreneurial Wall Street businesses, and her research focus made her an expert at what the market might think of Greenhill in the context of an IPO. We walked her, page by page, through a detailed presentation of our history, our strategy, our operating principles and even our view of what the "right" valuation would be. She was generous with her time and quickly assured us that our plan seemed workable.

For whatever reason, despite the encouragement Joan provided we convinced ourselves that we needed one more $100-million-revenue year under our belts before we dared pursue an IPO. So we determined to see how that year turned out before reaching out to prospective underwriters – the brokerage firms that might bring our deal to investors – in early January. In the end, the firm made $127 million of revenue for 2003, a respectable 12% increase over the prior year, a new record and a fourth consecutive year at or above $100 million. We thus looked to be not only highly profitable but also growing. Further, for a business that was by its nature both cyclical and prone to wild swings in revenue due to the random timing of deals, our brief financial history made our business look far more stable than it actually was.

Having achieved our revenue goal for 2003, on the first business day of January 2004 I reached out first to Goldman Sachs, the most prestigious firm to have lead our stock offering. We had obviously not been seen as an IPO candidate by any firm, as no banker had ever proactively approached us to suggest that idea and thereby solicit the lead underwriter role. But Goldman knew us as a competitor, was a perennial leader in equity capital markets and on top of that had done its own IPO just five years earlier. I called Rob Kaplan, a Goldman vice chairman who had previously run investment banking, would years later oversee Harvard University's endowment, and then become head of the Federal Reserve's regional bank in Dallas before resigning in the wake of a stock trading controversy and later returning to Goldman.

Rob and I did not know each other well but had worked together on the ill-fated (in that it rapidly ended up in bankruptcy) leveraged buyout of the iconic department store Macy's in 1986. At the time, he was a young rising star at Goldman, and I was a similarly youthful lawyer at Wachtell Lipton. That transaction had always been memorable for me in several respects: my wife Roxanne happened to then be a housewares and food buyer for Macy's, and the transaction's closing celebration at the Metropolitan Museum of Art's Temple of Dendur was the most lavish I would attend in my entire career. Macy's board member Henry Kissinger was among the notables in attendance. What became most amusing in retrospect was that the lead banker on the Goldman team had advised us lowly lawyers that the most junior debt financing the buyout (a "zero coupon" piece of paper where interest accrued over time rather than being paid in cash) was "perfect for an IRA" (the individual retirement account of that era). Of course, those bonds very soon turned out to be pretty much worthless, which provided laughs to my slightly more senior Wachtell colleague and me for many years to come.

When Rob and I spoke I asked him to send a team, not to present Goldman's credentials (their usual sales-driven approach), but rather to listen to our story as Joan Solotar had done and then advise us as to the feasibility of an IPO. We made similar calls to Lehman, Merrill Lynch and UBS. Each agreed to come to our office in mid-January and listen to our story. The other obvious name to add would have been Morgan Stanley, but we believed that there was too much history between our firms and that the relationship was too complicated for them to want Greenhill (the man or the firm) to become an even larger success. So we left Morgan Stanley out.

On January 12 our partner group gathered at "21," where Marty Lipton had invited me onto the Prep for Prep board. The Prohibition-era speakeasy was an old-school favorite of Bob's – every December he hosted a boozy Christmas lunch there for longtime friends, where attendees made bets on predictions of the next year's market results. Despite his outsized public persona, Bob was very much an introvert and rarely went to lunch with anyone, preferring a sandwich alone at his desk. But that annual gathering held great meaning for him. It was therefore natural that from the start that "21" became our go-to venue for formal gatherings in New York.

As we dined together that evening the partners remained fully on board and highly enthusiastic, ready to make whatever commitments needed to be made to ensure our IPO's success. In separate meetings over the two days that followed Bob, Simon Borrows, Bob Niehaus, John Liu and I delivered our pitch in separate meetings with the four potential underwriters.

Our 64-page (plus appendix) PowerPoint deck was persuasive. We began with the important albeit amorphous topic of "culture." While every company thinks its culture is unique, we believed ours truly was. The five descriptive words we highlighted were conservative, stable, collegial, analytical and meritocratic. "Conservative" meant that we did not take a lot of risk, either financially or regarding our culture. We could have used our early success to adopt a much more aggressive strategy, built a larger firm and perhaps made even more money, but we placed a higher value on the character and quality of our team than on scale. "Stable" meant that we minimized change. As with the best sports teams, there would be continual evolution in personnel around the edges, but we aimed to retain a substantial and strong core group to ensure long-term continuity of quality, brand and culture.

"Collegial" was our way of saying that we were the polar opposite of the typical Wall Street firm where "politics" was a way of life, client relationships were closely guarded, information was not freely shared and the internal competition as intense as the external. Ours was simply a nice place to work. How we achieved that differentiating characteristic is not entirely clear – perhaps it was the humble Midwestern roots of Bob, myself, Niehaus and many of our other early people. However we got there, once we established that culture we were committed to maintaining it, even if that occasionally meant foregoing a valuable recruit or exiting a money-making banker who made office life unpleasant or simply did not fit. "Analytical" meant that we were not predominantly salespeople. Our team cared deeply about the quality of our work product – perhaps even too much sometimes, to the detriment of winning more assignments or getting more deals done. Finally, "meritocratic" meant that we would avoid the rigid hierarchy typical of larger firms, where those in senior positions can lord it over younger partners and staff and pay themselves disproportionately to their contributions. We aimed to reward people according to performance, regardless of whether someone was part of the early founding group or a new arrival.

The IPO's key selling point was that we were "focused entirely on the areas of investment banking with the highest margins and lowest capital requirements." In other words, we had invested little (apart from our time and talent) in our business but still generated large profits that could be distributed to shareholders rather than reinvested in the business. Further, we had "consistently grown advisory revenues at the expense of larger rivals," had a restructuring advisory business that was countercyclical to M&A, demonstrated a "record of expense discipline and high profitability and cash flow even in difficult market conditions," and had numerous sources of future growth, led by increasing "demand by leading companies for independent advice." The bottom line was that we believed we could "grow earnings *and* return significant cash to shareholders via dividends and share repurchases."

The historic data on our growth was limited in duration but powerful. Every advisor of importance had generated huge fees in the tail end of the dot-com boom, but our presentation highlighted that the advisory revenues of Goldman, Lehman and Morgan Stanley had fallen by a range of 51–69% in the period of 2000–2003 while ours had grown 13%. In addition, the recent sharp decline in general transaction activity, which drove those weak results for our larger competitors, provided a further selling point in favor of the timing for new investors. Deal activity seemed poised for a rebound, and in each M&A cycle the highs in terms of number and size of deals had been higher than in the prior cycle.

We knew our business model would sound appealing and that our performance, particularly our relative performance, would look strong. But several points seemed likely to give investors pause. A large majority of our revenue was generated from the talents, relationships and efforts of fewer than ten people – what lawyers call "key man" risk was very real in our case. A related point was the complete lack of recurring revenue. In other words, a client that did a big M&A deal in one year might like our work and intend to use us for its next one, but that could be several years away. When our role involved advising on the sale of a client company that company would then be gone forever as a client. As best we could, we tried to turn that weakness into a positive, noting that our combined list of top ten revenue-generating clients for each of the past five years included forty-one different names. In other words, we did not have a coterie of recurring revenue sources, but rather relied on a collective network of relationships that each year seemed to generate new opportunities from an ever-evolving set of clients.

A further issue was whether the historically high fees paid for M&A advice would be sustained. There was no question that companies had traditionally paid lucrative, multimillion dollar fees for advice on important transactions. Why? Well, the difference to a company between a successful and failed transaction could be enormous. The primary role of a banker was trying to develop and negotiate a compromise that allowed buyer and seller to come together on mutually beneficial terms and thereby allow each side to achieve an important strategic objective. With the right financial incentive in place, bankers could be very clever in playing that diplomatic role.

While the fees paid were large in absolute terms – often multiples of the high hourly rates charged by top law firms or consultants – they were small in relative terms. A modest percentage "commission" seemed like a small price to pay for the right advisor, and cost was therefore not typically the determining factor in a company's choice of advisor.

Was that situation sustainable in the long term? In nearly every part of the financial services business, fees had been falling for years. That was true of brokerage commissions, mutual fund fees, stock and bond underwriting fees and so on. Yet M&A advisory work was essentially an artisanal craft role, where understanding human psychology was as important as financial analysis in advising management and boards on the largest and most complex decisions they might ever make. Technology cannot process a complex merger like it can a simple stock or bond trade. So high fees had been maintained for decades and likely would be going forward.

Finally, given the unpredictability of revenue we were not going to attempt to provide forecasts. Providing earnings "guidance" as many companies did would be impossible, so we would not try. Further, we would not hold a quarterly investor conference call to answer analyst and shareholder questions as almost all companies do with each earnings announcement. Our press releases would speak for themselves and contain all the information we felt able to convey. In part this decision was a function of the fact that I knew Bob wouldn't be as easily scripted as most public company CEOs – he was a man of few words who spoke in blunt, optimistic terms, without the caveats necessary in formal shareholder communications. Equally, given the positive "buzz" around our firm, we believed such a restrained, low-key marketing approach might help maintain a bit of mystery around our simple business, making investors, and perhaps clients and recruits as well, more intrigued by our success and more inclined to associate with us.

The reaction of our four brokerage firm audiences to our presentation varied. Of course, each believed that its own huge scale and highly diversified business model embodied the optimal Wall Street strategy. Hence they would almost have to be skeptical of our relatively new "independent advisor" business model that aimed to compete with them in a "David versus Goliath" fashion. Lehman, a trading-oriented firm where a big balance sheet was the primary asset, listened and was skeptical but still happy to go along. Our IPO was just another trade on which revenue could be generated. UBS felt the same. But Merrill, with its thundering herd of brokers and untold billions of assets under management, was more skeptical – so much so that we did not include it in the offering.

Goldman Sachs, on the other hand, was highly enthusiastic. Its head of equity capital markets for financial services companies said, "We think you're going to be just like us." In other words, just like Goldman Sachs in the sense of being seen as a premium player in our space, attracting investors for the same reasons that we attracted both clients and talented professionals. With Goldman as our lead underwriter we pressed full steam ahead, aiming to complete an IPO in just a few months.

To guide us through the transaction process we brought in Davis Polk & Wardwell, the law firm that had advised Morgan Stanley for years and helped with forming our private equity fund. It was a leader in executing equity offerings. Ulrika Ekman, a young partner of Swedish birth whom we would soon poach to be our first in-house general counsel, led the day-to-day work. A talented and pragmatic lawyer, she had a better sense than most about what matters were worth worrying about and what not. That approach, combined with a cheerful personality and can-do attitude, made her perfect for our entrepreneurial young firm. We made rapid progress on the requisite documentation under her guidance.

Along the way we needed to recruit a board of directors, including four "independent" members to go along with Bob, Simon and myself as employee directors. Forming such a majority was a New York Stock Exchange eligibility requirement for listing. Having served on several boards and advised many others, I knew that many executives and bankers of a certain age loved the notion of sitting on public company boards, often seeing that as the capstone of their careers. Doing so was also a way of keeping themselves "in the game" longer than was usually possible in full-time operating roles. At the same time I often cautioned friends that, despite the prestige most people attach to such roles, serving on boards was generally "either boring or scary."

When everything is going well the CEO does not really need or want your input, so the board role can be somewhat boring, consumed by financial audit reviews and other technical matters. However, very few companies avoid becoming "scary" at some point in their lives. Any of a regulatory misstep, civil lawsuit, accounting issue, controversy involving race or gender or inappropriate romantic relationships, accident, an untimely death or numerous other events can be the source of "scary" for a board of directors. Not to mention the recurring challenge presented by difficult economic conditions.

We reached out to friends of the firm, tried to portray ours as an exciting young company with limited risk, promised not to take too much of anyone's time, and people quickly signed on. First was Steve Key, an accounting expert who had advised bankers including Bob and myself on the accounting aspects of deals at Morgan Stanley while he was a partner at Ernst & Young, before later becoming chief financial officer of food business Conagra and still later the industrial company Textron. Once the IPO closed, Key would be joined by Jack Danforth, an Episcopal minister, former US Senator, Ambassador to the United Nations and friend of Bob's; Steve Goldstone, a former Davis Polk partner and later CEO of RJR Nabisco who knew Bob and myself; and Isabel Sawhill, an economist at the Brookings Institution whose late husband John had been a close friend of Bob's. I had randomly met John Sawhill once when he was managing partner of the huge global consulting firm McKinsey and generously gave me, then a lowly associate at Morgan Stanley, a ride to the Houston airport from the office of our common client Texaco. I had always remembered that, vowing that I would treat "junior people" like the one I then was in the same fashion.

With documents drafted, a board ready, our business performing well and capital markets continuing to rebound from a multiyear downturn we made our first filing with the Securities & Exchange Commission on March 12, thereby unveiling our plan to the world and seeking an SEC review of our prospectus. The offering was not going to be a large one: our initial filing indicated that only $86 million worth of stock would be sold– representing around 20% of the firm, with partners like me retaining the rest. But given the history and nature of our firm the announcement would garner much attention.

The New York Times reported that the filing offered a "rare glimpse into how lucrative running even a small company on Wall Street can be."[4] The story described Bob as a "swashbuckling banker" who "wears suspenders with dollar signs on them" – something I knew from Chernow's *House of Morgan* that he once did, but I had never seen in our seven years of working together. It further predicted that ours "could be the first of a wave of small firms similarly seeking to raise money from the public."

While we waited for SEC approval to begin marketing our offering my wife and I took the opportunity to see four Broadway shows – now that our kids were in school we had resumed our regular visits to the theater that began in London and came to characterize our many childless years. Entertaining stage productions provided a welcome distraction from the daily grind of business on hyper-competitive Wall Street.

As we bided our time with such pleasant evening diversions my Greenhill colleagues and I were spending our days planning a lengthy "road show" to market our stock as soon as we received SEC clearance. There are times when IPOs are easy to sell and times when they are nearly impossible. In addition, the IPO window can essentially close at any time, for a wide variety of reasons – some event related to a firm specifically or an industry generally, a Federal Reserve interest rate hike or simply a market decline. Hence we waited anxiously and hoped markets would remain favorable.

Filled with confidence but wanting to leave no stone unturned in look-ing for investors, we began our road show with a pitch to the Goldman sales force at its downtown New York headquarters. Future Goldman CEO David Solomon, the senior banker on our account, came by to wish us well. Thereafter our senior leadership group broke into two teams. Over the course of two weeks we visited five cities in Europe and eleven in the US. Bob flew the firm's Citation X to every meeting he attended, while the rest of us chartered planes to meet the rigorous schedule. In addition to large group meetings in New York, Boston, London and other major cities, we held sixty-five one-on-one meetings with prospective investors. Sandy Weill himself came to see what his friend and former employee Bob Green-hill was selling when we visited Citigroup's asset management team to offer our shares. Likewise, many a younger portfolio manager came out in part for the opportunity to meet an industry icon.

Bob typically said little in these investor meetings, although he delighted in pointing out to investors far too young to know that, while our firm was undeniably small, Morgan Stanley had fewer people and even less capital when he first arrived there. Then, after pausing slightly for effect, he would land his self-effacing punchline with a hearty chuckle, "but it was somewhat better known!"

The press was mostly favorable to our IPO plan, although *Barron's*, which liked to warn of what it saw as overhyped or overpriced stock deals, was skeptical, noting that "while the offering looks favorable to Greenhill and his team, it may not be so attractive to new investors."[5] It asked "why Greenhill & Co. needs to be public, other than to enrich Greenhill and key employees, because advisory firms require little capital." *Barron's* concerns were fair, and in fact had been anticipated by us. That was exactly why we had tilted every possible term of our proposed deal in favor of the outside investors we were seeking.

In the end, despite the skepticism of *Barron's* and the long list of "risk factors" described in somewhat frightening detail in our prospectus, investors bought into our pioneering IPO. As we would learn in many future offerings for our firm and others, in most deals there comes a tipping point where either almost everyone wants in or almost everyone wants out. In our case, increased interest in unconflicted "independent advisors," Bob's celebrity banker status, our diverse client base, our huge early success in Europe to complement success in the US, prospects of a rebounding M&A market after a few fairly quiet years and the development of a hedge against future downturns in the form of our restructuring business all worked to our favor. Add to that the fact that our stock would provide a meaningful 2.1%-dividend yield, offering investors the opportunity for both growth and capital return, two benefits rarely found in the same stock offering. Finally, it worked to our advantage (and would to firms in our sector that followed) that we were all skilled presenters of a financial deal. Indeed that is what we did for a living, usually on behalf of clients.

Nearly every investor we met placed an order for shares, and in total we received seventeen times the orders we needed to complete our offering. This overwhelming demand enabled us to price the offering at $17.50 per share, well above the $14–$16 range our prospectus had indicated – these being shares that my senior partners and I had acquired for less than one penny each.

The day before our offering, two-thirds of our firm was owned by just five of us. On May 5, as we gathered on the podium to ring the opening bell of the New York Stock Exchange following breakfast in its cavernous, ornate old dining room, we welcomed a large group of new shareholders from across the US and Europe and watched to see how the market would treat us.

On the first day of trading the stock benefited from the unmet demand for our shares, closing at over $20 and giving the firm a market value of $600 million. This was a remarkable valuation for an eight-year-old firm consisting of only 107 total employees. Bob's share was worth $180 million, while the next four largest holders owned stakes worth $43 million each. Collectively our partner group owned nearly $500 million worth of stock.

With personal balance sheets inflated far beyond our expectations, a few of us soon decided to indulge in Bob's longtime practice of utilizing private jets for business travel. We mutually agreed, however, to charge clients only commercial air travel rates, paying the tab for the sizable difference between that and the cost of flying privately out of our own pockets.

To keep the costs of this more efficient (and admittedly more luxurious) mode of travel from becoming too outrageous, we would charter flights rather than take on the far greater expense of owning aircraft. And, unlike Bob, we would certainly not serve as our own pilots, although our young partner Jeff Buckalew and a few more junior professionals found the possibility of further emulating Bob and sitting in the left-hand seat of the cockpit alluring and would soon take pilot lessons.

It felt like our whole firm was now ready to fly.

CHAPTER EIGHT

BRAINS AND BULL MARKETS

It's our time, breathe it in:
Worlds to change and worlds to win.[1]
                 – *Stephen Sondheim,* Merrily We Roll Along

An oft quoted bit of market wisdom warns, "Don't confuse brains with a bull market."[2]

We had brains at our firm. We also had experience that provided us both the credentials to win complex, high-profile assignments and the expertise to execute them skillfully. Plus we had a business model that differentiated us from our primary competitors such that we stood out from the crowd. Now, with our high-flying, first-of-its-kind IPO, our business model was turbocharged by generous amounts of free publicity that portrayed us in glowing terms to the broad universe of potential corporate clients.

Over and above all those factors we benefited enormously from operating in what was a powerful bull market. At the time we were getting started as a public company both the economy and stock prices were continuing to recover from the collapse that ended the dot-com bubble of the late 1990s. That kind of rebound invariably makes CEOs and corporate boards more confident, more ambitious and more willing to take risks. It is often as simple as this: if your business is struggling and/or your stock price is depressed, taking on a new challenge holds little appeal. On the other hand, if your business is humming along and you are feeling good about your stock price, you will much more readily take on the kind of new challenge that a significant acquisition inevitably involves.

Thus the continuing rebound in economic activity served as a powerful catalyst for robust growth in the types of deals on which we advised, substantially increasing our opportunity to earn advisory fees. In 2004 the total value of M&A deals announced globally rose nearly 50% from the depressed levels of 2002 and 2003, and the value of such deals rose sharply again in 2005. In 2006 the total combined value of all M&A deals increased even further, to an all-time high of $3.6 trillion – three times the level of the recessionary era year of 2002.

Deals were becoming larger as well as more numerous – in 2006, for the first time, there were more than a thousand deals globally with a value of at least $500 million, more than double the total from 2002. A deal of that size would typically produce a fee of at least $5 million for the advisor on each side of the transaction, and much more for deals that scaled into the billions of dollars as an increasing number of them did.

Our partners were therefore understandably highly energized when they assembled the September after our IPO for our annual partners meeting on Bob's island getaway Nantucket for what would turn out to be the last time. We again stayed at the Nantucket Country Club, the elite club that Bob, a member of the admissions committee, regularly used as a business development tool. Seemingly every corporate executive who acquired a summer home on that exclusive island wanted to become a member. After our few hours' long formal meeting I played what turned out to be a final round of my poor version of golf alongside my much more skilled partners. While I was once talented enough to play on my high-school golf team, years of preoccupation with work (and more recently, parenting) had made my rounds increasingly rare. Following this time I simply stopped playing.

Our stock that day closed at $23.55, up 35% in the four months since our IPO, which itself had come at a valuation level that we were thrilled to achieve.

Despite our firm's still relatively short history, the PowerPoint presentation I had prepared for our meeting had the audacity to lay out ambitious five-year objectives for what was a very small firm operating in a market impossible to predict even quarter to quarter. As we sometimes said to investors, we were not selling toothpaste – a mundane necessity the sales of which were presumably fairly predictable quarter to quarter and year to year. One should thus have looked at our plan with a high degree of skepticism, yet we accepted it as worthy of serious contemplation just like American school children of my era had once been led to do with respect to the similarly questionable five-year economic plans published by the old Soviet Union.

Putting aside the specific revenue and earnings forecasts, my presentation laid out a "virtuous circle" of factors that we hoped would drive continued success. Broader client coverage and a more recognized brand name, both boosted by our high-profile IPO, would help us grow revenue. That in turn would make our earnings grow, enabling us to pay higher dividends and achieve a higher share price. The resulting increase in the value of Greenhill equity held by our managing director group would both aid in retention of key personnel and help us recruit additional talent while bankers elsewhere watched with envy as we accrued wealth. That incremental talent would further increase our client coverage and embellish our brand, leading to further growth in revenue, and on and on around the circle.

The concept was sound even if the specific financial results to which it would lead were unpredictable. Nonetheless the presentation listed what felt like bold targets as to growth in headcount, revenue, earnings, dividend and share price. We aimed to recruit four or five new managing directors per year. Five years out we were projecting $326 million in revenue, $85 million in earnings, a dividend of $1.25 per share and a stock price of $55 – more than triple our IPO price. That would mean a total market value for our business of around $1.5 billion.

The presentation was candid in its assessment of the challenges inherent in meeting those objectives. In terms of revenue it noted that year to date our revenue was roughly flat, compared to massive growth at much larger firms like Goldman Sachs and Morgan Stanley, which we had hugely outperformed in the relatively quiet 2000–2003 period. We had expected that our bankruptcy and restructuring advisory practice – a business in which those large banks were essentially unable to compete – would result in our outperforming in weaker economic periods and then giving back some of that outperformance in stronger periods. Still, stagnant revenue even over a brief period was not comfortable for a firm that had recently sold investors an optimistic story of growth.

More concerning, the presentation noted that recruiting additional senior talent was proving difficult. Dealmakers have a nose for money, so plenty of prospects came by to kick the tires on our business in the immediate aftermath of our IPO. But those who make their living in the advisory business rather than as principals are notoriously risk averse. Our initial dozen or so partners were outliers – we were willing to bet on our individual and collective abilities to succeed. In contrast, most investment bankers like to earn substantial and increasing amounts of pay but are reluctant to put any of their personal capital, compensation or reputations at risk to do so. Rather than take a position in a small new business where one's contributions would be clear for all to see, most preferred the much lower level of accountability that went with working at a very large firm with an established brand and numerous products to sell. Corporations often act similarly when doing acquisitions – they would rather pay a higher price for what feels more like a sure thing than pay a bargain price during a time of greater uncertainty. This aversion to risk led to a relatively slow pace of senior banker recruiting when we were still private, and that phenomenon looked like it might continue post-IPO.

Beyond the potential to expand by recruiting individual bankers, being public created the opportunity to grow the firm more aggressively than is possible when hiring one person at a time: we could use our stock as a currency to acquire whole businesses. The first such opportunity presented itself only days after our IPO, when we received a lunchtime visit from the founder and head of an Australian firm called Caliburn that was a local version of Greenhill in that much smaller regional market. He was palpably interested in getting in on our success given that his own firm lacked the size and operated in too subscale a market to go public on its own. But as a savvy banker he intuitively knew that he would appear far too weak, even desperate, if he simply blurted out that he wanted us to acquire his business. So he took only the first tentative steps toward that goal, proposing a loose alliance to work together on cross-border deals between our respective regions.

As our share price and profile continued to rise an increasingly wide range of opportunities like that one found their way to our doorstep. In a variation of Bob's quip about our strategy for winning new clients, we would joke that our corporate strategy was to answer the phone when it rang. And it rang often.

One call was from a representative of the proprietor of a large but little-known asset management business called Lexington Partners. This highly lucrative business was a major player in the world of secondary private equity, where institutional investors commit capital to private partnerships that acquire limited partner interests in existing funds with visible portfolios rather than committing capital to new partnerships being formed to make unknown future investments. The firm appeared to be entirely owned by one individual who was intrigued by the concept of monetizing the future cash flow potential of his firm as we had done with ours. Over time, our IPO was to provide somewhat of a template for future IPOs of major private equity funds like Blackstone and KKR. Yet at that point ours was the only firm that had achieved a public market valuation based, in meaningful part, on a multiple of current and expected future investment management fees, including the speculative and volatile profit participation, or carried interest, element of those fees.

Given this fellow's very comfortable current position with annual income undoubtedly measured in the tens of millions of dollars, he moved slowly. He invited me to a series of lunches at Manhattan's exclusive Knickerbocker Club, where J.P. Morgan had himself once been a member,[3] to explore the concept of a possible combination. Over time my interest in the pursuit of this business faded given his lack of urgency and so many competing opportunities to divert my attention. Our dialogue soon petered out.

Time-consuming as it was to attract the best people, whether via recruitment or acquisition, we knew that we needed to succeed in those efforts at least to offset the attrition that would inevitably arise over time among our existing team members. Many bankers who thrived on large bank platforms would not succeed in a more entrepreneurial environment like we offered. Over time they would either proactively leave or have to be nudged out. We did not provide loans that could effectively force clients to give us further business opportunities. We did not have a century-old brand, nor did we advertise on television. We did not take clients to the Master's golf tournament or other prestigious sporting events to curry favor and win assignments. Ours was a fledgling business where one had to make things happen by dint of creative ideas, hard work and sheer force of personality.

Alongside near daily meetings with recruiting prospects or acquisition targets I remained busy working on deals for clients, as did all of my partners and colleagues. Initially, in those early days post going public, it took very little to keep our small firm productively and profitably busy. At the time of our IPO we were only involved in about four announced deals per quarter, and that was sufficient for us to be financially successful. In a bull market still gaining steam we could readily find that many opportunities, and in fact we had more than doubled the number of deals on which we were advising at any given moment already by 2005. As for the kinds of assignments we were winning, in the year of the IPO we advised on nothing as noteworthy as some of our earlier landmark transactions, the timing of such deals always being somewhat random. But during that time we helped industrial company Ingersoll-Rand sell an asset to private equity fund First Reserve for $1.2 billion, sold LNR Property (a real estate investment affiliate of the huge home-builder Lennar) to private equity fund Cerberus for $3.8 billion and sold the European pharmaceutical company Warner Chilcott to a consortium of such funds for $3 billion.

Given increasing concerns by clients in relation to the conflicts of interest that were inherent with big banks, we were quick to point out the intense loyalty that big banks had to the major private equity funds that provided them a steady stream of financing fees. It soon became clear that a specialty for us would be advising large public companies *against* such funds. As we put it to numerous prospective client CEOs and boards of directors, why would you hire Goldman Sachs or Morgan Stanley to advise you against one of its top clients? Apart from our early work for Hicks Muse, which had ended some time ago as that firm wound down its activities in the wake of declining performance, no major private equity fund had been an important client of ours. We were not even seeking business from that group. Thus we owed such funds, which were increasingly the proverbial 500-pound gorillas of the business world, no loyalty at all and could zealously represent our public company clients in negotiations across the table from them.

Even without many deals that were big enough to make the front pages, our efforts in our first partial year as a public company produced another record year for the firm, with revenue of $152 million, up 20% from the prior year. In the following year, 2005, we saw the return of higher profile transaction assignments, including another that was a direct product of the conflict-free nature of our firm. The New York Stock Exchange, long a "member-owned" institution held in small stakes by way of "seats" owned by numerous brokerage firms, developed a plan to go public via a merger with the upstart electronic trading firm Archipelago. Goldman Sachs was in the middle advising both sides of the deal – a highly unusual role that obviously undermined any notion of loyalty to either side. So we were brought in to bless (in other words provide an independent "fairness opinion" to) Archipelago, and Lazard came in to do the same for the other side.

We also advised telecom company MCI on its $8.9 billion sale to Verizon, airline America West on its $7.2 billion merger with US Airways and home appliance maker Whirlpool on its $2.7 billion acquisition of Maytag. On top of all that, given that some parts of the economy were still suffering the aftereffects of the recent recession, we remained busy on the restructuring side of the house, advising Delta Airlines on its bankruptcy and General Motors on the bankruptcy of its major parts supplier Delphi.

Alongside all the work advising corporate clients on large deals, Niehaus and I continued to develop our investing business. Our first Greenhill Capital Partners fund, launched just as company valuations were about to collapse, looked to be a major success. As we and our fellow investors began to be recipients of what turned into a steady stream of cash distributions resulting from various transactions we engineered for the fund's portfolio of companies, our thoughts turned to how we could build on that success to accelerate the growth of this business. Our investment track record seemed more than strong enough to enable us to raise additional funds, thereby increasing the management fees we would earn as well as the potential for carried interest, the 20%-fee kicker on whatever gains our investments produced. Just several weeks after our IPO, having by then put most of the capital raised in our first fund to work, we gathered at the Davis Polk law firm that had advised on both our IPO and the formation of our first fund for an organizational meeting to prepare for the launch of Greenhill Capital Partners II.

The prospectus provided to prospective investors in Fund II showed a "ROI," or return on investment, for Fund I of 2.2 times. In other words, while it was still relatively early days in the fund's history, we had already (on paper at least) more than doubled the money that investors had entrusted us to invest alongside our own. And we had done that so quickly that the annualized return generated for investors was an extraordinary 42% according to the industry standard "IRR," or internal rate of return, calculations. We had thereby far exceeded the ambitious goal we had boldly stated in the first paragraph of the prospectus for that fund.

In a sign of how critical the issue of timing was when it came to investments, we produced these extraordinary returns even though our early "science project" investments made during the tail end of the dot-com bubble had done very poorly. In fact, the $56 million we invested in eight different companies during 2000, the fund's first year of operation, had declined in value to only $8 million.

In contrast, our more numerous investments made post September 11, in the wake of the market's steep decline, had done remarkably well. Our barely two-year-old energy pipeline investment was now part of the publicly traded company Energy Transfer and worth six times what we paid – representing an annualized rate of return of a stunning 171%. The bankrupt wireless telecom tower investment that Niehaus had led at about the same time, now traded publicly under the name Global Signal, was worth five times what we paid – representing a 130% annualized rate of return. And our very first investment in what had clearly turned into a golden era, in the credit card transaction processor Heartland Payment Systems, was worth 2.9 times what we had paid, for a 43% annualized rate of return. Heartland was already contemplating its own IPO, which it would complete in the summer of 2005. Even the one-year-old investment that I had led in Texas insurer Republic Insurance showed a quick 35% gain, despite the tragic death of its CEO the day after our acquisition was completed.

Not surprisingly, our extraordinary early track record combined with a surge in investor capital flowing to private equity funds enabled us to raise a fund twice the size of GCP I. At $875 million we ended up well in excess of the $700 million target our prospectus indicated. Even as we looked for investments for GCP II to make, the first fund continued to prosper. By late 2006 the first fund had returned cash to its investors equal to 2.5 times the capital they had invested, and very significant value still remained to be harvested. Based on just the cash proceeds distributed to date, more than $100 million in carried interest proceeds had been paid out, primarily to the few of us who managed the fund, with a bit of that going to the firm itself and thereby further boosting its earnings and share price. Given our impressive investment track record, we began to explore the possibility of a European private equity fund that would build on the success of both our existing investment business based in America and our booming M&A advisory business in Europe. The goal, as always, was to find or develop more diverse streams of revenue to provide the firm with increased resilience against whatever challenges the market might present to us over time.

Our remarkable early achievements in investing as well as M&A and restructuring advice, and in both the US and Europe, prompted continuing free favorable publicity that further enhanced our profile and led to ever greater success consistent with the virtuous circle we had envisioned. Typically it was Bob Greenhill's iconic status and lifestyles-of-the-rich-and-famous persona that added color to the press's fawning stories.

In March 2005 *Bloomberg Markets* magazine featured a piece that began with a retrospective on our IPO less than a year earlier.[4] The reporter, an Australian named Brett Cole who would go on to author a book titled *M&A Titans* featuring Bob among many others of his generation, was clearly bedazzled by his subject. Hence the story began with Bob "climb[ing] into the cockpit of his Cessna Citation X and soar[ing] into the sparkling sky over Westchester County, New York." It went on to paint the larger-than-life image of a man with five glamorous homes and a "sun-creased face" who had "raised barns, hiked in the Idaho wilderness and canoed in the Arctic Ocean." Speaking of frozen oceans, the adventuresome imagery of the Antarctic Scott expedition portrayed in the photographs on our office walls was illustrated in great detail in Cole's story, providing exactly the metaphor for our business that we had intended when we hung those prints.

The story accurately highlighted that the firm was "riding a new wave of mergers ripping through corporate America." Further embellishing our reputation as a team with a bit of a Midas touch, it noted that our stock had doubled in just the ten months since the IPO, and that the market valued us at 32 times our 2004 earnings per share, far above the 12-times level at which the much larger and far more established Goldman Sachs was valued. Our total stock market value of $1.1 billion was only a fraction of that of the large banks with which we competed, but remarkable for a firm with no meaningful assets and only 130 people.

Many other flattering stories followed. In January 2006, *Investment Dealer's Digest* named the firm "Bank of the Year" in a cover story titled "Experienced, Dynamic and Not Conflicted."[5] The story featuring a photograph of Bob, myself and Simon Borrows, noted, "[o]ut of the gate, Greenhill was a smashing success." We did encounter the occasional critic amid the positive news flow – only a month after the *Investment Dealer's Digest* article, *Barron's* took another shot at us on valuation grounds, noting that our stock was by then up 270% since the IPO in which *Barron's* had advised against investing.[6] But even that skeptical story enhanced our image as stock market masters, and every other piece of journalism seemed to further add to our renown.

The very day after the *Barron's* piece caricatures of Bob and myself were featured on the cover of *The Deal* magazine.[7] Under the headline "Real Simple," playing off the name of a homemaking magazine of the day, the cover stated, "Legendary dealmaker Robert Greenhill and his right-hand man Scott Bok strive to recreate the old Wall Street partnerships of yore. The strategy appears to be working." The following month we were featured in the more prestigious *Institutional Investor* magazine in a story titled "Booming Boutiques."[8]

Relentlessly favorable coverage in multiple publications read by investors, prospective clients and recruits, on top of impressive financial performance in all corners of our business, added fuel to a raging fire of stock market optimism in relation to our firm. On a personal level, the increase in wealth for myself and other top partners was extraordinary. But for a full year those gains were only "on paper." The firm's partners had sold no shares at all in the IPO, as is the custom – any sign of owners selling out, as opposed to using an IPO to raise new capital to invest in their growing business, is typically read as a strong negative signal by prospective investors. In our zeal to provide the most investor-friendly IPO terms possible, we had volunteered for a full year's "lock-up" period post-IPO wherein we were restricted from selling any shares, twice as long as typical.

Meanwhile, in my desire to invest in our business and enhance both its growth potential and my future wealth, I had committed more than my entire personal liquid assets to our first private equity fund. I knew I would invest even more in our second US fund, a planned European fund and any other fund that we launched. Accordingly, after waiting patiently for the agreed-upon time period, only four days after the first anniversary of our IPO we completed a large "secondary offering" – so called because existing shareholders like me were the sellers rather than the firm itself offering new shares to investors.

The 4.6 million shares sold were allocated on a pro rata basis relative to our individual share ownership positions – around 10% for me and three other senior partners and triple that for Bob. Those shares were priced at $34 per share, around double the IPO price. And we did it all over again, selling another 4 million shares, after the stock doubled again during the next one-year lock-up period. In just two years our small group of pre-IPO shareholders had thus sold $440 million of stock. At the price of the second sale our still tiny firm of less than 200 people, of which we were collectively still the primary owners, was valued by the market at more than $2 billion.

Benjamin Graham, the investment sage often quoted by his long-ago student Warren Buffett, famously said that, in the long run, the stock market is a "weighing machine" (in other words, it indicates what a company is worth), but in the short run it is a "voting machine" (in other words, it indicates a company's popularity among investors).[9] Clearly our firm was getting a lot of votes in those first two years as a public company, as we had already exceeded the five-year stock price target we had boldly set at our post-IPO partners meeting. While our confidence was such that we were inclined to believe in the most optimistic of future scenarios for our growing business, we also had enough experience of the market's inevitable ups and downs that we knew to take advantage of our firm's extraordinary market popularity by "taking some chips off the table" as early and often as possible.

Despite all the busyness inherent in working for clients on major transactions, helping to invest and manage a private equity fund and dealing with the complexities of running a newly public company, I continued to follow my inclination toward even further involvement in a diverse range of activities outside the firm. As soon became clear to me, success in a public company context, wherein a significant portion of one's income and wealth becomes visible on the internet for anyone to see, meant that there would be no shortage of such opportunities to consider.

Only months after our IPO a dilapidated 1950s-era horse farm adjacent to our Connecticut weekend home came up for sale. This once-glorious breeding facility with its 20,000-square-foot barn featuring fifty-six horse stalls had slowly fallen into a sad state of disrepair as its owners aged – a testament to the way such enterprises (not ever really intended to be normal "for profit" businesses) can ultimately drain one's time, energy and resources until there is seemingly no choice but to give up. Roxanne and I knew a bit about that phenomenon from our continuing ownership of the White Hart inn, an increasingly common venue for Greenhill events that would soon celebrate its bicentennial. The maintenance challenges inherent in owning a large, aging, heavily used building were relentless.

Nonetheless, having a soft spot for rural land, old buildings and (especially in the case of Roxanne) animals of all kinds, we ended up buying the place. We dubbed it Weatogue Stables after the name of the road on which it sat, which in turn was named after an early Native American tribe said to have camped near that spot. Roxanne concurrently began writing a book[10] chronicling a renovation of the barn and outbuildings that was so thorough that scarcely a two-by-four survived, as well as her own journey from novice rider to accomplished equestrian. The result of our efforts was the creation of a first-class dressage facility – this from two people who only vaguely knew what dressage was when we began.

Shortly before we completed the purchase of that farm I was invited to a dinner for a group of University of Pennsylvania trustees and prominent alumni at New York's Metropolitan Club. I sat at the head table with Penn's new President Amy Guttmann and its board chair Jim Riepe, a leading executive in the mutual fund industry who helped index fund pioneer Jack Bogle found Vanguard before settling at T. Rowe Price for most of his career. I had already been serving on the subsidiary board of Penn's school of arts and sciences, but clearly now was being considered as a candidate for the board of trustees of the entire university. I must have cleared the vetting as later that year, just months before the twenty-fifth reunion of my college class, I was elected to that board as part of a new initiative to add some more youthful trustees.

No sooner had I completed my orientation as a Penn trustee than I was invited to lunch at midtown's Fresco restaurant by the chair of the trustees of the Chapin School, the elite century-old girls school on the Upper East Side where my daughter Jane was in kindergarten. Chapin's alumni included the progeny of many of Wall Street's finest, as well as Jackie Kennedy, Richard Nixon's daughters, Ivanka Trump and the granddaughters of cosmetics mogul Estee Lauder.[11]

With increasingly active roles at Penn as well as Prep for Prep I had a full plate of education-related philanthropic activities already. But how can any father resist the chance to be more involved in the life of his five-year-old daughter? So I agreed to join Chapin's board, setting myself up for eight years of frantic car rides from midtown to the Upper East Side to make late-afternoon meetings before then catching up on work afterward.

If it was clear that I had as many philanthropic board roles as I could carry alongside my day job, it would be even more obvious that with both a country inn and an equestrian operation I had all the outside business activities I could bear. Yet another interesting opportunity came along. Just as our newly renovated horse farm was starting to attract boarders and appear as if it might prosper at least to the extent of mitigating losses, on the other side of our Connecticut property another dilapidated farm became available.

Agriculture in New England had probably peaked a century earlier, but there were still plenty of dead and dying farms around, and we were suckers for the chance to help resurrect one where we could. As a Wall Street banker I must have seemed like the unlikeliest of farmers, but much of my grandfather's family had worked the land in Holland, and after arriving in America some of his brothers moved to South Dakota and created dairy farms. More specifically to me, I had worked on farms while growing up in western Michigan, picking tomatoes, asparagus and cherries – the last of those for a six cents per pound figure that was particularly memorable given the unbearable lightness of those tiny fruits!

This farm next door had a colorful history to say the least. Encompassed within the property was a small cemetery in which numerous Revolutionary War veterans had been laid to rest. Looking back even further, a sign on its entrance attested to the place's Dutch heritage, noting that the cemetery land was purchased by the town after the war from a Dutchman who had arrived in 1720 from the nearby Hudson River valley. The substantial farmhouse on the property was built in the 1850s for some prosperous but now unknown citizen. Much later, in the mid-twentieth century, the farm was owned by a descendant of Gilded Age robber baron Jay Gould, who as a young man had survived the sinking of the passenger ship RMS *Lusitania* during World War I.

Among current locals the place was best known as simply "Bing Crosby's brother's place." Underlining the Crosby connection from some decades ago, local legend had it that the house had served as the setting for Bing's familiar film *White Christmas* – the reality for that being a Hollywood stage set, as we discovered when our curiosity inspired my wife and me to rent the classic film. Now, a few decades later, the property was a collection of decaying buildings, with the roof of one of its two large barns having recently collapsed. Again we were motivated by the risk of landscape-marring development. This still beautiful piece of land, which stretched out along the Housatonic River, had fallen one zoning commission vote short of being turned into a golf course and seventy-seven-home subdivision in the 1970s. Now the current owner had planted septic test pipes around the property as an indication of his intention to pursue a similar development scheme.

Meanwhile, inspired by the writings of Michael Pollan, whose book *Omnivore's Dilemma* spoke passionately and convincingly of a need to return to old-fashioned farming methods, we had developed the fantastical notion that we might rotationally graze grassfed Black Angus cattle as well as raise ultra-free range chickens and grow a variety of fruits and vegetables on the property to turn our White Hart inn into a sort of "farm-to-table" operation. *The New York Times* would later sum up our plan under the headline: "Beef so fresh, it came from just down the road,"[12] although in trying to be witty the editor who wrote that title forgot that beef needs to be aged before being cooked and served to customers. We would call the place Twin Lakes Farm, after the road on which it sat, just around the corner from Weatogue Stables.

As Roxanne and I walked the property's circumference reflecting on the possible acquisition and resurrection of this second farm, we came across a weather-beaten four-inch by eight-inch sign inexplicably nailed to one of the innumerable rotting fence posts that would need to be replaced. It read, "Footprints in the sands of time are not made sitting down." We realized with a laugh that this was essentially our motto, so we took that sign as an omen and plunged ahead. With our inn and restaurant, horse farm and now cattle operation we had what I liked to refer to as a diversified portfolio of money-losing businesses. Fortunately, the funding for such follies continued to flow unabated from 100 miles south in midtown Manhattan.

CHAPTER NINE

VISITORS FROM JURASSIC PARK

Tradition, tradition! Tradition![1]
– Sheldon Harnick, Fiddler on the Roof

A s we navigated Greenhill's continuing rapid ascent on Wall Street there was no time for looking back at the firm we had left behind. Bob, never a contemplative man, was not one to look back in reflection on anything. He quite literally lived by his trademark phrase: "Keep moving." In particular he almost never spoke of his thirty years at Morgan Stanley – certainly not at all his ignominious end there – and by the time of our IPO he had already been gone for more than a decade. My own departure from Morgan Stanley, after a much shorter tenure, lacked the high-stakes drama of his exit. But I likewise did not look back.

The Morgan Stanley I was proud to have been a part of had largely ceased to exist. Now it was just one piece of a huge financial services conglomerate, which included Dean Witter's "Main Street" retail brokerage business and the Discover credit card alongside growing principal investment and trading arms. While the firm of my day had felt elite and exclusive despite its size, the larger conglomerate, initially carrying the cumbersome moniker "Morgan Stanley, Dean Witter, Discover & Co.," had tens of thousands of employees in hundreds of offices, most doing work that was far away from the Wall Street I knew in almost every sense. In straying so far from its historic role Morgan Stanley had created an opening for our firm to step into at least part of the void it had left. Thus in our business model, culture and daily interactions with clients we strived to assume its prestigious place on Wall Street.

Adding to my detachment from my old alma mater, those now in charge of the enlarged Morgan Stanley were different than those under whom I had served. Bob's old classmate Dick Fisher had stepped down as chairman upon completion of the Dean Witter merger, just after my own departure to join Greenhill. Within a couple years Fisher had retired from the board completely. Following his exit John Mack, Morgan Stanley's longtime CEO-in-waiting, was essentially pushed out of the firm, soon thereafter to become CEO of the competitor firm Credit Suisse First Boston, the investment banking business of the giant Swiss bank Credit Suisse that had stumbled when it bought DLJ.

Firmly in charge was Phil Purcell, the Dean Witter CEO, a former McKinsey consultant rather than an investment banker or trader. Perhaps because of that unfamiliar pedigree, his skills in boardroom politics had been underestimated by Fisher and Mack as they plotted the merger that brought these disparate businesses together. As a sop to the old Morgan Stanley crowd Purcell had hurriedly inserted investment banking veteran Robert (Bob) Scott as "president," theoretically his number two, just as Mack was leaving. But that secondary position was not a powerful one given Purcell's imperial CEO style, and after an uncomfortable stint of less than three years Scott was gone by the end of 2003.

While Purcell had succeeded in hanging on to his CEO position and expelling key Morgan Stanley loyalists who were potential successors, his years at the top of the firm had been far from easy. The leadership struggle with John Mack had to be painful given Mack's intimidating and aggressive style as well as the fierce loyalty he engendered from the troops. In addition, the integration of two very different businesses with very different cultures was awkward from day one. The bursting of the dot-com bubble further exacerbated the stresses within the firm. The sharp decline in high-flying technology stocks created challenges for all investment banks, but particularly so for Morgan Stanley given its leadership position in IPOs and mergers in that industry. Legal problems, ranging from Eliot Spitzer's investigation of corruption in equity research practices to embarrassing lawsuits relating to racial and gender discrimination, added to the firm's woes. Perhaps most important in the context of the recently consummated merger, the broad decline in stocks put heavy pressure on the inevitably cyclical retail brokerage business that Dean Witter had brought to the table, calling into question the original rationale for combining the two firms.

Seven months after the Greenhill IPO came a reminder of the Morgan Stanley that once was: the December 2004 death of Morgan Stanley's revered former Chairman Dick Fisher following a battle with prostate cancer. His passing came at a pivotal moment. Just a week prior to his demise a hedge fund manager named Scott Sipprelle who had previously served as head of equity capital markets at Morgan Stanley wrote a private letter to Purcell and his board of directors. He claimed that "the original rationale for the [Morgan Stanley Dean Witter] merger was flawed," that the firm's stock price had consistently underperformed that of peers and "that the current stewards of the firm [were] blind to the root causes of this affliction."[2]

Sipprelle argued for nothing less than the dismantling of the firm – the sale or spin-off of the Discover credit card, the investment management business and the retail brokerage business. These steps would pare back the firm to what it had labeled the "institutional securities business" – essentially the old Morgan Stanley. Failing to get a response from Purcell or his board, in early January Sipprelle leaked his letter to *The Wall Street Journal*.[3]

Like Morgan Stanley alumni everywhere, I read that letter with interest. While I did not know Sipprelle well, I had sat near him in my early days at the firm and knew he was a good friend of my partner Bob Niehaus, himself another interested Morgan Stanley alum.

While in years to come "activist shareholder" would become a familiar phrase in the corporate lexicon, at the time Sipprelle's move was highly unusual. "Corporate raiders" critiqued corporate strategies and tried to overthrow CEOs and boards to gain control of companies, but Sipprelle was not one of those. And companies like Morgan Stanley were not the kind typically targeted for such attacks. Morgan Stanley was supposedly in the business of telling clients how to structure and finance their companies to maximize shareholder value. Was it incapable of applying those same skills to itself? Worse, Sipprelle was essentially a member of the family, having spent years at the firm along with a brother who rose to a senior position in the junk bond group there – he and I had come into contact on the pig farm restructuring. Worst of all, there was a sense that Sipprelle was speaking for numerous people still on the inside at the firm. Given Morgan Stanley's history and high profile, the initial skepticism surrounding the merger with Dean Witter, the public battle that had ensued between Purcell and Mack and the intense corporate maneuvering ever since Mack's departure, Sipprelle's letter found a wide audience.

Just a week after Sipprelle's incendiary letter became public a memorial service for Fisher was held at New York's renowned Riverside Church – the timing of that missive being perhaps intentional so as to take advantage of what would surely be a large gathering of interested parties. Being of a different generation, I had experienced only one meaningful interaction with Dick, at the breakfast where he gently tried to coax me into staying at

Morgan Stanley several years earlier. Thus rather than join the throngs at Riverside I spent the day interviewing two prospective recruits, in a client meeting and in preparation for the upcoming IPO of Republic Insurance, where I sat on the board in connection with our private equity fund investment.

Somewhat more surprisingly (at least for those who did not know him well), Bob Greenhill, Fisher's business school classmate before spending thirty years working closely with him, did not attend the service either, although his wife Gayle did. Bob was not someone enamored of ritual or ceremony, nor was he a sentimental man. To the extent he felt anything there undoubtedly had to be some residual ill will from the way Fisher had maneuvered him out of the firm they had spent years building together. But nearly everyone else with a connection to the old Morgan Stanley did attend the service, and by all accounts[4] it was a highly emotional one – perhaps even more so because of the ongoing reverberations from Sipprelle's letter. Bob Scott, recently retired from the firm after his struggles with Purcell, was chosen by Fisher's widow as the firm representative to speak to the somber gathering.

When Red Sox pitching ace Curt Schilling was asked about the "mystique and aura" surrounding the storied New York Yankees baseball franchise, he scoffed that "those are dancers in a night club. Those are not things we concern ourselves with on the ball field."[5] But for the generations of Morgan Stanley employees and alumni gathered at Fisher's memorial service, the mystique and aura surrounding the Morgan Stanley franchise was very real. Dick Fisher embodied the firm's carefully crafted image – Princeton, Harvard Business School, a full career spent at the firm followed by devotion to philanthropy, an understated style and partnership ethos and, most of all, an abiding commitment to the founding father's ancient dictum about doing "first class business in a first class way."[6] For most of those present Fisher's memorial must have felt like the end of an era. The firm had fundamentally changed, its historic leaders were gone and it seemed like there was nobody left at the firm with the power or authority to reverse its slide into mediocrity and ultimately irrelevance.

Yet behind the scenes an unlikely mutiny led by the old guard was brewing. A series of conversations among key alumni, sometimes including current senior employees, took place. Five weeks after the memorial service Bob Greenhill received an unexpected call from his one-time boss Parker Gilbert, inviting Bob and myself to his Fifth Avenue apartment. Given his gentle nature there was no person less likely, yet at the same time no person more qualified, to lead a revolt than Parker. While he had been retired from the firm for well over a decade, he was a beloved former chairman who had literally descended from Morgan Stanley's founders.

Parker retired when I was still a very junior banker, so I had almost no personal recollection of him, but the understated even-tempered style I observed in this first meeting was entirely consistent with his legendary reputation. Parker explained that he and seven other former senior Morgan Stanley executives, soon to become known as the "Group of Eight", the "G8" or the "Grumpy Old Men", planned to push for change at the firm. Given their undying loyalty to the institution they were all still shareholders, but collectively they owned only about 1% of what was now a very large firm. In any event, their motivation was not financial. They felt an enduring allegiance to the firm in which they had grown up, and they simply wanted to set things right.

A week later the Group of Eight gathered at our office, mostly in person but with a few dialing in. For me this was as exciting as showing up at "Old Timers Day" at Tiger Stadium and meeting Al Kaline and the other long-retired baseball heroes of my Michigan youth. I had a personal history with only three of the group. One was Bob Scott, who had only recently left the firm and was coming off a high from having spoken from the heart at Fisher's memorial. As the youngest of the group and the most recent to have been full-time employed at the firm, Scott took an active hand in the group's efforts. It quickly became evident that, while all wanted Purcell removed, Scott hoped to personally fill the vacancy that would thereby be created.

Another member was Joe Fogg, head of the investment banking division during my formative years at the firm. Fogg had a powerful intellect and a ferocious intensity. People, including most managing directors, had lived in fear of him, yet his aggressive style was effective in making bankers like me continuously strive to produce their very best work. Many, including myself, had once assumed that he would one day lead Morgan Stanley. But timing is everything in a market-related business, and Fogg was a peer of John Mack, who ultimately prevailed over him given the ascendancy of the firm's trading businesses in that era. Hence Joe left the firm while still relatively young to start a small investment fund and now spent most of his time in Florida.

In sharp contrast to Joe, John Wilson, the consummate client man, was likely the most amiable of his generation at Morgan Stanley. Lacking any pretension and with ambition only for the firm rather than himself, Wilson was an earnest, salt-of-the-earth kind of banker who in my early years was regularly wheeled out for important client occasions.

The rest of the group was from an even earlier era and known to me only by reputation. There was Lewis Bernard, one of the four men who once led the firm along with Gilbert, Fisher and Greenhill. Renowned for his intellect, Bernard had stepped down from the firm fourteen years earlier, at only 49 years old. In commenting on his departure *The New York Times* called him the "chief conceptual strategist" of the firm.[7] He was now chairman of the board of the American Museum of Natural History among other philanthropic roles.

Anson Beard had led the equities division of the firm, and thus had deep connections to the institutional investors who collectively owned Morgan Stanley. Dick Debs had led Morgan Stanley's international business from the early days when it was just starting to expand around the globe. And Fred Whittemore had led what was called the equity syndicate, which managed stock offerings for corporate clients. He was the first of the eight to join the firm and was renowned for both his intricate knowledge of its history and his eloquence in retelling its stories.[8]

While in many respects most members of the Group of Eight had left the firm ten to fifteen years earlier, in another they had not left at all. Consistent with the firm's historic "Morgan Stanley for life" ethos, retiring partners retained the title "Advisory Director" and were provided modest office space, which they used to varying degrees. Those still fully employed by the firm referred to that space, in a mix of humor and sometimes mild derision, as Jurassic Park. Wall Street had indeed changed dramatically since this group was in charge of the firm. Little did current Morgan Stanley employees realize how important a role the Jurassic Park crowd, suiting up for one last corporate battle, would play in the next stage of the firm's history.

For our firm, the assignment to advise the G8 was a high-profile role that would further embellish our growing reputation at a critical moment. But at the same time that role was very unusual. From the G8's perspective an advisor was needed to organize the efforts of a group of men who had largely retired and for the most part did not even have an office from which to work. However, the group knew that Morgan Stanley parceled out all kinds of business on Wall Street, and finding an investment bank and law firm that were unafraid of what Morgan Stanley could do to them in retaliation would not be easy. The decision to call Bob for advisory assistance was one of many ironies in this peculiar situation. Some members of the group had played at least a tacit role in easing Bob out of the firm more than a decade earlier. Yet on a personal level they all liked Bob, admired his intrepid style and knew there was nobody better at leading a charge into battle.

"We want the man who can fire the torpedoes," Parker once exclaimed. Those bellicose words were a bit surprising coming from such a gentle man, but the metaphor was perfect given that Parker's predecessor as

Morgan Stanley chairman had done a stint as Secretary of the Navy, where Bob himself had also served. Hence Parker called "Greenie," as Bob was known to bankers of that earlier generation when nearly everyone at the firm had some sort of WASPy nickname, often carried over from playing fields of the elite boarding schools at which they were typically educated.

My role, as was often the case, was to provide the cautious and analytical counterbalance to Bob's "shoot first, ask questions later" style. I found the situation interesting enough on a personal level that I would have advised the group for free. Bob cared even less about money so would have done likewise. But as fiduciaries of a public company we needed to be paid for our work, so we shook hands with Parker on how we would be compensated and when, even if we had little clarity over who exactly would fund this obligation. Trust ran deep within the G8 and between it and our firm. I was two to three decades younger and previously unknown to most of the group but was seen by my elders as just as much a member of their tribe as anyone who had grown up at the Morgan Stanley they knew.

What was most unusual about our role was that the assignment was more about public relations than about the kind of analytics and negotiation that characterized our usual projects. As for financial analysis, it was far from clear that a complete break up of Morgan Stanley of the kind Sipprelle argued for was sensible, or even feasible. In any event, the public information provided in Morgan Stanley's financial reports was woefully insufficient to allow a detailed analysis of such possibilities. As for negotiation, it was clear that Purcell and his board would not be willing to deal with the G8, let alone with an advisory firm that had been founded by Morgan Stanley refugees and was a competitor of growing importance. So, with the help of Andy Merrill of the public relations firm Edelman, Bob, our younger partner and part-time CFO John Liu, our general counsel Ulrika Ekman and I planned a letter writing campaign.

On March 3, 2005, we launched our first missive to Purcell and his board. The letter, attacking his leadership and the firm's performance and warning of poor staff morale, was intended to remain private. Predictably, Purcell immediately sought loyalty oaths from those around him, and maneuvered to quickly purge the ranks of those he feared might be cooperating with the G8. Within a few weeks the head of the "institutional securities" business, a cerebral Indian PhD named Vikram Pandit whom I had known there, and his right-hand man were both gone.

At the end of March we fired off another letter, this time taking out a full-page ad in *The Wall Street Journal* to turn the heat up on Purcell. In an interview with *Bloomberg* Joe Fogg spoke of a "sense of outrage" at the firm, and Parker Gilbert defended the role the group was playing: "We're not a bunch of raiders. We helped build this firm. We have serious concerns."[9]

The Journal headline, "In Morgan Stanley Rebellion, Purcell Puts Up a Tough Fight",[10] said it all. Purcell was holding his ground. Given his intransigence, defections of old Morgan Stanley loyalists continued, and in early April the G8 formally proposed that Bob Scott replace Purcell, a notion Purcell and his board promptly, and not at all surprisingly, rejected.

Still, Purcell clearly realized he could not employ the classic "just say no" takeover defense that echoed Nancy Reagan's slogan for dealing with drug abuse and thereby reject every idea presented. So he indicated that the firm was looking at spinning off the Discover credit card business, thus accepting one small element of Sipprelle's original proposal. Despite that modest victory, we did not let up in our letter-writing campaign and watched through April as further defections suggested that seemingly a whole generation of Morgan Stanley leaders were fleeing.

Seeking to build support among Morgan Stanley's key shareholders, we convinced Brad Hintz, a Sanford Bernstein equity research analyst for the investment banking sector who had previously served as treasurer of Morgan Stanley, to host a meeting for institutional investors. On the early evening of April 6 members of the G8 spoke to a large room full of such investors at Bernstein's Sixth Avenue headquarters, just a few blocks from

Morgan Stanley's offices. Hundreds of other investors from across the country dialed in. As I left the building a CNBC film crew was waiting near the curb, adding to the circus atmosphere surrounding this project. Years later a bit of video footage from that evening would find its way into a lengthy Morgan Stanley-sponsored documentary posted on its website and thereby provide me with a very brief cameo appearance (albeit via a rear view) in this pivotal moment in the history of that storied firm.

Interest in the unfolding drama extended beyond the specialist business press. On May 1, *Newsweek* published a piece under the byline "By Newsweek Staff", titled "A War Without Winners", suggesting that "more may be lost in the battle than will ever be won."[11] The authors posited that "neither side can make a compelling case for why they're better than their opponents." They pointed out that many of the G8 had once supported Purcell, just as they had once *not* supported Bob Greenhill, and perhaps were upset mostly because the share price had fallen in half since the merger. In addition, they further suggested the proposal that Bob Scott replace Purcell indicated that the motivations underlying the debate were perhaps too personal. Pointing out the obvious alternative, they suggested John Mack might return to take the role. But Mack, whose time as CEO of Credit Suisse First Boston had already ended in something less than success, "said he wouldn't want the job if it became open." As for where the brouhaha would ultimately lead, the story speculated that Morgan Stanley might end up getting sold, and that someday thereafter the warring parties on both sides would look back with nostalgia at the firm that once was. Clearly *Newsweek* had fully bought into the firm's "mystique and aura."

From the perspective of our firm, the high-profile nature of the controversy served to further elevate our stature in the investment community at a critical moment. Throughout the entire saga Bob Niehaus and I were busy meeting investors to raise money for our second private equity fund. More importantly, while the battle was still raging a few of us spent the first week of May on an investor roadshow across the US in preparation for our first common stock offering since our IPO a year earlier. Spending some of my first stock sale proceeds several days before I actually had them, Roxanne and I closed on the purchase of our horse farm that same week.

In the weeks that followed the G8 continued to turn up on the heat on Purcell, and the continuing stream of defections began to wear down the resistance initially shown by a board of directors filled with Purcell loyalists. On June 2, Roxanne and I went to see David Mamet's play *Glengarry Glen Ross*,[12] a familiar favorite that we had first seen in London when I was there for Morgan Stanley. While the story revolves around salesmen in a classic "boiler room" land sale operation designed to sell far away vacation lots to naive buyers, the analogy to life on Wall Street is powerful. The salesmen's mantra "always be closing" is evocative of the relentless pressure to perform. And the play's sales contest where first prize was a new Cadillac, second prize a set of steak knives and third place meant you were fired was a perfect metaphor for the "winner take all" nature of working on Wall Street. As Bob Greenhill and John Mack had each learned twice and Phil Purcell was now learning, the competition was always most intense at the top. Getting to the CEO's office was extremely difficult and required a fair amount of luck relative to market cycles; remaining on top once that summit had been reached meant surviving constant challenges.

Finally, like Mamet's older salesman getting pushed out at a time when he felt he had so much more to give, Purcell lost the support of his board. In an announcement addressed to colleagues he spoke ruefully of the battle he had lost: "It has become clear that in light of the continuing personal attacks on me, and the unprecedented level of negative attention our firm – and each of you – has had to endure, that this is the best thing I can do for you, our clients and our shareholders."[13]

Later that month the board issued a press release saying that after a "thorough search" the board had chosen John Mack as CEO, describing him as "uniquely qualified" and with "strong ties to Morgan Stanley."[14] The choice of Mack was rich with irony. He was the engineer of the Dean Witter merger now largely seen as a failure and had allowed Purcell to take the top job as part of that deal. Replacing Purcell with Mack had certainly not been the intention of the Group of Eight. Yet as Joe Fogg put it after the saga was over, "None of us were thinking of replacing Phil with John Mack, but by the time Phil finally left, John was probably the only guy that could have turned things around."[15]

For certain Mack was the people's choice, as demonstrated by the lengthy standing ovation when he strode triumphantly back into Morgan Stanley headquarters like a deposed emperor returning from exile. Still the same General Patton-like figure I had observed in my years at the firm, albeit now a bit older and humbler given all he had endured, he spoke to the employee gathering with genuine emotion, his eyes at one point welling up with tears.

Various publications suggested Mack would "put the swagger" back into Morgan Stanley, despite swagger not being a characteristic to which Parker Gilbert or Dick Fisher or indeed J.P. Morgan would ever have aspired. More ominously, it was said that Mack would recreate the "culture of yes"[16] to replace Purcell's risk averse "culture of no."

CHAPTER TEN

ANOTHER YEAR OF MAGICAL THINKING

When the sky is bright canary yellow
I forget ev'ry cloud I've ever seen,
So they call me a cockeyed optimist
Immature and incurably green.[1]
　　　　　　　　– *Oscar Hammerstein II*, South Pacific

In every market cycle there comes a time when possibilities seem truly limitless. Animal spirits – the psychological energy that economist John Maynard Keynes identified as an economic accelerant[2] – run high among investors as well as with CEOs, boards of directors and their advisors. The pace of technological advancement and the evolution of industries seem so rapid, and the competition so intense, that simply maintaining the status quo feels risky to the point of recklessness. Taking bold action seems imperative.

In such a moment almost any price for a prized acquisition that would advance a key strategic initiative seems justifiable. Financing acquisitions in such an environment is not an obstacle – funds are readily available on attractive terms. Given the number of players facing similar challenges and opportunities, the fear of missing out leads to frenzied auctions, with prices spiraling upward. Deals come together in a rush, as market participants fear that some interloper might steal their target if they do not move quickly enough.

The year 1989 had been such a year. The roar of the Roaring '80s reached a crescendo not long after the infamous stock market crash of October 1987 – with its 22% decline in the Dow Jones Industrial Average in a single day – turned out to be nothing more than a speed bump on a long upward trajectory. But as a young investment banker buried in work and living fully in the moment I lacked the experience to recognize either the extraordinary scale of the opportunities then available or the fleeting nature of such a moment in time. With the advent of the first Gulf War, an economic recession, increasing defaults on corporate debt, declining deal activity, the first round of layoffs at Morgan Stanley in memory and the startling realization that a young banker's compensation would not increase every single year, 1989 was soon a dim memory of a golden era the likes of which one did not expect to see again.

Yet only a decade later 1999 had been another such year, when the dot-com bubble reached its maximum point of inflation three years after Fed Chief Alan Greenspan first warned of irrational market exuberance. With stocks soaring and deal activity on both sides of the Atlantic smashing records, our young firm had taken full advantage of the abundant opportunities then available, thereby solidifying its place in the Wall Street firmament. But as with the prior cycle, and indeed as with all economic cycles since the Old Testament's Joseph told the Pharaoh to expect harsh famine to follow years of bountiful harvest, soon innumerable tech start-ups failed, stock market valuations fell by half or worse, deal activity withered and in 2001 the September 11 terrorist attacks on New York and Washington added to the gloom.

As our still small team of 201 employees entered 2007, little did we know that economies, markets and our firm were all destined to scale heights well beyond those achieved in those prior epochs.

Our New York office kicked off the new year by hosting the "bake-off" (the colloquial term for a competition for investment banking business) to determine which of the world's major banks would be lead underwriter for the largest IPO in history. Two years earlier the chief financial officer of Charles Schwab, my longtime client and the source of inspiration for our own IPO, had recommended me to the CEO of VISA USA, whom he knew through their common San Francisco headquarters locations, to advise on a project that would be among the most complex assignments of my career.

VISA was essentially a cash machine, earning fees on millions of credit card transactions every day. The number of such transactions was growing inexorably, as consumers increasingly relied on cards rather than either cash or checks to make their purchases. At that time VISA was a collection of separate but affiliated regional entities around the globe. The hope was to negotiate a merger of all the various VISA entities into one, then take that combined global company public and let it operate as an independent business owned by a wide range of institutional investors in the same way that major companies normally are. The driver for this strategy was the pace of technological change in the financial services industry and the belief that VISA as a united entity could be nimbler than a confederation of separate companies in addressing competitive threats and taking full advantage of growth opportunities.

The various VISA entities were each controlled by the largest banks of their respective regions, and those banks typically were represented on the regional boards by their top executives given the high perceived value of their VISA ownership stakes. As we pressed forward on the project many months of negotiating sessions ensued in various world capitals, and the diverse venues, scale of conference room tables needed to accommodate the delegations and bevy of language interpreters on the sidelines whispering into the ears of their bosses via headsets collectively gave these occasions the feel of a United Nations (UN) summit. The slow pace of progress likewise seemed similar to that of a UN initiative, although we finally arrived at a merger announcement in October 2006.

That merger led to the IPO "beauty contest" in our office a few months later in January, around the time of Greenhill's annual partners meeting. That was probably the peak moment of my Wall Street popularity, as each major firm looked for any angle to gain a leg up in winning one of the prized investment banking assignments of that era. In the end I recommended Goldman Sachs, in large part due to my direct experience with its equity capital markets team on our IPO and subsequent offerings. And that was the firm that VISA chose.

Yet the VISA transaction was only one of many Greenhill deals that would have the word "largest" appended to them in that period. Just before the new year began my London counterpart Simon Borrows advised British tobacco company Gallaher on its $19 billion sale to Japan Tobacco, then the largest ever European acquisition by a Japanese company. A few months later in March 2007, our London team struck again, advising the ubiquitous British pharmacy chain Boots PLC on its $24 billion sale to American private equity giant KKR in the largest ever going-private transaction for a UK-listed company. Two weeks following, Bob Greenhill and I advised Sallie Mae, the primary student loan financier in the US, on its announced $25 billion sale to a private equity group led by former Goldman Sachs executive Chris Flowers; that sale would be the largest going-private transaction for a financial services company ever.

Only two weeks later I advised SSAB (the shorthand acronym for the leading Swedish steel company) on its $8.5 billion acquisition of Canadian steel maker IPSCO, in what was the largest ever North American acquisition by a Swedish company. We rounded out the first half with two more transactions with a "largest" designation. Bob advised telecom company Bell Canada on the announcement of a $52 billion sale to a private equity group led by media specialist Providence Equity, in what would be the largest Canadian transaction of that kind in history. And Simon advised the Belgian bank Fortis on its part of the $99 billion acquisition of the Dutch bank ABN Amro, on which it partnered with Britain's Royal Bank of Scotland and Banco Santander of Spain. That deal – the largest financial services transaction ever and for a client with which we had no prior history – came together in a matter of only a few months yet would generate the largest advisory fee in our firm's history – $49 million.

The competition for choice acquisition opportunities in that era was such that successful deals often came only after thrilling buzzer-beater finishes, resulting in several of the most memorable deals of my career. In the late autumn of 2006, I was entering the home stretch in selling Kos Pharmaceuticals, a multibillion dollar publicly traded company whose major product was a drug that elevated HDL – the "good" cholesterol, in patients, thereby reducing their risk of a heart attack. Kos, named for a Greek island, was controlled by the affable, elderly Greek billionaire Michael Jaharis, who – after being randomly introduced to the world of healthcare in his first assignment as a new US Army recruit – had made a career of building and selling innovative pharmaceutical companies. On Mike's board sat his close advisor Kevin Ferro, a young fellow from the hedge fund industry that I had met some years earlier.

Kevin called me looking for help, saying that Mike needed an advisor but did not trust investment bankers. I knew nothing about the pharma industry and had never heard of Kos, the headquarters of which it turned out was just ten blocks up Park Avenue from my office. But I did know how to run an auction of a highly sought after asset.

Mike and I hit it off immediately, and soon we were on the brink of selling the company to New Jersey-based drugmaker Schering-Plough before that company stunned us by abruptly walking away, just when final board approvals were expected. I was standing outside the Sharon Play-house in northwest Connecticut during intermission of a show I was watching with my wife and kids when my phone rang. It was the kind of call from the blue, of the sort that were all too common in a M&A banker's career, that can ruin a pleasant outing in a second. The trick is to keep your game face on and avoid ruining the day for the family or friends around you. As the Mafia boss Hyman Roth said in *The Godfather Part II*, "This is the business we've chosen."[3] In other words, there's no point feeling sorry for yourself. Or as Bob would put it, just keep moving.

Kos's leadership and my internal Greenhill team were understandably gutted by the last-minute collapse of such an important transaction, but as so often happens the seemingly dead deal soon came back to life with new prospective acquirers. On the first Thursday in November, following a second competitive auction process, the Kos board agreed to sell the company to a major Japanese pharmaceutical company. However, the Japanese company was a bit too relaxed about the timing for the deal's formal sign-ing and announcement. It proposed that we sign on the following Monday to allow time to prepare a public relations plan for such an important announcement.

That weekend was the annual autumn outing where I hosted the entire Greenhill New York-based associate group, those in their mid-twenties to early thirties, at the White Hart inn. Owning such a place, regardless of whether one is actually trying to make money, is a time-consuming affair. Innumerable challenges are involved in taking care of a 200-year-old building and overseeing a large and ever-changing staff of generally very young people. A kitchen snafu could lead to an evening full of unhappy patrons, an overused fireplace could set a chimney on fire, a chef could miss work because he got arrested for drunk driving – something I learned was an occupational hazard in the restaurant industry. However, the pleas-ure I derived from hosting events for colleagues at a historic place in which I took great pride made the effort worthwhile. That year I took our associate group on a big Saturday morning hike up Bear Mountain to the highest point in the state of Connecticut – not exactly Mount Everest, but still a good few hours of exercise.

After we climbed the "mountain" and returned to my home for lunch in the rustic party barn behind our house, I received an urgent call from the one associate who had been too busy to make the trip up from the city. He had just received a call from Abbott, the huge Chicago-based pharmaceutical company that had just lost the Kos auction. They had offered to do whatever it would take to top whatever deal we were about to sign. The law says that a board's fiduciary duties are such that until a deal is actually signed (and with public companies even beyond that) a board must consider any better offers that come along. Yet it is seen as a breach of ethics in our profession to blatantly inform an interloper of the terms of the current leading bid. We hurriedly arranged a call with the Abbott deal team, and I informed them only that their latest bid had been materially too low, that we could provide them an acquisition contract on which we would accept not a single word of revision, and that we needed a higher price and their signature on that document by no later than the next morning.

Clearly having been given a mandate by their leadership to not lose this deal, the Abbott team agreed to all my demands. To ensure that it would win the deal if it met all our requirements, that team insisted on personally delivering the signed contract to us in our New York office that Sunday morning. They demanded in return that we countersign within an hour, in time for them to return to Chicago via their waiting corporate jet to make the kickoff for the Chicago Bears football game later that afternoon. We happily complied, accepting their materially higher offer for the benefit of Kos shareholders and handing a huge disappointment to the befuddled Japanese company that was left standing at the altar. My former Morgan Stanley colleague advising the Japanese undoubtedly did his best to explain what had happened.

Six months later the SSAB deal was a similar come-from-behind thriller, this time with my client on the buy side of a deal. Like Kos, SSAB was a company we had never met, but somehow it found us through an American consultant with which it had a relationship – a fellow who happened to know one of our restructuring bankers. The Swedish company had a young, dynamic new CEO, Olof Faxander, who was keen to build a larger, more global business. He had a strong affinity for America, and so we quickly bonded and joined together in the quest for IPSCO, a leading North American steel company up for sale. Yet despite our best efforts, at the end of a weeks' long bidding process, we were informed that IPSCO was going with a higher offer than the one we had tabled.

Unlike the more relaxed Japanese acquirer of Kos, IPSCO and its acquirer had agreed to lock themselves in a late-night Chicago conference room until they emerged with a signed merger agreement. In the days before email that would have been sufficient to ensure the desired outcome. But in the wee hours of that New York morning, I sat in my Upper East Side apartment on the phone with Olof, who was six time zones ahead of me in Stockholm. I spoke in near whispers, hoping not to wake my wife or young kids in the dead of night. Together we conspired on how to trump the deal on the table, and Olof got quick board approval to make a higher offer.

I then emailed that offer to IPSCO's Goldman Sachs banker, who was sitting in the conference room in Chicago. Consistent with the fiduciary duties that had guided the Kos board, he had no choice but to convey the higher offer to the IPSCO board, and that board had no choice but to accept it.

A couple weeks after that thrilling victory Roxanne and I celebrated my May birthday with a night at the theater. We saw a newly opened play, *The Year of Magical Thinking*, based on Joan Didion's grief-stricken year following the loss of both her author husband John Gregory Dunne and their only daughter. The one-woman show starred acclaimed actress Vanessa Redgrave and was directed by the equally acclaimed David Hare.

This was one of many shows we enjoyed that busy year, as the efficiency with which we cranked out completed deals provided me a surprising amount of spare time to indulge in my favorite pastime. We saw everything from a revival of Stephen Sondheim's *Company* to that year's innovative new Tony-winning musical *Spring Awakening* to *Cyrano de Bergerac.* That French story had inspired my wife's mother, a teacher who tragically died from a brain aneurysm while still in her twenties, to name her Roxanne.

The notion of "magical thinking" felt particularly relevant to the moment in which we were living. In general terms, magical thinking refers to the belief that one's thoughts or actions can influence events, despite there being no logical basis for that causal connection. An example would be the belief that wearing a lucky shirt or following a set routine will make one perform better in an athletic contest or have a successful evening gambling in a casino.

Markets indulge in their own version of magical thinking, particularly in periods like the one we were living through in 2007. Participants in an inexorably rising market assume it is their skill, their hard work, their sheer force of will that is the source of their success. Cable television channel CNBC and various business publications amplify the propensity for magical thinking by featuring one commentator after another who explains the (apparently) rational reasons why the stocks they recommended have been going up, their business has been thriving, or their deal has been or will be a success. It is easy to sound like an expert when explaining what happened yesterday, but few have the skills to recognize a change in the tide of markets, let alone accurately forecast one. So the same fateful drama seems to play out with every market cycle.

At each crescendo of M&A deal activity there is typically a single transaction that represents the height of magical thinking and marks the peak of that cycle. Such is a deal that in its scale, strategic logic, pricing or all the above is simply a bridge too far. In 1989 that deal was clearly the failed buyout of United Airlines, which *The New York Times* dubbed "a costly fiasco" and nominated as worst deal of the year – one that arguably set off a decline in the entire stock market, and from which "no one emerged with an intact reputation."[4] Ten years later in 1999, the hubristic deal which defined that era was undoubtedly the $164 billion merger of internet upstart America Online (better known as "AOL") with staid old publisher and filmmaker Time Warner. That was the deal that helped Time Warner advisor Bruce Wasserstein get such a high price in selling Wasserstein Perella.

A very good nominee for the transaction that defined the worst excesses of the 2007 merger frenzy was the sale of the Dutch bank ABN Amro, a deal that involved twists and turns at least as dramatic as those of the Kos and Swedish Steel deals but on a much grander scale. ABN had been "put into play" by an activist shareholder who was pushing for management action that would drive up what he saw as an undervalued share price. Soon sharks began circling. Royal Bank of Scotland approached ABN about a deal involving itself, Fortis Bank of Belgium and Banco Santander of Spain. But then Britain's Barclays Bank outflanked RBS and reached agreement on a £67 billion deal, part of which involved selling ABN's large Midwestern US bank LaSalle to Bank of America. After some tussling back and forth, the RBS consortium ended up topping the interloper bid from Barclays and won the deal with an offer of £72 billion, equivalent to $98 billion.

How did a small firm like Greenhill, one with no specialist in the arcane banking sector, win a role in such an important transaction, and in doing so negotiate and earn the biggest fee in its history? The constraints created by conflicts of interest were again the primary source of our good fortune. By the time Fortis got around to identifying an advisor for its piece of that massive deal, which involved buying ABN's Dutch operations, there were almost no advisors left from which to choose. ABN had retained several advisors on the sell side of the prospective deal, as did both Barclays and RBS as lead parties for the alternative buy-side consortia. Add in advisors for Santander and Bank of America for their parts of the potential transactions, and nearly every prominent M&A advisory firm in the world was already involved. Thus we were brought in to advise Fortis, and in a remarkably short time the deal was signed and our unprecedented fee was thereby earned.

While the Fortis deal ended in apparent "success," not every deal we worked on in that period managed to get done. Personally, I spent time on a highly unusual potential project for AIG, the world's largest insurance company. Specifically, my work was for a unit named AIG Financial Products, which called itself "FP" for short and was run from Greenwich, Connecticut, far from AIG's downtown Manhattan headquarters, by a fellow named Joe Cassano.

I had suspected that much would have changed at AIG since the legendary Hank Greenberg, a diminutive but supercharged business leader whose office walls were decorated with pictures of him with generations of world leaders, finally exited his decades-long CEO role under pressure from the crusading New York Attorney General Eliot Spitzer. But I was shocked at the scale, breadth of investment holdings, profitability and apparent independence of Cassano's operation. He seemed to have the authority to commit billions of dollars with little supervision – something that would never have been allowed under Greenberg's legendarily hands-on leadership. Having said that, the project seemed to get tangled up in AIG's corporate bureaucracy and never progressed to become a formal engagement. The reasons for that were not clear to me.

Despite such occasional disappointments, in this extraordinary year most of the deals we worked on did manage to get done. And our string of major advisory roles on landmark deals, particularly in the extraordinary first half of that year, led to remarkable financial results for our firm. Nonetheless, in revenue terms 2007 started slowly. We booked only $43.5 million in first-quarter revenue, less than half the level of the same quarter in the previous year. The quote I penned for attribution to Bob in our earnings release explained that the results "illustrate[d] our consistent comment that quarterly results can fluctuate materially."[5] In other words, we essentially admitted it was a weak quarter but pointed out that we had repeatedly warned investors of occasional outcomes like this.

With numerous deal announcements already made or on their way, and with transaction closings and related fee payments to follow soon thereafter, we did what many companies do to distract investors from current anemic performance: we signaled a positive outlook by announcing a large stock buyback plan. The $150 million repurchase authorization we announced for the next twelve-month period was extraordinary in that it equated to almost six times our net income for that poor quarter. Looked at another way, it was 30% of the value of our entire company on the day we had gone public a few years earlier. Such was our confidence as to the tsunami of fees coming our way.

Consistent with the bullish signal we sent, the second quarter showed record results – more than $140 million in revenue. This was a stunning accomplishment for a firm of our size and well above our prior quarterly record. Just a few years earlier that would have been a record result for a full year.

In further good news for shareholders, we announced our sixth dividend increase in only three years since going public – far exceeding our ambitious five-year dividend target in a fraction of that time. Our dividend was now nearly five times its level at the time of our IPO, generating quarterly payments of several hundred thousand dollars for large shareholders like me and other early partners.

"Capital allocation," the common phrase for the decision on how to apportion accumulated corporate cash between dividends, share buybacks, repayment of debt and reinvestment in the business, is a challenging issue for any company successful enough to produce significant cash flow. At that quarter end we had a surfeit of financial resources, with $80 million in cash, $52 million in accounts receivable soon to be collected and

$123 million in private equity fund investments that should turn into cash over time. All of this was on top of a steady flow of incoming new fees. We had little use for all that cash, as reinvesting in a service business like ours meant simply hiring more people, and those people (if one chose reasonably well) quickly become generators of even more cash. So our choice was between letting the cash pile up on our balance sheet or paying it out to shareholders in some manner.

If we wished to pay out excess cash to shareholders, we could do so either via share repurchases or dividends, a choice that involves several considerations. Share repurchases can put a lot of money in the pockets of shareholders quickly. But buying stock obviously becomes less attractive at higher share prices, and the stock we had purchased the previous quarter was already at an average price of $66 – around four times the price at the time of our IPO. And of course money spent on share repurchases goes only to shareholders who sell shares. In contrast, dividends go to all shareholders equally, so the share price at the time a dividend is paid is irrelevant. However, while share repurchases can be "turned off" at a moment's notice, any reduction in a dividend is typically perceived by investors as a strong signal that something has gone terribly wrong. Thus one must be careful that any dividend increase announced is sustainable for the long term.

A final consideration related to the personal interests of our senior team: with share repurchases, the cash would all go to our outside shareholders, who collectively owned less than half of our firm. But if we paid out our cash via dividends, a proportionately large portion of that would go to our employees, particularly early partners like me who were large shareholders. Moreover, such dividends bore about half the tax rate of our salary and bonus income, so were an especially attractive source of personal cash flow either to plow back into the investment funds we were launching or simply to diversify personal assets. So, not surprisingly, we pursued a mix of share buybacks and dividends, with a significant emphasis on the latter.

Our third quarter was another strong one, resulting in back-to-back $100 million revenue quarters for the first time in our history. Our year-to-date revenue thus already exceeded the previous full-year revenue record. We had already topped our five-year dividend and share price goals and were now well on our way to also beating the revenue and earnings targets we had set out only three years earlier.

Amid all this good news we concluded that this was an opportune moment to tuck into our earnings release the news that Simon and I had been elevated from co-presidents to co-chief executives. While our press release quoted Bob as saying he believed this was the "appropriate time to pass the CEO role,"[6] in fact it took a bit of nudging from me to our lead independent director Steve Goldstone, and then from Steve to Bob, to get this done.

We all knew that the change had no substantive meaning – Bob loved doing deals for clients and had never shown any interest in managing the firm, so absolutely nothing was going to change in terms of how our business was run. But the public relations aspects of management transitions are complex, and the risk of a misstep in our case was heightened by Bob's status as a Wall Street legend. The key to avoiding an unfavorable market reaction is for all management changes to appear well-planned and gradual – that is what is considered "good governance." Hence my comment to Bob when we were preparing for our IPO that in order to create the right appearance, we would need a period with him as chairman and CEO, a period with him as only chairman (as he would be post this announcement) and later a period with him as chairman emeritus – a title with no meaning other than to convey some level of ongoing association with the firm. Now, at a time when we were achieving record results in a period of market euphoria, was the perfect time for the first step in this journey.

As we planned our announcement regarding the CEO position, it was clear that we would carry on with shared roles for Simon and myself. Such joint roles are unusual, and the cases where they work for an extended period are very rare. Clearly the shared leadership of Morgan Stanley by Dick Fisher and Bob Greenhill did not prove sustainable. But this approach seemed to make sense for our firm at this stage of its history, particularly given that titles had little do to with actual authority and responsibility at our firm.

With Bob's career having been twice upended as a result of him not holding the CEO title, he was clearly more comfortable, if he had to give up the title, with the concept of two people sharing the power inherent in that role rather than concentrating that in one individual. Further, while New York was our largest office and the home of our restructuring and private equity investing businesses as well as a large part of our M&A team, our London office was a huge generator of M&A fees, particularly that year. In addition, the geographic diversity of our revenue sources seemed to be a key ingredient in the special sauce that made the market love our stock. Further, Simon and his co-founder James Lupton had always been somewhat sensitive to the status of the London office within the firm, consistent with the transatlantic tension that often seemed to exist in international investments banks. Sharing the CEO title with a London-based partner seemed a small price to pay to avoid allowing that tension to turn into conflict as it historically had at many firms.

We finished 2007 with yet another strong quarter, falling just short of a third consecutive quarter of $100 million of revenue. The primary contributors were the Fortis bank deal and VISA's global merger. For the year we topped $400 million in revenue, with the lion's share of that being advisory fees and the modest remainder coming from our private equity investment business. It had taken nearly a decade of steady progress to get to a record $142 million in annual advisory fees only two years earlier, and the next year we broke through the $200 million revenue level for the first time. We were now at $400 million. That equated to $2 million per employee, pretty remarkable for a business consisting of nothing but phones, desks, conference room tables and some talented people.

What drove this amazing outcome was not only the abundance of mega deals among major companies but also the unusual strength of the British pound, which averaged an exchange rate of just over $2 for the year – far higher than what was typical. This hugely inflated the dollar value of UK fees we earned in a year when there were plenty of those, resulting in a third year when slightly more than half our total advisory revenue (measured in US dollars) came from clients outside the US. Some of that revenue, as in the case of my Swedish Steel deal, was generated from New York, but clearly the balance of revenue production between the two continents reinforced the rationale for maintaining co-CEOs and harmonious relations across the ocean.

Notwithstanding our extraordinary second-half revenue reflecting the closing of numerous large deals we had announced in the first half, we saw some moderation in deal activity as the year played out. Yet markets remained generally strong. In September, our private equity fund sold about half of its stake in Heartland, the payments company that had gone public two years earlier, generating a large gain for our investors and more cash for our firm and for ourselves in our capacities as both fund managers and investors in our own fund. A month later, in a sign of just how frothy stock markets had become, we received a visit from some bankers at Bank of America. They wanted to talk about something called a SPAC.

SPAC (pronounced "SPACK") was the acronym for a "special purpose acquisition company," sometimes referred to as a "blank check company." Such a company seeks to do an IPO to raise money for an acquisition to be identified later, after the fundraising has occurred – hence the term "blank check" in reference to the cash entrusted to the SPAC's managers.

Bank of America told us we were ideally placed to take advantage of the burgeoning market opportunity to create a SPAC. Greenhill was a business the primary purpose of which was facilitating acquisitions. We also had a private equity investing business that had built an outstanding investment track record over its eight-year life. Furthermore, we had a history of successfully completing IPOs, both for our own firm and for Heartland and other companies in our private investment portfolio. We knew the drill when it came to executing a successful IPO road show.

SPACs are peculiar entities that have a long history dating back to at least the early 1990s. While the SPAC structure had over time been modified to provide better investor protections, SPAC deals had remained largely limited to small transactions on the fringes of the stock market, engineered by some of Wall Street's minor players. Certainly the Morgan Stanley I grew up in did not participate in this market, and the New York Stock Exchange still refused to list SPACs, leaving that business entirely to the racier NASDAQ market. Even among lesser firms, the popularity of SPACs ebbed and flowed with markets. The structure faded into obscurity each time markets turned down before reappearing in the next bull market – "like Frankenstein arisen from the dead," as a *New York Times* columnist once put it.[7]

Bank of America's bankers, one of whom I had worked with at Morgan Stanley, explained to us that the extraordinary bull market of 2007 had resulted in a proliferation of SPACs, and larger SPACs than ever, ultimately drawing more mainstream Wall Street players like their bank into the game. The "too good to be true" pitch with SPACs was that investors were guaranteed to at least get their money back. By convention, all SPACs went public at $10 per share, and that $10 went into a trust that would return the funds to investors if no acquisition to utilize the capital raised was completed within a designated time period. The sponsor of the SPAC, Greenhill in this case, would put up a small amount of money to cover fees paid to the underwriters that executed the offering as well as some very modest operating expenses for the period leading up to an acquisition. The sponsor's hope was that an attractive acquisition would be found, and many new investors would then be drawn into the stock, essentially to buy out any initial SPAC investors who chose to then exit and get their money back.

This idea came to us at an opportune time, as we had been highly attuned all year to opportunities to expand our investing business. We wanted to develop a larger counterpart to our advisory business, so that we would be better positioned for the downturn in deal activity and related fees that would inevitably come at some point. To that end we had already raised a second US private equity fund, more recently added a European fund, and were exploring raising a venture capital fund to invest in early-stage companies. We had also held our talks with Lexington as a larger potential acquisition in the asset management space earlier that year.

Based on what we were hearing, a SPAC seemed like a quick, easy and natural way to further increase our funds under management and generate more revenue from a new source. Thus we quickly latched onto Bank of America's idea. Seeking to utilize as much of the Greenhill halo as possible, we called our SPAC GHL Acquisition Corp., named after the ticker symbol under which our Greenhill stock traded. Given my public company CEO experience, I would be CEO of the SPAC while continuing to carry on all my existing Greenhill roles. Bob Niehaus, as leader of our US investment funds, would be senior vice president – his role was intentionally slightly less prominent to avoid our fund investors thinking he would be distracted from stewarding the capital with which they had entrusted him. Our young M&A partner and part-time CFO John Liu would serve in that same CFO role for the SPAC.

We would become part of a huge wave of SPACs, with sixty-six of them having completed an IPO in 2007 and fifty-five more including ours in the queue for one as the year ended.[8] Always ambitious, we aimed to raise an amount of money toward the high end of recent SPAC deal sizes and filed our prospectus with the SEC seeking to raise $400 million.

As we entered 2008 we were finalizing financial statements that, relative to our size, would demonstrate a level of productivity and profitability unlike anything we or any of our competitors had ever achieved. At the same time, we were preparing the requisite materials to mail to investors for our annual shareholders meeting, showing that Bob, myself, Simon and Niehaus had paydays for 2007 of between $20 million and $25 million each. That was on top of the dividends we received on our Greenhill shares, the increasing value of those shareholdings and various intermittent gains on our personal stakes in the firm's private equity funds. We were all so flush that we did not even bother selling any Greenhill shares that year despite their robust valuation. Yet with cash continuing to pile up on the firm's balance sheet we could not resist raising our dividend again when we announced full-year results – the seventh such increase in three and a half years.

With the economy still strong and our new SPAC in process, it looked like 2008 might be just as spectacular as 2007. But perhaps that was magical thinking.

CHAPTER ELEVEN

SHIFTING TIDES AND TIDAL WAVES

It's time to try
Defying gravity.[1]

– *Stephen Schwartz*, Wicked

While our 2007 financial results were indicative of a year in which absolutely everything went right, 2007 was decidedly *not* a year in which everything went right. Amid all the market euphoria there were numerous indications that the economic tide was beginning to shift. That does not mean that there was a clear turning point – there almost never is such a thing in markets. The old broker's saying, "nobody rings a bell at the top" (indicating that it is time to sell), makes precisely that point. A financing that cannot be completed or an M&A deal that falls apart might indicate a fundamental change in market conditions or, equally, might occur for reasons very specific to that particular case. A stock market drop might represent an opportunity to "buy the dip" in advance of an imminent rebound, or it could be the beginning of a cataclysmic decline. An investor or analyst boldly declaring that a dangerous market bubble has formed might be just another among the cacophony of voices trying to attract attention in the business media. Only in retrospect, when numerous data points over an extended period of time can be evaluated, can one clearly identify a turning point.

My first observation of a potential turning point in markets that could affect our firm and Wall Street generally came in July 2007, just weeks after the Fortis bank deal that produced our largest fee ever was announced. As had happened several times in the preceding months, I received a call alerting me to a major transaction in progress where a company I had never met needed a financial advisor. The call came from our law firm Davis Polk – lawyers often were in a position not only to identify a client's need for a financial advisor but to recommend which advisor that should be. In this case, the deal was an approximately $10 billion leveraged buyout of a publicly traded Midwestern industrial company. The opportunity for us arose because that company's existing financial advisors were seen as too close to the several buyout funds looking to take it private.

Amid a wave of huge acquisitions by private equity funds that year we had won numerous new clients in exactly this way, as we continued to ask prospective clients in such situations why they would use Goldman Sachs (or a similar firm) to represent them against Blackstone, KKR or any of the other top buyout funds. Given the extraordinary growth of private equity funds those were literally Wall Street's most important clients. A public company might award one lucrative assignment to an investment bank in a year, maybe not even that. The buyout funds, on the other hand, would each award dozens of them. Thus it was obvious where the loyalties of the bank would lie. The pressure within those banks to avoid crossing the more important client was not overt – everyone knew that looking out for the interests of the party on the other side of the table in a negotiation would be completely inappropriate. But that pressure was nonetheless real and felt all the way down through the ranks. An unwitting client could be thereby disadvantaged in the course of a sale process in any of numerous subtle (and sometimes not so subtle) ways.

Given my own Midwestern roots I was always quick to bond with an industrial company in that region, where they don't always take kindly to New Yorkers. This case was no exception. For Greenhill, this project looked like it would result in an $8 million advisory fee for only a few weeks of work. Three different consortia of the largest buyout firms in the world were competing for what would be one of the biggest deals of its kind, so it seemed clear that our client would very soon end up being acquired. Nearly every major investment bank was somehow involved in the situation, offering to provide debt financing to one or more of those bidders for what would be a very highly leveraged acquisition made possible by the unusually accommodating status of credit markets.

Then, suddenly, not one but all of the competing buyout groups went quiet, and momentum for the deal completely died. The company management and board that I was now advising were as confused as the Japanese pharmaceutical company when it lost the Kos Pharmaceutical business I was selling. What had happened? Why did everyone lose interest at once? For those not riding the daily ups and downs of the capital markets, and in many cases even for those who were, the answers were not clear.

Several weeks later came another sign. The buyout group which announced in April that it was buying Sallie Mae for $25 billion backed away from that deal. The *Financial Times* reported that the "buy-out of Sallie Mae [was] one of a series of large private equity deals signed before credit markets froze that [were] in danger of falling apart."[2] Sallie Mae immediately responded to the buyout group's announcement, threatening to sue to enforce the terms of the original acquisition agreement.

The buyer, as buyers typically do in such scenarios, pointed to the clause of the merger contract referring to a "material adverse change," or MAC (pronounced "MACK") for shorthand. Specifically, the claim was that a planned change in federal subsidies for student loans constituted a MAC, meaning that it should be relieved of its commitments under the acquisition agreements. The seller, as sellers typically do in such cases, claimed that the changes were not material enough to justify invoking the MAC clause. They said the buyer was simply using the potential new regulatory development as an excuse for wriggling out of a deal that, given subsequent movements in the markets, now appeared to have been struck at too high a price. We continued to advise our client on possible compromise solutions, but this project was now largely in the hands of warring teams of lawyers.

Two weeks after the Sallie Mae news I came to understand why my work with AIG had stalled. Joe Cassano, the previously low-profile fellow at AIG Financial Products who had launched that project, was suddenly in the public spotlight. Investors in FP's parent company AIG were asking questions about risks in the huge portfolio of securities through which FP had essentially provided credit insurance to various counterparties in relation to high risk, so called "subprime," mortgages. Cassano was calm and reassuring in his public comments: "It is hard for us with, without even being flippant, to even see a scenario within any kind of realm of reason that would see us losing even $1."[3]

Three months later, in early December, AIG reported a $352 million unrealized loss in the portfolio to which Cassano had referred.[4] But the parent company CEO Martin Sullivan, the Englishman who had stepped into the giant shoes of longtime CEO Hank Greenberg, reassured investors that it was "highly unlikely" the company would ultimately lose money on the deals that it had made in this space.

Yet only a month later AIG upped its estimate of unrealized losses in this portfolio again, to more than $1 billion. Sullivan then repeated his assurances, saying that his team's risk modeling was "very reliable" and showed that there was "close to zero" chance of an economic loss.[5] Sullivan was distinguishing between an unrealized loss based on a "mark to market" calculation (in other words, the market value of an investment had declined, but that investment had not yet been sold) and an "economic" loss where the loss had crystallized and become permanent. His clear expectation was that the value of the investment in question here would ultimately rebound, thereby reversing the unrealized loss.

Nine days after the latest update from AIG our client Bell Canada announced that it would not renegotiate the buyout – the largest in Canadian history – that it had agreed to at mid-year, despite persistent rumors that the deal would be terminated or at least have its price reduced as a result of weakening credit market conditions.[6] The market price of Bell's stock had drifted down to well below the agreed buyout price, indicating that stock market investors were increasingly skeptical that the deal would be completed as planned.

Another warning that a storm might be coming came later that year on my daily twenty-seven–block commute from my office to home one evening. I was sitting in the back seat of a car provided by one of the ubiquitous "black car" services used by firms like ours to ferry bankers to meetings and airports in the pre-Uber era. The driver was one I had seen frequently, but our conversations had heretofore been limited to traffic, the weather and occasionally local sports.

"You know anything about that bank?" he asked. I looked out my window to see which of the numerous banks with branches on Park Avenue he was referring to.

"You mean Washington Mutual? Not much," I said. "Why?"

"They keep calling me about payments on two condos I bought in Florida," he said. "I told them, 'I can't pay if I don't have a tenant!'"

Joseph Kennedy, the business tycoon and patriarch of America's most prominent political family, has often been quoted as saying prior to the epic stock market crash of 1929 that "if shoe shine boys are giving stock tips, then it's time to get out of the market."[7] Likewise, if people who drive cars for a living are borrowing from a little-known financial institution based 3,000 miles west of them to speculate on real estate located 1,000 miles south of them, then it probably makes sense to get out of the real estate market. What's worse, as Joseph Kennedy could have told you, is that getting out of the illiquid real estate market is a lot trickier than getting out of the stock market, where shares can be sold instantaneously.

Despite the setbacks on some of our largest assignments and the ominous conversation with my driver, 2007 had indeed been an extraordinary year for our business. Yet as we entered 2008 it was becoming clear that market conditions had fundamentally changed. And that raised the question of whether we would succeed in completing the IPO of our SPAC.

Niehaus and I had been involved in numerous IPOs including Greenhill's, but the SPAC IPO was different. History shows that SPACs only succeed in the frothiest of markets. In attempting to take public our SPAC we were not selling an operating business with a management team, a track record of performance and a plan for the future. We were simply raising a pool of cash to invest in some unknown business that we would identify in the future. Numerous other groups were queued up to do the exact same thing. Further complicating the situation was the fact that our SPAC, at $400 million, was larger than most. We would need a reasonably friendly market *and* have to distinguish our SPAC from the many others then pending to attract the requisite number of institutional investors to fill out the order book for shares and complete the offering.

The marketing process for SPAC shares was far different than that for other IPOs. There was no worldwide road show to visit prospective investors. The limited number of specialized hedge funds that invest in SPACs seemingly all sat in either Manhattan or nearby Greenwich, so our road show was by car rather than plane. And strangely, unlike other investors we had encountered, these hedge funds seemed to be playing for pennies.

They were more like bond investors than stock investors. They were not even contemplating being long-term investors in whatever business we acquired. For the most part, the nature of their funds did not allow that. Instead, they planned to exercise their right to ask for their investment back later, once we had found an acquisition and attracted a different set of investors to replace them.

These investors hoped to eke out a few pennies on the dollar in profit by selling the warrant (i.e. the right to buy an additional share at a fixed price) that was attached to every SPAC share as part of the peculiar structure of such offerings. The better job we did in finding a good acquisition and attracting new investors, the more that warrant would be worth. On the other hand, if we failed to find a deal that would gain shareholder approval, the warrant would expire worthless, eliminating any hope for a profit by these funds.

There was thus not a lot of substantive discussion in any of these investor meetings. Whether or not investors would buy our SPAC was largely a function of simply how much capital they had to put to work – the more money flowing into their funds from their investor base, the more they could use that capital to place bets on SPACs like ours. Their hope was that a reasonable percentage of those would succeed in finding an attractive acquisition and thereby generate a profit for them.

In early February Niehaus and I set out on our road show. The increasing sense of nervousness among investors was palpable, but we were good salesmen and the track record of our funds and of Greenhill itself provided us a good product to sell. We must have seemed likely to find an acquisition that would attract investor support. Accordingly, on Valentine's Day 2008 we were relieved to complete our offering, raising the $400 million we were seeking at a moment when it felt like the window for deals like ours, and perhaps for deals of all kinds, was rapidly closing.

With that behind us we quickly pivoted to what we knew would be an even greater challenge: finding something in which to invest all that money.

Thus, less than a week after we collected our money, my first stop was at York Capital, the hedge fund run by my freshman year college friend, Jamie Dinan, whose tip had guided me toward my first job in the M&A business while I was still in law school. I wondered if Jamie might be interested in monetizing the value of his fund the way we had done with our firm.

As turned out to be the case with many other businesses we pursued with our SPAC, my approach to York got no traction. SPACs were considered to be on the fringes of the financial universe – not suitable for high-quality companies that had other financing alternatives. In any event, Jamie and his team were likely distracted at the time by increasing stresses in the market that were undoubtedly impacting York's day-to-day business of investing in stocks. Only two weeks after completion of our SPAC IPO, AIG reported that the losses in FP's portfolio for the prior year were $11.5 billion, not the zero it had expected six months earlier and more than thirty times the $352 million it had admitted to two months ago.[8]

Fortunately we already had our money in hand by time the window for SPACs firmly closed. A further bombshell hit weeks later when Bear Stearns agreed to be sold to J.P. Morgan for only $2 per share, a huge discount to its current market price and far below the $170 a share at which it traded only a year earlier. Bear announced that transaction with a statement that this ugly deal was the "best outcome for all of our constituents based on the current circumstances."[9] The fact that it was concurrently preparing a bankruptcy filing in case a sale could not very quickly be arranged clarified that its stunning statement was not hyperbole.[10]

Bear was a major securities firm with an eighty-five-year history but had always stood behind Goldman Sachs, Morgan Stanley and Lehman Brothers in the pecking order. As *The New York Times* accurately wrote, "Bear Stearns was never considered a white-shoe Wall Street firm and often operated on the edge of the industry."[11] Bear's was a scrappy business, focused on trading. Its modest M&A advisory business was distinctly second tier, so our firm rarely interacted with it. The recent exception for me was when Alan Schwartz, the

M&A banker who ended up being elevated to CEO of Bear when it was in its death spiral, represented Schering-Plough in its near purchase of Kos Pharmaceuticals. He also represented the telecom company Verizon when it acquired our client MCI some years earlier. Bear had been under increasing pressure, starting in 2007 when it became clear that it had huge exposure to the same subprime mortgage business that was plaguing AIG – but without the benefit of the stable insurance and retirement businesses that AIG had to help absorb losses.

The Times reported that Bear had been "pushed to the brink of bankruptcy by what amounted to a run on the bank." What it meant was that, as a firm that relied on trading for most of its revenue, Bear regularly interacted with other major trading firms. Those firms, the counterparties to its daily trades for itself or on behalf of clients, took the risk in accepting each trade that Bear would be good for the agreed purchase price at the time the transaction was completed (or "settled") a couple days later. That was referred to as counterparty risk, a factor that gets little focus in good times but increasing attention in unstable or declining markets. Just as a clothing maker will suddenly cut off shipments to a retailer that appears to be at risk of bankruptcy, trading firms will abruptly cease to trade with a weak firm, or at least require greater amounts of valuable collateral as protection in case of default. The former can quickly put a trader like Bear out of business, while the latter can stretch its balance sheet in a manner that can ultimately lead to the same place.

When a trader is put out of business there is a negative knock-on effect on every firm with which it has done business, further denting confidence in all of them. That is the "contagion" risk which the Federal Reserve and US Treasury had sought to avoid when dealing with the Long-Term Capital case a decade earlier. With the objective of avoiding such contagion in Bear's case, the government essentially pushed it into the arms of a stronger bank, not caring how much damage would thereby be done to shareholders or employees. The clear priority was protecting the financial system on which the global economy relied. In any event, few tears would be shed for Bear, which notably had refused to participate in the industry-wide bailout of Long-Term Capital that had successfully limited the contagion last time around. Hank Paulson, the fellow running the US Treasury at the time of Bear's demise, would have been fully aware of that footnote to financial history given he had been leading Goldman Sachs at that time and therefore deeply involved in that earlier bailout discussion.

While J.P. Morgan ultimately agreed to raise its price for Bear from $2 to $10 per share, the news of Bear's fire sale was a shock to all on Wall Street. This was the most significant failure of a Wall Street firm since Drexel Burnham's demise almost two decades earlier.

Why did major market reversals always seem to come as a surprise to nearly everyone on Wall Street? In part it was because the fires tended to start in unexpected places – Russia in the Long-Term Capital case, the Middle East for the September 11 attack and residential mortgages in the case of the 2008 crisis now being felt most acutely by AIG and Bear Stearns. What often further obscured any signs of approaching danger in cases like this was the high degree of specialization across Wall Street. As a mentor from my Morgan Stanley days once derisively said, "there are guys on the trading floor trading 10-year Treasury bonds who don't even know 5-year bonds exist!"

His comment was obviously sarcastic, but it would not be an overstatement to say that traders who bought and traded bonds for leveraged buyouts know little if anything about Russia, and perhaps even less about residential mortgages. Many were likely as naive as my driver who had taken out mortgages on the two Florida condominiums for which he was now struggling to pay. Thus a dangerous fire in one market segment can quietly spread to a point where it cannot be contained before being noticed by players in other market niches.

For Greenhill, the import of Bear's disappearance was far from clear. Bear was smaller than its Wall Street peers and had always been more aggressive when it came to risk, so it was not obvious that other firms would come under similar pressure. And while traders of all kinds were undoubtedly spooked, subprime mortgages were a very long way from the part of the financial services world in which we operated. Our business was not closely tied to day-to-day market activity the way a trading firm's is, and we had a very manageable debt on our balance sheet, which was more than offset by cash and other assets. Still, a shocking event like the collapse of a major financial institution can cause activity all across the capital markets to freeze up. That's what happened when Long-Term Capital was failing and again after the September 11 attacks occurred.

Just as Bear was in its final death throes, Roxanne and I went to see the first revival of Stephen Sondheim's *Sunday in the Park with George*, which had won a Pulitzer Prize for drama when it first premiered on Broadway just as I was starting my career as a young lawyer. It is hard to imagine two people more different than Sondheim and Bob Greenhill, yet the last song before the finale in *George*, "Move On," echoed Bob Greenhill's motto to always "keep moving":

> Stop worrying where you're going
> Move on
> If you can know where you're going
> You've gone
> Just keep moving on[12]

One critic called the song "one of Sondheim's soaring, searing explorations of the inevitability of imperfect resolution."[13] The song must have held great meaning for Sondheim as he, a composer and lyricist who rarely performed himself, sang what was described as a "very emotional"[14] rendition of the song just a few years after its premier at the memorial service for his friend Michael Bennett. Bennett, the choreographer and director who won two Tony Awards for the very first show I ever saw on Broadway, *A Chorus Line*, died at only 44 years old from an AIDS-related illness. Perhaps their common Depression-era birth was enough to have imbued in Sondheim and Greenhill a similar perspective on life – that it is inherently unpredictable, that unfortunate events come along with remarkable regularity and that one has no choice but to keep moving on in the face of whatever life brings.

In any event, the week that Bear effectively disappeared we took Greenhill's and Sondheim's advice and kept moving. I was busy advising bookseller Barnes & Noble, fast-food chain Wendy's and my longtime client Charles Schwab on active deals and was also preparing to take on a leadership role on the board of trustees of Prep for Prep – a role about which I was starting to feel some trepidation given the organization's almost-total reliance on fundraising from Wall Street firms and their employees. The next week my family and I escaped to the Caribbean island of Anguilla, as had long been planned, in accordance with the school spring break schedule that inevitably drove vacation timing for bankers in my age bracket.

Day-to-day work continued as usual in the months that followed, although clearly animal spirits had been dampened and the M&A market was therefore much quieter. In addition to my active projects at that particular moment, over the course of that year I advised on deals for credit-rating agency Moody's and children's book publisher Scholastic, and our London partners advised the British companies Cable & Wireless and supermarket operator Tesco on other transactions. But very few deals that year were large or otherwise notable. Clients were clearly beginning to hunker down, husbanding cash and shunning risk of all kinds.

Notwithstanding the slowdown in deal activity, in May several of us from the top to the bottom of our organization were interviewed for a cover story for *Dealmaker* magazine.[15] The very existence of a slick new magazine called *Dealmaker* was itself an indication that the deal-making party might be at a peak and soon coming to an end. And indeed the magazine itself ended up having a very short shelf life. Further, putting an M&A firm on the cover, as it did by picturing Bob, myself and Simon, brought to mind the oft-noted superstition that it is a jinx for an athlete to appear on the cover of *Sports Illustrated*. Regardless, the *Dealmaker* story was a puff piece with no substantive new content and certainly no criticism, and thus served as another bit of helpful publicity as we continued to build our brand. Bob was quoted in the article repeating his usual story about how lucky we were, how things had "just kind of happened" for us – something the author correctly noted he was "fond of saying."

Indeed that was always how Bob saw the business, and when that story was published that summer his remark about how things "just kind of happened" seemed truer than usual. However, what was happening at that point was not good. On the heels of Bear's demise hedge fund manager David Einhorn announced a large "short" position in Lehman Brothers stock, meaning that he was betting that Lehman stock would go sharply lower. He could then close out his trading position by buying the stock at a much lower price than he had sold it, the difference between the purchase and sale prices being his profit. That was the first salvo in a months' long war between Lehman and Einhorn, wherein he loudly and repeatedly proclaimed his belief that Lehman had dangerous exposure to illiquid real estate assets and used aggressive accounting practices that hid its true risk profile.

Einhorn was far from the only speculator seeking ways to profit from shifting markets, and that phenomenon resulted in markets of all kinds becoming highly volatile. Oil prices soared that summer, eventually hitting an all-time high of $147 per barrel just after mid-year. As it so happened, our private equity funds at that moment had a significant concentration in energy assets, and thus we were direct beneficiaries of the unexpected price spike. The peak price came almost exactly midyear, when we routinely measured the value of our private equity assets for purposes of calculating gains or losses for our second-quarter financial statements. Accordingly, after a respectable first-quarter revenue result of $75 million based largely on M&A advisory work carried over from the robust level of 2007 deal activity, our second quarter turned out to be the third best in our history. Despite a much-reduced level of advisory revenue, our total revenue for the three months was $109 million, including almost $60 million of merchant banking revenue – a record contribution from that business, driven almost entirely by a sharp increase in the value of our energy investments. Unlike in the case of AIG and its subprime debt exposure, here the "mark-to-market" accounting methodology had worked to our favor.

As often happens in commodity markets, almost as soon as oil prices peaked they began a decline just as steep as the increase had been. As a result, in the third quarter we had the previously unthinkable result of a negative *revenue* quarter. This was not simply negative net income due to costs exceeding revenue, but rather actual negative total revenue. That bizarre outcome came about due to two factors. First was a weak advisory revenue quarter given that market participants of all kinds were now taking shelter, and second was a negative $52 million of merchant banking revenue reflecting the sharp reversal of the oil price spike that had boosted our results only one quarter earlier. Essentially, our gains on paper the previous quarter had been almost completely reversed before we could turn them into cash.

For obvious reasons, we had serious concerns about how the market might respond to such a peculiar quarter. Nonetheless, I was relaxed enough that August to take my family on a sailing and hiking trip along the coast of British Columbia's Great Bear Rain Forest, where we were able to observe numerous whales and grizzly bears up close. To keep in touch with market developments from that remote location I took along a satellite phone from Iridium Communications, a private company originally launched many years earlier by Motorola that we were actively considering buying with our SPAC.

Notwithstanding our trepidation about a bizarre quarter's results, the problems we faced were nothing compared to those of the large banks. Before our disastrous third quarter had even ended Washington Mutual had been seized by federal regulators for having made too many bad mortgage loans to people like my driver. Far worse, the mighty Lehman Brothers filed for bankruptcy. I immediately recalled *Greed and Glory on Wall Street*, the influential book excerpted in *The Times* that I eagerly read my first year as an investment banker. The subtitle of that book was *The Rise and Fall of the House of Lehman*. The author turned out to be twenty-something years early in his eulogy but spot on about some deep cultural weaknesses lurking within that storied firm. The demise of Lehman, particularly via bankruptcy meltdown rather than in a fire sale, was a far greater shock than the loss of Bear. Lehman was a much larger firm, with far more assets, more employees, a higher public profile and a more august history.

Post-Lehman's collapse, the contagion risk was now very real, raising the specter of a domino effect across Wall Street. The US government, which had let Bear and now Lehman go, drew the line there, encouraging Bank of America to buy Merrill Lynch later the same day that Lehman failed and then the next day taking control of AIG via an emergency $85 billion loan. Days later, after the federal government made them an offer that couldn't be refused, both Goldman Sachs and Morgan Stanley applied to become bank holding companies, providing them immediate access to essentially unlimited low-cost borrowing from the Federal Reserve, the cheapest and most secure source of precious liquidity. In exchange, they accepted much closer regulatory scrutiny and tighter restrictions on the risk they could take with their balance sheets. Historically those creatures of the freewheeling capital markets would have been appalled at the notion of accepting all the constraints inherent in becoming a fully regulated bank. But now, grasping for a life raft in a raging storm, they quickly concluded that this was the best, and likely only, way forward.

The tidal waves set off by Lehman's failure extended well beyond America's shores – most of the British banks needed some form of government bailout and Fortis, our most valuable client of the previous year, was fully nationalized by the Belgian government in early October. We found ourselves wondering about our potential liability for having advised on the deal that helped lead to its demise, but governments, banks and investors were all fully preoccupied with the urgent task of surviving the here and now. Any autopsy to determine who was at fault for various corporate deaths and near deaths would have to wait.

My alma mater Morgan Stanley came particularly close to following Lehman and Merrill into a bankruptcy filing or sale. As events unfolded former colleagues and I quickly came to realize that the deferred compensation plans we had blithely signed up for decades earlier to defer personal income taxes were unsecured obligations of the firm, ranking behind nearly all other debt in the case of a bankruptcy. The degree of anxiety across Wall Street was so high that I soon moved most of my personal bank accounts from Bank of America (BofA) to J.P. Morgan. My fear was that even a bank as large as BofA might end up failing, particularly given its rushed purchase of Merrill. In the end, BofA managed to persevere, and so did Morgan Stanley, saved by the combination of its conversion to regulated bank status and a hurriedly arranged $9 billion equity investment from a Japanese bank.

My thoughts turned back to Morgan Stanley's long history, a saga I had first come to know via Ron Chernow's riveting (at least for a young Morgan Stanley banker like me) book *House of Morgan*, then as an employee and finally in the Group of Eight episode. Ironically, as events continued to unfold it became clear that John Mack, who had received a hero's welcome when the Morgan Stanley board brought him back in response to pressure from the G8, had not been the right man for the times. Mack, a salesman by trade, later had the humility to admit in his autobiography that he had misjudged market risks.[16] His "culture of yes" and his confident swagger would have been ideal for the years of economic recovery and expansion that came after the dot-com bubble burst. Equally, the risk-averse Phil Purcell with his "culture of no" was the wrong choice for that period but would have been a better pick for the years leading up to the financial crisis. Such are the vicissitudes of life on Wall Street.

If Mack brought anything to the table it was passion, and thus he resisted government pressure to accede to a fire sale that would have consigned the mighty Morgan Stanley to the dustbin of history along with Bear and Lehman. As much as for any other event in his colorful career, Mack would be remembered as the man who, in response to another call from Washington, intended to increase the already-excruciating pressure on him, shouted at his assistant: "Tell Tim [Geithner, then at the New York Federal Reserve and soon to become US Treasury Secretary] to get fucked!"[17]

As the crisis played out, every major financial institution followed Morgan Stanley in trying to increase liquidity, reduce risk and generally build a sturdier life raft for a storm that showed no sign of abating. Yet in sharp contrast to the crisis now engulfing all of our larger competitors, activity in our offices continued to feel largely unchanged by the string of startling events. The day Lehman Brothers filed for bankruptcy I flew to Minneapolis for an ordinary course business development meeting with the leading American health insurance company United Health. From there I flew on to Bermuda for two days of board meetings in relation to a large property and casualty insurance company investment held by our private equity fund. We learned there that what we had believed was a conservative insurance company investment portfolio was hardly that in light of the recent events. Any investment with any link to the housing market – even if a previously highly rated bond – was getting hammered in the market.

The rest of that eventful week was devoted to preparation for the announcement that our SPAC, after five months of looking, had found a place to spend the cash it raised in its IPO. GHL Acquisition Corp. was merging with Iridium Communications, a satellite communications company with a complicated history. Iridium made the phones that American soldiers used in

Afghanistan and I used on a sailboat in the Pacific – places with no cell towers to support ordinary mobile phones. With the worst possible timing, we announced that acquisition just a week after Lehman failed and only a day after the Goldman and Morgan Stanley announcements regarding their new bank status.

Against that highly unfavorable backdrop, we began a road show to present our case to shell-shocked investors. Among the market wreckage we hoped to find new long-term investors for a post-merger company that needed to raise billions more dollars to fund the development of new satellites to replace its aging network. In the midst of that challenging but ultimately successful road show I returned home to our farm to enjoy the first horse show, a dressage competition, at our newly renovated Weatogue Stables.

All things considered, our business was doing tolerably well – survival was the only appropriate goal for the moment, and we were doing much more than that. We were on our way to 2008 full-year results showing a worst-ever 45% revenue decline from the too-good-to-be-true 2007 level. But even at that much lower revenue level we generated strong profitability and sufficient cash flow to fund our generous dividend. Our advisory revenue was actually higher than it had been two years earlier, before the extraordinary 2007 year. But our investment business was – after years of generating substantial gains – now basically breaking even.

Notwithstanding our respectable financial results and the "business as usual" tone that prevailed in our offices, it was clear to me that our cash reserves might prove to be inadequate if the crisis was prolonged. The firm had made significant financial commitments to each of our private equity funds, which would be drawn down over time alongside those of other investors to pay for new investments. We also had significant capital tied up in our SPAC, which had not even closed on its Iridium acquisition yet, let alone had a timetable in sight for monetizing that investment. And the prospect of receiving any offsetting asset sale proceeds to help fund future investments seemed dim. Indeed, in the current depressed market it seemed unlikely that any of our funds would be generating meaningful gains of the type so common in recent years.

I worried about the financial health of our partners at least as much as I worried about the financial health of the firm. The previous year's bonuses had reached into the stratosphere for a handful of star performers but not for everyone. Looking ahead, it seemed likely that compensation for all would be down substantially for this year and possibly for years to come. Furthermore, like the firm itself, our partners had made substantial personal commitments to our various funds in an effort to be supportive of our strategy and help us attract outside investors. As I had done with our first fund back in 2000, many had likely committed more than they had available in liquid assets, on the theory that future bonuses and occasional investment sale proceeds would arrive in time to cover any shortfall.

Given the high degree of prevailing uncertainty, I soon concluded that the firm should raise cash by selling some stock – and that it should do so urgently, before markets could worsen further. We had already done two equity sales since our IPO, but those were entirely on behalf of partners like me, generating substantial cash for our personal benefit but none for the firm. The firm itself had sold no equity since the IPO itself – in fact, given the seemingly endless flow of large fees and investment gains coming our way, it had spent significant surplus cash buying back stock in the open market. Now, it seemed to me, was the time to do a stock offering both for the firm and for its large internal shareholders, providing both with the liquidity necessary to ride out the financial storm no matter how long it lasted.

On the question of the price for that stock offering, we received help from an unexpected source: the Securities and Exchange Commission. In the days following the Lehman bankruptcy, the SEC announced it was taking "temporary emergency action to prohibit short selling in financial companies to protect the integrity and quality of the securities market and strengthen investor confidence."[18] David Einhorn's hedge fund had eventually made big profits by shorting Lehman stock, and other funds were likewise seeking to profit from the crisis ripping through the financial services industry by shorting stocks of other financial firms. All that short selling was creating a downward spiral in stock prices that seemed to feed on itself, undermining confidence in every financial firm.

Greenhill had always been somewhat of a target for short sellers, as our stock's spectacular performance had understandably drawn skeptics from the start. Surely we were not of concern to the SEC. But the government was using every tool it had, no matter how blunt, to mitigate the crisis – going far beyond simply relying on interest rate cuts as it had in past downturns. There was no time for fine-tuning how each tool would work. So it turned out we were among the "financial companies" covered by the new rule, and that meant short sellers had to swiftly close out their positions by buying our stock in the open market. All their urgent buying resulted in a classic "short squeeze," which drove our share price to as high as $92.90 per share – a new all-time high and more than five times our IPO price from four years earlier. This was the very week that Lehman went bankrupt, the shares of financial services businesses were in free fall and the future of our firm was more uncertain than ever.

Clearly we were unintended beneficiaries of the SEC-driven short squeeze, but at the same time the resilience of our stock did not seem entirely irrational. The growing financial crisis created numerous risks for us – would companies have the courage to make acquisitions amid all the uncertainty? Would they be able to get financing for deals even if they did? Would our competitors slash their fees to win more business in a shrinking market for deal advice? The answers to those questions were unknown. But on the positive side it was clear that the crisis would also create significant opportunities for us, just as previous crises had. And those opportunities would encompass acquiring new talent as well as new clients.

Our phones those days were buzzing with refugees from all the big banks seeking a safe port in the storm. Just two weeks after Lehman's bankruptcy filing we hosted most of its Chicago-based investment banking team, a group focused on clients in the industrial sector in the Midwest, to talk about the team joining us en masse. The Lehman group and most other bankers had seen the value of company stock received as part of their annual compensation evaporate, along with their expectations for year-end bonuses.

For many M&A bankers, the fact that traders – their longtime rivals for capital, compensation and firm leadership positions – had put the very survival of their firms at risk was the final straw in breaking the always uneasy intra-firm alliance between those two groups. I was reminded of my old mentor's quip about bankers, traders, hot dog stands and casinos – operating a hot dog stand outside a bankrupt and shuttered casino did not sound very lucrative. As shell-shocked bankers looked around for alternatives, our firm must have seemed appealingly safe.

The unexpected spike in our share price provided a welcome psychological boost for our team at a time of uncertainty. But we never expected it to last, not with extraordinary volatility buffeting stock and bond markets and the resulting subdued state of M&A activity. So our share price soon dropped to well below where it had been the last time we did a share sale. Still, now was a time for protecting against downside risk, not for worrying about maximizing upside potential. So we proceeded with our share sale on the accelerated basis that was allowed by regulators for the more mature public company that we now were.

On the very day that Barack Obama was first elected president, two days after my annual weekend outing for Greenhill associates at the White Hart, we held a call with underwriters and recorded a video road-show presentation. No longer was a whirlwind trip visiting investors across the country necessary. Just ahead of the marketing process, as a way of piquing investor interest in the opportunities that the crisis might generate for us, we announced the recruitment of much of Lehman's Chicago team. By coincidence, the day after we launched I was at an investor conference in Manhattan sponsored by one of the research analysts who covered our stock, and that provided the perfect forum for marketing our stock. Only one day later I dialed into Goldman Sachs for the offering pricing call from the Harvard Business School campus after speaking at a recruiting event for MBA students.

In the end I was relieved to get $56 per share, reflecting a still impressive $1.7 billion market value for our small business. The firm came away from the offer with about $80 million in cash proceeds, while we raised well more than $100 million for our senior partner group including myself. No investor asked why the firm was selling stock despite our longstanding proclamations that ours was a business that consistently generated strong cash flow and thus needed no new capital. Given the astonishing headlines rolling out daily, investors knew we were smart to build up cash reserves for both the firm and its senior partners. What is less clear is how we found a group willing to invest significant new money in our business at that moment of maximum market volatility, compounded by the election of an unproven new president. Despite all the challenges we were facing, presumably ours looked like a better bet than almost every other financial firm at that moment.

With our corporate and personal coffers replenished we could confidently focus on the opportunities created by the financial crisis. There was plenty of recruiting to be done amid the continuing flood of talent from big banks, but we also needed to produce revenue to pay for all the new hires on top of the existing team. Generating that revenue was a challenge; M&A activity had slowed dramatically. Getting deals agreed during a time of great uncertainty was always hard and getting them completed in volatile financing markets was even harder. I was personally involved in numerous false starts, including a near miss in selling our old private equity investment and now public company Heartland.

One of many plays my wife and I saw on Broadway that year, Samuel Beckett's *Waiting for Godot*, provided an apt metaphor for our prolonged wait for renewed action. But we did manage to find some things to keep us busy while we waited. Six months after Lehman failed Bob advised on his biggest deal in the twelve years since he founded the firm, advising Swiss pharmaceutical giant Roche on its $47 billion acquisition of Genentech. Bob had met Roche Chairman Franz Humer via our London colleague James Blyth, and they had immediately formed a tight bond – they were like-minded, action-oriented men who generally got what they wanted by sheer force of will.

While the crisis reduced the flow of "regular" M&A activity like the Roche deal, most of our business at that time consisted of unusual advisory roles that were a product of the crisis itself. Dow Chemical brought Bob in to negotiate some kind of compromise to its poorly timed $19 billion acquisition of chemical company Rohm & Haas, a deal that was pending when financing markets suddenly deteriorated. The resolution was announced just three days before the Roche deal, making that likely Bob's best week ever at the firm. Meanwhile our London team advised the Norwegian government on a life-saving capital injection into the troubled airline SAS, and I advised automaker Chrysler and consulting firm BearingPoint on bankruptcy-related transactions.

Our most interesting and unusual role in those early days of the crisis was for Citibank, one of the many large banks that remained at risk of failing for an extended period. This was one of the few projects since our early days in business that Bob and I worked on together. Bob's protégé from his Morgan Stanley days, Vikram Pandit, was then CEO of Citi, having left Morgan Stanley a few years earlier when Phil Purcell was purging anyone from the old Morgan Stanley who posed a threat to his leadership. Vikram was an unflappable, analytically brilliant man, but his board of directors felt the need for some independent advice as it navigated its way through a financial crisis like no one alive had ever seen.

In that moment of turmoil there was probably no board of a major financial institution that was willing to rely entirely on its CEO to ensure safe passage to the other side of the crisis. The losses had been simply too large and too unexpected, proving existential in some cases and threatening to become so in many others. Reminiscent of my old dictum about serving on public company boards, serving as a director in the midst of the financial crisis was very scary at places like Citibank.

Citi's board consisted of folks with very impressive resumes, but all were clearly in shock as to the situation in which their company now found itself. One board member was the highly acclaimed former president of the University of Pennsylvania Judith Rodin. A psychologist by training, she was learning firsthand the risks to which academics and most others are typically oblivious when taking on corporate board roles.

The board also included former Goldman Sachs managing partner and US Treasury Secretary Robert Rubin, a man who had been at the center of resolving the Long-Term Capital crisis and had successfully managed various lesser crises that came before and after that one. He had undoubtedly come to Citibank following extended government service thinking it would provide a comfortable, prestigious and highly lucrative perch for his retirement years. Widely respected as a wise man and financial wizard but also known as someone highly protective of his reputation, he kept a low profile in the board discussions I witnessed. Certainly the last thing he would have wanted was to find himself in a leadership role at a troubled bank that had increasingly fractious relations with a government of which Rubin had recently been part.

At our first meeting with Citi's board Rubin came up to shake my hand during a break. "I know your father," he said. I politely shrugged off his comment, visualizing my father climbing telephone poles to repair storm damage in wintry Michigan yet saying only that I thought he was mistaken. But he repeated, "No, I know your father well." Of course he was referring to former Harvard University President Derek Bok, thereby adding to the lengthy list of people who for three decades had wrongly assumed that the two of us were related. I was always amused by the fact that, in America's modern celebrity culture, people were typically visibly disappointed to learn that I was not connected to the prominent university leader, even though that meant I had more likely earned my place by merit.

What the Citi board wanted was an advisor to provide an independent perspective on some of the ideas coming from management, as well as those being put forward by the federal government, as potential means to survive as an independent corporate entity. Vikram wanted any such advisor to be someone he trusted, so he maneuvered our firm into that role. Yet if the board would not fully rely on Vikram to navigate through the crisis, it also did not fully trust Bob, someone who had been Vikram's friend and mentor for many years. So I ended up working jointly with Bob on the project. Bob was the primary interface with Pandit while I became the principal liaison with Citi board chair Dick Parsons, a gregarious fellow who was one of the top executives in corporate America. An unflappable veteran of corporate battles from his years as a senior executive at Time Warner, he had successfully picked up the pieces after its disastrous merger with America Online just before the dot-com bubble burst.

Our Citi project lasted two years, all without the kind of major deal that was usually the focal point of our assignments. Our role was more one of hand-holding as the government rolled out new crisis-era programs and other inquiries were fielded. Some wild transaction ideas were being tossed about as financial institutions sought increased scale and balance sheet strength to absorb growing losses. But the unfortunate reality for the largest banks was that they were not only "too big to fail," as the phrase of the day indicated, but also too big for any quick fixes. The only viable solution was a long, grinding restructuring process, slowly dealing with the innumerable bad assets on the bank balance sheet and waiting for the rebound that history suggests always eventually follows such crises. The patient, even-tempered Parsons was well-suited to shepherd the bank forward implementing that strategy.

If economic downturns, and even more so financial crises, create opportunities for those who are well-prepared, they also have a way of uncovering those who have taken excess risk. As Warren Buffett famously put it, "Only when the tide goes out do you discover who's been swimming naked."[19] Likewise it is at those moments when financial frauds are usually uncovered, as the free flow of funds that has a way of hiding such frauds slows or even reverses. So it was following the dot-com bubble bursting when the fraud at Enron was uncovered. Other fraud cases of that era included cable company Adelphia Communications and telecom company WorldCom.

Ironically all three of those situations had led to opportunities for our firm. The debacle at Enron led to plenty of work with its Houston neighbor and energy sector peer Dynegy (a company that I joked had always wanted to be like Enron and in the end nearly succeeded), as well as to my assignment for the accounting firm Arthur Andersen. WorldCom's crisis led to our work with its acquirer MCI, both in bankruptcy and later when it was sold to Verizon, as well as our fund's fabulous investment in cell-tower operator Pinnacle. We also executed a multiyear assignment advising the creditors of Adelphia in its long-running bankruptcy process.

The biggest fraud unveiled by this latest, and much more serious, financial crisis came in December, three months after Lehman's bankruptcy, when investor Bernie Madoff was arrested in New York for operating a Ponzi scheme. Madoff's name was completely unfamiliar to me, but I along with everyone else who follows the news soon learned that he had managed billions of dollars for various people in New York, Palm Beach and indeed around the world. The owners of the New York Mets and one of Prep for Prep's most generous benefactors were two of his many clients.

On the very day the news broke my wife and I happened to be in Palm Beach with a local real estate broker looking at buying a home there.

We had acquired a small apartment on the island a year or so earlier, but Roxanne wanted to put down deeper roots and have more room for family and friends to visit. I was dragging my feet on that initiative given the chaos in markets, but was ultimately convinced to take a look. On the day we toured homes the famed high-end shopping street Worth Avenue was abuzz with the news about Madoff, whom we learned had been a long-time seasonal resident. His victim list was particularly heavily represented at the Palm Beach Country Club, an elite club established in the 1950s.[20]

I guessed that nobody I knew would be among Madoff's victims, just as nobody I knew had died in the September 11 attack – New York is a big place. But amid the flood of press coverage I soon learned of the close association between Madoff and a "feeder fund" called Fairfield Greenwich, a business built around raising enormous sums of money from investors around the world to invest in Madoff's funds, collecting generous fees for itself along the way. Fairfield Greenwich was founded by Walter Noel, a fellow who over the years had carefully crafted the perfect image for what was essentially an international asset-gathering business, not a hedge fund as it sometimes labeled itself.

Several years earlier the celebrity-loving *Vanity Fair* had published an article titled "Golden in Greenwich" about Noel's daughters – "five beautiful sisters with a Brazilian provenance" and "not a divorce or scandale among them."[21] Well, no "scandale" up until then anyway. The family, based in "the heart of WASPy Connecticut" but with outposts in London, Lausanne and beyond, seemed impossibly rich, and in the effortless sort of way that old money likes to appear. Just a year before the Madoff fraud came to light Noel had hired what must have seemed the perfect person to take his business to the next level and onward toward a lucrative IPO. That recruit was a former Morgan Stanley colleague of mine, Charles Murphy.

I had lost touch with Murphy thirteen years earlier when I left London to return to New York but had occasionally come across news of his movements. Murphy had been a good banker, but he was even better suited to

217

play one on TV. Tall even from my 6′2″ perspective, good-looking in a bankerly sort of way, and always impeccably dressed, he had from the start been an aggressive climber of Wall Street's social ladder. Morgan Stanley was one of several big banks for which Murphy had worked, seemingly always in search of a more prestigious and lucrative post. At the height of the dot-com bubble he left Wall Street entirely, as innumerable fortune-seekers did at that time, for an internet investment vehicle with the indecipherably trendy name "Antfactory Holdings." As was typical then, he reportedly received a modest salary and equity that would become worth many millions if events played out as planned. Yet the bubble burst not long after he arrived, dashing his hopes (along with those of a whole generation of kindred spirits) for a quick windfall and sending him scurrying back to Wall Street. Then, at the peak of the next upturn in 2007, he left London and moved back to the US to take the Fairfield Greenwich job. He celebrated the move by buying a $33-million Manhattan townhouse from an heir to the Seagram's drinks fortune.[22]

In January *The New York Times* wrote a biting story mocking Murphy's ambition, his bad luck and his ignominious fall from grace.[23] It was the kind of story journalists love to write about the fallen rich or famous. Murphy called me after the story appeared, asking to come to my office for advice. I was curious to see him after so long, but in any event had a policy of always being willing to meet with a former colleague wanting to reconnect, regardless of how close we had been or how long ago we worked together. There is a kind of fraternity among former Wall Street colleagues from the same firm. Even those who were not terribly close during the time they worked at the same place still have a lot of common history.

When I walked into our conference room to greet Murphy it struck me that physically he looked the same – dressed in a well-tailored pin-stripe suit as usual. Yet emotionally he seemed shattered. He wondered if there was any way he could get a job with our firm or indeed any investment bank. Clearly he had the requisite skills and experience, but I was honest and told him no. Any association at all with Madoff was not just toxic, it was more like radioactive. That he had been duped along with numerous other victims made no difference. His rueful admission that he had done no real "due diligence" on the Fairfield Greenwich story was not a surprise to me – the Noel family must have seemed as perfect to him as it did on the pages of *Vanity Fair*.

Given Murphy's predicament, I suggested that he seek a hedge fund role. Those funds are far more private and less regulated than investment banks, only care about making money, and are generally open to hiring anyone who can help them do so. Not long after, I heard that he had gone to work for John Paulson – a hedge fund manager who had recently risen to prominence as someone who had profitably bet against the subprime mortgage market that had sunk Bear, Lehman and AIG.

Paulson was a very rare winner in the financial crisis. In contrast, there were plenty of losers like Murphy, many of them nothing more than innocent bystanders. Heartland Payment Systems, the credit-card-processing company with a history closely intertwined with Greenhill and me, was prominent among them. Heartland was founded in 1997, shortly after I started at Greenhill. Our first private equity fund's $25 million equity investment, weeks after the September 11 terrorist attack, accelerated Heartland's growth and turned out to be the first in a string of wildly profitable investments by that fund. In August 2005, about a year after our own successful IPO, I stood on the podium of the New York Stock Exchange a second time to applaud Heartland's IPO at $18 per share – a price six times the roughly $3 we had paid for each of our shares. The business prospered and grew to the point where it served 175,000 small businesses, processing 100-million credit card transactions per month.[24] Consequently, in the years following the IPO the stock moved higher, ultimately peaking at over $30 per share. Recently we had nearly succeeded in selling the entire company at a substantial premium to that market price.

Then, on January 20, 2009, came yet another sudden reminder of the fragility of all businesses, as well as yet another case study for my old dictum that serving on a board of directors is generally either boring or scary. Heartland announced that it had been the victim of a security breach within its processing system. This was not an unfortunate accident, but rather a criminal attack thought to have been led by that shadowy group often referred to as "Russian hackers." Indeed, nearly a decade later, two Russians did go to prison for the assault on Heartland and other similarly victimized companies.[25] While the damages from the attack were initially unclear, early news reports said that tens of millions of credit and debit cards might be exposed to fraudulent charges in what would be one of the worst data breaches in history. My own card was one of them.

In practice what that meant was that my old client VISA, as well as MasterCard and others, would reimburse customers like me for losses, replace all those millions of compromised cards and simply send the bills to Heartland. Of course, on top of that Heartland would bear enormous expenses for information technology (IT) experts, lawyers and others to figure out what happened, and take whatever measures were necessary to ensure that the dangerous gaps in IT security that had been painfully exposed were firmly closed. Even if Heartland could withstand all the costs of the breach, there was a question whether key constituents like Visa, MasterCard and the banks on which it relied for credit would continue to do business with the company, given the heightened risks that the breach had made evident.

Heartland's stock collapsed to under $4 per share, down nearly 90% from its peak, and the company could very easily have ended up in bankruptcy. The biggest loser in the attack was Bob Carr, the visionary company founder and CEO in whom we had put our faith. Over time Carr had borrowed against his company stock holdings, in part to make generous charitable contributions, and ended up suffering painful margin calls as a result of the steep share price decline. That allowed his broker to unilaterally sell his shares at the worst possible moment, further driving down the share price and wiping out the personal wealth Carr had accumulated by building this great company.

For Heartland's directors this whole episode was the epitome of "scary." Fortunately, I had managed to avoid being one of those board victims. After years of early morning car trips back and forth to Heartland's headquarters on the edge of the Princeton University campus for board meetings I had recently retired from the board to free up more time for other commitments. My partner and friend, Bob Niehaus, however, remained on the board. He ended up playing an important role assisting Carr in ensuring Heartland's ultimate survival, thus keeping alive the hope that the large shareholdings we had retained from our original investment would maintain at least the potential for some future recovery.

Meanwhile at Greenhill, in contrast to Washington Mutual, Lehman, AIG, Citigroup, Charles Murphy and Madoff's innumerable other victims, Heartland and untold others, we muddled through. All our crisis-era projects helped us get away with only a 1% decline in 2009 advisory revenue from the already much-reduced level of 2008. That was far better than our peer group did in a period when M&A activity continued to be depressed, but it still meant we were at not much better than half of 2007's record level of advisory revenue. Yet with the help of a large gain on the completion of our SPAC's deal with Iridium and some other investment gains, we were able to report a 26% increase in total revenue versus 2008 as well as an extraordinarily high level of profitability.

SPACs epitomized the phenomenon encapsulated in that age-old Wall Street question: "Where are the customers' yachts?"[26] They produced windfall gains for their sponsors, even if outside investors typically saw very modest profits or even losses. Our SPAC, which we were barely able to get funded in the final days of the bullish pre-crisis era, had yet to generate any profits for other investors, but the gains it produced for us were sufficient to keep our little ship powering ahead in turbulent seas.

CHAPTER TWELVE

GREEDY PEOPLE WATCHING

Money makes the world go around.[1]

– *Fred Ebb*, Cabaret

There is generally a "first-mover advantage" in business, but the invisible hand of capitalism typically moves quickly to eliminate that edge. The late Austrian-trained economist Joseph Schumpeter, who immigrated to the US to teach at Harvard University before ultimately being laid to rest just down the road from my White Hart inn, popularized the concept of "creative destruction"[2] as a means of explaining this harsh phenomenon. Entrepreneurs conjure up innovations that generate wealth for themselves and, in aggregate, growth for the whole economy. Such innovations might even result in a highly profitable yet almost inevitably temporary monopoly, or near-monopoly, position for the innovator. The natural laws of capitalism are such that others observe the profit being generated and seek to copy or even improve on any innovation, ultimately undermining the position of the first mover. Thus wealth is both continually generated and destroyed.

Wall Street arguably represents capitalism in its most pure form. Its inhabitants seem more motivated by money than their counterparts in the industrial, healthcare, technology or other spheres. Furthermore, unlike in those other realms, the "raw material" with which Wall Street works, and indeed its only product, is money itself. Substantial fortunes are created for the winners in each successive generation of Wall Street participants. But scan the list of Wall Street firms from any era, and it quickly becomes clear that few of those winners prevail for long. And even at those firms that do persevere for extended periods, the need to continually evolve in order to adapt to ever-changing market conditions regularly results in the abrupt ouster of leaders who were once held in the highest esteem. Thus, not surprisingly, the ongoing financial crisis that began in 2008 added more names to the long historical lists of failed firms and discarded CEOs.

Looking back over my career, I could see how the process of creative destruction had driven the evolution of Wall Street. There was first a massive consolidation that resulted in an industry dominated by a small number of global mega banks and then the rise of firms like ours that sought to take advantage of the flaws endemic to those sprawling institutions.

When I started in the mid-1980s most firms were relatively small and highly specialized. Winding back the clock just one generation further, Morgan Stanley-already by then a prestigious firm with a decades-long history – had only around 100 employees when Bob Greenhill joined it in the early 1960s. Yet even when I went to work there a quarter century later no firm even attempted to be "global" or "full service" in the manner those terms later came to mean. For one, investment banks then did only investment banking – essentially, corporate stock and bond offerings along with M&A advice. As for other financial services, if a company wanted a loan it would go to a commercial bank. If an individual investor wanted a checking account or credit card he might go to that same commercial bank, while if he wanted to trade stocks he would go to a retail brokerage firm. As a result of some combination of regulation, historic business practice and the varying cultural attributes of those who populated these diverse businesses, there was little crossover between the various specialists.

The generation that led the industry as I was starting out foresaw the benefits of scale, globalization and diversification, along with the ever-growing use of technology to help the resulting larger, more complex entities function. The late Dick Fisher – the last of Morgan Stanley's old-school patrician leaders, the man who nudged his HBS classmate Bob Greenhill out of that firm and some years later tried to convince me to stay – was particularly eloquent on this topic.

Scale was important because it enhanced one's ability to survive the inevitable market declines that throughout history had so often ended the lives of such firms. Lehman Brothers, it turned out, even at $600 billion in assets lacked the scale either to ride out the financial crisis or be seen as worthy of a government bailout. Globalization was important because the clients themselves – major corporations across industries – were increasingly global. If you were the primary investment banker for a global consumer goods company based in the US, you would be wise to develop the capability to help raise capital or execute an acquisition for that client anywhere in the world. If you did not, someone else might help your client with its next foreign acquisition, and then try to leverage that experience into a role in its future domestic deals as well, displacing you from your historic position. Diversification was important because it provided streams of cash flow that were uncorrelated. One business activity might do very poorly in particular market conditions, while another might benefit from those same conditions. Together they would create the more consistent aggregate profitability that both reduces borrowing costs and increases stock market valuations. And ever-increasing investment in technology was needed to help these increasingly complicated

225

businesses communicate globally, operate efficiently and both measure and manage risk of all kinds.

The pursuit of the strategic objectives of scale, globalization and diversification led, via numerous mergers and acquisitions, to a consolidation of the financial services sector over the course of the first decade or so of my career. Investment banks vastly expanded both headcount and balance-sheet size. They reached across borders to create global businesses. They moved further into the principal investment business rather than simply serving as advisors, brokers and market makers who handled other people's money. As legal restrictions allowed, the lines between lending and investment banking businesses (once codified in the Glass-Steagall Act that forced the creation of Morgan Stanley during the Great Depression) became blurred and ultimately disappeared. Consumer-focused businesses like retail stock brokerage and credit cards were then also added into the mix.

Entrepreneurs like Sandy Weill, the serial acquirer who eventually enlisted Bob Greenhill – first as an M&A advisor, then as a senior executive – in his effort to build a vast financial empire, started speaking of building "financial supermarkets." Those could provide "one-stop shopping" for all the financial products that a company or individual might need. Increasingly, small or regional players could no longer compete effectively against the resulting larger entities that had more capital, more expertise, more services to offer, more connections to key clients and more diverse sources of income with which to prosper throughout market cycles. Some niche players thus went out of business, but by far most of them were simply swallowed up by acquisition as part of the continuing sector-wide consolidation. Ultimately, by the early 2000s, the entire global investment banking business was dominated by just nine firms: Citibank, Goldman Sachs, J.P. Morgan, Lehman, Merrill Lynch and Morgan Stanley in the US, and Credit Suisse, Deutsche Bank and UBS in Europe.

Our new firm purposefully went against the prevailing trend. We aimed to compete with giants by intensely focusing on a narrow business specialization and maintaining a close alignment with clients. In doing so we avoided the real and perceived conflicts of interest that inevitably came with huge scale. We eschewed any notion of employing a supermarket approach to "cross-sell" various financial services products that may or may not be in a client's interests. Our throwback business model was energized by an entrepreneurial spirit and an ownership mentality that harkened back to the days not long before, when Wall Street firms were small partnerships owned entirely by their senior employees.

To the behemoths with which we competed and the people who worked in our industry, our upstart firm must have seemed like little more than a curiosity – a quaint but inconsequential relic of another era. However, that changed when we decided to do an initial public offering and become a publicly traded company. When we accomplished that, the man once hailed by *Business Week* as the "King of Wall Street"[3] wryly commented to *Bloomberg* that "I'm sure many other greedy people are watching."[4]

John Gutfreund, an important client of my former law firm who was long retired by the time of our IPO, knew a thing or two about the pursuit of money on Wall Street. A bald, blunt, cigar-chomping caricature of a man in charge of a 1980s bond-trading house, he lived so large that, at the apex of his power, he became entangled in a lawsuit over the use of a crane to hoist a large Christmas tree up to his palatial Park Avenue apartment.[5] The Salomon Brothers firm he ran was thought to have provided the model for the trading floor in Tom Wolfe's *Bonfire of the Vanities*. For sure it was the setting for Michael Lewis's entertaining bond-trading memoir of the same era, *Liar's Poker*. Gutfreund was the longtime boss of the ace bond trader and central figure in Lewis's book, John Meriwether – that is, until they both got embroiled in a Treasury bond trading scandal which forced them out of Salomon. Meriwether, of course, then rose to even greater infamy at the high-flying but ultimately doomed hedge fund Long-Term Capital.

Why was our IPO so interesting? Because we were a mere handful of investment bankers, mostly still in our forties, who had invested almost no capital in our firm yet somehow convinced investors to assign a $500 million value to our still unproven enterprise. Over the next 18 months that firm, still largely owned by fewer than 10 partners and still with not much more than a 100 total personnel, rose to a more than $2 billion market value. Not surprisingly, that proved to be a sum large enough to attract much attention across Wall Street.

Bruce Wasserstein, by then at his final posting as "Head" (his peculiar title) of Lazard, was one of the greedy people watching. Lazard historian William Cohan noted that the filing of our IPO prospectus "was a watershed event, and not lost on anyone at Lazard, least of all Bruce Wasserstein."[6] Lazard was more than a century older than our firm and a much more significant player in the global advisory business. But despite its illustrious history, prominent brand and numerous offices scattered across the globe, it consistently fell short of achieving its potential by tolerating a culture renowned for its internal fiefdoms and rivalries. Recruiting the high-profile and strong-willed Wasserstein to lead the business solved some problems but created others, as Cohan's richly detailed history of the firm clarified. Wasserstein, looking for a way to get greater control of the unruly Lazard firm, needed the capital that an IPO could provide to buy out Lazard's historic European owners.

While our IPO had to overcome the fact that our business was small and unproven, Lazard had a very different problem – a lack of profitability. Cohan quoted one partner speaking of "costs spiraling out of control" and a board member of that era saying that "he saw no profits for Lazard anywhere on the horizon."[7] Nonetheless, in the end Wasserstein – the brilliant deal tactician whose derisive nickname "bid-'em-up Bruce" was evidence of a sullied reputation well before he joined Lazard – was able to achieve his IPO dream. He did so by restructuring Lazard's businesses to exclude unprofitable activities from the public company, slashing costs and liberally using "pro forma adjustments" to the firm's audited financial statements to show investors a bridge from a loss-making recent history to a theoretically profitable future. Lazard completed its IPO in 2005, around the first anniversary of ours. The market valued it at a premium to the large investment banks but at a significant discount to our firm, which had, according to Cohan, "become the gold standard of boutique investment banking at least as far as its public valuation was concerned."[8]

One powerful factor in the proliferation of firms following our path to the public market was the role of our lead IPO underwriter Goldman Sachs. Goldman, arguably the most intensely profit-seeking entity on Wall Street and maybe on the planet, was bold in seeking the mandate to manage our offering while other underwriters were more cautious about our prospects. And its view that we would be seen as meriting a premium valuation proved correct from the moment we started our road show to sell shares.

But Goldman's motivation in seeking that assignment was not merely its share of the roughly $6 million fee that we would pay for the execution of our offering. Goldman knew that if it led the first IPO in our space it would be in the pole position to win many similar mandates to follow. It was not shy about seeking out other IPO candidates or about helping them modify their businesses to better appeal to the market. In seeking a path to a successful IPO for Lazard's unprofitable, debt-laden, much more complex business, Goldman explicitly told Wasserstein that Lazard "should look as much like Greenhill as possible."[9] That advice led Lazard to exclude its unprofitable capital markets business, much of its private equity investing business and various other assets and liabilities from the vehicle in which public investors would buy shares.

Goldman led most but not all of the IPOs that followed ours. In early 2006 the technology-focused investment bank Thomas Weisel Partners (TWP) led its own IPO. The TWP story had some overlap with ours, but in other ways was different. Weisel, a fiercely competitive banker best known as an avid bicyclist and sponsor of the later discredited seven-time Tour de France winner Lance Armstrong, was head of Montgomery Securities when it was sold to Nationsbank. He then found his firm unexpectedly married to its crosstown rival Robertson Stephens, after we sold that firm to Bank of America shortly before it then merged with Nationsbank. Weisel used the chaos created by that series of transactions to break away with some of his key people to form the new eponymous firm.

His timing initially seemed excellent when he launched the San Francisco-based, technology-focused boutique investment bank in early 1999, just as the dot-com boom was cresting. However, Weisel had two major disadvantages relative to a firm like ours. First, his business specialized in only one sector and a particularly volatile one at that. Just how volatile soon became clear, when the air started going out of the tech bubble only about a year after his firm's public launch. Second, Weisel's firm was more focused on underwriting IPOs than on M&A. Unlike the advisory business, equity underwriting required significant capital. Further, it was a business where scale mattered, as a bigger sales force can distribute more stock than a small one can and hence will attract more clients wanting to raise money by selling equity. Even worse, the market for raising equity can shut down on a moment's notice when a downturn comes.

Amid the continuing euphoria from the Greenhill and Lazard IPOs, TWP was able to get an IPO done in early 2006, and its stock even rose 30% on the first day of trading. But the challenges that firm faced were fundamental, and it ended up struggling until it sold out to the low-profile retail brokerage firm Stifel Financial in the wake of the financial crisis. In announcing the April 2010 transaction *The Wall Street Journal*, noting that TWP's stock was down 80% over the prior four years, called it an "unlikely marriage between a St. Louis brokerage and a San Francisco high-tech investment bank."[10]

Evercore Partners was the next "boutique" bank to pursue an IPO, around the second anniversary of ours. In doing so it followed Lazard's cue by adhering closely to our business model – one based on advisory and investing businesses that generate high profit margins yet require almost no capital. Thus the bounty of future revenue could simply be divided between employees and investors, with little need for reinvestment in the business.

From the start Evercore had much in common with our firm. Like Greenhill, it was founded in early 1996. Also like Greenhill, it had a founder who was somewhat of a Wall Street celebrity – one, like Bob, who was seeking a fresh start with his own new firm after a bit of a career mishap.

The celebrity in Evercore's case was Roger Altman, well known for his work in Washington for both the Carter and Clinton administrations, as well as for his time on Wall Street with Lehman Brothers and Blackstone. Having a foot in both realms had served him well as a banker – given his history, CEOs and boards were interested in his views on everything from the economy to markets to government economic policy. That kind of access to the inner sanctums of corporate power was a valuable tool in the hands of a skilled investment banker seeking advisory assignments.

Bob Greenhill's career mishap was the failure of his brief sojourn with Sandy Weill's Smith Barney after three decades of success at Morgan Stanley. Altman's was his August 1994 resignation as Deputy Secretary of Treasury in connection with the long-running political controversy that became known simply as Whitewater, the name of a real estate investment entity with which President Bill Clinton and First Lady Hillary Clinton had been connected. Altman – a good man by reputation and based on all my interactions – was not charged with any substantive impropriety regarding Whitewater, which in fact never resulted in any criminal charges against the Clintons either. But he was accused of both mismanaging conflicts of interest and the misuse of information. *The New York Times* summed the matter up with words that did not reflect well on bankers: "Mr. Altman hewed to a standard of behavior that on Wall Street would be acceptable but in Washington often is not."[11]

Evercore was launched with a business model more akin to that of Blackstone, the private equity powerhouse where Altman had worked after he left Lehman, than that of Greenhill, which began as a pure client advisory business. But watching our growing success, Evercore increasingly focused on developing its advisory capability. As a result, with a reasonably sized M&A advisory team in place alongside its private equity investing business, it looked a lot like Greenhill by the time of its IPO. In an effort to look even more similar, Evercore had sought to develop an international footprint, something that was appealing to stock market investors given the notable early success our London office had enjoyed.

Evercore, however, lagged far behind us in the process of building a real business outside America. In 1998, just a few months after we opened what quickly became a highly successful office in London, Evercore made its first move by announcing a joint venture with Robert Fleming, which *The Wall Street Journal* referred to as "one of the last remaining independent investment banks in London."[12] But the venture with Fleming did not produce any meaningful results, and by the time of Evercore's IPO there was no mention of that alliance in its prospectus.

Meanwhile, in a second attempt to create at least the appearance of an international strategy, Evercore agreed on the same day as its prospectus filing with the Securities and Exchange Commission to acquire a small Mexican investment bank that had generated less than $20 million in revenue in its most recent year. Mexico had never been seen as a substantial market for investment banking services, but this particular company did at least have a high-profile leader in the form of a former central bank head who lent some international luster to the offering.

Given Evercore's initially heavier focus on the investing side of its business and modest progress in developing an international footprint, it was much slower than Greenhill to demonstrate significant advisory revenue. Reading its IPO prospectus,[13] it was now clear to me why, back in 2003, Altman had quickly slid my presentation back across the table when he came to see Bob and me to discuss a possible merger of our firms. Evercore was headed for a $60 million revenue year at the time of that visit, while we were on our way to slightly more than double that revenue. Despite starting its IPO prospectus with the bold claim that it believed "Evercore Partners is the leading investment banking boutique in the world," Evercore had only eleven of what it called "senior managing directors" in its advisory business and continued to lag behind us in advisory revenue. In 2005, the most recent year for which data was provided in its prospectus, Evercore's advisory revenue crossed the $100 million mark for the first time. That same year was our fifth consecutive year at that level, and our annual revenue remained slightly more than double that of Evercore's.

Given the tailwinds created by our and Lazard's successful IPOs, Evercore's IPO was well received but at a valuation of only $570 million. By comparison, just days before Evercore filed its IPO prospectus we completed our third equity offering at a valuation over $2 billion, with our senior partner group selling a small portion of its personal shareholdings for more than $280 million in cash.

Those first three IPOs of investment banks – each inspired by ours – had little impact on our business, which continued to power ahead. Yes, each competitor would compete with us for clients, talent and investors. But there appeared to be plenty of investors to go around, and in the wake of the financial crisis, the large investment banks were hemorrhaging so much talent that there were also far more recruiting prospects than we could possibly absorb. As for competition for clients, Evercore had been around as long as we had, and Lazard more than a century longer. So they presented nothing new in terms of competition. However, the "greedy people watching" our IPO also included many prominent bankers across Wall Street who believed that perhaps they too had the potential to create a new advisory firm that could achieve a high market valuation and thereby produce a financial windfall for themselves and any co-founders.

The barriers to entry for such new enterprises were low. All it took was a founder or two who was a bit of a star in the Wall Street firmament – someone with a "name brand." What gave one such a brand in the world of

M&A was some combination of experience in executing major transactions, a personality suitable for building relationships with key corporate decision-makers and a style that engendered trust. That last element was critical – only if the CEO or board really trust their banker will they let him lead the delicate process of "making" a deal. All who would attempt to launch a new firm like ours bore those characteristics in varying degrees, and most – like Bob Greenhill, Roger Altman and Bruce Wasserstein before them – had suffered enough Wall Street trauma that they were motivated at least in part by the feeling of having something to prove.

Not surprisingly, the proliferation of new entrants to our business reached a crescendo just as Greenhill was hitting a $2 billion valuation in the market. In June 2006, a month after we completed our first sale of stock at that remarkable price level, Perella Weinberg was formed by Joe Perella and Terry Meguid. The two senior Morgan Stanley executives who had fled in the last chaotic months of the Phil Purcell regime teamed up with Peter Weinberg, a cerebral but affable banker who was a member of the Weinberg clan that had led Goldman Sachs for generations yet had begun his career with a brief stint at Morgan Stanley. Weinberg had most recently served as London-based head of Goldman Sachs International and as co-head of investment banking at Goldman Sachs, where his grandfather Sydney Weinberg began as a janitor in 1907 and rose to serve as senior partner. Adding further to the family legacy, his uncle John Weinberg had been co-managing partner of Goldman in the late 1980s.

Perella, the charming but eccentric banker whose arm-waving histrionics on the day I resigned from Morgan Stanley I would never forget, had been Bruce Wasserstein's co-founding partner for Wasserstein Perella. Given that firm's declining fortunes, he soon moved to Morgan Stanley, where it was hoped he would help fill the large gap left by Bob Greenhill's exit. He thus ended up missing out on the blockbuster price that Wasserstein later negotiated when he sold his firm to Germany's Dresdner Bank.

Unlike Greenhill and other advisory firms that were founded with senior banking talent but no outside capital, Perella Weinberg raised more than $1 billion from prominent global investors to launch a combined advisory and investment business based in New York and London.[14] Perella quickly attracted a significant number of Morgan Stanley alumni to his new firm, all undoubtedly also in search of IPO riches. However, many were from outside the advisory business. Hence it appeared initially to be attempting to create somewhat of a variation on our business model of M&A and related advisory work alongside private equity.

Only a month after Perella Weinberg's debut, a new firm called Centerview Partners was formed. The three founders, Steve Crawford, Blair Effron and Robert Pruzan, each came from separate firms and had diverse backgrounds. Crawford was a Morgan Stanley financial services sector specialist who later moved into a management role. He benefited from several promotions amid all the turmoil around Phil Purcell, rising to a very brief co-presidential role in Purcell's dying days before exiting soon after Purcell did. Having cast his lot with Purcell, Crawford was no longer a popular man with the Morgan Stanley crowd with which he had grown up and thus needed to find a new perch.

Pruzan had likewise experienced some career turmoil. He had risen up through the ranks at Wasserstein Perella as generations of older bankers eventually grew tired of partnering with Wasserstein. By the time Wasserstein Perella entered its lucrative but ill-fated merger agreement with Dresdner Bank, Pruzan was Wasserstein's right-hand man. He then became head of the investment banking business for the combined firm. He stayed longer than Wasserstein, but it was not surprising when he ultimately left. That deal was a shockingly good one for the sellers, but the combined company was not a viable platform for a talented banker still in his prime. In the end, the firm Wasserstein sold essentially disappeared.

Blair Effron was the highest profile of the three co-founders, lacked the kind of career setback that both Crawford and Pruzan had endured and was the best-suited to form his own firm. He had spent nearly two decades at the Swiss bank UBS and its predecessors, rising to become the leading banker in the consumer products sector. That was a particularly important sector for bankers, as the clients for which one executed transactions – with names like Pepsi, Phillip Morris and Kraft – were well-known all across the whole business landscape given the fact that every executive is, in his personal life, a user of consumer products.

Effron, who was also deeply involved in Democratic Party politics, took a circuitous route to where he ended up at UBS despite never changing jobs. He began at Dillon Read, a small but prestigious boutique investment bank of an earlier era – a kind of forerunner to firms like ours. Among its alumni were not one but two US Secretaries of Treasury – Douglas Dillon, who served in the Kennedy Administration, and Nicholas Brady, who served in the first Bush Administration. But despite being a renowned brand in old-school investment banking, Dillon Read had a checkered history in managing its own affairs. At one point it was owned by the Bechtel Corporation, a large, privately held engineering and construction firm, and later by the major insurance firm Travelers, both very odd homes for such a business. In 1991 Travelers, under financial pressure in that recessionary period, sold the business to a joint venture of management and the British merchant bank Barings. There Effron and his colleagues collaborated on international deals with Barings top bankers, Simon Borrows and James Lupton, the duo that went on to launch Greenhill's London office.

But that transatlantic partnership ended abruptly when Barings went bankrupt in 1995, resulting in Dillon Read returning to ownership by its employees and setting off the chain of events that sent Borrows and Lupton to Greenhill. Two years later Dillon Read sold out to Swiss Banking Corporation (SBC), which had recently acquired the leading British investment bank S.G. Warburg, resulting in the short-lived investment banking brand of Warburg Dillon Read. But SBC the next year merged with fellow Swiss bank UBS, and the Dillon Read investment banking brand faded away in favor of UBS Warburg. Through all those various ownership regimes Effron persevered, building his personal brand in the consumer products space.

Having not done much myself in the consumer products industry, I had never met Effron until he visited our offices on the day before Thanksgiving 2005. Earlier that month our stock had crossed the $50 mark for the first time, meaning the firm had tripled in value in our 18 months as a public company, giving us a $1.5 billion valuation. Given our high-profile success, our offices saw a continuing parade of bankers looking to be recruited and businesses hoping to be acquired. Effron found his way to us via Tim George, the Greenhill partner who joined the firm just two weeks before I did and was himself a consumer products specialist. Our senior London partners, not fellows who were easily impressed, were enthusiastic about our meeting Effron based on their recollections of working with him when Barings had its short-lived partnership with Dillon Read. Further, the consumer products area was of great interest to them and to me – it had been the source of some of the landmark deals in our firm's early history, helping to create our own prominent advisory brand. Yet it had now been nearly five years since we did our last major deal in the space: the $11.5 billion acquisition of Ralston Purina by Nestle.

Effron's visit came at a very busy time. I was working on a US acquisition for the British water company Kelda and just getting started in our role advising Sallie Mae on what would much later become a $25-billion buyout announcement for a deal that would, unbeknown to us, never be consummated. The closing dinner for the Heartland IPO, a big win for our private equity fund, had taken place earlier that week. And on a personal level, having barely completed the renovation of our Weatogue Stables horse farm, I was deeply involved in pursuit of what became Twin Lakes Farm for our planned grassfed cattle operation. That would be a major preoccupation over the Thanksgiving weekend ahead, which we would spend at our expanding farmstead in Connecticut.

Despite all the distractions, my meeting with Effron, a polished Princetonian who had a brother in the hedge fund business who had been in my class at Wharton, was very positive. I immediately came to the conclusion that we had much in common, and that he would be both a productive addition to the partnership and an excellent fit within our collegial culture. Bob Greenhill felt likewise. However, Tim George expressed strong reservations, concluding that we already had a consumer products specialist (him) and did not need another. While the rest of us had a different view, there was a reluctance to force anyone into the senior partnership ranks. Our business was functioning well in every possible way, our stock price was soaring and interesting new opportunities seemed to come our way almost weekly. There was not a burning need to do anything differently. Thus, we acted like one of those private clubs where any member can block a new entrant and went with Tim's view, letting the dialogue with Effron peter out.

Clearly Effron at the time was intent on finally stepping away from UBS and had come to our office, at least in part, seeking to learn more about the new business model that we had pioneered and others were moving swiftly to emulate. Only several months after our meeting he came together with Crawford and Pruzan, neither of whom he had worked with before, to form Centerview. As *The New York Times* would later note in a retrospective on our burgeoning industry niche, "Greenhill was the first in the new wave of boutique firms," and was "the model for Mr. Effron's and Mr. Pruzan's firm."[15]

A year after Perella Weinberg and Centerview were launched, just as the boom of the mid 2000s was about to come to an end, yet another independent advisory firm was formed: Moelis & Co. Moelis was founded by Ken Moelis, who like the founders of Evercore, Perella Weinberg and Centerview had been directly involved in many of the twists and turns in the investment banking business in recent years. Ken, who was a year ahead of me at Wharton, began his career at Drexel Burnham where he worked for the famed junk bond innovator Michael Milken in the firm's Los Angeles headquarters. Given that heritage, it was not surprising that he was a savvy banker who had a big following among the kind of private equity players that Drexel financed.

When Drexel collapsed in the late 1980s Moelis took refuge with many other Drexel alumni at Donaldson, Lufkin & Jenrette. In 2000, when Credit Suisse First Boston acquired DLJ, he was named head of investment banking. But soon he moved to UBS, taking dozens of bankers with him. There he joined Blair Effron and others from Dillon Read, Warburg and the various other firms that UBS had merged together in its quest for investment banking greatness. He enjoyed success there for six years, rising to become head of the global investment banking business.

In mid-2007 Moelis left UBS along with several colleagues to form his eponymous firm. The reason for his departure – per chatter in the market – was that UBS's conservatism, consistent with its Swiss heritage but the polar opposite of the risk tolerance at the Drexel firm where Moelis began his career, kept that firm from competing for the large and highly leveraged private equity transactions with which he wanted to be involved. But given Moelis's presence at pivotal moments in recent investment banking history, he could not help but be intrigued by what was happening with our firm. Indeed, his objective in going public was clear – "I thought about going public from day one," he later told *Inc* magazine.[16] In commenting on his launch, *The Wall Street Journal* said Moelis wanted to "get the ball rolling by conducting M&A and restructuring advisory work, then building up a private-equity or merchant banking operation"[17] – the very same strategy that was driving Greenhill's stock market success.

The late economist Schumpeter would have struggled to identify a better case study for his "creative destruction" concept than what happened around our firm. Just when it looked like the entire investment banking industry was going to be dominated by giants, Bob Greenhill and the rest of us had tried something different. Our little firm was nimbler, hungrier and narrowly focused on the business of advising clients on deals. Clients saw us as being invariably on their side, while the dominant large firms increasingly looked like sales-driven organizations striving to "cross-sell" them as many products as possible. Not surprisingly, our differentiated business model – one common in an earlier era – quickly gained traction. Then, when the stock market validated our early success by assigning our nascent business an initial valuation measured in the hundreds of millions of dollars, the inevitable capitalistic response was activated.

Every prominent banker must have given some thought to whether he was capable of replicating our success, and many of the better ones gave that a try. But as new firms were formed they created incremental competition, thereby diluting our once nearly unique status as an "independent advisor" without the conflicts inherent in the big bank business model. Most adhered closely to the strategy that was working so well for Greenhill: an almost pure focus on transaction advisory work for clients, a smaller but complementary private equity investing business and a quest to become "global," which initially meant being active in the two key markets: New York and London.

All were fundamentally on the same path – to acquire and assimilate investment banking talent as quickly as it could be absorbed, with the ultimate goal of serving clients in all major industries in all important countries around the globe. In a busy market there would be plenty of opportunity for all the new players, especially with our large bank competitors still reeling from the financial crisis and coming under greater scrutiny from both clients and regulators. For Greenhill, however, there was no doubt that the creation of so many new competitors meant winning – especially in periods when deal activity was subdued – would not be as easy as it had been.

CHAPTER THIRTEEN

NOT TOO BIG TO FAIL

You're gonna need a bigger boat.[1]

– *Peter Benchley*, JAWS

Our firm was a whirl of activity in the financial crisis years. We took advantage of the massive dislocation at our large bank competitors by embarking on a major expansion, opening offices in Chicago, Houston, Los Angeles, San Francisco and Tokyo, and recruiting specialists in consumer products, energy, insurance, retailing and other industry sectors. As of mid-2009 we had nearly doubled our number of managing directors in just 18 months. Meanwhile, in the investing side of our business, our private equity funds weathered the storm better than most, and our SPAC won approval from its shareholders for the acquisition of the satellite telecom company Iridium, generating substantial revenue for the firm.

All that activity in a period when our largest competitors were under severe financial pressure, subject to increasing regulatory scrutiny and hemorrhaging talent helped us produce respectable financial results while maintaining the appearance of strong momentum. The stock market continued to applaud everything we did and, in the year following our somewhat panicky sale of Greenhill shares at $56 on the day of President Obama's election in November 2008, my senior colleagues and I were able to sell more large blocks of stock, at $76 and $83 per share, in two offerings at the highest prices at which we had ever sold.

Still, despite our relative outperformance, our aggressive expansion and the sizeable lumps of cash our senior team garnered from those share sales, there was no escaping the devastation of the worst financial crisis since the Great Depression of the 1930s. Merger and acquisition activity was the lifeblood of our business, and the combined value of all M&A deals globally fell from $4.25 trillion in 2007 to less than half that in 2009. That was not much more than the level back in 1997, when I joined Bob in the firm's early days. Only now there were many more competitors fighting for those advisory assignments. Yet given the much greater number of mouths we now had to feed as a result of our continuing expansion, we actually needed to win far *more* business than in our early days.

In 2008 our revenue had fallen 45% from the extraordinary level of the year before. That was less than the decline in global deal activity and a better outcome than we had achieved only two years earlier. Yet it was still painful for a firm accustomed to relentless upward momentum. Our total revenue rebounded 35% in 2009, but that masked the fact that our advisory revenue had actually fallen slightly further. Our successful SPAC transaction drove the positive headlines for us.

Importantly, our SPAC revenue windfall was not yet in the form of cash, and the value of our Iridium shareholding would fluctuate every quarter based on that company's share price until we sold our stake. The operative phrase was again "mark-to-market," the same accounting methodology that had sent us on an earnings roller coaster in 2008 with the quick boom and bust in oil prices and had continued to pummel large banks as the asset values on their highly leveraged balance sheets fluctuated wildly with markets. In our SPAC's case, the mark-to-market had so far worked to our benefit, but our own experience taught us that paper gains can be quickly reversed.

While our SPAC's success obscured challenges in our core advisory business, it hid even greater challenges in our investing business. In 2008 we lost money there, as the decline in the value of the firm's investments exceeded the management fees that we earned for managing our various funds. In 2009, we did only a little better, with very modest gains on our investment portfolio on top of collecting management fees.

The outlook was even more concerning than the recent performance. Management fees, which are directly based on the scale of funds under management, were trending downward as we sold fund holdings without raising incremental capital for new investments. Given shrinking valuations for all asset types and the consequential difficulty of raising new funds in this period, that trend seemed likely to continue. Gains on the firm's investments in our funds were a second source of income, but those also seemed unlikely in the foreseeable future. Our first fund had performed spectacularly, and Niehaus had wisely liquidated the bulk of our holdings at big profits prior to the onset of the crisis. Now there was little value left to extract. As for carried interest, the third source of income for this business, the prospects were dim. It seemed unlikely that we would generate large enough gains on our newer funds to exceed the required minimum rate of return for earning a share of profits that flowed to outside investors.

The troubling outlook raised many questions. Would we be able to raise additional capital in the more challenging environment, or would our funds under management continue to shrink? Even if there was the potential for external fundraising, would the firm have the liquidity to seed new funds with corporate cash? Even more uncertain, in a period of reduced personal wealth and much lower compensation, would our team be in a position personally to support our fundraising efforts as our senior bankers had always done? And if I was right about the outlook for this business, would we even be able to generate enough revenue to retain the investment team, or would the advisory side of the business – then facing its own significant challenges – need to subsidize that group?

By late 2009 it was clear to me that the firm needed to exit the private equity investment business that had served it so well since we launched it a decade earlier. Doing so seemed unlikely to cost us any meaningful profitability, at least for a while, and appeared likely to bring us numerous benefits. For one, if Niehaus and the investment team would pay something for this historically very attractive business, the purchase price would be an immediate revenue item to boost our current anemic financial results. More importantly, a sale would enable us to avoid funding additional investments from the firm's balance sheet, freeing up cash for operating expenses, dividends or share repurchases. Furthermore, in addition to selling the management company that operated the business, we might then also be able to find a buyer in the secondary market for the firm's substantial existing investments in our funds. That would generate further cash to bolster our financial position in the face of what could be a prolonged period of challenging market conditions. Perhaps most important of all, getting out of this business would free up management time to focus on what were plenty of challenges, as well as some opportunities, in our core advisory business. As military history teaches, fighting a two-front war can lead to overstretched forces and ultimately to defeat.

The notion of shrinking in any way is always risky for public companies, particularly those seen and valued by the market as a growth company. But, at least at this moment, we had an easy way to rationalize to shareholders the strategic move I was contemplating. We had never run into conflicts between our advising and investing businesses – the latter focused almost entirely on much smaller companies so the two groups largely operated in different spheres. On the other hand, the benefits of being a purely advisory business, with no other activities and absolutely no real or perceived conflicts of interest relative to clients, had been highlighted in the financial crisis.

Leaders of our large bank competitors had been pilloried for putting their own interests ahead of those of their clients. Congress had grilled big bank CEOs on the topic – unfairly so in my view, as politicians seemed incapable of understanding the difference between a client (someone to whom an advisor owes loyalty) and a counterparty (someone who is simply on the other side of a purchase or sale transaction). Goldman Sachs CEO Lloyd Blankfein, a brilliant, Brooklyn-born trader with a quick wit, became a particular target of Congressional ire and public disapproval. This was largely due to the extraordinary profitability Goldman had reaped through clever trading bets in advance of the market's decline. Under the headline "Clients worried about Goldman's dueling goals," *The New York Times* chronicled the stories of numerous unhappy clients, noting, "Goldman's many hats – trader, adviser, underwriter, matchmaker of buyers and sellers, and salesperson – [had] left some clients feeling bruised or so wary that they have sometimes avoided doing business with the bank."[2]

This seemed the optimal moment for highlighting our single-minded focus and complete alignment with clients, particularly given the significant expansion of our advisory business over the previous couple of years. Meanwhile, on the other side of the transaction that I was planning, I believed Niehaus and his team could also better weather the continuing storm on their own, without the distractions involved in being part of a larger, more complex enterprise that had to answer to public shareholders.

Despite the unassailable logic of my planned strategic move, this decision was the most difficult that I had made in my twelve years at Greenhill. This business had been a huge success in its own right and a major contributor to the firm's extraordinary early performance, and I had personally been intimately involved in every aspect of the operation. On top of that, Bob Niehaus, the leader of this business, remained my closest colleague and had been a true partner in building and managing our entire business.

Friendships on Wall Street are generally very transactional – a colleague can seem like a close friend, but when he is no longer a colleague the relationship often ends abruptly and completely. As famed corporate raider Carl Icahn, someone I encountered on my very first M&A project as a young lawyer, once said, if you want a friend in this business, "get a dog."[3] The quip summed up reality so well, and so chillingly, that Oliver Stone put the same words in his villain Gordon Gekko's mouth in his film *Wall Street.*[4]

I hoped things would turn out differently between Niehaus and myself. We had made a pile of money together and had plenty of fun doing so while surmounting innumerable obstacles. We would undoubtedly continue to interact, both at the GCP funds and with our ongoing Iridium board roles. And given our close friendship and a strong shared belief in philanthropy, we would continue to be major supporters of each other's favorite charities. Furthermore, I was prepared to spend some money to smooth things over, by making significant corporate and personal commitments to his team's next private equity fundraising effort and getting Bob Greenhill to match my personal commitment. I hoped those steps, on top of our long history, would provide a basis for continuing friendship.

My very first conversation with Niehaus on the topic of separating made clear that my hopes would be fulfilled. He had a deep understanding of markets and accepted that conditions change and strategies must evolve to reflect the ever-changing reality. Further, he had always been the ultimate pragmatist, and once he had pivoted was capable of quickly accelerating to full speed in a new direction. We both knew how to execute deals, so we worked out all the transaction details in a matter of a few weeks, thus meeting my objective of being finished in time for the separation to favorably impact the firm's 2009 results.

We did not get a big price for what we were selling – doing so would not have been justifiable or appropriate given the outlook for that business. The purchase price would be in our own highly valued shares – a small portion of those Niehaus had accumulated during his time at the firm. In the end, the separation created $22 million of revenue to add to the gain on our SPAC's Iridium deal, transforming our 2009 financial results into a positive outcome that clearly stood out from those of our very troubled competitors. On top of that, the firm also retained $178 million in accumulated fund investments and Iridium shares, which could be liquidated over time and paid out to shareholders or used to reduce debt.

We put a lot of effort into packaging the news of our retreat from principal investing, hoping that and our long history of glowing press coverage would translate into a favorable response to the plan. To avoid attracting too much attention, we announced the completion of the deal in the press release for our year-end financial results. We made a virtue of necessity by stating that a more focused, purely advisory strategy would be "a great source of strength for the Firm going forward," and that it would avoid "any distraction of our management or client advisory teams," as well as "any meaningful commitment of capital to principal investments or new ventures."[5] As we hoped, the press, analysts, stock market and our internal team all accepted our story as positive news without any reservation.

The other aspect of our business that felt permanently impacted by the financial crisis was Europe. Almost from the start, Europe had represented a major part of our firm. Of our first seven partners, four were in New York and three in London, and the third office we opened was in Europe, not North America. In the decade after we opened our London office we earned almost exactly half our advisory revenue from European clients, some via New York-based partners, but much of it sourced locally across the Atlantic. However, the businesses we added to our original M&A practice – restructuring advice, private equity investing and most recently the SPAC – were all US-based, tilting the weight of the firm heavily toward the American market.

Furthermore, the financial crisis seemed to have hit the European market much harder than the US market. Europe is a less dynamic economy than the US to start with – Morgan Stanley's longtime investment strategist Barton Biggs, who seemed to enjoy wordplay as much as investing, once got in trouble with his European colleagues for deriding the Continent with the quip that it was the world's largest open air amusement park (rather than a place for business). My personal observation dating back to my time there for Morgan Stanley in the early 1990s was that in every downturn Europe was impacted more deeply, and for a longer period, than the US. European companies seem to be more cautious by nature, and any economic or market downturn tended to make them even more defensive. Worse, European governments seem more tentative – much less aggressive than the US – with the kind of fiscal and monetary stimulus that can get an economy going again. Furthermore, European law lacks the efficient bankruptcy process that America's has, as well as the extensive network of "vulture" investors that deliver much-needed capital to financially distressed companies, thereby assisting in economic recovery. Given a financial crisis that was far more painful than anything in living memory, the situation in Europe appeared even more grim than in the past downturns I had witnessed. As a result, by 2009 European clients were contributing only about one third of our shrunken advisory revenue and less than a quarter of our total revenue, down substantially from the roughly equal contribution prior to the crisis.

While there was little we could do about the fact that our revenue opportunities in Europe and indeed globally had shrunk, there was plenty one could do in an effort to offset the financial impact of that reality. My view was that we not only needed to seek new sources of revenue but that we needed to manage the expenses inherent in our business more aggressively than we had historically. We particularly needed to more rigorously evaluate our team and both terminate senior bankers who proved unable to thrive in the new normal in which we were living and "right size," to use the common human resources euphemism for culling, the support team below those senior bankers. Such moves would seem obvious to most businesses, but investment bankers are notorious for their single-minded focus on revenue and lack of attention to costs. To me, my London-based co-chief executive appeared to be such a banker.

Simon Borrows was one of the most talented M&A advisors with whom I had come in contact in my entire career. He had been a huge revenue generator in his more than a decade at the firm. He was also an affable partner – I had enjoyed all my interactions with him. From the time we first met, I felt like we had much in common. But now, after years of great success, our European business was struggling mightily, and he seemed reluctant to make the changes necessary to adapt to what I expected would be a prolonged period of difficult conditions. As my frustration grew, I came to believe that our shared chief executive role no longer worked – just as Dick Fisher's and Bob Greenhill's shared leadership ultimately had not. I felt that I needed clear authority over the entire global business. Our board of directors was likewise increasingly concerned with the performance of our European business and agreed, albeit with a degree of trepidation given that this move could rock the boat in a way that our little vessel had never been rocked before, and in very stormy seas no less.

We all agreed that Bob Greenhill would have the requisite conversation with Simon, hoping Simon would quickly choose to "make this his idea." Bob's terse, man-of-few-words style likely made that conversation awkward. The only thing he reported back was that the job was done but that, in his response, Simon had warned Bob that I had removed Niehaus, now him and would soon go after Bob himself. That certainly was not my intention, and Bob clearly felt secure in his position. However, I can imagine how the evolution of events must have looked from Simon's very different perspective. From my viewpoint, we were living through a war that had destroyed some major financial institutions in the US and Europe, and others had survived only through government rescues. Nobody was going to rescue a small, pure advisory firm that represented no risk at all to the broader financial system. We needed to fend for ourselves.

We planned to announce our management reconfiguration with the next set of quarterly results, which would be the first since the one in which we announced that we were exiting the private equity investing business. This would make two quarterly press releases in a row containing major strategic news. As was our custom, we put as positive a spin as possible on the news. Our release said that the move was "designed to position the Firm for continued global growth and further develop its next generation of leadership."[6] Further, we stated that Simon had asked for the move, and that he would take on a new role, "less than full time," as chairman of our international business. He would "focus on advising the Firm's major clients in Europe." Clearly this was not going to be a long-term position, but we hoped Simon would stay onboard long enough to avoid signaling either internal strife or increased risk.

In the meantime, we laid the groundwork for future leadership of the firm by elevating Jeff Buckalew to head of North American corporate advisory, encompassing our M&A and restructuring activities in our largest market – thus, making him my eventual heir apparent as CEO. Jeff's long-time compatriot John Liu would have joined him in that role but in early 2008 had left the firm to help manage money for a client – a family for which he had recently completed a hugely lucrative asset sale. Meanwhile, in Europe we elevated Brian Cassin and David Wyles, the fellows who had come to us from Barings as young bankers underneath Borrows and Lupton, as well as the founder of our Frankfurt office, to become heads of the European corporate advisory business. James Lupton, meanwhile, would become "Chairman" of Europe, a role focused on clients rather than day-to-day management of the business.

In making major announcements we had always sought to deliver anything that could be construed as bad news stapled to something that was indisputably good news. We did that in 2007 when announcing, alongside record results in the best ever M&A market, that Bob would step out of the CEO role. We had done that again just recently in announcing our exit from the private equity business together with significant one-time gains from both our SPAC and the sale of that business to Niehaus. Now, alongside the change in Simon's role, we announced the completion of a large acquisition in Australia that we had signed up only weeks earlier.

Australia had long been an interesting market to consider for expansion. The Anglo-American markets of the US, UK, Canada and Australia are ones where M&A is central to the business culture. Equally important, it felt like having a large presence in Australia, on top of a recently established beachhead in Japan and large teams in North America and Europe, would finally make us the global firm we had always claimed to be. I often joked that at the time the firm started "global" meant only the US and Western Europe, consistent with the way American schoolchildren of my generation were taught "world" history. But as economies and markets had grown and corporations sought new customers, over time "global" had come to mean actually global.

An acquisition in Australia, of a regional Greenhill lookalike called Caliburn, was the perfect complement to our announcement of a management reshuffle. It increased our global reach and scale while diminishing the relative importance to the firm of the troubled European market. Caliburn was almost as old as our firm. It had six partners and about forty employees in Melbourne and Sydney and did exactly the kind of work we did. Simon Mordant, the dominant partner among the three Caliburn founders, was much like Bob in that he was both hyperactive and strong-willed. Both could be single-minded and absolutely relentless in pursuing an objective, whether that was winning a new client or executing a deal.

Mordant had been maneuvering for years to get us to buy his firm. He had first approached us through our London founders Borrows and Lupton, both of whom repeatedly warned us to be cautious in our dealings with him. We therefore moved slowly. Initially we put in place a loose "alliance" between our firms, pursuant to which we would work together on any transaction work that straddled Australia and the markets in which we operated. But there were few such cases, so the alliance proved fairly meaningless. Yet Mordant had a way of regularly putting himself in front of us, such as arriving in New York for lunch just a few days after we had completed our IPO – an event that clearly further whetted his appetite for monetizing the value of his own firm. But Caliburn was far too small to go public on its own, and we learned over time that there had been significant dissension within its small founder group. Thus he was undoubtedly anxious to get something done while his firm was still intact.

In late 2009 it became clear to me that, given the pressure on our advisory business globally and especially in Europe, now was the time to acquire Caliburn. The business was sizable, averaging about $70 million of revenue in US dollar terms, over the prior three years. That meant this business would have contributed about a quarter of our global advisory revenue had it been part of the firm in the past year or two. As such, this deal constituted a meaningful step up in scale and risk-mitigating diversification. Australia was a very different market closely linked to both China and natural resources like oil and minerals, so it could serve as a favorable counterbalance at times when there was not much action in Europe.

Apart from the longer-term strategic merits of the acquisition, the deal's structure made it particularly attractive at that moment. The purchase price would be paid entirely in the form of our stock. We did not have the excess cash to contemplate a cash deal, and in any event we wanted the Australians to be fully aligned with us via shared equity ownership.

Further, almost half of the agreed purchase price was conditional, via a so-called "earnout" structure, on Caliburn's revenue in the three- and five-year periods following the combination. And even if we paid out the maximum amount over five years we would be buying the business at a fraction of the lofty level at which the market valued our own business.

Best of all, our firm's already high share price took off just as we were negotiating final terms, in part because of the positive reception to our exit from the investing business. In an era where the value of almost all types of investments had been dropping, the market seemed to love the notion of our getting out of that business. Mordant half-jokingly begged for mercy on the deal terms as our share price kept rising, but our simple response was that the market value was what the market value was. On the day we finally struck the detailed deal terms he and his partners agreed to accept our shares at a value of almost $83 per share,[7] close to their all-time high (apart from the few days surrounding the government-induced short squeeze in our shares in the days after Lehman Brothers collapsed). This price reflected a value for our firm of around $2.5 billon.

The stock market responded enthusiastically to news of our Australian acquisition, which represented another important step in our expansion and diversification. It paid no attention at all to our management reshuffle. Accordingly, we immediately began preparation for yet another stock sale by our original partner group. In recent months we had already completed two such sales, having typically waited one to two years between offerings in the past. But we had a good story for the market as to why yet another offering was appropriate: we needed to give our new Australian partners some liquidity, given that they received none at all from the sale of their firm to us for stock. So within weeks we did our largest stock offering ever, at the highest sale price ever, generating $250 million in cash for our early partner group. We had now done three offerings at record stock prices since our discounted sale on Obama's election day, generating more than $700 million of cash for those partners in only a ten-month period. All this occurred at a time when the world was in the midst of the worst financial crisis in my lifetime.

Greenhill was not alone in trying to reconfigure its business to get through the financial crisis and prepare for whatever might be on the other side. Almost every business was doing the same and, whether with Citibank or other major companies, facilitating that process represented a large part of the day-to-day activity of myself and our whole firm. But small businesses were impacted by the crisis even more severely than larger ones.

Much as I enjoyed weekend dinners on the porch, the annual village Christmas tree lighting that we hosted and the Memorial Day parade where we served free ice cream to the community after the names of the war dead were read and "Taps" was played at the cemetery down the road, it was clear that my own White Hart inn was one of innumerable small businesses languishing in a weak economy. While making money had never been my objective in owning the place, the scale of losses had crept up over time. Demand for its twenty-six rooms was limited mostly to weekends in "the season" and for various events at the nearby Hotchkiss School, Parker Gilbert's alma mater and where my son was now enrolled. Those rooms were hopelessly outdated in terms of style and of an economical size better suited to 1950s travelers. Increasingly they sat empty, generating little income to fund prodigious heating and cooling bills and support the large staff needed to run the place.

The inn's restaurant saw reduced traffic too, given both the recession and more local competitors. Hope springs eternal in the restaurant business, so there are always new openings funded by ambitious chefs or people who simply think it would be fun to own a restaurant. But few such entrants last long. In our case, the "farm-to-table" idea prompted by our development of Twin Lakes Farm had sparked some interest locally, but not enough to offset the reduced traffic that results from a serious economic recession. And our environmentally friendly approach to food had turned out to be far more difficult to implement than one would have guessed. While "supply chain" is not a factor in the white-collar services business of investment banking, seeing firsthand the challenges of coordinating between a small kitchen staff and a modest farm only four miles away helped me understand why our firm's manufacturing clients obsess about that issue. Simply put, most chefs prefer getting their food from a truck dispatched by a faraway wholesaler than from a nearby farm – it's simply easier.

Meanwhile, although the inn and restaurant still looked good in an old New England version of "shabby chic," underneath the surface every single mechanical aspect of the 200-year-old building needed a thorough overhaul. As Roxanne and I began looking behind walls, it struck us that the whole place was like a Hollywood facade – attractive on the surface, but only held together only by the occasional new layer of paint or wallpaper. Given the combination of my recent highly lucrative Greenhill share sales and the fact that closing the place for a while in a weak economy would not cost much in terms of lost revenue, I decided that now was the perfect time for a complete reboot of this venerable rural institution.

In starting down this path I knew I would never get a satisfactory monetary return on my new investment. But it wasn't about that. We knew from renovating multiple architecturally interesting but structurally collapsing barns at our farms that resurrecting such buildings is far more expensive than starting over from scratch. Additionally, the place was simply too large, in too small a village and in too seasonal a community ever to repay what I would have to put into it. Nonetheless, I decided I would throw caution and common sense to the wind and turn this into a giant art project. Roxanne, who had always left the lunacy of trying to run a busy country inn part time from a hundred miles away to me, joined in as a collaborator. More importantly, we brought in a friend, a top New York designer who had owned a home in the area for years, to work with the local builder who had handled all of our personal building projects. They would oversee a wide range of local craftsmen who would execute the project.

In just a few months we transformed the place from twenty-six cramped rooms into fifteen far more comfortable suites, replaced the roof, improved energy efficiency and building safety, updated the kitchen and refinished nearly every surface, using reclaimed old wood where preservation was not feasible. We decorated the place with antiques, old maps of the area and paintings by local artists. Yet we were careful to preserve the inn's old New England character by avoiding any changes to the features of the inn that everyone treasured, like the "tap room" with its worn wooden floors, paneled walls and two brick fireplaces. We started out with somewhat of a budget, but in the end simply did whatever was needed, ultimately pouring $5 million into the place – five times what I had paid for the entire property twelve years earlier.

Concurrent with the renovation, we undertook a national search for a talented, energetic chef who was willing to oversee a 364-day-a-year (all but Christmas) operation. We had been through a string of chefs who left because they couldn't handle the work, burned out over time or, most recently, left to serve a mandatory jail term for a second drunk driving arrest. Still, we thoroughly enjoyed the whole process, and also took some pride in securing the long-term future of an inn that sat prominently on Main Street overlooking a village green featuring a statue that commemorated local folks who had fought and died in the Civil War.

Well, it did not take long to realize that change of any sort is not easy in a rural community populated with a diverse mix of multi-generational Yankee families, wealthy weekenders from New York and sundry workers who earned a living catering to the needs of both. The local weekly newspaper chose to host a months-long debate over what we were doing. That paper, *The Lakeville Journal*, had always seemed to take a perverse pride in avoiding being the local booster that most small-town papers are. The fragile local summer stock theater we had long supported knew this first-hand. It had been the recipient of some devastating reviews that had intermittently crushed ticket sales over the years. While the paper was positive on our building renovation, a reporter who was sort of a critic-at-large blasted the new chef's food under the headline "Change Comes Hard...To a Community Treasure."[8]

The reporter managed to find room in her third paragraph to note that I was "a New York finance executive whose annual compensation was estimated recently at seven figures," as if someone of lesser means might have been able to take care of such an enormous old building, let alone fund its desperately needed renovation. She accurately declared that "people have a proprietary attitude about the place," and made clear that she was one of those people. She took particular issue with our new 28-year-old chef, ending her piece with a quote from him: "I'm not from Mayberry." That made him sound like a snob even though the remark really only signified his unfamiliarity with local ways. The reality, of course, was that our critic was the elitist. Our chef was simply an unsophisticated young man from Tampa Bay, Florida, who knew nothing of New England's sometimes haughty culture. Regardless, in my view there was nothing wrong with Mayberry – I was born in a place that in some ways resembled that mythical rural town, and *Mayberry RFD* was one of my favorite TV shows as a kid.

That critical piece along a few others prompted various letters to the editor, some very supportive but others bemoaning changes like our plan to allow diners to eat on the beautiful front porch overlooking the green. One writer, obviously a fan of the old *Bob Newhart Show*, offered that it would be good if I could be on hand personally to greet guests at the inn like the innkeeper Newhart played did. While I obviously needed to keep my day job to cover ongoing losses at the place, perhaps the new chef did need some more guidance and maybe even to be replaced. In any event, now that the renovation was complete, I decided that I should let someone else make the next decisions on the inn's future. With my hands full helping Greenhill get through the lingering financial crisis I concluded that now was the time to end this chapter of my life.

As with various aspects of Greenhill's business, not everything was meant to be forever. In the case of a two-centuries-old institution like the White Hart, there's no such thing as permanent ownership anyway. One merely steps in as temporary caretaker – one in a long line of owners that stretched from 125 years before my grandfather arrived at Ellis Island and would undoubtedly stretch forward far beyond the end of my own lifespan. Thus on Election Day 2010 we had the inn manager tape a piece of paper to the White Hart doors indicating that the inn was closed and now for sale – knowing full well that it could take years for a new owner to appear and repay even a fraction of the money I had invested in the place. As the note explained: my wife and I had "owned the inn for over 12 years. While much of that time was a pleasure, it was also a heavy responsibility and time commitment to oversee a 24-hour, 364-day-a-year enterprise, despite having a young family and a full-time job 100 miles away."

I chose the timing of the closure to coincide with the end of the busy season, trying not to inconvenience anyone. In that regard, I was soon sorry to learn from the staff that the Oscar-winning actress and nearby neighbor Meryl Streep had booked all our rooms for the upcoming wedding of one of her daughters. However, I knew that she would be able to find alternate accommodations. And I was bemused that the inn's staff was so protective of a customer's privacy that they had not even shared that interesting tidbit of celebrity news with me until after we closed.

To my surprise I received a call from a *New York Times* reporter a few days later while sitting in my Manhattan office. With some trepidation given the flak I had taken in relation to the inn from the local Connecticut press, I spoke openly. In the end, the piece summed up the situation eloquently, stating that "[t]here's a lot of selective memory at work" and that "[w]hat people want is often what they have, had or thought they had."[9] As for my decision, he noted that "there's not much mystery to the closing.... Running a beloved local institution is like being in elected office but having to pay the bills yourself." He closed the piece with a few "lessons." I was amused by one aimed at the local community: "If you're dependent on the largess of people with money, it doesn't come with a lifetime guarantee." And I took to heart one aimed at me: "If you're promising change, you had better do it right."

In the end I left the inn behind with nothing but good memories, the antique maps that we had recently hung there and the tap room's beautiful but worn British pub sign from a much older White Hart inn across the Atlantic – those would be my expensive souvenirs from this illuminating journey into small business ownership. As the *Times* reporter wrote, "[s]ometimes you need to invest in the future, even if it doesn't pay off on your watch." I was fine with that.

Only a few weeks later Roxanne and I pivoted to the next chapter of our life. We spent some more of my recent Greenhill share proceeds buying a historic 1930s house in Palm Beach, Florida. We would continue to enjoy our Revolutionary War-era Salisbury house, operate our horse stables, welcome the dozen or so calves born each year on our farm and maintain the veritable petting zoo of chickens, ducks, goats, sheep, miniature donkeys and diverse other creatures that friends and their children loved to visit. But by shedding 24/7 local management responsibilities, we had gained the freedom to pursue new adventures.

In the months that followed, it became increasingly clear that the financial crisis would not spare Greenhill. On the positive side, the crisis itself continued to create some opportunities for us. Just a few weeks after closing on my White Hart acquisition the US Department of Treasury hired a team led by myself for a two-year advisory assignment assisting on its sell down of the huge stake it had acquired as a result of the bailout of the insurance behemoth AIG. The project was interesting, and it felt significant to be visiting the US Treasury headquarters building in Washington to play some small role in addressing the financial crisis.

But despite some notable wins like that one, 2010 had started slowly for the firm. A *Barron's* story, prompted by our announcement of a meager first-quarter profit of two pennies a share, clarified that, after all our success (indeed perhaps because of it), the press was now eager to shine a spotlight on even the slightest sign of weakness. The reporter wrote with what felt like some degree of determination that the "rare earnings shortfall…could begin to break the spell that [Greenhill had] cast over the investment community."[10] The piece further stated, perhaps with some degree of envy, that our going public had "been a boon to insiders, who ha[d] sold stock at a huge premium." And it noted, one sensed with some frustration, that the firm had long "confounded skeptics" as well as short sellers (those who make financial bets that a stock will fall sharply), the breed of investors who had profited from Lehman's demise. The article's author admitted that ours "arguably [had] been Wall Street's best-managed firm in recent years" but cautioned that, as a result, we had been "rewarded with the sector's highest price-earnings ratio," perhaps setting us up for a fall. The article ended with a word of warning: "[l]ooks like one of Wall Street's sharpest firms may be about to lose its edge."

Despite the ominous warning from *Barron's*, for 2010 as a whole we produced a 17% increase in global advisory revenue. That strong result was despite a further sharp decline in European revenue – now down to only 18% of our total advisory revenue. Fortunately our recently acquired Australian business offset that decline. Despite being a far smaller market, Australia produced almost as much as revenue for the firm that year as Europe, even though it had been part of our firm for only a portion of that period. Although our aggregate advisory performance far outpaced the modest growth in overall global deal activity, our increase in advisory revenue was more than offset by a decline in investment revenue following our sale of that business at the end of the prior year. As a result, our total revenue for the year was down 7%.

While in the end we managed to recover from a slow start in 2010 and post tolerable full-year results, we kicked off 2011 with another weak start, reporting a first-quarter loss. *The Wall Street Journal* pounced on that news, declaring that we were "facing a 'put your money where your mouth is' moment,"[11] as our huge expansion of the previous three years had yet to pay off. The weak quarter and related news commentary sent our share price down further from the lofty levels at which we had three times recently sold significant shares to below $50 per share.

A few months later in July 2011, Simon Borrows resigned from his "less than full time" role at the firm to take a senior position with one of our British clients, the decades-old investment firm 3i. He had stayed with us longer than I had expected post his being nudged into a new role. Our series of hugely lucrative recent share sales had given him and all of the firm's early senior partners the wherewithal to do whatever they chose with the remainder of their careers. And Simon made a great next move, given that over time he went on to become CEO of 3i and achieve much success there.

But even with Simon's exit our carefully orchestrated crisis-era retrenchment was still not over. A month later, Tim George walked into my office just a few hours before I was to leave for what would literally, at age 51, be the first two-week vacation of my entire career. I was heading with my family to Kenya, joined by a couple senior people from The Nature Conservancy who had accompanied us on our earlier nature-focused adventure along the coast of British Columbia.

Tim, who had joined Greenhill just before I did and indeed prompted my own move to the firm, said he was leaving to join our much larger competitor Lazard. Over time he had grown disenchanted with his shrinking role at our firm. From my perspective, this was not a meaningful loss – Tim had been a major contributor in the firm's early years and played a supporting role on the recent Coca-Cola deal, but it had been a while since the last landmark deal or large fee event that he originated. Our dialogue was entirely cordial, and I asked only that he hold off on announcing his move until I returned from my vacation.

Days later, toward the end of my trip but while I was still in remote Kenya, *Bloomberg* published a story on a Friday that had obviously been planted for maximum effect.[12] The timing of the move was reminiscent of when Bob left Morgan Stanley for Smith Barney at a time when he knew both Dick Fisher and John Mack were out of the country and would be unable to react. Having enjoyed lavishly positive news coverage for most of our history, here we finally got our first real taste of hostile coverage. We did not even get a chance to respond, given that I was more difficult to reach than I had been in the entire firm's history.

The piece declared that Tim was a major loss in that he had been with the firm since shortly after its founding (true – he joined thirteen months after Bob launched it), was a member of our management committee (also true, but he was on the committee only as a vestige of his early partner status) and had "advised on some of the firm's biggest deals" (true, but almost all of those had occurred many years earlier). The story mentioned Simon's recent departure, as well as recent losses of one less prominent partner and various junior people – an unavoidable feature of life in firms like ours filled with ambitious strivers.

The story's negative tone sent our stock down sharply, prompting *The Wall Street Journal* to add fuel to the fire with the headline "Greenhill stock getting hammered"[13] and the undeniable comment that it had "been a very, very bumpy year" for our firm.

In the midst of a six-million acre nature preserve in northern Kenya I managed the crisis by talking on my Iridium satellite phone while standing on a stump behind our lodge to get a better signal, occasionally pausing to evade undue attention from small groups of elephants that randomly sauntered by. At the time we were only a few days from announcing our quarterly earnings, which I knew would convey very positive news that should allay the unjustified fears that *Bloomberg* had created. Our advisory revenue was actually up a whopping 38% versus the prior year quarter. But given the misinformation in the market, we felt compelled to put out our good news early. In an unusual move, we did so on a Sunday while I was still on safari, prompting the shrill *Financial Times* headline "Greenhill rushes out results after departures."[14] Further, we decided that for the first time in our history that we should not simply publish a news release regarding our quarterly performance but also hold an investor call, as most other public companies routinely did.

I wrote a lengthy script for the call from a tent on the coast of Kenya – the last stop on our tour. When we transferred aircraft in London I sent Roxanne and our kids directly on to New York while I traveled to our London office to host that call. It went well, and we managed to calm the market's worst fears, but it felt like our relationship with the press had suddenly, and fundamentally, changed. Members of the press know that "bad news" sells papers and seem to particularly relish taking down a person or institution that the press itself helped build up. *Barron's*, our old nemesis that investors had always seemed to ignore in the past, piled on, with the claim that, even after a sharp decline, our shares were still "too pricey."[15]

In worse news, just after I finished the investor call I took a call from Roxanne, who was in a panic after landing at JFK. Our son Elliot had fallen ill on the flight and was doubled over in pain in our car's back seat while en route northward to our farm. It was a nasty reprise of a stomach illness he had picked up in the early part of our trip. She did not have to describe how bad it was – I could hear his moaning loud and clear over the phone line. Ten days earlier we had been exploring finding a helicopter to get him to a Nairobi hospital before the illness seemed to subside. Now we found ourselves fretting about unknown tropical diseases. Fortunately, after two days with infectious disease specialists at Westchester Hospital it was clear that Elliot would survive. Despite our own gut-wrenching year, I felt like our business would do likewise.

CHAPTER FOURTEEN

ZAMBONIS AND ICE

One minute you're here
Next minute you're gone[1]
　　　　　– *Bruce Springsteen*, One Minute You're Here

The calendar year has always meant more on Wall Street than it does in most other businesses. Historically, employee compensation on the Street has been much higher than in most other industries. However, that higher pay is very heavily weighted toward discretionary year-end bonuses. In almost all cases those bonuses are closely linked to performance within the relevant calendar year. Aggregate firm performance drives the size of the "bonus pool," and individual performance determines how that pot is divided up.

"Performance" on Wall Street often means little more than revenue generation. Thus whether a particular deal is completed, and the related transaction fee earned, in late December versus early January can make a tremendous difference to an individual's compensation for the year. Bankers have always joked about savvy colleagues who endeavor to get paid twice for deals that close just after year-end – once when they overconfidently convince their superiors during the late-year compensation process that the deal in question will close before year-end and then again the next year when it actually does close and generate revenue for the firm.

While the calendar year is paramount from an employee perspective, for a public company it also has great meaning. Annual financial results are the primary measure by which a company's performance is judged. It is generally accepted that seasonality and a degree of somewhat random variability make quarterly results less meaningful in any business, particularly one that is closely linked to volatile financial markets. But full-year performance is closely watched.

Given the competitive and striving nature of those who populate Wall Street, the importance of the calendar year thus leads to intense year-end efforts to get projects completed and often equally intense politicking to maximize one's personal share of the bonus pool. If one's job description includes both reporting to outside shareholders the firm's annual financial results and allocating the employee bonus pool, as a CEO's does, the year-end can be particularly fraught. Getting to the point in December where everyone disappears for the holidays can feel like running through the tape at the end of a marathon.

One of the Morgan Stanley Group of Eight, former investment banking group head Bob Scott, often used an even better sports metaphor to describe the year-end process. Perhaps someone who had spent a great deal of time in hockey rinks either as player or parent, he referred to year-end as "The Great Zamboni." On Wall Street as in a hockey game, the teams go at it with great intensity, often building to a frantic crescendo of competitive action as the clock runs out. At that point, the ice typically looks pretty chewed up, reflecting the intense battles fought there.

Then, out comes the Zamboni to scrape and polish the ice, making it like new for a fresh start in the next period.

For Greenhill in 2011, the Zamboni metaphor seemed even more apt than usual. The financial crisis had destroyed or at least severely damaged nearly all our major competitors already in 2008, and their pain had lingered since then. In contrast, our firm had until very recently managed to carry on largely unscathed, growing in multiple directions. Our stock remained in the stratosphere most of the time, enabling senior bankers like me to monetize significant shareholdings at attractive prices on four occasions. Importantly, we had come into the crisis very strong on the back of an extraordinary 2007 performance, which relative to our tiny size was undoubtedly one of the best years any firm ever achieved in our business. Then, as the economy and market turned sharply downward and transaction activity dried up, we benefited from some debt-restructuring work for companies in financial distress as well as various crisis-related advisory roles like our assignment for Citigroup.

But what had really deferred our day of reckoning with respect to the financial crisis was not our ongoing core advisory business but rather three rabbits we had pulled from our corporate hat. The first was our successful 2008 SPAC IPO that we completed just before that perennially fickle market closed. The second was our highly accretive 2010 Australian acquisition, which was paid for in heavily overvalued stock and completed just before Australian deal activity boomed, with the benefits of resulting fees magnified by a soaring Australian dollar in foreign exchange markets. The third was our well-received exit from the private equity investing business. Yet notwithstanding all our efforts, a business that depends entirely on the completion of large transactions could not fully escape the clutches of a financial crisis of once-in-a-century magnitude.

The year 2011 was when that crisis finally caught up with us. Deal activity had remained weak, especially in Europe. And I had failed to conjure up another rabbit, like an acquisition, divestiture or new initiative, to follow the previous three. Exacerbating the challenge created by stubbornly weak markets was our high-profile resignation episode that summer, which had resulted in a lot of damaging "fake news" long before a future president made that phrase common. The press coverage of that event marked a painful shift in reporting on our firm, from a historically almost absurdly flattering tone to a critical and even sometimes ominous tone. Given bankers are insatiable consumers of financial news, that shift had in turn caused a fair degree of angst among our managing director group, which included numerous recent recruits who were big bank refugees still smarting from their bruising experiences in the early days of the crisis before they joined us. Nonetheless, despite all the tumult, as the year wound down it was clear that we would continue to persevere.

In fact, we would do much more than that. Despite the senior banker exits – most notably including my former co-CEO – and all the skepticism from the press that followed, we generated a 20% increase in global advisory revenue for the year, getting us back over the $300 million level for the first time since our 2007 revenue peak. That occurred despite that our business in Europe had continued to be very weak – producing only around 20% of our total revenue, with the Australian business now surpassing the European contribution. Our global team was justifiably proud of what we had collectively accomplished, yet most were somewhat shaken by the tumultuous events of that year. Thus, as December wound down, I was truly looking forward to a long holiday break and then starting fresh on new ice in the new year.

Monday, December 19, was to be my last full day of work for that year. The next day Roxanne would drive our two kids, then ages 11 and 16, from our northwest Connecticut farm for an early afternoon rendezvous 80 miles south at Westchester Airport, from which we would fly to Palm Beach for our first Christmas visit to our new place there. We had first laid eyes on our newly furnished home a few weeks earlier at Thanksgiving and were excited at the prospect of a lengthy break there after what was, at least for me, a trying year. Roxanne meanwhile was feeling very good about life, having just the month earlier published her book *Horsekeeping: One Woman's Tale of Barn and Country Life*, the story of our resurrection of the old horse farm that became Weatogue Stables and her learning to ride at a competitive level (while I chose to remain safely on my own two feet). There was just one more business day to go in this trying year, although I knew that the last day in the office before an extended break was always a frantic one. There are inevitably numerous loose ends to tie up on a variety of client and internal matters.

For my younger partner and putative heir to our firm's leadership Jeff Buckalew it was also a jam-packed day, as it was also to be his last one in the office before heading off to a final client meeting en route to holiday time with his extended family. Nevertheless, he invited me to join him for lunch at the century-old Racquet & Tennis Club a few blocks up Park Avenue from our office.

Jeff and I were close and spoke multiple times a day. He – the lanky Southerner who was a favorite golfing partner of Bob Greenhill – had become my primary consigliere in running the firm since the year-earlier departure of Bob Niehaus along with our private equity business. Yet we almost never ate lunch anywhere together, let alone at a place as grand as the Racquet Club, which served country club-quality cuisine in a formidable structure built in Italian Renaissance style. We were simply too busy, and if not with clients would typically settle for a hurried sandwich or salad at our desks.

But this day, having survived that exhausting year, Jeff decided that a somewhat celebratory lunch was warranted. As we sat in window seats in a main dining room that defined the word "clubby," we spoke with relief regarding the year now ended and with excitement about what lay ahead. At 52 I felt like I had a lot of gas left in the tank. Jeff, at 45, was my right-hand man and in every way well-suited to be my ultimate successor.

The next morning I headed to the office for just a few hours before a car would take me up to Westchester to meet my family and catch our flight. The weather was cool and a bit damp but not rainy – true New York winter weather had not yet arrived. Shortly after 10 a.m. I was sitting at my desk when my assistant Maureen called out that our longtime public relations advisor Jeff Taufield, a very frequent caller on media matters whom she often encountered on their shared commuter train from Greenwich, was on the line.

Jeff, in a much more serious tone than usual, skipped the usual small talk: "Scott, a TV reporter just called me and said Bob Greenhill's plane just crashed in New Jersey."

"What? That can't be. I just walked by his office, and he's sitting in there."

"Well, the guy says a Greenhill plane just went down. Could it be someone else?"

"I don't think so"–nobody but Bob ever took the Citation X, and that was the only aircraft the firm owned. "What kind of plane did he say it was?"

"A Socata."

Not too concerned, I said I would do a quick investigation. Being neither a pilot nor someone who thought much about what brand of aircraft I was traveling in, I had never heard of a Socata. But I remembered that Bob Niehaus and Jeff Buckalew, no longer partners in our business but certainly still friends, jointly owned a plane that they each used for business trips. I called Niehaus who, since the separation of our businesses, had been subleasing some space from us on a separate floor for his team.

"Bob, is that plane you and Jeff own a Socata?"

"No. We have a Hawker. Why?"

I explained the call I had just received. Niehaus replied somberly that, while he and Jeff did indeed share a Hawker, Jeff separately had a smaller single-engine plane, a Socata, that he used primarily to go back and forth between New York and his recently acquired home in Charlottesville, Virginia, to which his young family had relocated to get closer to his Southern roots.

There are no words to describe the feeling when some sudden, completely unexpected event occurs that, in an instant, you know has fundamentally and permanently changed your life. Such an incident will never be forgotten, and there will be no recovery – just a sort of muddling through. For my wife it was when, before her tenth birthday, she lost her mother to a brain aneurysm. For friends I have known, it was a child's tragic fall down stairs, a bike accident, a suicide.

All were unfathomable, gut-wrenching tragedies for which there is no rational cosmic explanation. Upon hearing news of such an event there is a numbness to be sure, but also confusion, as relevant facts tend to present themselves in fragments. There is a desire to learn more, to better understand. And further, a desire to do *something*. Thus, despite the numbness and confusion I was feeling at that moment, I sprang into action, wanting to avoid the scenario where the most emotionally impacted people would first hear about this tragedy in the wrong way or from an unfamiliar source.

My first call was to Jeff's assistant, Leanne. While Jeff and I had been together for lunch only the day before, and each had mentioned that we would be flying out of New York the following day, we did not discuss the details of our respective travel arrangements. I had not been aware that he was personally piloting his flight. The incremental facts that Leanne was able to convey to me were devastating. I had known Jeff was going to visit Primerica, an Atlanta-based financial services client that was a piece of Sandy Weill's empire when Bob Greenhill was part of that. What I did not know is that he would be flying with Rakesh Chawla, a 36-year-old partner who had worked with me on the Charles Schwab project that had indirectly led to our firm's IPO. Rakesh was an unabashedly enthusiastic young man who had grown up in an Indian immigrant family in Mississippi of all places. He had joined us from Blackstone eight years earlier, and from the start took literally the notion that our firm was like a family. He had been named a managing director (a role we still referred to as partner) just a year earlier, and I knew he and his wife Cathy had three very young girls at home.

Even more devastating was the news that Jeff's wife, Corinne, and their children Jackson and Meriwether, ages 10 and 6, were also on that plane. Apparently, after a short client meeting in Atlanta, Jeff and his family were planning to fly onward to visit family for Christmas in North Carolina where he and his wife were born. There were multiple layers to this grim story, but at least now I felt like I understood the full extent of the calamity even if not how exactly it had played out.

I walked into Bob Greenhill's office a few steps from mine to share the news. Nobody would understand the risks of traveling in a small private aircraft better than Bob. He owned and personally piloted at least three planes at the time including a seaplane for landing on water. Bob calmly explained what might have gone wrong, correctly guessing icing despite the dry weather on the ground that morning. Moments later I was stunned to hear him say, either because he was in shock or more likely simply because he was always such a stoic, that "I guess we have to keep moving."

It was jarring to hear that phrase he had used so often in the case of broken deals and other business disappointments, events utterly trivial relative to this situation. Bob in turn was startled by my sharp reaction to his remark, and his demeanor immediately changed as he realized that there was going to be far more emotion for everyone around us to process than either of us had previously witnessed.

I, in turn, quickly realized that in some respects Bob was correct. There was much to do. So, between brief tearful visits to my office from Jeff Taufield and Bob Niehaus, I got to work. I first dashed off a brief memo to be emailed to our global team, being careful to be clear on exactly what we knew and did not know. This was no time for implicitly assuming anything. I also wrote, with Taufield's help, a very brief press release to inform our public shareholders. I sent a message to my wife, then en route to the airport, asking her to call me as soon as she arrived. Obviously I was no longer flying to Palm Beach that day, but I did not want to share the heartbreaking news – she knew Jeff, Corinne and Rakesh well – while she was driving herself and our kids on a busy highway. Most painfully, as those broader communications were being prepared to go out I concluded that I was the obvious one to convey the heartbreaking news to Jeff's father and Rakesh's wife.

I had never met Jeff's dad, a North Carolina physician and Wake Forest professor who in his professional capacity had undoubtedly seen more than his share of death, but I got his number from Leanne, called him in his office and introduced myself. He said he recognized my name from conversations with Jeff. I briefly conveyed what I knew.

Undoubtedly stunned, his response was even more brief. Remarkably, the wise doctor and obvious man of faith said what he could to relieve my sorrow, knowing my loss and recognizing the difficulty of my making that phone call. I found myself contemplating the unimaginable grief there would be in his household in the hours to come as he passed on the news to Jeff's mother, Corinne's parents and their extended family and friends.

I then called Cathy Chawla, whom I did know, and fairly well. It was a confusing phone call. As I knew was often the case with my wife, Cathy was not aware of the details of Rakesh's travel – after some years one loses track of the specifics of the unending trips of a road warrior spouse. I later learned that Cathy was opposed for safety reasons to Rakesh flying privately and guessed that, in his usual zeal to fully participate in every activity related to our firm, he had perhaps hidden such travel plans from her. Certainly she, like many people in her place, would have objected to a flight like this one, in a single engine, single pilot, turboprop with a harried investment banker at the controls.

Following those emotional and awkward calls I decided I should take the elevator down to the seventeenth floor, the largest floor of the five we had leased in our building, where Jeff and most of our bankers sat. All eyes were on me – clearly none of our shell-shocked troops were working at that moment – as I strode past the silent bullpens of twenty-something junior bankers who filled that floor toward Jeff's corner office, straining all the way to hold back tears. Leanne sat in Jeff's chair and others were gathered around his desk, trying to piece together what had happened, still hoping to figure out that the news report was somehow mistaken.

After briefly conveying our mutual condolences we called a town hall meeting for the whole New York-based staff, which *Bloomberg* later reported in a lengthy story under the headline: "Greenhill Grieves for Two Managing Directors Amid 'Outpouring of Support.'"[2] I told the assembled group that our firm was like a family; that we should take some comfort from all the warm messages received from clients, competitors and friends; that we would always remember our two partners, and that we would find some way to honor their memory. I encouraged others to speak as well. We also freed everyone to answer press inquiries, both to help them voice their own grief and to give Jeff and Rakesh the loving send-off they merited. Each deserved to be portrayed in the many news stories that would come as full human beings – good and beloved people – not simply as bankers in the way the press might if not provided with more color.

At the meeting's end Bob closed with a few words, a simple sort of benediction to what felt like a religious occasion. Afterward, with tears in her eyes, Leanne told me that the day before, amid his rush to wrap things up before leaving for the holidays, Jeff had said several times leading up to our lunch that "I just want to see Scott before I go." Clearly he meant before he left for the holidays, but in that emotion-filled moment we were both dumbfounded at the larger potential meaning.

The next morning we awoke to a *New York Post* cover featuring pictures of Jeff and Rakesh from our website, as well as a close-up of the mangled wreckage of Jeff's aircraft, all under the bold headline "Death Dive."[3] The paper described a horrific three-mile-long spiraling descent, with the plane breaking up in mid-air and spreading debris over half a mile alongside the always busy Interstate 287 in northern New Jersey. Miraculously, despite the speeding highway traffic, there were no injuries on the ground.

The Post said there had been reports of "moderate rime" – rime being a word unfamiliar to me that was apparently used by pilots to describe the ice that can rapidly accumulate on an aircraft from water vapor in clouds or fog. It noted that while in flight Jeff had been in conversation with flight controllers about the ice in a conversational rather than urgent tone, although other reports said he seemed to be declaring an emergency as the transmission died.[4] Jeff was careful by nature and an experienced pilot with 1,400 hours of flight time. Only the month before he had completed his annual two-day training refresher course. But perhaps he had been caught off guard by unusual weather conditions or simply underestimated his margin for error.

More than a year later a National Transportation Safety Board (NTSB) investigation report indicated that conditions had indeed been difficult, with three crews that day referring to the icing as "severe," one crew member saying it was the worst icing he had seen in thirty-eight years of flying and another noting the accumulation of four inches of ice on his aircraft's wings in just five minutes.[5] Apparently Jeff's plane was qualified to handle light or moderate icing, but not severe icing. Thus the NTSB's concluding statement implied that Jeff should have reacted more quickly and have exercised his "command authority," rather than asking twice for permission to move to a safer altitude. A couple of precious minutes were lost waiting for that permission before his last truncated transmission, which sounded like the beginning of a declaration of an emergency. Jeff was an even-tempered, polite, agreeable man, perhaps in this instance tragically to his detriment.

No event could have struck closer to the heart of our firm. We once had a partner from the Nordic region who stood out for his upbeat, sunny disposition yet took his own life. And on another long-ago occasion Jeff sent around a mass email with the subject heading, "Sad News," explaining that Corinne had lost a baby, their first child, only a day before its expected arrival date. Those were terrible events, but for our firm they obviously paled in insignificance relative to this loss. While the Nordic partner had been with the firm only briefly and was not widely known, Jeff was the only banker besides Bob Greenhill whose tenure at the firm exceeded mine, and his Southern gentility and easygoing charm made him very popular with people ranging from CEOs and junior bankers to country club locker-room attendants and shoeshine men.

His wife Corinne, a regular fixture at firm social events, was the kind of vivacious woman who loved to laugh and did so often. Their two children were as adorable as kids can be, both featured along with their mop-haired dog who also accompanied them on the ill-fated journey, in a Christmas card we had received by mail just days before the fatal crash. I recalled the time at our farm that Jackson and my daughter, Jane, less than a year apart in age, returned to our home after collecting eggs from our chicken coop a half mile away. They were so soaked from a heavy rain that the egg cartons they carried had literally decomposed en route. Jane later disclosed that her first kiss came from Jackson that day.

And on top of all that was Rakesh. Which is worse, for an entire family to be erased in a single moment, or for a wife and three daughters likely too young to remember much of anything to be suddenly left fatherless?

While the holidays could be seen as a particularly difficult time for such a terrible event, they did provide a welcome break for people to get away from the office and grieve with their own families. Yet there were also numerous ways that we came together in the weeks that followed. On December 30 several of us gathered amid an overflow crowd at the Holy Trinity Episcopal Church in Greensboro, North Carolina, for the Buckalew funeral service. Bob Greenhill, not a comfortable speech-maker, rose to the occasion as did several other speakers previously unknown to me. Just before the priest's final words the huge congregation stood and sang the children's gospel song, "Jesus Loves Me." While my mind was fixated on my friend and partner Jeff, that song served as a grim reminder that, even more sadly, this was a funeral service for two little children as well.

A larger group from our firm gathered for a memorial service in Manhattan that week for Rakesh. His wife Cathy purposefully planned an uplifting service, much more "celebration of life" than funeral. I was pleased to share with the assembled group my thoughts on a young man about whom I cared deeply. Given the fact that many people were unable to make holiday-time services due to other family commitments, after the start of the new year there was a second service for each of the two families. The numerous New York friends of Jeff's family packed the cavernous Saint Thomas Church on Fifth Avenue in midtown. The firm then hosted a sort of memorial cocktail party for friends and colleagues of Rakesh at the University Club just a couple blocks from there. Our annual partners meeting was planned to coincide with both events, so that our partners from around the world would be able to attend.

While those early weeks post-tragedy were appropriately focused entirely on the emotional and psychological aspects of our losses, it is always remarkable how financial matters come to the fore even in situations where thinking about money seems somewhat crass. I have often found apt, usually in a humorous context, the words spoken by George Bailey, the small-town banker played by Jimmy Stewart in Frank Capra's Christmas film classic *It's a Wonderful Life*. When informed by the angel, Clarence, that there was no use for money in heaven, George exclaimed, "Well, it sure comes in handy down here, Bub!"[6]

Recognizing that, our immediate reflexive action was to set up a scholarship fund for Rakesh's three daughters, with Bob and myself kicking off that effort with substantial checks, which were quickly followed by those of many others from within the firm and far beyond. Hard as it would be for most Americans to believe, sending three Manhattan-based kids to private schools from kindergarten through college would cost millions of dollars. We gathered these funds without thinking about what level of financial damages Rakesh's family might be able to garner in a lawsuit, nor about whether we ourselves might have had any liability. We simply wanted to place Cathy's mind at ease on at least that one issue. For Jeff, sadly, there was nobody left who needed any financial support. Still, we wanted to make some kind of gesture, as people without better alternatives can sometimes find some comfort amid tragedy through the generosity inherent in giving away money. So we decided to establish a scholarship in Jeff's name at his alma mater, the University of North Carolina.

This being America, a lawsuit between Rakesh's family and Jeff's estate did ultimately materialize. I have never been a fan of "plaintiff's lawyers" – the type of attorneys who had preyed on Arthur Andersen and handle airplane-crash cases, even though I spent my second year of law school doing part-time work for such a firm. My time owning the White Hart inn only solidified my view. We were victims of multiple egregious claims, including one from a family we knew through our kids' schools relating to an elderly grandparent tripping on a carpet. Another came from a local real estate broker who claimed to have fallen off the inn's front porch while sitting there enjoying her lunch – she actually wanted to continue her lunchtime visits while suing us!

My faith in mankind relative to such matters, however, was somewhat restored in the case of an elderly gentleman who had tripped down the two steps leading from the lobby to the inn's tavern, staggered off balance across the room, hit his head on the ancient fireplace, and died. Even though I rarely involved myself directly with inn customers I did the opposite of what any lawyer would advise and called the family, complete strangers to me, to convey my condolences. In the end the family sought no damages at all. It turned out that the unfortunate victim was a retired judge from Indiana who apparently shared my dislike for plaintiff's lawyers.

Notwithstanding my personal biases, I was completely comfortable with the lawsuit ultimately brought by Rakesh's family, seeing it simply as a means to an equitable transfer of wealth from Jeff's family, which sadly no longer needed it, to Rakesh's family, which had lost its primary source of financial support. Any lawyer worth his salt would certainly have also pulled our firm, the proverbial "deep pocket," into that litigation – maybe would have named me personally as well. After all, we did allow Jeff to pilot himself in a small plane on a business trip and Rakesh to travel with him, even though neither of those were conscious decisions on our part.

In the end neither family chose to drag the firm or me into the dispute – I like to think because they knew that Jeff and Rakesh loved our firm and, like the elderly judge in the tavern, would not have wanted that. Even though our firm was insured and certainly could have absorbed any reasonable loss from such litigation, I nonetheless took some comfort in that belief. If our firm was anything like a family, then these men were two favorite sons. The losses we sustained took a toll that extended far beyond the financial realm.

Little did the *The Wall Street Journal* know what an understatement theirs was, some months earlier, to declare 2011 a "very, very bumpy year" for our firm. The Great Zamboni could not scrape the deadly ice from the wings of Jeff's plane. And whether it would be able to help get the rest of our team back up on its skates for a new year was far from clear.

CHAPTER FIFTEEN

CLOUDS OF DUST

Walk on through the wind,
Walk on through the rain,
Tho' your dreams be tossed and blown.[1]

– Oscar Hammerstein II, Carousel

Most business histories focus on either the thrill of victory or the agony of defeat, to use the old *Wide World of Sports* tag line. With our frequent front-page M&A deals, a first-of-its-kind IPO and years of remarkable stock market success, we certainly knew the thrill of victory. With the tragic loss of Jeff and Rakesh coming at the end of a year in which we had already endured the messy departure of long-time colleagues and taken a beating in the press, we had now also known the agony of defeat. And only seven months after Jeff's plane crashed along a New Jersey highway we felt the agony of defeat again when a 23-year-old analyst from Texas, still in his first few weeks as a trainee, was killed in a terrible accident on that same state's Garden State Parkway.

Each year in midsummer a new class of analysts, all newly minted college graduates, travel from around the world for a few weeks of training in the New York offices of the leading investment banks. It's fair to say that these aspiring bankers play hard as well as work hard. That is the nature of that coveted role – precisely what draws thousands of bright young people to New York each year for starting positions on Wall Street. Like Sinatra sang, "If you can make it there, you'll make it anywhere."[2]

On the fateful night, following a firm-sponsored social event in Manhattan – one of many during the training period – our young recruits decided to extend their fun-filled evening. On the spur of the moment they booked cars to the Atlantic City casinos 129 miles away. One could do that sort of thing in what was the new age of Uber, and certainly that alternative was safer than self-driving after an evening fueled by alcohol. Ultimately a bathroom pit stop was needed, and in the dark of night the cars pulled over to the side of the quiet highway. The precise details from there were unclear at least to me, but amid the maneuvering in and out of cars Jack Roloson, the younger brother of a highly regarded Greenhill analyst from a few years earlier, was struck and killed by a passing car. His traumatized classmates not only saw the gruesome accident but spent much of the rest of the night explaining to the local police what had happened.

The next day our firm was back in the *New York Post*,[3] which reported "an after-party celebration gone horribly wrong" and noted the painfully close juxtaposition of this event to the recent plane crash. For our global team this was another horrifying event. Yet apart from those who witnessed what happened, all of whom were in a state of shock for some time, this loss did not hit that team as hard as the plane crash did. Most people had not even had the chance to meet this promising young man before he was gone. Still, another tragic loss of life in a firm of only 300 people so soon after an even larger loss reopened wounds that had yet to heal.

What then followed our firm's extended thrill of victory and more recent agonies of defeat was far less dramatic than either. Extending the sports metaphor, the years that followed were more like what Woody Hayes, the legendary Ohio State football coach of my Big Ten youth, referred to as "three yards and a cloud of dust."[4] In fact, for the four years following the devastating plane crash we failed to pick up even the three yards. Rather than rebounding as hoped, our annual revenue for those years hovered just under $300 million, with year-to-year movements ranging from a token 3% increase at best to a 5% decline at worst.

This was nothing about which to be embarrassed. We had only achieved a $300-million revenue year a single time in the pre-crisis years. Somewhere in the range of $200–$250 million was more typical for us then, apart from the uniquely spectacular year 2007. Further, that relatively flat revenue was sufficient to keep the firm highly profitable, just as the Ohio State of the Hayes era generally fielded a winning, albeit not terribly exciting, team. We were thus easily able to pay out around $55 million per year in dividends, a significant portion of that going to employees on their shares, including on the stock grants they received as part of their compensation each year.

Yet all of that was of limited consolation given that revenue growth had been the primary driver of our firm's valuation over the years. Thus through that period of stagnant revenue our once lofty stock price ground relentlessly lower over time. Clearly the spell that *Barron's* once claimed we had cast on the stock market had been broken. My admonition to our team that "the stock price only counts on the days you're selling," while undoubtedly true for individuals who do not need to mark the value of their holdings to current market prices the way professional fund managers must at each quarter end, was of limited comfort to our bankers. Many had already seen their stock grants from previous employers get battered by the financial crisis.

In fairness, there were understandable reasons for our anemic revenue growth. For one, the market for our services had shrunk. In 2012 the aggregate value of M&A deals globally was barely half of what it was in

2007. And that proved very slow to change. In Europe, the news was even worse. While by the metrics of deal numbers or deal sizes that market had been about the same size as the US market prior to the crisis, by 2013 even a shrunken US market was around 40% larger. That gap grew even greater in the years following. Europe was simply hit harder by, and took longer to recover from, the global financial crisis – all consistent with my personal observation from past economic recessions and crises of various ilk. Indeed, there seemed to be a continuing series of uncertainties in Europe that essentially prolonged the financial crisis there. Would Greece be pushed out of the European Union? Would the Euro survive as a currency? What about Italy's burdensome debt load? Later, in June 2016, came "Brexit," the surprising British vote to leave the European Union that further exacerbated the gloom hanging over European financial markets.

Given the resulting subdued pace of European deal activity, that market produced less than 30% of firm revenue in this period, down from roughly half in the years prior to the crisis. So, while our flat total revenue production made the firm's performance look sluggish in those years, under the surface there was intense activity. We continually changed personnel and entered new businesses and markets to offset the unrelenting decline in Europe's contribution to the firm's results.

Apart from these prolonged challenging market conditions in Europe, the firm's larger issue was the heightened level of competition globally. In the firm's early days our strategy was close to unique. We were an independent firm – one with no conflicts of interest and no ancillary products to sell. We were unfailingly on the client's side. When that kind of advisor was needed, which happened more often in an increasingly complex world, the call for assistance from a CEO, a board director, a lawyer or whomever would often come to us. Yes, there was still competition from the much older and larger Lazard firm as well as some smaller players. But Lazard continued to be preoccupied by internal intrigue and lacked the kind of international cooperation across offices that brought us so many large cross-border deals. Meanwhile, the array of smaller advisory firms in the market lacked our recognized brand – the valuable imprimatur our name could bring to a boardroom or to a group of institutional investors who wanted to see a qualified independent party "bless" the terms of a particular deal.

The number of direct competitors with a similar structure and strategy to ours proliferated in the years following our wildly successful IPO. Seemingly every investment banker of note sought to get in on the game. The number of competitors expanded further after the financial crisis. In 2014 the leading private equity investment firm Blackstone announced that it would spin off sits advisory business into a separate public company, simultaneously merging it with the start-up M&A firm PJT, which was named for the initials of founder Paul J. Taubman, a telecommunications and media banker who had been in my managing director promotion class at Morgan Stanley. Rather than do a traditional IPO they went public by simply distributing ownership shares in the advisory business to Blackstone's existing public shareholders. Blackstone, which had begun in the late 1980s as an advisory business as well as an investing business, had over time seen the latter grow dramatically while the advising side of the business was constrained by perceived conflicts in relation to companies in the firm's enormous investment portfolio. The move to separate the two businesses made strategic sense – we ourselves had made the same decision in separating from Niehaus's business a few years earlier.

Creating yet one more publicly traded competitor, in 2015 Houlihan Lokey took public its advisory business, a much older one even than our own, shortly before the PJT spin-off was completed. We had never seen Houlihan as a close competitor, but it operated in the same neighborhood of M&A (where it focused on much smaller transactions) and restructuring (where it generally served lenders rather than financially distressed debtors). Going public would facilitate its expansion in ways that would make it more of a competitor over time.

While several firms followed our strategy and aimed to outdo us in terms of scale, there were also new competitors with an even narrower focus and specialization that aimed to outflank us on the other end of the size spectrum. One such firm, based in London, was founded in 2013 as Robey Robertson, named after my former Morgan Stanley London colleague Simon Robey and Simon Robertson, the former head of the UK merchant bank Kleinwort Benson before it was sold to Germany's Dresdner Bank. I had spoken to Robertson about leading our planned London office before we engaged with Borrows and Lupton to fill that role. Instead Robertson moved to Goldman Sachs for several years before joining up with Robey. While their partnership lasted barely a year before Robey teamed up with a younger fellow to form Robey Warshaw, this small firm had considerable success aiming to be a more specialist version of our firm. They sought to serve exclusively FTSE 100 companies in London on M&A matters, rather than a global client base with a wider range of advisory services.

More important than the simple proliferation of competitors was the fact that, with a few exceptions like Robey Warshaw, all followed the same basic strategy. We were the first of this generation of new firms to open in London, first to move into Continental Europe, first into Canada, first with branch offices across the US, first to go to Australia and Japan, first to expand to restructuring advice and first into the capital-raising business for private equity funds. In each case our move inspired numerous followers, diluting the market opportunities we had been first to identify and pursue. As Schumpeter had explained, that is simply how capitalism works.

Ironically, our extraordinary early success likely contributed to the eventual outcome that several of our newer competitors ultimately grew to become much larger than our firm. We were the first of this new generation of advisory businesses, formed at a moment when corporations seemed to be yearning for a respected investment banking group focused solely on providing them with high quality advice on their most important transactions. From almost day one, we produced very high revenue per employee, generating cash sufficient both to fund outsized pay packages for our senior bankers and to pay generous dividends to shareholders, including those same bankers. In due course we attracted a stock market fan base that – in just a matter of months – drove the value of ownership interests held by early partners like me sky high. But that early success meant that star bankers were less likely to join us than our newer competitors – why become a partner in an entity where the valuation was already hugely inflated rather than a newly formed one where there was greater remaining upside potential?

At the same time, it is probably fair to say that our early success also led, perhaps understandably, to a degree of complacency on our part – why complicate life by building substantially greater scale when things were going so well and our existing team was being so richly rewarded? Thus ours remained a business with a global brand name and reputation far out of proportion to its modest headcount, while our many competitors that got off to much slower starts took a more methodical approach to building scale and generating value for their owners. Over time, consistent with the children's fable, many of the tortoises thus ended up surpassing the hare in the race for team size, revenue and stock market valuation.

Our lack of revenue growth eventually raised questions as to whether our generous dividend, which provided some degree of a floor under our share price in the absence of meaningful growth, was sustainable. During our glory years, we hiked our dividend seven times in rapid succession, fully cognizant of the fact that any future dividend cut would be very poorly received by the market. Thus I tried to shut down any talk among analysts or investors of an impending dividend cut with glib remarks like "you would have to water board me to get me to cut the dividend,"[5] an inappropriate and impolitic reference to allegations of torture in the ongoing US war in the Persian Gulf. In fact, our modest cost structure and the ongoing liquidation of our large portfolio of fund investments along with Iridium shares resulting from our SPAC meant that we almost certainly would be able to sustain our dividend for the foreseeable future.

My "day job" throughout this period of running in place remained as an investment banker to a variety of clients. In 2012 I finished my long-running assignment for the US government in relation to the resuscitation of the insurer AIG. That same year I helped a colleague advise the healthcare services company Coventry on its $7.3 billion sale to Aetna. The next year I was introduced to Gracia Martore, CEO of the prominent media conglomerate Gannett, which owned numerous media assets but was best known as publisher of *USA Today*, the colorful national newspaper placed daily outside hotel room doors across America.

Gannett would turn out to be my most prolific, and loyal, client ever. I ended up leading a team that advised on its sale of apartment rentals information business Apartments.com, its spin-off of online auto retailer Cars.com as a separate public company and the similar spin-off of America's largest newspaper publishing business. I also advised on several broadcasting acquisitions for its television business that was labeled TEGNA (simply a scrambling of the letters in the historical Gannett name) following the newspaper spin-off.

That same year I advised Masco, the Michigan-based maker of Delta faucets and Behr paint, on the spin-off of its installation services business. Spin-offs like what Blackstone did with its advisory business were very much in vogue as companies increasingly recognized that their various business segments would often be more highly valued if traded on the stock market separately. Then late in 2015, I advised on a deal for Heartland Payment Systems, which had come back from the near dead after the 2008 Russian hacking episode to achieve even greater success than before. We sold that company to Atlanta-based Global Payments, a larger player in the business of processing credit card transactions, for $4.2 billion. The sale price was around $100 per share – thirty-three times the price our fund had paid for a one-third stake fourteen years earlier. The deal's legal documentation required the public disclosure that I had retained much of my personal equity holdings for that entire period, resulting in a significant personal investment gain on the sale along with a deal fee for Greenhill of around $17 million.

But alongside my busy day job I spent plenty of time trying to find or develop the next new thing – something that would spark renewed interest in our firm like our SPAC deal, the spin-off of our investment business and our Australian acquisition did. In addition to searching for another such rabbit that I could pull out of my hat, recruiting new senior bankers was a constant activity in our effort to spur increased revenue growth, or at least offset the ongoing and inevitable depreciation and attrition of existing senior personnel. As I had tried to explain to shareholders on our very first quarterly investor call while en route back from Africa, "[n]o well managed business is or should be static."[6] Sometimes we nudged people to leave because they simply had failed to become successful in our business model. Other times we did so with bankers who had enjoyed a period of success with us but had seen their productivity over time wane to a point where, if they were not yet ready for retirement, they needed to make a fresh start elsewhere.

In dealing with such matters I often commented to my wife that I felt increasingly like my job was that of a psychologist for middle-aged men. I limited that comment to men both because our senior team (consistent with our entire industry) was overwhelmingly male, and because I would never dare claim the ability to be a psychologist for the opposite gender. The best of bankers start out smart, energetic, hungry and nearly single-minded in their pursuit of business success. Over time, with experience, they should become even smarter. But with age eventually energy dissipates. With increasing financial success the hunger starts to go away. And as the years go by problems relating to personal health, aging parents, troubled kids or crumbling marriages can fragment what was once intense focus.

As these challenges accumulate, at some point in the life of most professionals comes the moment when they realize that their reality will fall short of their initial hopes and dreams in terms of responsibilities, title, compensation and wealth creation. They will not have one of Mamet's Cadillacs in their future. They will get the steak knives, or maybe even end up getting fired and leaving the Street with no prize at all. Or, even if they did get the Cadillac at one stage of their career, they ultimately have to face up to the cumulative depreciation of their capabilities and indeed to their own mortality and thus step away. Proof that the struggle with this reality is universal across cultures was the bizarre case involving the head of our Tokyo office. As polite and gentle a man as I had ever known, he flew to New York on the eve of his long-planned retirement to convince me that I should terminate his handpicked successor and allow him, at the ripe old age of 78, to run the business for several years longer while he looked for another one.

At times the notion of an acquisition seemed like a more effective way of returning to growth than a continuing series of individual recruits. The most interesting of the opportunities we came across led to a 2012 flirtation with the legendary, late, former Secretary of State Henry Kissinger in relation to the potential affiliation of his Kissinger Associates international advisory firm with our business as part of an expansion to China. I had been introduced some time earlier to Kissinger's right-hand man, Joshua Ramo, a committed Sinophile and former journalist who years earlier wrote *Time*'s "Committee that Saved the World" cover story after the Long-Term Capital crisis was resolved. Over several months we chatted about whether our respective firms could be put together in some manner.

This informal dialogue led to a June breakfast at Kissinger's River House apartment on Manhattan's east side, with just Bob, me, Henry and Joshua attending. Hearing up close the rumble of Kissinger's unmistakably deep, German-accented voice was a bit of a thrill for someone who had followed international politics and recent US history as I had. He clearly retained much of the gravitas for which he had been known for nearly my entire lifetime. He was 89 at the time, which made a serious commitment to our firm for any meaningful time period likely infeasible. But even if he were much younger, his unflinching aversion to ever seeking a fee from a Chinese entity, on the theory that doing so would undermine his credibility with that longtime counterparty, was a serious obstacle. Needless to say, Bob could not relate to that discomfort with fee-paying work and given his taciturn style the breakfast therefore consisted mostly of our listening to Henry talk. But the visit was worth it just to see that Henry had a softer side than I would have guessed, evidenced by his repeatedly dipping into a generously proportioned bowl of bacon that sat next to his breakfast plate to hand feed the large, rambunctious canine under the table.

Less interesting was our expansion to Brazil in 2013. We had historically eschewed so-called developing markets, believing that more economically advanced countries were where the action was in terms of large, complex mergers and acquisitions of the kind on which we advised. Nonetheless, in our continual quest for the next frontier we spoke to numerous prospective teams and businesses in that market before landing on a former Goldman Sachs partner who looked like he could build a business for us. Coincidentally, he had been an exchange student in Grand Rapids, Michigan, in his youth, so we quickly identified multiple points of personal connection. In moving into Brazil, undeniably a very large market that had intermittently enjoyed rapid growth, we overlooked a history of economic booms and busts, the latter with the potential to hammer the local currency to the point where the dollar value of any advisory fees earned would be trivial. Emboldened by journalistic chatter that Brazil's time had finally come, we decided to take a chance on our first expansion to a so-called "emerging market."

In a reflective moment soon after that office opened, I thought back on what was now ten years since the firm had gone public, asking one of our analysts to do a comparison of how our stock had performed relative to that of our competitors. The PowerPoint chart he created showed bars for each of our large competitors but none of the smaller independent advisory firms that had followed us down the IPO path given that none of those had been public for that full period. In any event, I knew that none of those newer firms had stock that had performed anything like ours had.

What the chart showed was pleasing enough that I had it laminated. I would keep it along with the other random bits of memorabilia I had collected along the way, like the printed program for the Morgan Library event I attended years ago for newly minted Morgan Stanley managing directors and the medallion the New York Stock Exchange gave me, as it routinely does to corporate executives, to commemorate our firm's IPO.

The data displayed on the chart was a reminder of what a tumultuous decade it had been in our industry. Lehman Brothers, for example, had obviously lost 100% of its value since we went public – it went bankrupt and was still in the process of being painstakingly liquidated for the benefit of its unfortunate creditors. Bear Stearns did a bit better by getting J.P. Morgan to buy it for a fire-sale price, resulting in an 86% decline in value over the period. That was slightly better than Citigroup's 87% decline. My alma mater Morgan Stanley did considerably better than those, losing only 19% of its value over that decade. The large European banks with which we competed had all lost value as well. Only Goldman Sachs (up 87%) and J.P. Morgan (up 93%) had gained any value at all over a full decade. Meanwhile, our Firm's value, including dividends, had increased 373% over the decade despite our stock price now being far below its peak. Clearly, notwithstanding the trials and tribulations of recent years, we had much for which to feel thankful.

A year later came another opportunity to look back with gratitude, as the firm and I were honored by the Museum of the City of New York (MCNY) at its annual Chairman's Leadership Award dinner. Most major Wall Street firms had been similarly honored over time, including the once mighty but now defunct Bear and Lehman firms. Ours was the first firm of anything close to our small size to win the award. But it was perhaps natural given both our long history of success and the fact that my old friend Jamie Dinan was chair of MCNY's board of trustees. Such awards feel like an honor, even though the cognoscenti regarding such events know that the purpose of the festivities is essentially for the honoree to help Jamie raise money for the museum, which I was happy to do.

I stood before a crowd of friends and museum supporters gathered on the patio in front of the museum facing Fifth Avenue and began with some light-hearted words, saying I wanted to "spend just a minute reminiscing about the ways in which the city of New York is entwined with my life, with Jamie's life and with the life of the Firm I lead, Greenhill." Continuing, I added,

> I wish my New York story had begun with my Dutch ancestors coming over in the early days of New Amsterdam. But for reasons unknown they decided to stay in Holland for two or three centuries longer, by which time all the really great Manhattan real estate acquisitions had been made. Worse yet, when my grandfather finally landed at Ellis Island about a century ago, rather than come to Manhattan he took the longer journey to a rural part of Michigan.[7]

I went on to speak of how New York had impacted my romance with Roxanne and my friendship with Jamie, as well as the formation of Greenhill and my decision to "leave a perfectly good job" and join the firm in its early days. I went on to tell the story of our firm, feigning jealousy by noting that Jamie's hedge fund business had achieved far greater success than ours had. I closed on a note of sincere gratitude: "Seriously, I have no complaints, and if I did, I should be struck dead by lightning as I stand here tonight." And indeed, I should have.

But there was not a lot of time spent in those days looking back with nostalgia. By the time of the museum event, we were again ready to consider M&A as a means of catalyzing the next chapter for our firm. There was some reluctance to return to that alternative, as our Australian acquisition had proven far more challenging than we initially expected. We completed that deal in 2010, and the business was a major contributor in the first couple years that followed. It even outpaced our much larger European business one year. But the two key founders of the business we acquired had proved increasingly difficult in terms of cultural fit.

To be fair, they had some reasons to be less than thrilled with the deal they had done. First, they had accepted an all-stock purchase price at a time when our stock was near an all-time high. When the effects of the financial crisis finally caught up with us, the value of their holdings declined precipitously. Further, they had agreed to an onerous transaction structure with two performance-based earnouts, pursuant to which they needed to achieve robust regional revenue targets to be paid the full purchase price. They easily hit the first target given their strong early performance, but it then quickly became clear that they would miss the second. The combination of these deal terms meant that the actual value they received ended up being a small fraction of the headline figure on the day we announced the acquisition. Given that our London partners had long warned us to be wary of the fellows who ran this business, it was no surprise that as time passed and the value of their deal proceeds withered, the relationship grew more uncomfortable. True to our historic policy of protecting our collegial and collaborative culture, I ultimately concluded that the leaders of the Australian business we had acquired represented a clear and present danger to that ethos.

Given the nature of those who populate Wall Street firms, we had parted ways with many bankers over time, including some highly talented ones. Not long after our IPO we separated from our star restructuring banker Michael Kramer. Notwithstanding a history of tension in that relationship, there wasn't any drama in the divorce. It was "just business." Much later came the amicable parting of ways with my gentlemanly co-CEO

Simon Borrows. But this one would be more difficult. For one, these two Australian fellows and their team worked 10,000 miles away – there was no way we could manage that business from New York, even on a short-term basis. Accordingly, I determined that we would plan for a slow-motion departure in which they would make the final move.

At the end of our annual partners meeting, when all managing directors including the Aussies were in New York, Bob and I invited the two into a small room in Davis Polk's large conference room facility, which had served as our meeting venue since our crisis-era expansion meant we no longer could fit in our own offices. Having been agitating essentially to recut the deal they had agreed a few years earlier, they undoubtedly walked into that conference room expecting to hear an offer that would kick off what for me would have been a painful negotiation. Instead they were handed a draft press announcement. They would be given important-sounding new titles but forfeit all management responsibility. With that news set to be disseminated imminently, they were left with no choice but to go along with our plan.

There was no doubt in my mind that these fellows would in due course leave the firm, and eventually they did. But I equally knew they would take time for them to plan their next move. That gave me the chance to transition our Aussie franchise to new regional management. To aid in that transition, I sent a young New York-based partner, Kevin Costantino, to help run the business. Kevin was a loyal young lieutenant who shared with me both a Michigan youth and a stint at the Wachtell Lipton law firm. The transition would not be easy, and our efforts to rebuild the Australian business would take some years to pay off, but nonetheless it was prudent to proactively start that process rather than wait for our adversaries to make a surprise exit.

I endured all the unpleasantness relating to our Australian acquisition only by regularly reminding myself that it was a record stock sale on the heels of that very well-received deal that directly funded my purchase of the beautiful Palm Beach retreat that would over the years serve as my refuge from crises of a personal, corporate and global nature.

In 2015, I was lured into another acquisition. This one was smaller – around $100 million in size.

My knee-jerk response was negative when first approached about buying Cogent Partners, a Dallas-based global business focused on advising pensions, endowments and other institutional investors on sales of investment interests in private equity funds. They sold to buyers like the Lexington Partners fund we once looked at buying when we were still in the investing business ourselves. It might seem surprising that someone like me whose career had been devoted to M&A would be skeptical of the wisdom of acquiring an attractive business. But the unpleasant Australian experience on top of a few near-misses over the years with various other acquisitions we considered had convinced me that "people businesses" – those where the primary assets of the business went down the elevator and home each night – were unusually difficult to make work.

On the other hand, there were obvious reasons to consider buying Cogent. While the clients (institutional investors versus corporations), assets involved (passive investment interests versus operating businesses) and counterparties (investment funds like Lexington versus other corporations) were all different from those of our historic M&A business, the basic function the Cogent team performed was very similar to that of our M&A bankers. And with European deal activity still subdued and our Australia business going through a difficult management transition, adding a new source of revenue sounded very appealing. In addition, the Dallas-based senior leaders of the business seemed like fairly uncomplicated, loyal Midwesterners similar to me who would be easier to manage than the Australian fellows had turned out to be. So, following a year of playing hard to get, I decided to press ahead with this acquisition.

Throughout our prolonged period of going sideways the firm's key outside director was Steve Goldstone. He was the only board member who had personal experience as CEO of a public company – one that encompassed the tobacco giant R.J. Reynolds. Along the way Steve repeatedly told me in sympathy that the CEO job is by nature a very lonely one. That had to be particularly so for the leader of a tobacco business in the anti-smoking era, but there was no doubt that he was also right in my case.

Bob remained our nominal chairman and was engaged with a limited number of clients, but now played a modest role in the life of the firm. From the start he had not been a terribly social human being, preferring to eat a sandwich alone at his desk than go out for lunch and avoiding evening events as much as possible. As the firm grew, he thus failed to make much of a personal connection with anyone beyond the small group of us who had joined the firm in its very early days. In recent years, Bob's beloved wife Gayle unfortunately began suffering from Alzheimer's disease. The ultimate stoic, he was never able to acknowledge that fact to me or even to many people he had known much longer. Yet this grim reality seemed to cause him to withdraw further into himself, dissipating his already limited engagement at the firm.

For a decade I had relied primarily on Niehaus as a true partner in leading the firm. Once he departed along with the private equity business he led I turned increasingly to Jeff Buckalew, my putative successor, as my consigliere. Jeff's fellow associate from year one John Liu had also been a close colleague, but he had left the firm to work for a client a couple years before Jeff's plane went down. Likewise our first general counsel, Ulrika Ekman, decided at a youthful age to join her older husband in retirement, in part because our exit from the private equity business made her in-house legal role smaller and less interesting. That left me with no sympathetic ear or sounding board within the firm. And at some point it even becomes inappropriate to drag one's spouse through all the twists and turns of leading a public company – especially once all reasonable personal and financial goals have long since been exceeded. So Goldstone was right.

There were moments when an escape from a prolonged period carrying the solitary responsibilities of being CEO of a public company seemed appealing. One possibility arose when Evercore's new CEO initiated a series of conversations about combining our firms – we met for a series of breakfasts and lunches at midtown's Brasserie restaurant in 2011 and 2012. But the complexities entailed in combining two very similar firms with significant overlap sounded more like an increase in responsibilities than an escape, so I never showed any real interest.

More interesting to me was the notion of combining with the still-private firm Centerview. Steve Goldstone reconnected me with Centerview founder Blair Effron, who had advised him on various consumer-sector transactions relating to another board role he held, as chair of the food company Conagra. I liked Blair when we first met back in 2005 to talk about him joining our firm. Since then he had launched what had become a formidable competitor. But his firm's activities were then largely limited to the US market and to certain industry sectors – most notably the consumer goods sector where we had enjoyed modest success since our early years. The overlap between our teams would be limited while the synergies available in a combination might be considerable.

Blair and I met for dinner at star chef Jean-Georges Vongerichten's restaurant in the Mark Hotel a couple blocks from my apartment in May of 2014. Over several months, we followed that up with occasional phone calls and a couple of breakfasts at E.A.T. – a nearby place more popular with Upper East Side moms stopping for coffee after school drop-offs than with investment bankers trying to make deals. Each meeting solidified my positive view of Blair, and it was clear that he was intrigued by the notion of a combination as well. But he was not CEO of his firm (as with the old Morgan Stanley, nobody was) and therefore needed others to go along with the concept of a potential merger. Ultimately it became clear that, perhaps influenced by the volatility that all publicly traded investment banking firms had suffered in recent years, he and his senior partners preferred to remain privately held for at least some time to come.

Notwithstanding these various flirtations, I was quite comfortable continuing on as leader of an independent advisory firm, even with the complications of operating in public company form. I often thought back to our original goals for the firm – to create a platform for a career working on large, complex and interesting transactions; to develop a brand that stood for quality advice on such transactions; to build meaningful scale; to become global; to persevere for the long term. And of course to create some wealth along the way. Certainly all of that, and more, had been accomplished. So I soldiered onward and kept moving. And I continued my practice of diversifying my activities to provide alternative means of fulfillment for those times when work felt, for lack of a better term, like work.

After exiting the Chapin School board once my daughter Jane had followed her brother to Hotchkiss for high school, I sought other opportunities beyond my continuing board roles at Prep for Prep and the University of Pennsylvania. In 2013 I turned down Steve Goldstone's request to join the board of Roundabout Theater, the nation's largest nonprofit theater group, which he had chaired for some years. As much as I loved theater, in those early years post the financial crisis the finances of performing arts groups – particularly ones that owned and operated Manhattan theaters – seemed precarious. I was reluctant to get embroiled in a potential rescue project given the challenges I was facing at Greenhill.

But I did accept the 2013 request of Group of Eight member Lewis Bernard, the man *The New York Times* once correctly called the "wise man" of Morgan Stanley, to join the board of the American Museum of Natural History (AMNH).

AMNH is one of New York's most prominent cultural landmarks, perched on Central Park West and then easily identifiable by the large statue of Teddy Roosevelt, son of one of its founders, mounted on a horse at the top of the stairs to its front entrance. The Museum had an illustrious history dating back to the early post-Civil War era. J.P. Morgan was a founding trustee alongside Roosevelt senior and other notables. Important scientific research took place at the Museum, but it was also a popular tourist attraction, drawing more visitors each year than all New York sports teams combined. The wildly popular 2006 film *Night at the Museum*, in which characters in various Museum exhibits – including Teddy Roosevelt, played by comic genius Robin Williams – came to life overnight, didn't hurt in that regard.

For major Museum donors like I would have to become upon joining the board, the highlight of each year was a glitzy late-autumn fundraiser held under the great blue whale that hung in the Museum's Ocean Life Gallery, with entertainment generously arranged by longtime board member Lorne Michaels of *Saturday Night Live* fame. At the same meeting I was elected the board also voted in the comedic actress and *SNL* alumna Tina Fey. That somehow seemed appropriate – as had been the case since the onset of the financial crisis some years earlier, maintaining a sense of humor would continue to be a most useful survival skill.

CHAPTER SIXTEEN

STARTING OVER

Many a new day will dawn[1]
                    – Oscar Hammerstein II, Oklahoma

The formula for investment success can be simplistically boiled down to "buy low and sell high." Yet few are able to put that strategy into practice. Doing so involves the Herculean task of suppressing the powerful cognitive bias, inherent in the human brain, to do exactly the opposite.

My father provided me with a real-life case study of this phenomenon. He knew nothing about economics or finance. Lacking even a high school diploma, he never took a course or read a book on either subject. And he preferred a TV diet heavy on the political rantings of Fox News rather than the investing advice of CNBC. Yet given a savings ethic rooted in his post-Depression upbringing and a long career in a company with generous pension benefits, when he finally "took early retirement" in one of the downsizings typical of major companies in that era he left with a nest egg measured in the mid-six figures. I advised him to roll that into a retirement account at the leading retail brokerage firm Fidelity. Knowing that he would fret about every little market downturn given the decades of hard work and persistent thrift that accumulating this sum had required, I told him to put half the money into risk-free long-term US Treasury bonds – then yielding around 8% – and half in a highly diversified index fund that held the stocks of 500 large American companies.

Over the years that followed he repeatedly implored me to move some of his money into the heavily marketed funds that were top performers for the most recent period. Why would he want to do that? The answer is obvious: because successful funds for the most recent period generated extraordinary profits for investors and were celebrated as winners, so why wouldn't one want to get on that kind of bandwagon? Conversely, why would one want to invest in companies, sectors or markets that had been performing particularly poorly?

Of course, left to his own devices this approach would have resulted in him catching the top of every market – NASDAQ tech stocks, emerging markets, energy, real estate and all the rest, as each took their turn at the top of the performance rankings. Conversely, he would have missed all the really good buying opportunities, when various assets had fallen out of favor and were therefore on sale at marked down prices.

What is perhaps more surprising is that many Wall Street bankers who graduate from the top business schools and spend their entire careers in finance sometimes have instincts nearly as bad as my father's. It always proved easiest to recruit bankers using grants of our stock when the price was high rather than when it was low. Even annual grants as part of bonus compensation seemed more welcome when the price was high than when it was low. We needed to give away a full percent or more of ownership in our firm to attract a new partner right up to the moment we went public, but the price of recruitment dropped to a fraction of that as soon as it was possible to ascertain the value of our business in the stock tables of *The Wall Street Journal* or on a *Bloomberg* terminal. People like what feels like certainty, and they like investing in what look like winners, often to their own detriment.

Particularly memorable were the investments our first private equity fund made just as the dot-com bubble was bursting and market values of almost all assets were in free fall. My partner Bob Niehaus chose that moment to invest in the particularly downtrodden energy and telecom industries in the wake of the Enron and WorldCom frauds, which helped decimate values in those sectors. It was initially far from certain that we would make a profit on those investments, but at least it was clear that we were following Warren Buffett's oft-repeated advice to "be fearful when others are greedy and greedy only when others are fearful."[2] In November 2016 that fund finally sold off its last asset, and Niehaus sent fund investors like me a letter noting that, according to a prominent industry data source, the fund was the highest returning private equity fund of the entire decade, providing investors with 3.8 times their money, equating to an annualized return of a staggering 46%. That was even after subtracting the lucrative fees and profit participation that we collected as fund managers.

Following that same advice, when we raised $400 million for our SPAC on Valentine's Day of 2008 we were selling shares in a new company with a completely unknown future at the tail end of an era when investors were feeling particularly fearless. Only weeks later Bear Stearns became the first prominent victim of the worst global financial crisis since the Great Depression of the 1930s, sending the investing herd stampeding from the greedy to the fearful end of the psychological spectrum. Thus the window to raise money for these blank-check investment vehicles was abruptly closed soon after our successful withdrawal.

Our 2010 Caliburn acquisition provided another instructive case study. The founders of that Australian business began their pursuit of a sale to us several years earlier and accelerated such efforts after our IPO.

In ensuing years they watched our share price climb to five times its initial price while they continued their chase. Even in the days immediately prior to our locking in a purchase price, the stock kept climbing, but that only served to further whet their appetite for those shares. In the end they were glad to accept stock that was trading near an all-time high in exchange for their business, ultimately to their detriment.

In the case of my own share ownership in Greenhill, it would have been easy to get caught up in the euphoria that prevailed the several years following our IPO. The potential for escalating success seemed endless. If the future was so bright, why sell shares and pay significant taxes on capital gains when it was possible to retain an asset that seemed to rise inexorably in value? Yet my senior partners and I managed to restrain ourselves from believing too fervently in our own marketing story. We executed six stock sales, for well over a billion dollars, over a five-year period starting just days after the 2005 expiration of our post-IPO lock-up restriction enabled us to do so. Having acquired our shares for a fraction of a penny each, my fellow pre-IPO partners and I sold at an average share price of nearly $67, with the last sale at $84.45 in the weeks following our Australian acquisition.

In the years that followed the market pendulum with respect to our shares swung far in the opposite direction, as the market's pendulum is wont to do. To be sure, there were good reasons for the steep and pro-longed decline. For one, the stock should never have reached the lofty heights it did. Valuing our firm at $2 billion when we had only around 100 employees in 2005 made no sense, nor did our stock hitting an all-time high the very week that Lehman Brothers collapsed and the entire financial world was teetering. Likewise for another all-time high in 2010, when it was becoming clear that the financial crisis was finally catching up to us despite the excitement of our attractively priced Australian acquisition.

Still, what had once felt like excessive market optimism now felt like undue pessimism. I began to wonder if it might be possible to repeat our past success, by buying low and someday again selling high. Then in late 2015 came a completely misleading *Financial Times* story with a painfully negative slant. That provided the catalyst for my first acquisition of Greenhill shares since my initial bargain purchase back when I joined the firm eighteen years earlier.

Around the time that we were announcing some unsatisfactory quarterly financial results we took the difficult but entirely appropriate decision to terminate three senior European bankers. Despite coming to us with impressive pedigrees from leading firms, they proved unable to succeed on our platform. In exiting people in such circumstances we always aimed to let people go without any sort of public announcement so that they could put whatever "spin" on the move they chose and thereby more easily find a new perch. But that lack of full disclosure could sometimes lead to inaccurate external perceptions, as reflected in the *FT* headline "Trio of top Greenhill bankers exit as boutique misses M&A boom."[3]

The reporters had obviously leaped to the conclusion that a weak quarterly earnings report, followed by the exit of three senior bankers, must mean that the bankers had chosen to bolt, thereby suggesting that the firm was unable to retain key talent. This ancient logical fallacy described by the phrase *post hoc ergo propter hoc* (after this, therefore because of this) was about all I remembered from high school Latin. The story noted that our shares were down 40% for the year to date, and of course that article itself knocked the price even lower.

To me, the shares now seemed ridiculously cheap, so I bought $5 million worth at just under $25 per share, less than a third of what I had sold my last tranche of shares for five years earlier. This was partly an investment and partly a show of faith, putting my money where my mouth was. And partly it was simply to make the game more interesting. Having more "skin in the game" would make the attempt to prove the naysayers wrong more fun, in the same way that making even a small bet on a sporting event makes watching that contest more exciting.

From time to time I considered a much grander share repurchase. The most extreme form would be to acquire all the shares held by the public – the operative phrase being "going private," the opposite of "going public" in an IPO. Typically going private requires very substantial debt financing, hence the familiar term "leveraged buyout." We were paying out well over $50 million in cash annually in the form of dividends at that time, and dividends were paid out of after-tax profits (unlike interest on debt, which provides a valuable tax deduction). That was a lot of cash that could be redirected toward debt service, which implied the potential for a very large amount of debt financing given interest rates were then unusually low by historical standards.

A buyout where that cash was redirected to servicing debt incurred for the acquisition would be a fabulous outcome for shareholders and our team – as well as for me. I would thereby shed all the unappealing aspects of running a public company. Debt alone, however, would not be sufficient to fund such a transaction – to finance a full acquisition some equity would also be needed. But I knew I was willing to put up some cash, assumed Bob Greenhill would do whatever I did, and figured others would at least roll over whatever stock they currently owned into equity in a newly private company.

Just as my initial interest in doing an IPO had been piqued by work I was doing for my client Charles Schwab, the catalyst for exploring this new possibility also came from a client interaction. In late March 2016 I had lunch at the midtown Italian restaurant Fresco, a regular lunchtime spot where a decade earlier I had been asked to join the Chapin School board. My guest was Simon Freakley, the newly appointed CEO of Alix Partners. Alix was not a competitor of ours, but it was similarly in an advisory business, in its case focused on corporate restructuring and various aspects of consulting. James Lupton, my longtime London partner (now in a very part-time role given his House of Lords membership and other activities), made the introduction to his fellow Englishman

Freakley. He thought we might help find acquisition possibilities for Alix, which had grown in various directions since its 1981 founding as a narrowly focused, Detroit-based, debt-restructuring specialist. While I came to lunch that day hoping to provide some insights and provocative ideas to a prospective client, I came away from the table with more than I had brought to it.

Alix had initially been wholly owned by founder Jay Alix. Over the years it had remained a privately owned business with significant employee ownership, but in recent times had attracted three successive generations of private equity investors. The first was the prominent San Francisco-based private equity firm Hellman & Friedman, but its current outside ownership group comprised two Canadian pension funds and a Middle Eastern investment fund. Such institutions were increasingly trying to make private equity investments directly rather than through funds that charged high fees.

As Simon casually described his most recent transaction facilitating another smooth transfer of ownership in Alix, I was struck by the extraordinary leverage he was able to put on his business, and even more so by the very low interest rate he was paying on that debt. I loosely monitored debt markets in the context of client M&A projects on which my colleagues and I were working but had never considered that a pure advisory firm like ours, with no tangible assets or recurring revenue, might be able to borrow such large amounts at such low cost.

Only two days later, as if to underline the "easy money" epoch in which we were living, my wife and I went downtown to the Public Theater to see *Dry Powder*, a play *The New York Times* described as a story of "rapacious wheeling and dealing in the world of high finance."[4] The "dry powder" referred to in the play's title was familiar shorthand for the capital that an investment fund has available but not yet deployed. At that moment there was plenty of dry powder in nearly every fund's coffers, making financing for a possible going-private deal unusually plentiful by historic standards.

A couple decades earlier, as I contemplated my move from law to investment banking, a *Sunday Times Magazine* cover story signaled that my personal plans tracked a major trend then in motion. A Public Theater play starring Clare Danes of television spy drama *Homeland* and John Krasinski of the popular sitcom *The Office* sent just as clear a signal. Highlighting how Wall Street was seen by the type of people who write plays for the theater that launched *Rent, Hamilton* and numerous other productions of a somewhat left-leaning nature, *The New York Times* said that Danes' character was the kind of person who, "rather than come to your aid… would probably step over your bleeding body to sidle into a town car and head to her next meeting." Caricatures can be amusing.

I left the play wondering if we might take advantage of all that dry powder to lock in the "buy low" part of the investment equation for a second time around at our firm. As with our long-ago IPO, confidentiality while exploring this concept would be imperative. Despite the obvious abundance of money then available, it was not clear to me that we could actually accomplish the transaction I was contemplating. A buyout rumor could instantly push up our share price to a higher level than we would be willing or able to pay, rendering a deal impossible. And a failed deal could be devastating, regardless of the reasons for that failure. It would signal to the market – and to both our clients and employees – that we had "needed" to do an extraordinary transaction yet were unable to make that happen. Hence I kept our plans confined to a very small group of my closest colleagues.

In the midst of those few weeks of preparations came another reminder that, even in a firm of fewer than 400 people, unforeseen real-life dramas will frequently disrupt the day-to-day focus on business. I was working from our farm on a Friday, something I did when I needed space to grapple with the larger strategic issues like the possibility of taking the firm private. Clients and colleagues could find me when needed wherever I was. While Roxanne and I were eating an early breakfast one of the firm's assistants reached out to me by email, and I immediately responded by phone to what looked like an urgent message. A partner's high-school-aged son had taken his own life. Taking a deep breath, I walked away from the breakfast table into another room to dial that partner. We both wept openly as he told the story, in my case much more so than I had when Jeff Buckalew's plane went down.

Like Bob, I had always been a bit of a stoic – unflappable being an adjective many had applied over the years. But the horror of the plane crash and all that followed had pierced my psychological defenses and left me a more emotional person going forward. This news struck particularly close to home. There is nothing worse than the death of one's child, and losing one in this manner had to be the worst of all fates for a parent. My own daughter was only a couple years younger than my partner's boy, giving me some sense of the anguish he must have been feeling. Many years earlier one of my cousins had taken her own life after years of struggling with depression. At the time I was too focused on my early career and too ignorant about such matters to feel the appropriate degree of empathy. But that was before the plane crash.

It is an understatement to say that a tragedy of that scale can absolutely knock the wind out of you. But, as Bob's old mantra indicates, one ultimately has no choice but to keep moving. There is no better alternative, and sometimes work can feel like a form of therapy, or at least a helpful distraction. So I got back to work.

By early July our buyout presentation was ready. After first sketching out my plan to my friend Ed Herlihy, a Wachtell Lipton partner who was the leading M&A lawyer to financial services firms of all types, I ventured alone to visit two funds that specialized in lending for highly leveraged deals.

One was HPS, the successor to a hedge fund called Highbridge that J.P. Morgan had owned for a period. I had some long-ago history with the Goldman Sachs alumni who ran the place, and I also happened to be an investor in one of their funds via my banking relationship with J.P. Morgan, which still acted as a fundraiser for that firm. The other was Fortress, the fund with which we had partnered long ago on our wildly successful investment in the bankrupt cell tower company Pinnacle. I was also a personal investor in three Fortress funds. While in principle financial investments ought to be made with the singular goal of generating attractive returns on capital, I had often invested in part as a means of building or maintaining a business or personal relationship. Doing so felt good, and one never knew when such a relationship would become useful.

Both funds gave me a serious audience of senior decision-makers as I described my simple plan to acquire complete ownership of our firm on behalf of our employees, essentially by converting after-tax dividends into pre-tax interest payments that would fund enough debt to finance the buyout of our public shareholders. Both conversations were illuminating, yet ultimately convinced me that this was not the right path for our firm.

There are many surprisingly distinct pools of capital on Wall Street, and each has its own very specific objectives in terms of transaction structures and target rates of return on investment. Often getting to the right transaction outcome depends on knocking on the right door to access the optimal source and form of capital. The groups behind the door on which I had knocked wanted very high rates of return, which meant they required some degree of equity ownership alongside the costly debt they were offering. That would enable them to share in whatever value we were ultimately able to create.

I did not want expensive debt, and I definitely did not want new shareholders. Our existing public shareholders, with whom I was fully aligned by virtue of significant equity ownership myself, were largely passive. In fact a large percentage of our shares were held by index funds that were literally passive other than in regard to the required "say on pay" vote on executive compensation required by regulators as part of every annual shareholder meeting. That vote was a somewhat time-consuming exercise in navigating a specialized bureaucracy spawned by overzealous regulators, but it imposed very little by way of real constraints on managing our business. Otherwise, our shareholders allowed us to run things as we saw fit, knowing that our interests were largely consistent with theirs. Replacing them with the kind of hyperactive overseers who populated the private equity world would not be an improvement. So I quickly put the idea of going private aside.

Fortunately, there was no particular urgency to do any sort of transformative deal, as our business at the time was performing surprisingly well, particularly in contrast to the gloom-and-doom scenario that the press had become prone to portraying. In January 2017 the *Financial Times* followed its misleading story from a few months earlier with a more-balanced piece, perhaps because the reporter felt some guilt for what he ultimately admitted was an inaccurate portrayal (for which he blamed the headline writer when we spoke) of the personnel departures that were the focus of that earlier story. Titled "Greenhill & Co a Survivor in the Volatile World of Boutique Banking,"[5] the new story made an obvious point that could have been applied to almost any Wall Street business – that "the road has not always been a smooth one." Illustrating the volatility referred to in his headline, the reporter noted that the previous June, when unbeknown to him I was privately talking to investors about going private, our stock had dipped to an all-time low, even below our original IPO price from thirteen years earlier, yet since then had rebounded 70%.

Further illustrating both our earnings volatility and the fact that surprises could come on the upside as well as down, three days after this latest story ran we reported a particularly strong fourth-quarter performance, resulting in a larger year-over-year percentage increase in advisory revenue than that reported by any of the fifteen large and small publicly traded competitors that disclosed an advisory revenue figure as part of their reported results. In fact, despite the slow start that year, 2016 turned out to be the second-best revenue year in our history, as well as showing a high profit margin and sufficient cash flow for both substantial share buybacks and continuation of our generous dividend.

Events of the early weeks of 2017 prompted recollections of past crises of both a corporate and personal nature. In February Roxanne and I saw the new Broadway musical *Come from Away*, which told the story of travelers stranded in Newfoundland in the wake of the September 11 terrorist attacks. Much more poignantly, as I scanned the news while on a trip to San Francisco in late March I was reminded of the larger crisis that came some years after that one.

My long-ago Morgan Stanley colleague Charles Murphy had committed suicide. I had not laid eyes on Murphy since he came to me in the wake of the Bernie Madoff scandal during the early days of the global financial crisis. Before that I had not seen him for over a decade. But he had left a lasting impression from our time together in London. After we reconnected I heard that he had taken the advice that I (and probably others) offered in early 2009 and landed an advisory position with a hedge fund. I then later heard from a colleague about some specific work he was doing in relation to that fund's investment in AIG, the once mighty insurance company that we had helped get back into public ownership after its crisis-era bailout by the US Treasury.

The news said Murphy had jumped from a high floor of midtown Manhattan's Sofitel Hotel,[6] the place in which I had once holed up for two weeks trying to find a buyer to rescue the Andersen accounting firm in the wake of Enron's collapse. Perhaps Murphy was never able to recover from the personal humiliation that flowed from the Madoff scandal, despite his managing to find a new foothold on Wall Street. According to *The Wall Street Journal*, at the time of his death Murphy still lived in a nineteen-room townhouse and had a net worth in the tens of millions of dollars, yet friends said he nonetheless struggled to find a path forward. The press stories noted that Charles was dressed in a business suit when he jumped to his death – remaining, even at this moment of ultimate tragedy, the picture of sartorial elegance for which I had always remembered him.

When 2017 started off slow for us and our stock swooned again my thoughts returned to some sort of extraordinary transaction to take advantage of the market's inability to accept the kind of revenue volatility inherent in our business. While my inclination was toward some kind of large share repurchase that would substantially enhance employee ownership while we continued as a public company, before going further down that road I decided I would first explore one other possibility. Several weeks earlier over breakfast at midtown's Casa Lever restaurant, I had met with Antonio Weiss, a former Lazard banker I had come to know and like on a deal involving Coca-Cola several years earlier. He was a cerebral, even-tempered fellow who had recently come off a stint with the US Treasury under the Obama Administration, a role he had stuck with even after members of Obama's own party blocked him getting the appropriate title for his position – such was the disdain in which Washington types held Wall Street bankers in the post-financial crisis era.

I was hoping to lure Antonio to our firm and was far more willing to dangle my CEO position than Senator Elizabeth Warren had been to hand over a Treasury Department title. But while the discussion over breakfast was a pleasant one between two friendly former competitors, it quickly became clear that Antonio had no interest in such a role at our firm or at any of its many peers, including his former employer.

"Why would anyone want to be CEO of a publicly traded advisory firm?" he asked, noting the inherent volatility of deal flow and revenue, as well as the challenges of managing the kind of ambitious, striving people who populated such firms. His comment was well-informed by many years near the top of Lazard, the oldest, largest and therefore likely most stable of such firms.

When asked for advice regarding our firm's future he offered it in two words: "Bury it." Not as in "kill it," but rather in the sense of letting it be subsumed into some much larger organization with a greater diversity of cash flow that would obscure its day-to-day operations and performance from public view. "Just sell to some Japanese bank," he said. "Then you can keep doing what you're doing without all the noise" that goes with managing a public company in such a peculiar industry.

I wasn't ready to bury the firm in that manner yet, but I did decide to explore a combination with Houlihan Lokey, the advisory firm that was a quarter-century older than our firm but only recently had gone public. I knew Los Angeles-based Houlihan well, as my first boss at Morgan Stanley had left that firm in the late 1980s to open Houlihan's first New York office. Houlihan pursued the low profile but more stable business of advising on much smaller transactions than we typically took on, as well as advising creditors on bankruptcies and the more mundane business of providing innumerable formal valuation opinions for a variety of tax, estate and other purposes. For several years following our IPO a senior Houlihan executive would intermittently stop by our office to chat when he was visiting New York. It was always clear to me that he was looking for insights as his firm tried to chart a course toward its own IPO.

Weeks earlier, my son Elliot had graduated from Penn. In the last hurrah of his college athletic career he would soon head west to near Sacramento to be part of its varsity heavyweight rowing team at the national collegiate rowing championship, known as the "IRAs" for the Intercollegiate Rowing Association that governed the sport. Roxanne and I were obviously going to travel there to watch. We took immense pride in his having "walked on" to the team freshman year after being a high school wrestler and cross-country runner with no rowing experience at all, then worked his way up to the first varsity boat over the next few years.

After a few glorious days in dry and sunny early summer weather watching my son's rowing career end with Penn achieving a respectable thirteenth place national finish, my wife and I made the short flight to Los Angeles. Trying to make the work-related detour fun for her, I booked us an over-the-top suite at one of my favorite hotels, the Bel-Air, a 1920s era boutique hotel owned by the Sultan of Brunei that exuded old Hollywood glamor. We ordered room service for dinner both because we were tired from the early morning boat races and because we wanted to maximize our enjoyment of the opulent accommodations. The next morning I took a car for the short drive to Houlihan's office and met with its CEO, Scott Beiser, a friendly, low-key fellow I had gotten to know at various industry events.

On a conference room floor crowded with a large class of summer interns arriving for their first day of work, Scott and I spent a couple hours talking frankly about how our respective firms functioned and whether they might somehow fit together. On paper, the combination seemed obvious. We had the bigger name in the corporate world, as we worked on the kind of deals that got reported in the business press. Ours was also a global business, with a brand as strong in Europe or Australia as it was in the US, while Houlihan was essentially a domestic US business. On the other hand, Houlihan brought a very high volume of smaller transactions, which resulted in a granularity of revenue that smoothed out results over the quarters and years. Plus it had a much more significant bankruptcy restructuring business than we had, providing a larger counterbalancing source of revenue in periods where M&A was slow due to economic weakness.

Notwithstanding the good fit on paper, it quickly became clear to both of us that the cultural differences between our businesses were substantial. Advising on small deals was very different from advising on large ones, and the advisors who played those respective roles were likewise very different creatures. Getting them to work together harmoniously would not be easy. Furthermore, Houlihan seemed much more intensively managed than our place – more bureaucratic, as Bob would surely have said had he been there.

While a professional sports team had always seemed like the best metaphor for our business, Houlihan's operation felt more like a factory. In some respects I envied the consistency and lack of drama in their seemingly well-run factory, but I struggled to imagine how that could be effectively melded with our sports team. Even agreeing on a name would be problematic. They were the larger firm in several ways, but our numerous international colleagues would see Houlihan as a name completely unknown to their client bases. So we parted amicably, and I flew back to New York with the intention of returning my focus to a transaction where we could be masters of our own destiny to an even greater extent than had been the case throughout our years of public ownership.

Only a couple weeks later I reached out to the same firm that had helped us with our IPO thirteen years earlier: Goldman Sachs. Among other connections, I knew the head of Goldman's investment banking group for financial services companies, as he was married to a Greenhill alumna who had once worked in our CFO Hal Rodriguez's back-office finance group. As had been the case last time around, I saw Goldman as a tough competitor but also as an organization that was the best at getting difficult deals completed for clients. The prestigious Goldman brand could be extremely useful in lending credibility to the first-of-its-kind transaction I was contemplating, just as it had been in our first-of-its-kind IPO. Meanwhile, looking at the relationship from Goldman's perspective, I knew we had been significant fee payers in our several equity offerings starting with the IPO, believed they saw us as formidable competitors for certain clients and deals and hoped they would continue to see us as a smaller but similarly successful version of themselves.

With all the shared history between our firms providing a useful prologue to our meeting, on July 17 Rodriguez, myself and another colleague traveled south to Goldman's relatively new downtown headquarters on West Street. Goldman assembled a large group to hear our idea. We took its team page by page through a thick presentation, a revised version of what I had used for the going-private discussions fourteen months earlier. The primary focus was again the substantial cash flow a business like ours generated – compensation constituted the bulk of our expense, but a meaningful portion of that was in the noncash form of our stock. Proof of our substantial cash flow continued to be the hefty dividend we had been paying for years.

Consistent with my going-private discussions the previous year, the plan was to convert those after-tax dividends into pre-tax interest payments that would support a large amount of debt. But unlike in the prior discussions, the plan this time was to maintain our public listing while buying back enough stock to dramatically increase employee ownership and leverage the potential future upside for internal and external shareholders. This type of transaction is called a "leveraged recap," short for "recapitalization," which refers to a complete reformulation of a balance sheet. Back in the 1980s when I was starting my career, these were sometimes called "public LBOs" given their high leverage, similarity to a buyout and continued (albeit much reduced) public ownership.

As with our IPO, the intention was to pull out all the stops in maximizing the probability of success by making this transaction as appealing as possible to investors – this time to investors in debt, in other words lenders. Most importantly, we planned to avoid going too far in our use of leverage so we would get a decent credit rating from the Standard & Poor's and Moody's rating agencies. This would keep our interest costs low and the investment appeal of our debt high. Second, employees would refrain from selling their shares in the transaction, thereby providing them with a greater percentage ownership of the firm and stronger economic incentives to perform going forward. In furtherance of that theme, Bob Greenhill and I would each make a large new equity investment – initially we said $5 million each, but I later told Bob we should each do $10 million to make an even stronger statement of confidence. I even came up with the idea of cutting my annual salary for the five-year life of the loan by about 90% to only $50,000, with the amount forfeited being rolled into a form of restricted stock that would pay off only if the debt was successfully repaid in full. I saw little risk in that exchange yet knew from experience that was the kind of grand gesture that would attract significant attention from investors.

Within an hour it was clear that this time I had knocked on the right door – the one that led to the cheap and passive debt for which I had been looking. Behind this door was the "leveraged loan" market, which differed from the "bond" market in that the debt had a floating rate that was appealing to us, given that rates were very low then and seemed like they would stay that way for a while. The scale of funds available in the leveraged loan market had exploded in recent times, and Goldman was working hard to become a major player in that market. As was the case way back with our IPO, Goldman was enthusiastic about handling our transaction – it would be the first of its kind in our sector, and whichever bank executed ours would likely get hired for those that followed.

The Goldman team suggested we aim to seek $300 million from investors. What we really wanted was $350 million, which would enable us to repurchase enough stock, given that employees like me would not be selling, to increase the aggregate economic ownership of our firm by employees to around 50%. But as is often the case in capital markets, the right tactic to get there was to start lower in our talks with rating agencies and investors, then upsize our debt offering on the back of excess investor demand.

As I knew would be the case, Goldman was well-prepared for our meeting. Even after a near lifetime on Wall Street, I came away having learned much I had not known about modern capital markets. For one, I learned that approximately half of our stock was held by passive index funds like the one into which I had long ago directed my father's retirement money. Of course I knew that the major index fund players Blackrock, Vanguard and State Street were among our largest holders, but I was unaware of the aggregate scale of such passive holdings. Goldman's team said our stock was part of more than 100 different indexes relating to various size, sector and regional characteristics. Separate from this very large index fund group were the "quant funds," which were funds that used quantitative analyses to manage money via computer algorithms. The most prominent member of that group was Renaissance Capital, a massive fund started by mathematician James Simons and staffed with fellow PhD mathematicians rather than by financial analysts with MBAs.

My quaint old idea of an investor in our stock was someone who analyzed what countries and sectors to invest in, settled on our sector, then studied our various peers before deciding to invest in our stock and then monitor our performance on an ongoing basis. But between the index funds, quants and our own employee holdings there was almost nothing left for investors of that traditional type. I had been feeling like we were going through a period when the stock market hated us. The strange reality was that, at least in our case, the stock market consisted of machines that did not even know who we were.

A completely separate group of investors was in the business of investing in what were called leveraged loans. While I had mistakenly thought I understood the stock market, I fully recognized that the leveraged loan market was completely unfamiliar to me. There were a few names I recognized, like Blackrock and PIMCO, both dominant players in nearly every aspect of debt investing. But most funds had names I had never heard of, such as Sound Point, MJX, Benefit Street and Marble Point. Most of this group managed highly specialized, extremely diversified funds and many looked for only tiny $1–$5 million slices of huge numbers of different deals. These passive investors were the debt equivalent of our stock index fund investors. Completing a financing like ours would require more than fifty such investors, although we hoped to reduce that number with a few larger lead investors.

Goldman said the way to begin marketing, in parallel with the rating agency process, was to hold a series of confidential meetings with fund investors that had the scale to play such a leading role. If a few of the right ones could be persuaded to take a sizable piece of our deal, then it was reasonable to assume that the many small ones would follow and get us to the total investor demand we needed. And as with our IPO, the key was to create excess demand. Investors want there to be unsatisfied demand when the loan is initially placed to ensure there will be buyers in the secondary market afterward.

For a variety of reasons, we really needed to get this deal done – doing so would resolve a number of challenges, essentially "reboot" our business and regenerate the excitement we had felt after our IPO. With the nod from Goldman that we should be able to succeed, we were intent on sprinting to the finish line just as we had done with our IPO thirteen years earlier. So only five weeks after that first introductory meeting with Goldman we met with Moody's and Standard & Poor's on separate days in late August. Those meetings went extremely well, clearly aided by the fact that, as members of the financial services industry, the ratings teams at each agency saw M&A advice as a premium service and were very familiar with our firm given the high profile we had developed over more than twenty years. We ended up with ratings one notch better than Goldman had told us to expect – "BB" from S&P and the equivalent from Moody's.

While still working to finalize those ratings, which were at the better end of the "below investment grade" (once referred to as junk) bond market, in mid-September we had a series of one-on-one meetings with potential lenders at the new Park Hyatt hotel in west midtown. As is typical for such affairs, Goldman ordered lavish snacks for each session, even though most people were so focused on the task at hand that they didn't touch the food. Certainly our team didn't. Given all that was at stake, the smell of warmed Brie cheese baking on a service table behind me as I made my pitch in one afternoon meeting struck me as particularly ridiculous.

The first reactions we received from the meetings were very positive, and it looked like we were home free. But Goldman's daily marketing updates the week of September 18 indicated that interest was flagging as various investors struggled to get the necessary investment committee approvals to invest money into our deal. Our story was a good one, but our weakening share price and recent negative press raised doubts in the minds of some. While our historic financial performance was more than adequate to service the debt we were seeking, some people wondered if they were missing something. Our stock had just touched an all-time low of $14 per share, down more than half from earlier in the year.

Ironically, I saw the low share price as favorable, given that we were getting ready to set a price at which to buy back ownership of most of the firm. This would be the "buy low" half of repeating the "buy low/sell high" strategy. But we had to get the financing to do that first. Finally on a Friday in September we won over just enough of the support we needed from the lead investor group to formally launch the larger marketing process.

As fate would have it, by the time we got to that point a new hurdle had materialized, created by what had become my nemesis: the press. In mid-September I met with a longtime *Wall Street Journal* reporter who had reached out through our PR advisor for an interview. *The Journal* had paid scant attention to us in recent years, but it was clear that the reporter was geared up to write a very negative story focused on how our post-financial crisis performance had been weaker than that of the glory years that came before that. She was pushing for an interview with Bob Greenhill, whose role in our business had steadily declined in recent years, and I feared that encounter would not go well. Bob had always been unpredictable in interviews, and in his 80s, he was obviously no longer as sharp as he once was. Making matters worse, it seemed, as is often the case, like the reporter had her story written before she even asked me the first question.

I knew that a negative story in a high-profile publication like *The Journal* could poison the well for our financing, which already felt fragile. We needed to convey our plan to the market in our own way and at a time of our choosing. Fortunately the reporter did not appear to be in a hurry, and I tried to slow walk her by stringing out our meeting dates and dribbling out the information she requested.

I was just able to stretch out our dialogue, and thereby defer her publication plans, until Monday, September 25, the day on which we were scheduled to announce our recapitalization plan after the market closed at 4 p.m. As a matter of courtesy, I reached out to her that mid-afternoon to preview the contents of our press release. She immediately realized what I had done and was understandably not pleased. She still went ahead with her story, conveying our news but focusing heavily on Bob, as had clearly been her plan all along. She framed the story as if it were "breaking news" that an 81-year-old man had lost his fastball. The approach seemed needlessly cruel, but I guess that was the press's pay-back for years of fawning stories filled with anecdotes like his snowmo-biling across Maine to find cellphone reception for a client call. Remarkably, she even repeated that oft-told story in her article.

The headline ("Legendary Dealmaker Greenhill's New Assignment: His Own Struggling Firm"[7]) and her lead (that the firm was seeking a "lifeline from its founder") were both misleading. This deal was not his assignment – he was barely involved in the firm at that point. And we were not throwing the firm a lifeline. We were simply offering to buy out one group of investors (shareholders who were assigning what we saw as an inappropriately low value to the firm) using money from another group of investors (lenders whose confidence in our business led them to offer ample funding at remarkably low cost). Plus we were throwing some per-sonal money into the deal – a token portion of what we had taken out of the firm over time – simply to demonstrate our commitment.

The admission further into the story that the deal was essentially "a partial leveraged buyout" clarified what was really going on. But the report-er's goal had been a gratuitous takedown, and while I had preempted her attack she salvaged as much of her planned story as she could. She even ended it with an inaccurate suggestion that major industrial company and longtime Greenhill client Emerson Electric no longer used our firm for advice. That prompted an unsolicited call to one of our bankers from

Emerson wondering why she would have written that, given that only a year earlier we had advised Emerson on its largest acquisition ever.

Notwithstanding my critique of her story, I understood the reporter's job – to write stories that attract readers. And I knew that *schadenfreude* regarding fallen Wall Street legends sold well. But I hoped she likewise understood my job. If our firm was anything like a family, then my job as CEO was to protect that family.

But whatever labels the press wanted to put on our move did not really matter. Without any warning, I had unveiled our plan with exactly the spin I wanted. Even though I was jettisoning our big dividend our stock immediately popped on the news, creating precisely the kind of positive momentum I was seeking as we sought to complete the marketing of our loan. Just two days later, we held the main loan marketing meeting a block from our office at the W Hotel. What had started as a hipster boutique hotel felt like a peculiar location for a business meeting, but it was adequate for the task at hand. Only a few investors were in the room. Dozens of others dialed into the meeting. They had massive funds to invest in very small increments to create the highly diversified loan portfolios they sought, so a deal like ours did not merit a trip across town, let alone a flight from wherever they were based.

My one-hour presentation went extremely well. The logic of our plan – converting dividends into tax efficient interest payments – was understood by everyone. And the scale of my personal commitments – $10 million in cash plus swapping 90% of my salary for five years in exchange for even more stock – had exactly the impact I intended. In the day or two after this main meeting we held one-on-one sessions with potential large investors, but before those even started our deal was massively oversubscribed. As I had observed with our IPO and in many client transactions since then, in a successful deal there comes a tipping point when everyone wants in.

This phenomenon is the fear of missing out, and it existed in markets long before psychologists and marketers coined the acronym FOMO for its application to other aspects of life. In this case we took advantage of FOMO to upsize our deal to the $350 million we had originally hoped for and were able to bring down the interest rate we were paying to only 3.75 percentage points over the benchmark bank-lending rate, which was then very low by historic standards. After the tax benefits of interest expense our new loan would have an effective interest rate of less than 4%.

We had now succeeded in executing our creative plan, "flipping the script" to replace a group of investors who no longer seemed to like us much with another group that seemed to love us. The benefits we had hoped for became evident immediately. Our team was reenergized. We attracted new talent. Within just a few days of the recapitalization announcement, one of the top restructuring bankers in the business, then head of Rothschild's group, reached out through a mutual friend to discuss joining us. That led to a major expansion of our restructuring advisory team. And our stock, far from declining on news of a big dividend cut, more than doubled in the several months that followed.

Having successfully refueled our balance sheet with new capital from a novel source, it felt like we might just be ready to take off again.

CHAPTER SEVENTEEN

SUCCESSION

Sunrise, sunset,
Sunrise, sunset,
Swiftly fly the years[1]

– *Sheldon Harnick*, Fiddler on the Roof

The bounce in our stock price in response to the announcement of our recapitalization was gratifying, but that transaction was never intended to be a get-rich-quick scheme. I hoped instead it would be somewhat of a get-rich-slowly scheme for those who joined us long after our IPO, which had unexpectedly produced a windfall for early partners given the quick quadrupling of our initial share price. In simple terms, the recap was a clever arbitrage of markets: we used cheap financing from an aggressive new constituency (the leveraged loan market, which was supercharged by the expansionist, "free money" monetary policies of the Federal Reserve) to buy out an old constituency (the stock market) that had come, at least for the moment, to assign a low value to our business. Far more important than any short-term move in our stock price, the goal of the recap was to put into place an ownership structure that, without either the cost or the risk that normally accompanies a full-leveraged buyout, would take us about halfway back to the private firm we once were.

People both inside and outside the firm asked me, why not just buy *all* the stock and go completely private again? To me, the answer to that was obvious. In a full buyout I knew that, rather than acquire shares at about the current market price as we would do in our recap plan, we would have to pay a substantial acquisition premium over that price. In addition, I knew from my explorations the previous year that the debt needed to finance such a move would be far more costly than the very inexpensive funding we were utilizing as part of the recap.

On top of those differences in economics, there were advantages to retaining a public stock listing, including maintaining a liquid market into which employees could intermittently sell the shares granted as part of their compensation. Going fully private would inevitably lead to a search for some alternative way of providing such liquidity, or maybe even right back to a reprise of the IPO alternative.

Our transaction was crafted with the aim of getting employee ownership up to around 50% of the firm. That increased ownership stake was meant to further incentivize our senior team to perform well and thereby, with any luck, create equity value for that group as well as outside investors. That was the "carrot." The "stick" was an increased level of debt that would act as a further incentive to improve every aspect of our business. Individual performance at all levels of the firm would come under greater scrutiny. Lower-performing managing directors would need to be let go, or so starved of compensation that they would leave on their own volition. More junior resources would need to be reallocated from slower to more active areas. We would try to get smarter about all our operating expenses as well.

In sum, we would behave like private equity funds do after completing a leveraged buyout of a company. We aimed for both more revenue and higher profit margins, and then to let the power of a leveraged capital structure, fueled by cheap debt, amplify the benefits thereof in terms of higher earnings per share and an increased share price. In managing our private equity funds years earlier I had seen up close the extraordinary value creation that could develop if all went according to plan. Now we would try to work that same magic on our own firm.

Despite the many parallels between our plan and that of the typical leveraged buyout, there was one fundamental difference. While private equity-owned businesses operate predominantly in the private sphere, our continuing status as a public company meant that every move we made would take place under the watchful eye of stock market investors, equity research analysts and … the press.

Our stock price initially suggested that investors approved of our move, although we learned while structuring our transaction what a peculiar bunch our shareholders were. They were more like computer algorithms than the analytical human beings who dominated the stock market of yesteryear. The pressure created by our own very large buy order thus had much to do with the ascent of our share price. Index funds had to follow their own peculiar protocols and were therefore unable to sell until our stock's weighting in the various indexes was revised downward as we reduced the number of outstanding shares. In addition, our employees (with a few exceptions) were also not selling. Given the large proportion of our stock held by those two groups, there were few shares available for us to buy. And the algorithms used by the "quants" knew exactly what that meant and pushed our share price higher with more buy orders of their own.

Equity research analysts are supposed to be experts at determining the value of companies, but in reality they are more like TV sports analysts – better at explaining why one team won yesterday than predicting which one will win tomorrow. That had become even more clear since the revenue-generating potential of analysts was gutted by Eliot Spitzer's reforms, which drove small research firms out of business and led the big banks to dumb down their research product to reduce costs. So, in the face of the overwhelming buying pressure that drove our stock price higher, most analysts followed the cue of our investors and became more positive, or at least less negative, about our business.

But the press, especially *Bloomberg*, which continued to apply far greater resources to covering our industry than the traditional newspapers that reported on business, remained a thorn in our side as we executed our makeover. *Bloomberg* held tight to its doomsday thesis like a dog with a bone, writing three highly critical opinion pieces in the six months following our recapitalization announcement. Fair enough that, for no particular reason other than the randomness of timing when it comes to major M&A deals, the year in which we launched our plan (2017) had turned out to be a relatively weak year for the firm. That's precisely what enabled us to advantageously launch our stock buyback when our stock price sat near its all-time low. And also fair enough that an outsider would often not be able to tell the difference between a senior executive departure that was a beneficial cost-saving measure quietly engineered by us and one that represented the undesired loss of a major rainmaker. What was harder to forgive was the intensity of the journalistic scrutiny. That excessive attention seemed unfair, even though I recognized that we had benefited from such disproportionate coverage – then almost fawning in its positivity – for more than a decade following our founding. Live by the sword, die by the sword, I guess.

In early 2018 came a lengthy feature in *Bloomberg*'s monthly glossy magazine titled "Greenhill's Bok Seeks to Prove Critics Wrong about M&A Boutique."[2] This latest story contained no startling revelations. It noted that our firm "was the first of its kind to go public...blazing a path for others." It accurately pointed out that our market share had fallen as the number of competitors had substantially increased. It quoted disgruntled former employees "on the condition they not be named," alluding to "a series of missteps" in relation to undefined "strategy and recruitment" matters. But in the end nothing of substance was new in the article, and on the positive side it did point out that our recapitalization was something "that many on Wall Street found clever." In any event, I knew that *Bloomberg's* slick magazine was distributed primarily by free distribution to every user of a Bloomberg computer terminal. It was a magazine written about Wall Street for Wall Street. That meant our employees and competitors read it but very few clients. So I chose to focus on the substance of running our business rather than the background noise of its critical commentary.

That stoic attitude turned out to be the right stance as, interestingly, this latest story ended up being the last story in the series. *Bloomberg* soon sharply reduced its reporting on our firm and all our independent advisor competitors. Clearly someone on the management team of Mike Bloomberg, an extraordinary business builder as well as an outstanding three-time mayor of the city of New York, had finally figured out that his team was devoting a disproportionate share of resources to this small segment of Wall Street.

While the last of the hostile *Bloomberg* stories seemed to have little impact in the face of a rising share price and increasing momentum in our business, one important reader did take notice of the one-sided commentary. That reader was one of my oldest colleagues, James Lupton. The series of stories prompted him to place a call to Bob Greenhill and to write to our recently appointed board member and former colleague from his era, John Liu.[3]

His objective was my removal from the leadership of our firm.

By then James was only a very part-time member of our team, bearing the honorific "senior advisor" title to go along with his similarly honorific membership in England's House of Lords. Regardless, his intentions were noble even if his timing and approach were both questionable. And that was not too surprising given his long track record of being a passionate colleague capable of occasionally launching a provocative electronic missive.

While such emails were somewhat disconcerting when he first joined us in the late 1990s, over time we learned to take them in stride, knowing that he always meant well. In this case I knew that one catalyst for James's outreach, on top of the *Bloomberg* article, was his recent appointment to a board role at one of England's oldest and largest financial institutions, Lloyds Bank. He clearly saw that as a prestigious appointment, just as he had years earlier when appointed treasurer of the UK's Conservative Party and then later as a member of the House of Lords.

In a sign of his enthusiasm for this newest role he wrote to Liu with fervent admiration for the "meticulous succession planning" that was regularly undertaken at Lloyds. Never mind that Lloyds had nearly failed in the financial crisis only a decade earlier, and that its share price was still about 90% below its peak level from way back in 1999. And never mind that Lloyds, unlike Greenhill, was a heavily regulated business with hundreds of times the employees of our firm, making a large bureaucracy with ongoing detailed planning of all kinds appropriate.

Putting aside the substantive merits of his plea, the manner of James's approach was peculiar. He began with a phone call to Bob, "in his capacity as Chairman of the Board," as he wrote to Liu later that day. Bob was the legendary founder of our business and once had the energy of a force of nature, but in recent years his role had faded considerably. He was 81, had been slowed by some health challenges the previous year and had just lost his wife of 59 years following her long battle with Alzheimer's disease. Gayle had managed all aspects of Bob's life outside of work, until her prolonged and debilitating illness prompted him to devote nearly all his energies to her care. Understandably, he had been looking listless and a bit lost since Gayle's demise, an event from which it seemed he would likely never really recover.

The timing of James's outreach was also curious. Our recap plan, ironically enough, had been inspired by a client to whom James had introduced me. In the face of less than satisfactory recent business performance, it was my personal credibility with Goldman Sachs and the credit rating agencies, my personal pitch to leveraged loan investors and my symbolically critical $10 million personal investment that had gotten that done. James had an old-fashioned British dislike of leverage, and I heard he had sold all his remaining shares, no longer then a significant holding, upon announcement of the deal. But the general reaction of our shareholders had been very positive, as indicated by our rising share price. Our board thought I had pulled off a Houdini act. Steve Goldstone said admiringly that the recap was the second-best idea of my entire career, after that of our 2004 IPO. But even if the board had felt I was completely incompetent, removing me then would have seemed strange to numerous constituencies at best and prompted lawsuits at worst – claims based on a failure to disclose such an important management change at a time when the firm was placing new debt securities with investors.

While the tone of James's communication was shrill, suggesting the firm was "dangerously poised to fail" and claiming that the board "may only have a few weeks left" to act, his words fell on deaf ears. Bob had never really acted as a traditional board chairman, and at this stage of his life he was not looking to take on more responsibility of any kind. Furthermore, he and I had never had a meaningful disagreement on any management issue. So he immediately informed me of James's call, a conversation that clearly had pained him given that he had always been uncomfortable with internal conflict. Bob told me he would inform the board of Lupton's approach but be fully supportive of me. John Liu, who avoided a face-to-face meeting when James was in New York on business unrelated to our firm, was likewise supportive.

As a member of the firm's inner circle of corporate governance, John had a lot more facts to work with than James did. He knew that I was far from clinging on to the CEO role. Unlike the prototypical public company CEO, I had little economic interest in staying on. I had put much more money into the firm than I had taken out in the preceding few years. In fact, I had not asked the board for a cash bonus in nearly a decade, choosing to be paid in stock so that more cash compensation could be allocated to others. On top of that, I had recently traded the bulk of my base salary for even more stock, which would be forfeited if we failed to successfully repay the debt that we had taken on for our recapitalization plan.

I was not hanging onto my leadership role for reasons of ego either. In the years since my presumptive successor went down in an airplane I had initiated, with the appropriate board support, numerous discussions with potential successors, potential merger partners, even occasionally potential acquirers. This was all appropriately unbeknown to James and others outside the firm's leadership. John knew that what drove me was a stubborn form of idealism – I had joined the firm with dream as to what it might become in terms of quality, culture and prestige. The dream had in many ways come true, and it was of paramount importance to me that this dream have a happy ending, in contrast to the outcome for so many other Wall Street firms and their leaders over the course of history.

Despite the last gasp of negative noises from the press and the related friendly fire emanating from the House of Lords, 2018 turned out to be an outstanding year for the firm. We announced a string of important transactions for clients throughout the year. We helped retail giant Walmart put in place a new credit card program with the bank Capital One and advised on a $6 billion merger for the American engineering firm McDermott International, a $5 billion sale of the British gaming company Ladbrokes and a $600 million acquisition of a German business for leading American industrial firm Emerson. That last deal disproved *The Wall Street Journal's* unsubstantiated claim that we had lost Emerson as a client. Most noteworthy for a generally Calvinist type like me was our work advising Canadian cannabis company Canopy Growth on a $5 billion investment from the American drinks company Constellation Brands.

We ended the year with $352 million in total revenue, the second-best result in our history. In achieving that outcome, we set a number of firm records: highest number of fee-paying clients ever, highest number of transaction announcements and so on. At the same time, we also made huge progress on implementing our recapitalization plan. Buying back shares on the scale we were seeking is technically very difficult, simply because of the limited availability of shares for sale in the market and the fact that liquidity declines with each share that is purchased and thereby removed from the market. Nonetheless by year end we had managed to acquire almost 90% of the total shares we had targeted.

Following year end, rather than convening our usual global partners meeting in New York in January, I began the new year with a whirlwind tour of many of our offices – Chicago, London, Madrid, Toronto, Dallas, Houston and San Francisco. Our teams everywhere seemed reenergized by the recapitalization plan and the positive market reaction it had prompted.

Yet despite all our accomplishments Lord Lupton was directionally correct, in substance if not in style, that leadership succession was an appropriate topic for consideration. In reality, nothing lasts forever, and so succession should be an ongoing concern for any organization. Indeed, little did I realize that I would be at the center of several different successions over the course of the upcoming year. All but one would be difficult – each in its own way. But perhaps that difficulty should not have been a surprise.

From what I have seen in my career, well-conceived and executed successions are almost mythical in their rarity. One can aim for "meticulous succession planning" like Lloyds Bank and other major companies do but, as the old Yiddish saying goes, "Man plans, and God laughs." Most often, a sudden shift in economic or market conditions, merger, business setback, scandal, some sort of conflict at board or management level, illness or death, or any one of innumerable other forms of major or minor crisis upend orderly plans. Triggered by one of those unexpected events, the moment of succession often comes like a thief in the night, and a carefully crafted plan lying in the desk drawer often turns out to be not quite right for that particular moment.

My close observation of numerous successions at my alma mater Morgan Stanley illustrated the challenges well. Following a brief period of transitional leadership by the patrician Parker Gilbert, the succession to shared control between Dick Fisher and Bob Greenhill clearly did not work. The later pivot toward John Mack in preparation for the next succession cost the firm Bob Greenhill and considerable other talent, yet Mack's succession of Fisher was never even consummated. Instead it was disrupted by a merger with Dean Witter, after which its leader, Phil Purcell, succeeded Fisher. But Purcell was the wrong man for the times and represented too great a deviation from the firm's historic culture. Deep internal conflicts developed, which prompted the return of long-retired Morgan Stanley elders to form the Group of Eight and successfully push for Purcell's ouster. That group had no intention of bringing back John Mack as his replacement, but as they advanced closer to success they realized that Mack was the only plausible candidate, and he finally got the job he had first sought years earlier.

Mack's aggressive style would likely have been perfect for the bull market of the previous few years, but he was clearly the wrong man for the period leading up to the greatest financial crisis in nearly a century. Indeed, under his leadership the firm came perilously close to following Lehman Brothers into bankruptcy. It was saved only by a big investment from a Japanese bank and the decision by the US government to provide the firm access to cheap and plentiful Federal Reserve funding by suddenly making it a regulated bank – a status it would have seen as completely unworkable for its entire prior history. In a final irony, the firm's successful resurrection was completed following Mack's retirement by a former consultant who was a Purcell protégé who engineered the further expansion of its retail brokerage operation by adding Smith Barney and later E-Trade to Dean

Witter. All of that was in line with the strategy that Phil Purcell had advocated.

Succession missteps could be seen as a matter of the wrong man for the job, but more often it is a matter of the wrong time for that man (or woman, in the modern era).

It would be easy to think that Morgan Stanley was unique, or that Wall Street is a uniquely fractious place given the tumultuous histories of leadership at most of Morgan Stanley's peers. While there is likely some truth to both notions, corroborating case studies for the challenges inherent in smooth succession are everywhere. For example, General Electric's leader Jack Welch was undoubtedly the most admired American business leader of the first decades of my career, and his board's methodical succession planning was regularly spoken of in a reverent tone by a wide variety of executives, academics and journalists. Yet the board ended up making a disastrous choice, passing over several executives who ended up successfully leading other major companies in favor of a man whose failed leadership ultimately resulted in the dismantling of that once-proud industrial colossus.[4] Such stories are commonplace. Indeed, the concept of fractious corporate successions prompted the creation of a popular long-running HBO television show named simply *Succession*.[5]

For me, the first succession to focus on that year related to the continuing evolution of our firm's leadership. Initially, Bob Greenhill wanted to hold the key leadership titles, even though his status as founder and largest shareholder with his name on both the proverbial door and on all our business cards made any title superfluous. His holding those titles for an extended period also made sense for our team and our various external constituencies. Later, in 2007, when every possible thing about our business was going well, our board and I nudged him to accept the first step in management transition, giving up the CEO role. That torch was thus passed almost without notice, which is exactly what we had hoped.

Now, as Bob's activity at the firm had wound down further, it was time for another nudge, to move him to emeritus status, with the chairman title to be added to my CEO designation just as it originally had been to his. In governance terms, the move was long overdue, as Bob had always held formal board meetings in disdain as mere bureaucracy and typically said only a few words at those gatherings. Even at our board dinners, for years held in an upstairs room at the 21 Club the evening before quarterly board meetings, he would depart for his Greenwich home early, and we usually left the most substantive discussions for after his exit.

The board and I considered moving Bob out of the chair role at the 2018 annual meeting, at which time it again appeared that – as in 2007 – every possible thing about our business was going well. Yet there is a healthy fear of any kind of leadership change that takes place in the public realm. Particularly so with respect to a man whom, despite decades of interaction, none of us felt like we knew on a truly personal level. As Bob's rival John Mack later wrote in his autobiography, acknowledging the need to plan for one's own succession "is an existential acknowledgement that [one] will not always be present."[6] That's not easy for anyone.

Uncertain how Bob would react to such intimations of his mortality, we decided instead to be patient and let 2018's annual meeting that spring be the last at which he would stand for election as chair. Later that year, when that delicate conversation between a couple of directors and Bob finally took place, it went well. He was finally ready.

A second succession that year took place in the "not-for-profit" world. One would expect that nonprofit boards of trustees would be less drama-prone than corporate boards. However, that was not my experience. Corporate boards are generally very carefully managed. There are reasonably clear parameters as to what makes a good board member, candidates are carefully vetted before being appointed, there are usually clear retirement ages, and – although this move is not common – board members can be quietly dropped from the list nominated for reelection at any annual shareholders meeting. Corporate boards are also relatively small, meaning they are of a manageable size.

Nonprofit boards, by contrast, tend to be very large, simply because nearly every member is an actual or prospective major donor to the organization. Every quality organization seeks to maintain appropriate standards for its board, but the criteria can be vague. Even for the largest and most prestigious organizations, simply a significant level of financial support – and that standard isn't even always very high – can land one a place on a board. Finally, exiting a board member, even at a reasonable retirement age, is difficult for organizations that cannot afford to risk losing even one meaningful supporter.

My first experience with a successful nonprofit thrown off course by its own board occurred several years earlier in relation to a small, rural, summer theater company based not far from our farm. I wasn't even a member of that board, but my wife was, and we had been the organization's largest financial supporters. From our perspective, everything at the theater was going along swimmingly, meaning that the organization was providing fine local entertainment and education while keeping its head slightly above water each year financially. Realistically, that is how success is defined in the theater "business."

Over time a small board faction, and ultimately the board leadership, came to the view that what was good could be made even better. So it booted out a beloved longtime artistic director who was well-known in the local community in favor of what seemed like a more exciting prospect from afar. The new fellow may indeed have been brilliant, but he was unknown to, and never really tried to engage with, the local community in a meaningful way. Financial support from those close to the former artistic director, including for a lengthy period from my wife and me, fell away. To top it all off, not many years later the new fellow received a more alluring opportunity to work his magic elsewhere and resigned, forcing the board to find another new leader. Multiple iterations of leadership played out in the ensuing years.

Prep for Prep provided yet another unfortunate case study of challenging board dynamics among nonprofits. In my decade chairing that entity's board, the view from around the board table was that Prep ran like a proverbial Swiss watch. Each year it continued to find gifted young people of color to enter the program, prepared them for success at the top private schools in New York and throughout the northeast, and ultimately sent them off to leading universities and then successful careers. Over time, many reached the pinnacle of their professions in business, law, education and other fields.

Because the schools to which Prep sent kids provided the necessary scholarship money to cover tuition and related costs, we only needed to raise about $10 million a year to fund the intensive program necessary to prepare students for those very challenging schools. But there was no natural constituency from which to raise such funds – no wealthy alumni or parents like those who funded New York's elite private schools or Ivy League universities. We fretted every year about how we would hit our goal. Fortunately, my long-ago law firm boss Marty Lipton and a compatriot of his from the private equity world developed a broad funding base from successful Wall Streeters, one my generation of leadership had built on. We typically not only achieved our annual goal but exceeded it, enabling us over time to accumulate a modest endowment in preparation for whatever rainy days the organization might someday encounter.

Yet despite the joy brought about by repeated inspirational stories of poor kids from the Bronx finding their way to the Ivy League and beyond, a degree of dissension developed within Prep's board of trustees. It was only a tiny bit of discord at first, but like a pebble in one's shoe it caused increasing discomfort. Indeed even one dissident board member can be enough to wreak havoc.

In the corporate world, boards almost always act in unanimity. Apart from cases where an activist investor has forced his way onto a board by seeking election with a stated intention of forcing change, I had seen only one case in thirty-plus years where dissension on a public company board became widely known because of a board vote that lacked unanimity. That was in the case of my Houston-based energy client Dynegy. Dynegy was an "independent power producer," meaning it generated electricity without having the captive client base of the large, regulated utilities to which most Americans pay their monthly electricity bills.

Without that reliable client base, Dynegy's business was highly volatile, driven largely by movements in the price of the natural gas that its plants used to generate power. Thus after years of ups and downs as a public company, in one case to the point that a bankruptcy filing was drafted shortly after its crosstown competitor Enron collapsed, the board concluded that it made sense to take the company private. So, following an auction process, in 2010 I helped Dynegy put in place an agreement with the private equity giant Blackstone to do just that. The company had been valued at much higher levels at various points, but given all the circumstances (including the fact that it was the best bid received following a broad auction) we advised that this was a deal well worth pursuing.

The Dynegy board agreed with our advice, with one stubborn exception. One Dynegy director simply had a much more positive view of the company's future and therefore refused to go along with the board consensus as collegial directors almost always do. Reluctantly, the board proceeded with the Blackstone deal anyway. But that one highly unusual negative vote, which under applicable securities law needed to be publicly disclosed, caught the eye of powerful activist investor Carl Icahn, whom I first came across way back in my time as a lawyer at Wachtell Lipton.

Icahn figured something fishy must be up if the board could not get to consensus, simply because of how extraordinary that scenario was. He virulently opposed our deal, at one point conveying to Dynegy's

CEO and me, as we sat in his spacious conference room overlooking Central Park that was decorated with framed magazine covers featuring his face, his simplistic theory that, "if [Blackstone founder and CEO] Steve Schwarzman thinks it's worth $4.50, it must be worth more." Icahn and some smaller hedge funds with which he became aligned ultimately succeeded in blocking the deal, and the company ended up in bankruptcy within a year, much to the detriment of Icahn and everyone he prevented from taking the Blackstone deal. That's exactly how dangerous dissent in a board room can be.

At Prep we had a similar situation. As a whole, the board was more than content. Indeed, most of the board was completely unaware of any dissension within its ranks. And as in the case at Dynegy, the source of the dissident trustee's unhappiness was not easy to grasp. Despite all the organization's continuing success, his vague sense was that the current executive leadership had been in place too long. He felt leadership had paid too much attention to Prep's patrons and to the schools supporting the organization and too little to the alumni who had graduated from the program over the years and were rapidly growing in both number and prominence.

Race is inevitably a difficult topic to discuss, even among a group consisting entirely of white people (which all involved in this debate were), but one source of the trustee's discontent was his view that an organization that serves people of color ought to have a leader who is likewise of color. The current, longtime CEO was married to a black man and had mixed race children but was herself white.

As chair, I agreed wholeheartedly with the objective of installing leadership that looked like Prep's student beneficiaries. There was no doubt in my mind that the next leader of the organization should be, and would be, of color. But I did not want to rush into a leadership change that would push out a proven and capable CEO at a time when the organization felt, as such institutions often do, somewhat fragile.

I strained to keep the dissension on the board quiet, to avoid distracting the incumbent CEO from her challenging job. Equally, I wanted to avoid scaring away any of our key donors, who each year gave generously thinking that the organization was performing well and in a harmonious manner. Accordingly, I sought to mollify the trustee in question through patient listening and a commitment to future change. Even on the evening of our huge annual celebratory event, the "Lilac Ball" held in midtown Manhattan's largest banquet space, a couple key board colleagues and I met beforehand with the disgruntled trustee in a side room at the hotel, pleading for patience and peace before exiting with smiles on our faces to greet the thousand patrons who had gathered for the dinner.

Further complicating the planning for management succession at Prep was a separate succession looming on the horizon – this one relating to my possible selection as the next chair of the University of Pennsylvania's board of trustees. For me, that appointment would be both a great honor and the culmination of a lifetime of involvement at Penn, where I had earned three degrees, met my wife, sent both my children and been a trustee for over a decade. As that prospect began to seem like a real possibility I realized that there was no way I could fulfill that demanding role plus my "day job" running Greenhill while also continuing as chair of Prep (which coincidentally had over the years sent more of its graduates to Penn than almost any other university in the country). So in order to be ready for the possibility of chairing Penn's board I began to plan my own succession at Prep. As part of that preparation I wanted to have a new CEO in place at Prep before my time there was finished.

There was one last succession process – the one most primal in nature – that came into play for me just as 2018 ended. I had always been terrible at remembering birthdays. I never attached particular importance to my own, and regrettably failed to do so with others (even my wife) as well. But my father's birthdate, December 20, became impossible to forget once Jeff

Buckalew's plane went down on what was my dad's 73rd birthday. So that day I placed a call to my parents' Grand Rapids home even though I knew I would see my dad in person shortly. He and my mother were already packed for their annual post-Christmas sojourn to the small Palm Beach condominium we had made available to them for seasonal visits after Roxanne and I upgraded from there to a larger family home a few miles away.

The tone of the call was palpably different than usual. He had always been among the most contented men I had ever known. Furthermore, he had been remarkably healthy apart from a long-running battle with rheumatoid arthritis and, in any event, was definitely not a complainer. Yet, his strained voice quickly betrayed his discomfort. He said his stomach had been bothering him, and that he was heading to his doctor the next day to see if he could get something to help with that.

At that doctor visit he learned that his aching stomach signaled a pernicious cancer that had quietly spread to virtually every organ in his body. The disease's broad reach created some confusion as to its origin – at first it was identified as pancreatic cancer, but later the diagnosis was changed to lung cancer of the small cell carcinoma variety. Either way, the prognosis was dire. Although we would of course pursue all the obvious steps – chemotherapy, radiation and so on, the oncologist he had just met was clear that my dad was unlikely to have even one more year. Yet even in the face of the type of news that nobody is ever prepared for he retained his easygoing, uncomplaining manner. Indeed, his primary concern was the impending end of his ongoing role as companion and healthcare aide to my slightly younger brother and only sibling, who himself was in the eighth year of a battle with a less aggressive, but no less stubborn, form of cancer.

The impending succession of the patriarch of our little family made the several other successions in which I was engaged pale, at least to some extent, into insignificance.

CHAPTER EIGHTEEN

"WE'RE GONNA DIE"

Good health is the most important thing.
More than success, more than money, more than power.[1]
– *Francis Ford Coppola and Mario Puzo,* The Godfather II

In early 2020, as Greenhill began its twenty-fifth year in business, mortality was on my mind. A few months earlier my father had passed away at 81, having persevered for eight fairly satisfying months following his out-of-the-blue cancer diagnosis. He was fortunate to be granted the time needed to say a proper goodbye.

Not knowing exactly when he would pass, over those months my family and I made intermittent trips in various configurations back to Grand Rapids to be with him. In what turned out to be the final time we said goodbye Roxanne and I were departing on a flight from there to Lexington, Kentucky. We were going to watch our daughter Jane compete in the national championships for eventing, a three-day equestrian competition that involved dressage as well as numerous challenging (sometimes, to a father, frightening) jumps, both on a cross-country course and in a stadium. He was at peace when we parted, ready for whenever his time on Earth might finally come to an end. And not long after that it did.

Even unto death he exemplified the virtues that he had always held highest – faith, devotion to family, quiet satisfaction with his lot in life, equanimity in the face of adversity and optimism. An outside observer might think that, based on the lives he and I led, we had little in common. But undoubtedly he, along with his mother Katherine, a woman who experienced both the Great Depression and the Dust Bowl growing up on a small farm in South Dakota and had passed away only the prior year at age 101, were the primary sources of my own unflinching optimism.

Not long after my father's demise, Bob Greenhill, another confirmed optimist who was born just two years before him, abruptly emptied his office in our New York headquarters, sold his longtime family home in Greenwich and relocated to his place in Palm Beach. From there he planned to dial into our quarterly board meetings for one final year.

With his peer group and nearly all his historic clients long since retired, it had been at least a few years since Bob had been a meaningful contributor to our business. So his exit was not an economic loss to the firm, nor was it much of a personal loss for our team. Given the reclusive manner that had always belied his larger-than-life public persona, Bob did not have any relationship at all with most of our partners, let alone staff, by the time he departed. There was no celebratory farewell dinner, and he left quite literally without saying goodbye, using his old friend and personal financial advisor, the father of one of my long-ago Morgan Stanley colleagues who now lived in my Manhattan apartment building, to work out the details of his exit with me.

Still, Bob had continued to be a familiar albeit quiet presence in our office long after his operating role had wound down, coming in early most days for a few hours before beating the traffic back to Greenwich. Thus the sudden disappearance of this towering founding figure marked a poignant moment in our firm's history and in my life.

For many years Bob had defied the aging process, literally adhering to the philosophy inherent in his trademark phrase, "keep moving." He was the epitome of the swashbuckling dealmaker – an action hero flying his nearly supersonic plane across continents and oceans to advise clients on the greatest feats many of them would ever attempt. Nearly every day that he was in our office his personal trainer put him through a rigorous work-out in our in-house gym. Bob once told me that the key to successful aging was to continually ratchet up, rather than scale back, the intensity of one's exercise regime as the years went on. Indeed, that approach worked for him for a long time.

Only three years earlier he had eagerly insisted that he make the same new $10 million equity investment into the firm that I was making as part of our recapitalization plan. He even pressed our board (unsuccessfully) to give him the same five-year compensation deal, trading future salary for Greenhill stock, that it was giving me in alignment with the term of the substantial loan we were taking on as part of that plan. Clearly the board sensed then that there were not five years left on the clock in terms of Bob's connection to our business.

Time catches up with all of us. Two years earlier, Gayle, on whom Bob had so heavily relied, had died. The one and only truly personal conversation that Bob and I had in our entire twenty-three-year relationship came shortly before he moved out, when he spoke of his loneliness without her. That unguarded and surprisingly emotional moment was shocking to me given that he had never once acknowledged to me, nor even to some people he had known decades longer than me, that Gayle was not well, let alone the seriousness of her illness.

Around the time she passed he had also failed to get his pilot's license renewed following his annual weeklong training trip. If there was a love in Bob's life besides Gayle, it was his Citation X. Some elderly folks grumble when the car keys are finally taken away – what Bob lost was the ability to fly himself from New York to the West Coast or London on a whim, and in just a few hours. The ability to make such trips was central to his self-image and critical to a psyche characterized by an inability to remain in any one place for long. Add to those blows the inevitable physical ailments and medical repair work that come with later age, plus – I sensed – some specific health-related catalyst the details of which I did not know, and it was no surprise that Bob was finally, and suddenly, ready for retirement.

Following his practice of always being in a rush to close whatever the deal of the day was, Bob moved swiftly from his conceptual decision to both a sold Greenwich homestead and a completely empty Park Avenue office. His last official act (other than to dial into a few more quarterly board calls, on which he would rarely utter even a single word of greeting) was to appear at the firm's annual holiday party, held as usual in one of the ornate meeting rooms in the New York Public Library's landmark main building on Fifth Avenue and Forty-Second Street – a place named for the Blackstone founder whose investment prowess had prompted Carl Icahn to block my Dynegy deal. Accompanying Bob as he entered was a younger fellow I had not seen before – he reminded me of the kind of aide who had stood quietly alongside Gayle at such events for a few years before she stopped attending completely.

Early in the evening, at his customary time, Bob made his familiar speech of less than one-minute duration. As always, he held notecards with his script written out in large print. The words, and indeed the notecards on which they were printed, had been essentially unchanged for years. And anyone there other than our newest employees could have recited the speech from memory – the story of the secretary, the driver, Gayle hanging pictures and our getting lucky.

Rather than quietly let his brief speech stand and allowing everyone to return quickly to cocktail hour chatter, this time I added my own speech, as I was urged to do by both my wife Roxanne and my assistant Maureen, praising Bob for all he had accomplished at our firm. Given the stealth manner in which he was exiting, almost nobody in that room had any idea this would likely be the last time they would lay eyes on Bob. Nonetheless, I felt compelled to try to make that moment somewhat memorable for him, if not for them. Given his inscrutable nature, I have no idea whether he recognized or cared what I was doing.

As a kind of lovely farewell gesture to New York, the city where he had earned a billion dollar fortune, Bob made a donation to the Museum of Modern Art (MOMA), which it described as a "monumental gift of photographs from the Gayle Greenhill Collection."[2] The gift, uncharacteristically generous for a man whom I had seen show little interest in philanthropy other than to his and his three children's Harvard Business School alma mater, comprised of 300 works by 103 photographers. Gayle had always brought out the best in Bob.

In its announcement of the gift MOMA highlighted the themes we had tried to portray through the art in our offices, noting that Bob and Gayle "had a keen interest in exploration, collecting extensively in the area of early aviation." The Steichen photographs from World War II and many of the other pieces that hung in our New York conference rooms were part of the gift, although not to be removed until we made our planned office move across midtown nearly a year later. Importantly, while the originals documenting the Scott expedition to Antarctica were included in the gift, the copy prints hanging in our New York and other offices would remain with the firm.

Only weeks after Bob decamped to Palm Beach, to a home not more than a couple golf shots from my own (if you could clear the palm trees and a water hazard known as the Intracoastal Waterway), news of a life-threatening virus out of China began to appear. As with past crises that our firm had encountered, this one was completely unexpected by all but a very few. One exception, Microsoft founder and leading global philanthropist Bill Gates, had warned of it with great clarity and specificity in his 2015 *TED Talk* aptly titled, "The next outbreak? We're not ready."[3]

When the virus appeared on our shores its significance was initially unrecognized by our political leaders and to some degree even by scientists. But the speed with which the situation then evolved, both generally and for our business, was such that a detailed account may be illuminating.

The World Health Organization (WHO) declared a "public health emergency of international concern" on January 30. But based on historical precedents, I and the vast majority of other American business leaders paid this little attention. Indeed, in the week thereafter we announced the firm's year-end financial results without any reference to the news, and Roxanne and I attended three Broadway plays. There seemed no need for alarm – during our firm's history the WHO had made similar declarations regarding SARS in 2002, H1N1 influenza in 2009, Ebola in 2014 and Zika in 2015.

While I had paid cursory attention to the news flow on each of those, I vaguely remembered the initially frightening forecasts for each. None ultimately had consequences that were nearly as significant as those first feared. Indeed, I never participated in a single conversation internally with colleagues nor externally with clients or investors regarding the potential business impact from any of those health crises. Most tellingly, in each case, domestic and international travel for our team and our clients continued unabated, with no consideration of limiting that in any way. The only changed behavior of any kind that I could recall was that, given the risk to unborn children, child-bearing aged women within families of some friends chose to avoid vacationing for some time in tropical climates where Zika might possibly be carried by mosquitos. But even that response of trivial inconvenience faded fairly quickly.

Over the last two days in February I attended a Penn board of trustees meeting in Philadelphia, not yet as chair of that group. Several dozen current and emeritus trustees were there. Given the nature of those appointed to such roles, most were senior executives in major businesses and the others mostly retirees from such positions, in many cases well-advanced in age. In the various formal meetings and related social events there was some talk of the virus but not much. Scheduled activities carried on as usual. Outside, the campus buzzed with activity, as is typical that time of year. Spring break was about to start, and students including my sophomore daughter Jane planned soon to leave and then return a week later as usual. Her plan was to meet my wife and me at our home in Palm Beach.

Just two days later, on Sunday March 1, the first case of the new coronavirus that became known as COVID-19 was reported in New York. Still my partners and I, along with our clients and our competitors, paid little attention. New York Governor Andrew Cuomo's statement announcing that infection was reassuring, stating that "the general risk remain[ed] low in New York."[4] Accordingly, given an unusually full social calendar, on five of the next six evenings Roxanne and I attended events involving several hundred people each.

On Monday it was the annual gala for Roundabout Theater, where she had become a board member some years after I turned down my board colleague Steve Goldstone's request that I take on such a role for fear that the theater group might end up in financial distress. Just how far New York's theaters had rebounded from that financial crisis era conversation was clear that night. There was not an empty seat in midtown Manhattan's Ziegfeld Ballroom for what had become one of the most entertaining annual New York charity events. That year's special entertainment was Cyndi Lauper, of "Girls Just Want to Have Fun" fame, and the related fund-raising auction was even more raucous than usual. The attendees being predominantly theater people, there was plenty of hugging and kissing throughout the evening. An after-party followed at a crowded nearby nightclub. Alan Cumming, the prominent stage and screen actor who was a devoted supporter of the theater, was the master of ceremonies.

The next evening was another theater outing – this time to see a new play called *We're Gonna Die* at Second Stage Theater Company, an off-Broadway venue. At the time the play's title seemed neither noteworthy nor ironic. The evening after that we were in yet another jammed Broadway theater, this time with our son and his longtime girlfriend (and future wife) to see *Girl from the North Country*, the hit musical based on the work of Bob Dylan, which we had first seen at the Public Theater downtown. Going to the theater three nights in one week was not particularly unusual for us, except in summer, when Roxanne generally stayed at our farm.

Later that week, in Palm Beach where we planned to meet Jane, we were hosted by some new friends at the annual Preservation Foundation dinner dance, again without an empty seat in sight. Given the location, there were numerous octogenarians in attendance, including US Secretary of Commerce Wilbur Ross and Retired Army General, Heisman Trophy winner and Rhodes Scholar Pete Dawkins. He and I had briefly sat together on the Iridium board of directors following its acquisition by our SPAC. During an extended cocktail hour before dinner people shook hands as one normally would, although by that time often while making a light-hearted joke regarding the virus. The power of that virus was still unknown, or at least unappreciated.

A day earlier, before I flew south for that event, we had held a Greenhill board meeting to approve the mailing of materials for our upcoming annual shareholder meeting. While there was some generally skeptical chatter about how serious the virus threat was, one director had a more ominous point of view. John Liu, who joined our board years after having been one of the firm's earliest employees and then its first chief financial officer as a public company, predicted that within days both schools and businesses would be shut down in New York and perhaps beyond. The rest of the group marveled at his bold statement, which he uttered with an air of quiet confidence, but none disputed him given that John is not known for either rash statements or hyperbole.

The very next day the governor of New York declared a state of emergency, although the import of even that in terms of day-to-day activities was initially unclear. Given the wisdom of crowds, markets have a way of detecting and reacting to risk well before most individuals do. Thus, a few days later on Monday, March 9, world oil prices – often indicative of the outlook for economic activity – collapsed by nearly one third.

Two days later, less than a week after the Greenhill board had met, I was in Houston for a day of client meetings. That same day the WHO declared a global pandemic and German Chancellor Angela Merkel became the first world leader to sound an alarm loudly, stating bluntly that 60–70% of all Germans would ultimately become infected. *The New York Times* noted that the estimate by this "no-nonsense" leader was "probably a worst-case scenario, though not wildly out of line with those of experts outside Germany."[5] At this point I first felt some degree of personal concern. Nonetheless, at a large client lunch meeting at Houston's Coronado Club, a favorite of energy sector movers and shakers, I shook each hand that was extended to me before we sat down for lunch. This was Texas, and it would have felt rude not to do so. Yet as we were sitting down to eat I slipped out of the room to wash my hands in the men's room – a step I would not normally take in the brief transition between drinks (in this case, iced tea, given it was a lunchtime event) and sitting down to a meal with clients.

Later that afternoon I flew out of an eerily quiet Houston airport to Palm Beach. My original plan had been to stay there for a four-day weekend at the tail end of Jane's spring break, but by then it was clear that I would be there much longer – admittedly, this was not initially a distressing revelation given the balmy weather in south Florida that time of year. While in flight I wrote the first of what would be many email notes relating to the virus, addressed to either all seventy-some Greenhill partners globally or to our full 400-person employee group. In my regular monthly business update emailed to partners two weeks earlier I had made a brief first reference to the coronavirus, noting that we were monitoring developments but still mostly working and traveling as normal, albeit avoiding international travel.

The only discernible impact of the virus up to that point had been in relation to market activity. The US stock market had been at an all-time high as recently as a month before, but by this point had begun what would become the steepest descent in history. Our stock, which had recently risen above $20 per share following a strong 2019 year-end earnings announcement, had already fallen by more than half. For the first time ever, it was in single digits.

As for deal activity, I knew firsthand that the downward spiraling market volatility was wreaking havoc. We were in the final stages of the negotiation of a large media transaction on which I was playing a lead advisory role, the potential sale of my longtime client TEGNA. Having sold or spun off the various newspaper and digital media assets of the old Gannett, the renamed TEGNA was now purely a television broadcasting business. Now facing some of the same competitive pressures that newspapers, radio and other forms of "old media" had earlier suffered, the broadcasting industry was rapidly consolidating into fewer, larger players better able to compete against newer forms of media, represented by names like Facebook, Google and Netflix. We were close to selling TEGNA to one of two enthusiastic bidders when our progress suddenly began to slow. Other deals on which my partners were advising were being impacted similarly.

At my end of February update, written just before the week packed with crowded social activities, I had stated hopefully that I believed we as a firm were "reasonably well positioned for most scenarios" – the word "most" being carefully chosen.[6] Only two weeks later, as I typed that first special COVID-focused note en route to Palm Beach from Houston, it was becoming clear that the scenario heading our way might prove to be extreme. Most of all there was uncertainty, as a blizzard of confusing data led to continually evolving commentary from scientists and equally rapidly changing proclamations from government officials at all levels. Given the political posturing that soon began to color the recommendations of scientists, in private conversations with friends I said I would make only one prediction with regard to the pandemic, which I was certain would prove accurate: in the end everyone would say "I told you so."

To our Greenhill team I was more serious, writing that our firm had "seen a veritable flock of black swans – a once-in-a-century financial crisis, [the British vote to leave the European Union known as] Brexit, and now a virus ha[d] prompted a panic like none of us have ever seen."[7] But I also noted that "the virus will at some point pass," and predicted that "the amount of [government] stimulus applied to revive the economy and markets will be extraordinary." Trying to provide encouragement, I wrote from the heart that "I find myself the most motivated, the most energized, the most committed to our success, in times like these."

Notwithstanding my attempts to calm the waters within Greenhill, on my first day in Palm Beach I heard that panic was setting in back at our Manhattan headquarters. That morning Mayor Bill de Blasio, the somewhat hapless successor to three-term mayor Mike Bloomberg and a man unlikely to engender confidence even in the best of times, declared a state of emergency for the City of New York. He said in a CNBC television interview that day that the prior night "it just seemed [like] the world turned upside down in the course of a few hours."[8] What exactly a "state of emergency" for the city meant was not immediately clear, although the mayor explained that he now had the authority to take steps like establishing curfews and shutting down mass transit. Later that day one of our young analysts told my assistant Maureen that a rumor was circulating that the bridges and tunnels might soon be closed, trapping Manhattanites in the city for an indeterminate period. News of that possibility, which in fact never materialized, sent our junior team into a frenzy of packing. Many bolted to parental homes or other perceived safe havens across America.

A few days later I dialed into an unusual Sunday night call hosted by Goldman Sachs, for what was undoubtedly an enormous number of its private wealth management clients like me. I wasn't a major Goldman client, but I did enough investing with the firm to be included. Given Goldman's vast resources, top medical, economic and market experts were on the call.

The Goldman experts spoke with high confidence, largely devoid of caveats, which was typical of commentators in the early days of this crisis. They claimed that 50% of Americans would get the virus, echoing Angela Merkel's even more startling estimate for Germany. They said there was really nothing to be done about that, as the new virus was seemingly as communicable as the common cold. They said three million Americans (2% of those who contracted the virus) would die, noting that those deaths would be focused on the elderly and were not necessarily all incremental deaths – in other words, many of those people might soon have died from common influenza or other ailments if COVID had not felled them first. In my insatiable hunger for data and insights I took it all down to pass along to our senior team, which I sensed was craving information as anxiously as I was.

By then my daughter's spring break had been extended, and the remainder of her sophomore year was to be conducted "virtually" rather than in person. Likewise, I chose to remain in Palm Beach for what would turn out to be ten weeks. Many of our firm's offices were essentially closed at that point, as most people began to work exclusively from home. A week later New York City was shut down in what, after some haggling over semantics between New York's perpetually feuding mayor and governor, was labeled a "pause." The Goldman call had suggested that a quarantine was unlikely to be effective, and would cause substantial economic distress, but might be needed to slow the spread somewhat and thereby reduce the stress on the healthcare system. The phrase du jour became "bend the curve," meaning taking steps such that the virus would impact the population over an extended period rather than all at once.

Our team seemed to appreciate my notes. Everyone was groping in the darkness for understanding, and any form of personal connection, even if not particularly illuminating, was of value in what was quickly becoming a period of isolation for most. In response to my first COVID communication, one European partner wrote back that it would be helpful if I spelled out my thoughts on the worst-case scenario. I joked to my wife that this would be easy: from this fellow's perspective the worst-case scenario was that a devastating market decline and related economic contraction would put the firm out of business and then the virus would kill him.

Gallows humor aside, this question prompted me to send a note to our entire global staff, in which I highlighted some tips from the world of "positive psychology," a field with which I had become familiar years earlier by reading the work of Penn professor Martin Seligman, a pioneer in the area. Positive psychology focused on ways of enhancing the well-being of mentally healthy people rather than on treating mental illness. Seligman's seminal book *Learned Optimism*[9] noted that evolution had established pessimism as the default mode for humans – in essence, the cautious ones survived and parented the next generation while the reckless ones did not. In a crisis situation, people thus have a natural tendency to mentally leap to the worst-case scenario. In a COVID-focused piece published in a Penn alumni publication that month Seligman recommended responding to that natural tendency by also consciously thinking of the best-case scenario, then of the most-likely scenario and then of what concrete steps one could take to increase the chances of that relatively favorable outcome.[10]

My note to partners took people through that exercise for myself: the worst-case was that the virus would kill me (I was in the allegedly "at risk" 60-plus age group after all), best case was that I would remain unscathed and the most likely case was perhaps that I would get the virus, but given my otherwise good health, suffer only a relatively mild case. The steps I could take to make that outcome more likely were taking care of my health, practicing good hygiene and following any other healthcare advice. One could go through the same thought process for our firm. It was all pretty simple stuff, but I thought it was worthwhile sharing with our global team, much of which was young and inexperienced in crises of any kind.

In fact, there were early signs that the worst scenarios would not materialize for our firm. On the very day that oil prices collapsed our London team, led by one of our original London employees and now head of Europe David Wyles, miraculously got to contract signing on a $10.6 billion sale of a Thailand-based business for our longtime UK retail client Tesco. In addition, our newly expanded restructuring team was being flooded with new advisory opportunities from companies in financial distress, mostly in the retail and energy sectors that were bearing the brunt of the early economic impact of the virus. We also did what we could do to reduce expenses – at a minimum we would be saving a lot of travel dollars given the restrictions flowing from the health crisis.

Our cost-saving efforts received a further boost when our Brazil team abruptly announced its plan to leave the firm and set up a small independent operation. That was a very welcome bit of news, and surprising given that the virus appeared likely to wreak havoc in that seemingly permanently troubled country. Despite our high hopes, Brazil had been a tough market in the seven years we were there, in part due to the local habit of sending senior political leaders to prison and the economic and market chaos that inevitably resulted from that. As the sarcastic old saying goes, Brazil is the country of tomorrow, and always will be. Our Sao Paulo office had been unprofitable, and our team there had proven an uncomfortable cultural fit. So it was a relief to part ways reasonably amicably.

In the early days of the pandemic most US businesses were reeling. The CEO of a company with a $4 billion market value and a fair amount of debt rather urgently asked me to reach out to Warren Buffett's Berkshire Hathaway to see if it would be interested in buying his company, which had recently plummeted in value. I spoke to one of Buffett's right-hand guys that same day by phone, but there was no interest. Not even Buffett had the courage to buy at the most uncertain moment of the pandemic, and he was not alone. Many other stars of the investment world went on CNBC day after day and shared their dire outlooks.

Given the isolation of our team members and the extraordinary degree of uncertainty with regard to all aspects of life, I continued sending frequent notes to either our partner group or entire team, imploring them early in the crisis to "[b]e smart. Stay safe. And once we've done what we can to take care of our health, let's also take care of our clients, so we come out of this as a Firm stronger than ever."[11] I sensed that fears of the virus were somewhat overblown, at least for our predominantly very young and healthy team, but I tried to be gentle in my exhortations to not abandon our posts. Our team rose to the occasion for the most part, and as time passed I gained more confidence that our business, despite all the turmoil, would perform surprisingly well. Even in the depths of the crisis, I wrote that "our aggregate level of business activity fe[lt] largely unchanged," given a surfeit of restructuring work to offset reduced M&A activity.

Many of my notes were repetitive – there was not much new to say, but I wanted to try to keep our people connected and positive. Trying to add some levity to a grim situation, I recommended the bizarre Netflix series *Tiger King*, and in April shared with our global team a picture of my beloved canine Buster, a not-so-custom blend of Yorkshire Terrier, Poodle, Pomeranian and Chihuahua that was very much the product of an unplanned pregnancy. That prompted a flood of pet pictures shared globally across our offices. Many people, including perhaps myself, proved to own very different pets than one would have expected based on their office personas.

Amid all the business turmoil, every nonprofit I was involved in was under even greater stress, leading to emergency financial appeals from nearly all. Penn abruptly closed its campus along with most universities, but fortunately was so well endowed that it could continue to thrive in any realistic scenario. The American Museum of Natural History, with a much smaller endowment and heavily dependent on admission fees from visitors, had to close, and soon was forced into significant staff reductions. The closure would be the longest in its 150-year history. Roundabout Theater likewise closed all five of its Manhattan venues and watched revenue, other than contributions from supporters like us, drop to nothing. Prep for Prep canceled its annual benefit dinner, of which I had been scheduled to be the honoree, putting at risk much of the income needed each year to fund its important work preparing successive generations of minority kids to thrive in the most rigorous and competitive of schools. We were then in the early stages of our search for a new Prep CEO and ended up selecting a candidate from Chicago whom we never got to meet in person but merely interviewed via Zoom, an online video app that had suddenly become a business (and household) necessity.

The Prep community, being based in New York City and by definition made up of people of color, was far more impacted by COVID than the broader population. With families based largely in the more crowded outer boroughs and generally of modest means, it suffered greater illness and death, as well as larger economic losses, than the broader population. Thus news of the senseless killing of George Floyd while in the custody of Minneapolis police that May, fully captured on film, was a powerful blow to a community that was already reeling. The resulting stress was soon further exacerbated by news that a young Prep alumnus, a lawyer who had graduated some years earlier from Princeton, was arrested at one of the protests in response to Floyd's death. The specific allegation was that a woman in a car he was driving had thrown a Molotov cocktail into a NYPD police car in Brooklyn.[12] The police car was empty, and nobody was hurt, but still the federal charges levied against him were serious.

Situations like that raise complex questions for the leadership of an organization like Prep. Should the organization be silent on its association with the fellow in question, knowing that adverse publicity in relation to one of the program's beneficiaries could negatively impact its ability to raise the funds necessary to continue to fulfill its noble mission? If it supports him, should it do so quietly behind the scenes or publicly? Given that Prep served young people who, like young people universally, are prone to frequent and sometimes life-altering misjudgments, the Prep leadership had faced numerous complex questions on such matters over the years. In this case, the understandably high emotions surrounding the Floyd case, the lack of a prior criminal record for the young man and the absence of any injuries made that decision easier than it could have been. Accordingly, leadership at Prep both openly sympathized with and comforted its community while also trying to get the young man the best legal assistance possible.

Far beyond impacting organizations like Prep that served the minority community, events surrounding Floyd's death abruptly elevated the issue of racial justice and equity throughout the American business community in a way that had not previously occurred, at least not in my career. As one small step in the right direction, I was glad that a plan was already well advanced to appoint Prep's first CEO of color, and for me to then step down as board chair to make way for a next generation of leadership that would be made up of alumni of the program who were by definition also of color.

Clearly my twenty-plus years of service and millions of dollars of donations to Prep indicated that my heart was at least directionally in the right place on matters of race, but my historic policy was that our business focused solely on business. I had always avoided any commentary on broad political or social matters. Nonetheless this time I felt the need to make some statement to our global team, just as many business leaders were then doing. I wrote in one of my emailed team updates that I was "appalled by what happened to George Floyd" and that I "fully support[ed] the right of people everywhere to peacefully protest...and to seek reforms," although I added that I did not support "the violence that ha[d] arisen in conjunction with some of the protests."[13] While many of my notes over the years, even those on fairly emotional topics, failed to generate much of a direct response, this one prompted many grateful comments from a global team that was clearly under increasing duress from a toxic mix of health, financial, personal and now societal issues.

As if my father's still-recent passing, the depressing daily news of the global pandemic and the killing of George Floyd were not sufficient tragedy for one year, my younger brother and only sibling then succumbed to prostate cancer after a decade-long ordeal. He had run out of hopeful options and had suffered enough, so it was time. Given all the pandemic-related travel restrictions, there was no opportunity to see him for a final visit, and a memorial service had to be deferred to a future, healthier time. While I did not broadly disclose Steve's passing (our people had enough of their own problems at that moment), his death undoubtedly impacted the tone of my team note, which concluded by saying that our firm strived to provide "a bit of a refuge from the tumultuous world that surrounds us."

By the end of June I had made my way from Palm Beach to our Connecticut farm but still not back to New York, which I had not set foot in for fourteen weeks – by far my longest time away since I returned from London twenty-five years earlier. Local virus infection numbers had plummeted by then, so restrictions around bringing people back into the office were being relaxed and returning seemed reasonably safe. Furthermore, it was clear that psychologically many people needed to get back to something resembling normality. I also knew that, despite our surprising success while nearly the entire global team operated remotely from their homes, our continued success would ultimately require bringing people back together for greater collaboration and productivity.

On the other hand, most of the activities that made New York appealing (restaurants, bars, sporting events, theaters, gyms and so forth) were still largely shut down, and many residents had fled to suburban or rural locations. Memories of a temporary tent hospital in Central Park and the continual wailing of ambulance sirens across the city while the virus was at its peak were still fresh, so most were not in a rush to return. And the recent race-related protests, some leading to vandalism or violence, had only added to the anxiety infecting the city.

I decided I should go see for myself what things were like before trying to convince anyone else to return.

I went knowing that New York had emptied out, at least of most of those who had the means to escape. Early in the pandemic the fabulously skilled and reflexively protective Slovakian immigrant farmer who took care of our cattle and most of our Connecticut land and buildings called to complain of numerous city folk randomly walking across our farmland. One couple actually drove their car a few hundred yards across a hay field to get closer to the forest. Their first words when he asked what they were doing, "We're from New York," failed to specifically answer the question but in effect said it all: they were part of a diaspora from the city far greater than what had followed the September 11 attack. They assumed they would be sympathetically received just as that earlier generation of urban refugees had been and had no clue that the hay they had driven across needed to be left to grow undisturbed to provide sustenance for our cattle the following winter.

Notwithstanding my low expectations, I could not have imagined the degree of emptiness and desolation that would greet me when I arrived in Manhattan – "dystopian" was the overused but in this case accurate word I utilized to describe it to friends who were still away. As a test of what getting around the city would be like, I decided to walk during the historic afternoon rush hour the mile and a half from my Upper East Side apartment to our midtown Park Avenue office, then a few blocks across town to our recently leased but not yet built out new space in the Rockefeller Center complex, then back home. En route I saw almost no pedestrians or vehicles, and nearly every commercial establishment was closed. That evening I met a friend for dinner in midtown and then walked the entire thirty blocks up Lexington Avenue to home without seeing a single one of the previously ubiquitous yellow taxis.

Still, to set an example and to connect personally with members of our team who wanted that, I started coming in four days a week. At the same time, I told my wife that she should stay away from the city until likely the following spring, then nine months away – not for health reasons but simply because life there was not very appealing. Indeed, on our weekends together in the country I noticed that the cacophonous early morning bird song made it harder to sleep than the now deathly quiet of the Upper East Side.

The road to anything like life as we knew it in New York would be a long one, if indeed that were possible at all. New York had been wrongly written off in past crises, and Morgan Stanley's long-ago investment strategist loved to say that the four most dangerous words in investing were "this time is different."[14] But it felt like this time might *actually* be different. For weeks nearly the only people I saw in midtown Manhattan were construction workers erecting the massive new J.P. Morgan headquarters two blocks south of our office.

One day when my assistant Maureen was away I ventured out at lunchtime to grab a sandwich. As I walked through the Colgate Building's revolving doors I saw a woman crouched in an odd manner next to one of the large planters that had lined our front sidewalk as a form of security since just after the September 11 attacks. As my brain was reflexively contemplating whether she needed help I noticed that she was squatting against the planter to urinate, her short skirt hiked up and providing an unobstructed view that I had not seen on Park Avenue in twenty years in that location.

Bewildered and embarrassed, I quickly averted my eyes and hurried past, though once there was both some distance and the planter between us I looked back trying to make sense of the situation. Upon first accidental glance I had not believed my eyes. But my initial impression was accurate. Coming at a time when so many aspects of life in my adoptive home seemed alien, I struggled to comprehend what circumstances had led to this. The woman did not look ill and was not poorly dressed – at some distance I would have believed she was an assistant for some mid-level executive in the neighborhood. Yet on second look she did have the somewhat emaciated appearance that one sometimes associates with drug addiction. I felt a deep sadness for her and for my adoptive city.

In the weeks that followed midtown Manhattan, as well as many of the other places in which we had offices, slowly began to reawaken. On the day after Labor Day I put on a suit and tie as a symbol of the return to office and was pleased that after a six-month hiatus the suit still fit and I could remember how to don the necktie. The following week I took my first commercial flight in six full months, heading back to Grand Rapids for a memorial service for my brother that had already been delayed twice due to the virus – once right after he died and a second time at the last minute when several clergy at the church hosting the service suddenly contracted the virus.

While driving up to LaGuardia Airport after such a long time away felt familiar, walking into the large Delta Airlines terminal and finding it empty did not. There was literally not a single person buying a ticket, checking in baggage or standing in any of the security lines. Where normally there were hundreds of people, on this day there were none. On the other side of the security checkpoint were some signs of life, but the crowd looked to be only about ten percent of what had been typical before COVID. Once I boarded my plane I realized it was the exact anniversary of my last trip to Grand Rapids, for my father's memorial service.

Sitting in the Detroit airport on my way home the next day, I received a call from the head of the Cogent business we had acquired five years earlier. He was resigning after receiving a supposedly unique offer relating to a very different career path. He said he wanted to exit in the most constructive, nondisruptive way possible. On the other hand it would have cost him nothing to have provided ample notice of his plan so that together we could have planned for new group leadership. Having been down this road before, I took the ill-timed news in stride. I did, however, allow myself a brief moment of satisfaction when the head of the group, a devoutly religious fellow who undoubtedly had historically thought of himself as far from the kind of person who would do what he was actually now doing, realized he was dumping a mess in my lap not only in a pandemic but at a moment of obvious personal grief.

We had just passed the contractually agreed employee "lock-up" period post our acquisition of Cogent, so its leader was not the only one to go. Six other bankers also exited within a few weeks. For five years these guys had all seemed like I had first perceived them – solid, loyal, not terribly ambitious types. Yet bolting out the door as soon as their commitments had expired was entirely consistent with the most cynical Wall Street approach. Undoubtedly the sudden pandemic-related collapse of business activity in their area and resulting fears of what near-term compensation might look like played a major role in their decision-making.

In this case, what happened neatly illustrated both the reason that we had made acquisitions only twice and why we had repeatedly rejected buyout approaches to our own firm. The lack of loyalty I had observed following both our acquisitions is not unusual. And as for selling our firm, I simply lacked the cynicism of many Wall Street bankers and would feel compelled to do all that was in my power to make any organization I joined succeed. And if I was going to maintain that degree of commitment, why not just retain control? But this was no time for philosophical musings. Being handed the management task of sorting out a rebuilding program for this group just as I was leaving my brother's memorial service jolted me back into work mode.

Despite the loss of some who fled at the first sign of hardship, as the year wound down it became clear that being an optimist had once again been the correct stance. With regard to public health, infections were widespread and continued to flare up in varying degrees all over the world. Death rates, resulting in millions of lost souls globally, were stunning but likely to fall short of initial fears as doctors figured out how to treat infected patients better and the pharmaceutical industry developed several effective vaccines, including the highly effective mRNA versions that researchers at Penn played an instrumental role in creating. Gradually (very gradually) people returned to work in offices, although in New York our firm experienced another odd hiatus when we became homeless for twelve weeks when our existing lease ended before our new office space was ready. The build out and preparation had been significantly delayed by pandemic-related restrictions and consequent supply chain disruption.

As for the economic downturn, Federal Reserve Chairman Jay Powell declared it the most severe "in our lifetime."[15] Seemingly each new crisis our firm had faced managed to attain that status. Among the many victims was "21," the renowned midtown restaurant at which our firm had held so many partner and board events. Up near our farm, the *Lakeville Journal* appealed to the local community for donations to help it stay afloat – an ironic move given how it had squandered opportunities to support important local community organizations like the White Hart or the local summer stock theater. And big businesses were often as impacted as much as small ones. As one example, my college friend Jamie Dinan announced he would wind down his decades' old hedge fund.[16]

There were many other such casualties, even though central banks and governments provided massive monetary and fiscal stimulus well beyond what I initially expected. But all that stimulus meant most companies damaged by the pandemic survived. And not every company was damaged at all – many turned out to actually benefit from the pandemic as consumers spent money that might have gone to travel or entertainment on technology upgrades and other improvements to the homes in which they were now spending so much time.

As a result, the stock market quickly erased its first half decline, and the steepest ascent in history quickly followed the steepest decline. The stock of the company I had offered Warren Buffett nearly tripled in just a few months, confirming both that our client's CEO had prematurely hit the panic button and that Buffett had missed a real bargain.

As for our firm, despite the declaration by *Financial Times* that the "pandemic [had] abruptly ended a seven-year mergers and acquisition boom,"[17] our business proved resilient. We finished the year strong, leading to a very respectable full-year outcome. Indeed, the fourth quarter, almost all of which I spent with my family within a 10-mile radius of our Palm Beach home, turned out to be the best in our history, with $141 million in revenue. For the year, we earned $312 million of revenue, our third-best annual result ever, thanks largely to our big bet a year or two earlier on expanding our debt-restructuring advisory business. By the end of the year M&A activity was heating up as well.

Serious people began to ask whether the end of the pandemic might usher in a second "Roaring '20s." That sounded good, albeit a little too optimistic even by my standards.

CHAPTER NINETEEN

NOT DEAD YET

"One more dawn
One more day
One day more!"[1]

– Alain Boublil, Jean-Marc Natel and
Herbert Kretzmer, Les Misérables

A ny hope that we would leave the pandemic behind in 2021 and segue to a new "Roaring '20s" era was dashed – for me at least – on the second day of January when my daughter Jane suddenly felt ill and closed herself into her bedroom in our Palm Beach house. She was obviously young and sounded okay as we chatted through her closed door, so I wasn't particularly concerned. Her mother, however, lacks my equanimity on health matters, so she rushed to the local pharmacy and soon returned with several thermometers, a gadget for measuring blood oxygen levels and a variety of over-the-counter pharmaceutical products.

I pointed the most newfangled of the thermometers at Jane's forehead, saw a 104 figure pop up on the screen and reflexively declared "This thing is broken." I then pointed it at my own forehead, saw the figure change to 98, and realized that the thermometer was just fine. Jane, however, was not.

We then did what good citizens were supposed to do in the pandemic and hurried to get tests from the new concierge doctor service for which Roxanne had recently, and presciently, signed us up. Proving yet again that life is not fair, she – the one who had been more inclined to take all possible precautions – tested positive while I did not. Like Jane, she then closed herself into her bedroom solely for what would be ten days, entertaining herself by watching every season of the Showtime network detective show *Ray Donovan*. In the end Roxanne experienced a mild if not completely asymptomatic case, Jane recovered from her more serious symptoms quickly and I ferried trays of food to them both for the duration of their quarantine while managing to avoid contracting the virus myself.

Many others were not so lucky. One of my Greenhill partners, also temporarily based in Palm Beach, was hospitalized with serious COVID symptoms. Roxanne's new doctor service, of which I had admittedly been initially skeptical, came to the rescue again and was instrumental in getting him the care he needed. Like many people displaced by the pandemic, he was at the time far from his own doctor and did not know where to turn. Worse, within several weeks Paul Kelly, the Penn trustee from the generation before mine who years earlier had been instrumental in helping me gain my first leadership position at the University, succumbed to the virus. Of the million or so Americans who would ultimately die from COVID, he would turn out to be the only one in my own business or social network.

When a new iteration of the virus emerged the Greenhill team – after partially reconvening the previous summer and into the fall – again scattered across the globe, using the power of modern technology to work from homes, vacation homes, parent's homes or elsewhere. I hunkered down in Palm Beach, spending long days on Zoom video conferences working with clients, talking with our team members around the world, attending board meetings for the American Museum of Natural History and connecting with Penn's various deans and top administrators as I prepared to assume the role of chair of its board of trustees at mid-year. Relative to most, I had nothing to complain about, often doing my various video calls with my lower half dressed for a tennis match, bike ride or beach walk during whatever break might materialize over the course of the day.

Roxanne and I remained camped in Palm Beach until the last day of April, making for a more than six month stay – my longest time away from our Connecticut farm in the near quarter century we had owned the place and my longest absence from Manhattan since we returned from London almost three decades earlier. During our extended time away two landmark events in the history of our firm passed quietly, without the fanfare that would have accompanied them in more normal times. One was the firm's twenty-fifth anniversary, in January. The other was the opening of our New York office's new space shortly thereafter, following a few months in which we had no headquarters at all given that virus-related construction delays meant it was not yet ready by the time we had to vacate the old space we had occupied for twenty years in the Colgate-Palmolive Building on Park Avenue. Remarkably, having no corporate home for a few months wasn't even a mild inconvenience given the working arrangements to which we, like office workers everywhere, had already become accustomed.

On the first Monday in May I finally returned to New York for our usual monthly meetings with various industry sector and regional groups, in person, at least for those based in New York, for the first time in several months. As my car service drove me down Fifth Avenue along Central Park toward my new office destination the city appeared even quieter than it had been when I returned from the first phase of the pandemic the summer before. In blocks where there would normally have been dozens of joggers, mothers or nannies pushing strollers, dog walkers exiting the park after the early morning period when leashes are not required and executives in suits and usually ties walking toward midtown skyscrapers for the workday ahead, there was almost nobody. It was as if the proverbial neutron bomb had been dropped, eliminating all the people but leaving the structures still standing.

The building to which I was commuting for the first time was symbolic of a very different Manhattan – one expanding, pulsing with energy and exuding a bit of glamor – quite the opposite of the gloomy quiescence I observed as I traveled unobstructed through empty streets. Sitting across Sixth Avenue from the entertainment venue Radio City Music Hall that I visited on my first trip to New York a half century earlier and across Fiftieth Street from what was the Exxon Building when I began my years of work there for Morgan Stanley, it was the former Time-Life Building. Longtime home to the iconic print publications that bore those names, it was part of the Rockefeller Center complex that was developed during the Great Depression by John D. Rockefeller Jr. on land acquired from Columbia University. From the start, Rockefeller Center was one of New York's most distinctive architectural landmarks as well as headquarters to leading American companies like Exxon, the Associated Press and Radio Corporation of America.

Our new building, which came along a few decades after the first group of structures was erected, was the first of several that constituted a substantial expansion of the complex along the west side of Sixth Avenue. It was built specifically to house the two publishers for which it was named, which had until then been based nearby in one of the older Rockefeller Center buildings. The 1950s sex symbol Marilyn Monroe appeared at the groundbreaking ceremony for the new construction,[2] and the building later served as the fictional location of the advertising agency central to the long-running television show *Mad Men*. Having seen its charm fade over more than half a century of use, the building had been completely gutted and rebuilt. It was just now taking in its first tenants, including our firm as well as the executive management of Major League Baseball, the private wealth manager Bessemer Trust, a couple of law firms and a major Japanese bank called Mizuho.

As I walked up for the first time to the shiny new skyscraper that would be my new work home I was amused to see the numbers 1959 chiseled into the cornerstone, just below a gigantic baseball card-style picture of Yankees slugger Aaron Judge and a handful of other MLB stars. The place had opened for its first incarnation in the very year that I was born.

Notwithstanding the ongoing health crisis and the still largely empty office buildings throughout the world's financial capital, the stock and bond markets were partying like it was 1999, 2007 or any of those rare years that came to mark the peak of an economic cycle. Since at least the Long Term-Capital crisis that materialized in our first couple of years in business it had seemed to me that economic recessions were getting shorter with each successive cycle. The low pain threshold of American politicians and central bankers was such that the spigots of fiscal and monetary stimulus were opened wide at the very first sign of trouble. Given the unfamiliar horrors of the pandemic, this time veritable firehoses of liquidity had been deployed in an attempt to revive the economy and reawaken the animal spirits that powered markets. Interest rates were slashed, unemployment benefits amped up, student loan payments paused, childcare subsidies enhanced, food stamp benefits expanded, government checks mailed out to a majority of adults and novel programs set up to provide forgivable loans to a vast array of American businesses and nonprofits.

In sum, it was the equivalent of the "helicopter money" (cash tossed out the open doors of hovering helicopters onto the citizenry below) that previous Federal Reserve Chief Ben Bernanke had talked about as a last resort option for breathing life into the economy. Prep for Prep, the American Museum of Natural History, Roundabout Theater and my favorite bakery in West Palm Beach were each among the innumerable organizations that received aid, partly replacing lost revenue resulting from the shutdown of the economy. In a sign of just how comprehensive and undiscriminating the aid programs were, even *Hamilton*, the most successful Broadway hit of all time, for which I had multiple times paid more for a single ticket than I did for the not-so-gently-used Chevy Nova that was my first car, received at least $30 million in federal aid to support several of its touring productions.[3] That should have served as an early sign that the economy might not only shift back into a forward gear but could soon end up traveling at an unsustainable speed.

There's an old cliché that history doesn't repeat itself, but it does rhyme,[4] yet it struck me then that in the case of markets, this time history might quite literally repeat itself. Just before the year began *Bloomberg* had reported that "a speculative frenzy [was] sweeping Wall Street and world markets."[5] Special purpose acquisition companies were back. Remarkably, however, SPACs did not represent the height of market excess this time around. *The New York Times* reported, "from crypto art to trading cards, investment manias abound[ed]."[6]

Among more tangible assets, one of the greatest beneficiaries of the pandemic and related response was residential real estate in Palm Beach. There the confluence of comparative health, weather and tax advantages meant the house that Roxanne and I had purchased during the financial crisis a decade earlier using proceeds of a Greenhill stock sale was now worth multiple times what we paid. Meanwhile, that same Greenhill stock, which rose on news of our strong performance to end 2019 before plunging in early 2020 in response to the pandemic, crawled back up to a respectable level.

Putting aside the indecipherable gyrations of the stock market, it was clear that our firm was another beneficiary of booming markets. Our restructuring advisory team started the year with some work remaining on the numerous bankruptcy assignments that had arisen amid the very brief but calamitous drop in markets that occurred when the pandemic first hit. Our new assignments since that time had been almost all M&A related, with many closely tied to prominent themes of the pandemic period. For one, our health-care team advised Cigna on the acquisition of a business in telehealth – a growing channel for providing healthcare services, the development of which was accelerated by the perceived risks of a physical visit to your doctor's office during a pandemic.

Another pandemic-related opportunity arose in March. My old friend Rob Dyson (the man who gave me my first corporate board role) called, wanting to sell his manufacturing business that catered to the recreational vehicle market. That business was going gangbusters as Americans fled cities and hit the open road, staying in their own often luxurious vehicles to avoid the risks of walking into a hotel and encountering people who might be silently carrying a deadly virus. We had nearly sold that business for Rob more than a decade earlier, just before the calamitous global financial crisis hit, and this time he did not want to wait too long to pull the trigger.

In the months to come we would succeed in completing that sale; the buyer was one of the innumerable private equity funds that were prospering in this era of easy money. Another fund similarly prospering was the Lexington Partners vehicle that I had looked at acquiring many years earlier – the one with the arcane strategy of investing in the secondary market for private equity interests. It was sold to the giant West Coast-based asset management firm Franklin Templeton for $1.75 billion,[7] proving that it was indeed the highly attractive business I perceived it to be way back then. It would have been quite the catch had I been able to land it, but the owner was too wily to let his growing business be captured prematurely.

I gave some thought over the course of the year to supplementing our advisory income by sponsoring another SPAC, or two. Or even more, as many others with some degree of profile in the financial world were then doing. I even briefly raised the topic with my former partner Bob Niehaus over lunch at the same San Pietro restaurant where we long ago first discussed him joining Greenhill. Yet before that meal was over we both concluded that, notwithstanding the windfalls that SPACs were then providing to their sponsors just as one had done for us many years earlier, the transaction structure was so flawed that we had no appetite for attempting to reprise our previous success.

Neither of us had forgotten just how much work it took to extract gains from our SPAC investment in the wake of the collapse of Bear and Lehman. Ironically, Iridium, for which Bob had remained chair of the board of directors, had ultimately proven itself to be one of the most successful SPACs of all time. After struggling in its early years, it was now valued at more than four times its initial market price. In comparison, most other SPACs of its era had long since disappeared or were languishing in obscurity.

Amid all the government manufactured prosperity, the one thorny challenge that businesses like ours faced was finding and retaining enough employees to take advantage of the plethora of opportunities then available. In a sign of the times that echoed the 2000 Smith Barney analyst memo that was issued on what turned out to be the eve of the bursting of the dot-com bubble, a similarly youthful Goldman Sachs analyst published on social media a presentation to senior management complaining about ninety-five-hour workweeks and threatening to quit if working conditions didn't change.[8] Apparently the extraordinary volume of SPAC transactions, tantamount to a twenty-first-century gold rush, was a key driver in creating such excessive workloads.

Many workers did more than merely threaten to quit. Across all industries people resigned en masse in what was dubbed the Great Resignation.[9] Even our horse farm was affected, so much so that on several occasions Roxanne and I discussed closing the place for lack of help. Psychologist and star Wharton professor Adam Grant dubbed the new cultural zeitgeist "languishing,"[10] while others spoke more alarmingly of a nationwide mental health crisis.[11]

At Greenhill, for the first time in memory, several people quit simply because they wanted to "go home" – to Detroit, Milan, Los Angeles or wherever they had grown up. Perhaps the goal was a less frenetic lifestyle, or maybe the objective was escaping what felt like post-apocalyptic New York.

Possibly it was just a desire to be closer to aging parents at a time when life for older folks seemed more fragile and fleeting than before. In any event, we experienced far greater turnover among our junior and mid-level ranks than ever before yet were able to fill open positions fairly quickly as the people working at our competitors were at least as restless as our own.

One open position that would be considerably more complicated to fill than that of a horse farm barn hand or fledgling investment banker was that of the presidency of the University of Pennsylvania. I had known when accepting my appointment that as the next chair of Penn's trustees I would be tasked with finding a successor to longtime president Amy Gutmann – her twice-extended contract was set to expire in only a year. But the time to start looking arrived sooner than expected when President Joe Biden nominated Amy as Ambassador to Germany. Thus on July 1, my very first official day in the chair role that Benjamin Franklin himself first held, I informed the board's executive committee that she would be leaving.

Notwithstanding the ongoing public health crisis that meant meeting people in the flesh might be difficult to arrange, I knew Penn was well-positioned to attract the very best from across academia. It had just finished a major fundraising campaign, rising stock markets had driven its endowment to the $20-billion level and it was beginning to become more widely known that Penn researchers had been instrumental in creating the miraculous mRNA vaccines. That latter point achieved the trifecta of demonstrating Penn's research prowess, accomplishing something highly impactful to benefit humankind and generating enormous royalties that would fund future such research initiatives.

By September the presidential search process was well under way. That's when I made my first trip to the campus in nineteen months, for both the first in-person meeting of our search committee and a celebration of Penn's recently completed $5.4 billion fund raising campaign. Booming stock markets had clearly positioned alumni to be even more generous than expected, leading to that outsized result.

The journey via Amtrak to Philadelphia, one I had taken dozens of times over the years, was one of my first trips to anywhere other than one of my own homes since the onset of the pandemic. The streets of Manhattan were again empty as I drove south toward the new Moynihan Station, the beautiful former post office building then in the process of replacing the decrepit and depressing Penn Station.

The first meaningful sign of life en route was when the driver turned right off Park onto Thirty-Third Street. A three-quarters of a block long line of homeless people came into view. Almost all men, they were queued up to get a meal at the St. Francis of Assisi Church. This was a poignant reminder that, as with every crisis, the people at the bottom of our society were far more affected by the pandemic than those a bit further up, let alone those with my perch.

Having missed our regular theater trips and determined to do whatever we could to try to revive the aspects of life that had long-made Manhattan uniquely fabulous, Roxanne and I attended no less than seven Broadway and off-Broadway shows between when most theaters first reopened around Labor Day and the Thanksgiving holiday ten weeks later. One was *The Lehman Trilogy*, an entertaining gallop through the history of that storied firm that, until theaters all abruptly closed, we had been scheduled to see eighteen months earlier. Wall Street firms always seemed to involve a lot of drama – all that striving by smart and ambitious people trying to get to the top of the pile for what is almost inevitably a brief stay. I was familiar with that recurring story, having read histories of every firm from Barings and Bear Stearns to Goldman and Rothschilds. But Lehman had generated even more drama than most, right down to its undignified end when employees carried cardboard boxes containing their personal belongings out of the midtown headquarters that had been its home since the September 11 attacks pushed it northward from downtown. I found the new show, written by an Italian novelist and playwright, highly entertaining as well as more true-to-life than most stage or screen portrayals of the business world.

We also saw two excellent Roundabout productions focused on racial themes, a more common subject matter on stage given an increased focus on creating greater diversity in all aspects of Broadway. In addition we saw *Moulin Rouge*, a new musical based on the movie from some years back. It starred Danny Burstein, a Broadway regular whom we had met a few times through his work in various Roundabout productions. We enjoyed the show, for a second time, with one empty seat next to us. We had scheduled the return trip to bring our son Elliot and his girlfriend, both of whom joined us for a nearby pre-theater dinner before he suddenly declared that he didn't feel well enough to continue to the show. Later that evening he learned that he had COVID – a moderate case, which nonetheless meant we would all have to both miss the next night's Museum of Natural History gala and spend the approaching Thanksgiving holiday apart. I thereby became the family's lone survivor in terms of avoiding COVID infections.

Also memorable was a creative new downtown production of Stephen Sondheim's *Assassins*, a show we had first seen way back in 2004. I was admittedly a Sondheim groupie, finagling to see nearly every revival of his work that came along. We already had tickets to a new production of my favorite of his shows, *Company* – the first version ever done with the lead ("Bobby") played by a female. Thus I was deeply saddened in the time between seeing those two performances to learn of his passing, at age 91, at his home in Litchfield County.

I had always found it amusing that this consummate New Yorker landed in the same rural retreat that Roxanne and I did. We had enjoyed meeting "Steve," as his friends called him, on a couple occasions at the country home of Donna and Ben Rosen – Ben being a long-ago Greenhill client with whom I had reconnected through friends who had known his second wife Donna for many years through their mutual New Orleans connection. I always fondly remembered Steve's admonition in *Sunday in the Park with George* to "move on" that echoed Bob's mantra to "keep moving."

But getting through day-to-day life in urban post-pandemic America sometimes made it difficult to heed Bob's and Steve's admonitions. On December 3 I found myself alone in our office on a Friday, there because I had a series of interviews of Penn presidential candidates scheduled for that day and into the weekend. I looked out at a largely vacant midtown cityscape below. One of our young Asian American analysts had recently been pushed down the stairs at a downtown subway stop – one of many recent hate crimes targeting his ethnic group. By some tortured logic such crimes were thought to be increasing because the COVID virus originated in China. In another sign of deteriorating urban life, some young professionals in our Chicago office had recently been roughed up when leaving our office in Chicago's prime business district. Fortunately, our people involved in those incidents suffered no permanent harm.

Others were not so fortunate. At Columbia University, just a few miles north of my office, a graduate student was stabbed to death near campus,[12] echoing another fatal stabbing there just two years earlier. For the father of a college senior in Philadelphia, a city with considerably higher crime rates than New York, that news struck particularly close to home.

Beyond these specific cases of violence there was a general sense of lawlessness in the city that seemed an unwelcome further obstacle to getting people back to the office and fully reengaged as the pandemic wound down. One major contributor to that feeling flowed from the vast proliferation of bike lanes on streets across the city. Mike Bloomberg, a mayor I had deeply admired for his management skills, had launched the project over his unprecedented three terms as mayor, and Bill de Blasio continued the effort during his two terms that followed. Occasionally Bloomberg, and more routinely de Blasio, exhibited the overly exuberant tendency of progressives to continually tinker with how the city worked in an endless quest for "improvement."

My guess was that Bloomberg originally envisioned something like what I used to see driving into Amsterdam, Copenhagen or Oslo after arriving on a morning flight from London during my early 1990s sojourn there: law-abiding citizens pedaling away in a manner that both improved their health and reduced pollution. While this was well before people came to know the phrase "climate change," there was already a concern with auto emissions.

What ultimately materialized in New York was something quite different. Mixed in alongside those on old-fashioned bikes there were soon innumerable motorized vehicles ranging from lightly powered skateboards, scooters or mopeds to minibikes like those owned by some of my friends who grew up in rural Michigan with less-cautious parents than mine. Sometimes I even saw the larger and more powerful dirt bikes to which many of those same kids later graduated. All these vehicles, largely unregistered, unlicensed and uninsured, used not only the new bike lanes but also car lanes and sometimes even sidewalks. "One-way" designations were not a limitation either, as many times I watched as motorbikes raced southbound on the northbound-only Sixth Avenue.

Many of the bikers had good intentions – mostly they were delivery people in the age of Amazon and simply in a hurry. But others seemed to take pleasure in intimidating both pedestrians and automobile drivers. I once saw a few of them sidle up in a menacing way to two attractive young women who were traversing a wide avenue in a pedestrian crosswalk. Another time I came across what must have been 150 of them roaring up and down residential streets in the Upper East Side, not bothering to even pause at red lights. The only reason this kind of behavior was somewhat tolerable at the moment was that there were still so few automobiles or pedestrians on the streets.

The City had overcome near bankruptcy in the 1970s. It had recovered from the September 11 terrorist attacks in 2001 and, several years later, from the worst financial crisis in eighty years. Obviously it had also persevered through the long-ago Spanish flu pandemic that arrived just as World War I was ending. So it would probably recover from the current one. But I harbored doubts it would ever return to the era of peak prosperity that I had so thoroughly enjoyed. For me, *Hamilton*'s Schuyler sisters summed it up when they sang that New York was "the greatest city in the wor-or-or-or-or-or-or-or-orld!"[13] Even if I looked back to a much harsher time, when I first visited as a child in the dirty and dangerous 1970s, there was an appealing grittiness to the city. Now it just seemed empty.

Notwithstanding my fear of death by two-wheeler, somehow I managed to dodge all those unruly motorized vehicles, learning to look both ways on one-way streets just like American tourists do in London, while Greenhill likewise evaded its own pandemic-related threats. Thus we both got through that second year of the plague mostly unscathed. The economy maintained strong momentum, and equity and credit markets remained ebullient. Our stock climbed all the way back to just about where it had been before the pandemic hit. Furthermore, it felt like the trend lines on softer issues were also moving inexorably in a positive direction: the winding down of the health threat, the return to some degree of office life and a revival of the performing arts and other vital aspects of urban life. Maybe 2022 would finally mark a return to normality, or at least to a "new normal" not too far from the world as we had known and loved it prior to the arrival of COVID. At least one hoped so.

CHAPTER TWENTY

IT'S
(NOT ALWAYS)
A WONDERFUL
LIFE

I know that the clouds must clear
And that the sun will shine[1]

– Julie Taymor, The Lion King

T he new year opened on a hopeful note. On January 13, 2022, Penn put out an announcement under my name that its new president would be a legal scholar named M. Elizabeth Magill. She went by Liz. Currently the University of Virginia's provost, the chief academic officer position that is essentially the number two spot in a university hierarchy, she had previously served as dean of Stanford Law School.

The presidential search process through which we found her had efficiently come to completion on our original timetable of about six months.

Elite American universities can appear to be the most resilient institutions in our human ecosystem. Great corporations come and go, many of the most respected ending up diminished, acquired or in bankruptcy within just a generation or two. The entire banking system almost went down in the great financial crisis, and many banks disappeared. The media world has been upended by new technology and new businesses like Netflix, Facebook, Google and X (formerly known as Twitter). The church's authority has been undermined by sex scandals and cultural evolution. Government institutions at all levels long ago lost the respect of most.

In contrast, the leading universities today are by and large the same as when I applied for admission almost half a century ago. Applications for places in each year's freshman class have grown by leaps and bounds, as students across America and around the world go to increasingly greater lengths to get into the most prestigious institutions. So inelastic is the demand for spots that universities have been able to increase the price of tuition faster than the general rate of inflation for as long as I can remember. Supplementing that growing tuition revenue, a booming stock market – up around 40 times since I graduated – has helped boost contributions from alumni and resulted in endowments of a magnitude that rivals the greatest pools of wealth on the planet. Single donations can be $50 or $100 million or more, and individual contributions each year number in the thousands.

Yet what is expected of these great universities has also expanded in ways once unimaginable. As a starting point, each year they must assemble a diverse class of talented and highly credentialed students. No longer acceptable to anyone is what I remember of my freshman dorm floor: around twenty-five students, all white and none from further away than my home in Grand Rapids. And incoming students are no longer satisfied with the same education that earlier generations received – they want to learn marketable skills and gain qualifications that will justify the time, effort and money they invest in their degrees. Many aspire to a highly compensated first job on Wall Street, in consulting or at a leading technology firm.

While on paper these carefully selected prodigies can seem so accomplished as to be almost superhuman, many turn out to be remarkably frail – perhaps ironically as a result of the cumulative psychological wear and tear from the years on the hamster wheel required to build the resumes necessary to gain admission. The demand for counseling services provided by universities is thus seemingly insatiable, and many students are already on one or more forms of medication for their mental health by time they arrive on campus.

Apart from providing those specialized services to individuals as needed, today universities are expected to show care and concern for their entire community by speaking out in comforting and empathetic tones on an increasingly broad range of social, political and cultural phenomena, whether they occur in their neighborhood or on the other side of the globe. Even the quality of basic accommodations students expect for their undergraduate stay has escalated mightily – the dusty old room that nearly brought my decidedly middle-class mother to tears on my long ago move-in day is no longer seen as tolerable.

During our search for Penn's next president I often compared the job to that of the mayor of New York City – a management position that I see as more demanding than any but the president of the United States. Apart from the city of Philadelphia, Penn is the largest employer in its region, with sprawling physical facilities in constant need of refurbishment and upgrading. While the primary focus is the care and feeding of a large and ever-changing student body, there are numerous other constituencies to serve as well. The faculty want time and funding for research. Given the sharp disparity of wealth between tax-exempt universities and their generally prosperous students on the one hand and under resourced surrounding communities on the other, the surrounding neighborhoods and indeed entire city want to see some economic benefits flow their way as well. In addition, maintaining a high ranking among universities also requires having a global impact, as Penn did when its research led to effective COVID vaccines.

In order to provide adequate funding to pursue all those objectives, relationships with alumni must be cultivated and nurtured for their entire lifetimes – and indeed beyond, in the case of "planned giving," the euphemism for testamentary bequests. As a result, over time a vast apparatus of time- and attention-consuming "boards" and councils has been created to foster affinity and convey status upon those most able or willing to contribute.

A complicating factor in trying to manage the diverse and growing demands on an elite American university is the peculiar governance of such institutions. Corporate governance in the business world is complex and often leads to conflict, but the basic hierarchy is clear – shareholders elect a board of directors, which appoints management, approves strategy and monitors performance. If at any point the shareholders are not satisfied with the board or management, they have the right to remove them. Or if an outsider comes to think that the company is not performing as it should he can seek control by acquiring shares in the market and then push for changes. I had spent my entire career facilitating – or sometimes helping to resist – such transactions.

In contrast, at a university the board of trustees – usually consisting almost entirely of alumni, often chosen for their generosity to the institution rather than for any particular skillset – is nominally in charge. Most fundamentally, it approves where money is spent. But for most trustees, in practice their role is a fairly modest one – more of an honorary position, a networking vehicle or an exclusive social club than a weighty responsibility. Tenured faculty, which generally speaking have near-lifetime appointments like those of Supreme Court justices, see themselves as embodying the institution in many ways. Historically they have held a prominent role in governance alongside trustees. And students, while their stay at a university is relatively brief, are the "customers" that must be satisfied. With their youthful energy, idealism and passion, they are not shy about making their voices heard.

If something goes awry, there is no analogue to the situation at a public company. Private institutions have no shareholder equivalents or owners of any kind that can assert control. Members of both boards and managements tend to serve for extended terms, with little real oversight of either. For a board to prematurely or abruptly force change would create too great a risk to the "brand" that attracts fervent loyalty from student applicants, faculty, staff, alumni and donors.

While making the "best" choice from a surprisingly small pool of candidates qualified to fulfill the myriad roles of a university president is far from easy, the success of a search today is not defined solely by that outcome. It is equally important to get the process for landing that candidate right. Every constituency needs to feel heard, and in the end one hopes to get to unanimous acclamation as to the ultimate choice. Thus as a starting point we assembled, per requirements laid out in detail in the university's statutes, a search committee of trustees and faculty of diverse backgrounds. And before that group even looked at a single resume we ran a consultative process, involving a much larger group including more faculty as well as deans, staff and students, that served as a sort of listening tour of representatives of all the groups that appropriately wanted some say in the search.

Each candidate our search committee looked at over the six months that followed had fabulous academic credentials from the higher echelons of American education. One would expect that given we were seeking to fill one of the top jobs in all academia. Liz was unusual in that she brought leadership experience from two institutions, UVA (as the University of Virginia is known) and Stanford, which were remarkably like Penn. These were big, complex places that encompassed undergraduate education as well as several graduate schools, liberal arts and science programs along with professional schools, and a large associated hospital complex to boot. She had played both key academic leadership roles – provost, the internally focused and faculty-orientated position, and dean, a role involving the kind of constant interaction with students and alumni that university presidents had. By all accounts she was a great leader. Most recently, she had excelled in the provost position during the brutally difficult pandemic period.

Beyond her sterling resume, what was uniquely appealing to me about Liz was her warm, authentic, accessible approach to leadership, which was undoubtedly rooted in her upbringing in Fargo, North Dakota – a place so prototypically Midwestern that I jokingly told her it made my hometown of Grand Rapids seem like Paris, France. She showed a human touch unusual among senior executives by insisting on picking up myself and another committee member at the Charlottesville airport in her family SUV for a casual discussion over dinner at a crowded restaurant near UVA. Apart from of the appeal of her leadership style, her politics seemed moderate and pragmatic, not overtly "woke" or otherwise controversial. In an increasingly contentious world, that seemed to me particularly apropos.

In building a broad consensus across the university community that Liz was exactly the right candidate, I knew that the clincher for many would be that she had clerked for Supreme Court Justice Ruth Bader Ginsburg. Modern American culture reflects an obsession with celebrities – hence the innumerable times I was asked if I was related to the former Harvard president with my surname. The late RBG, as she became widely known over time, was a fabulous name brand to have on your resume – far more differentiating than the usual list of credentials from top universities. In her later years Ginsburg became perhaps the highest profile justice of modern times, thanks to her feisty style and two widely viewed films – one a documentary and the other a dramatized version of her early years.[2] Her legendary status among the East Coast elite, particularly among women given the pioneer story portrayed by those films, provided the perfect complement to Liz's gracious Midwestern persona.

Fortuitously, and completely unexpectedly, coming to a timely conclusion on the Penn search opened the opportunity for me to play the very same role closer to home, at the American Museum of Natural History, less than thirty blocks north of my office at Greenhill. A couple months earlier, as the Penn search was entering its final stages, Museum board chair Lewis Bernard, the Morgan Stanley alum, Group of Eight member and man who had invited me onto the Museum board eight years earlier, called me in my office.

"Scott, do you think alongside what you're doing at Penn you might have room for another similar role?"

"No" was my reflexive and immediate response. I was not at all surprised that Lewis was looking for his successor. Although he looked to be in good health and remained as intellectually sharp as I had ever known him, I figured he had to be around 80 years old and knew he had held the chair position for two decades. Given where I had come from, I was hugely flattered even to be considered a candidate to chair the board of one of New York's landmark institutions. Despite appropriately feeling an element of impostor syndrome just as I did when Amy Gutmann first broached the idea of my chairing Penn's trustees, I felt that I had many of the attributes needed to play such a role. A financial background is useful given that the most fundamental responsibility for a board is to serve as financial steward – to ensure the long-term viability of the institution. A legal background is also helpful, given that so many of the most complex and controversial issues facing such an institution today are legal in nature. Lastly, board leadership experience at a place like Penn or even at a much smaller organization like Prep for Prep was essential. Realistically, one's first board leadership role could not be at a place with the scale and complexity of the Museum.

But perhaps what was most suitable about me for such roles was my long career dedicated to advising innumerable CEOs and corporate boards.

For the most part, I had not spent my career as a principal – one who has the authority to make decisions unilaterally. I generally played quite a different role, as an advisor – a consigliere whose task could be fairly described as building a consensus as to how a board and the institution it governed should respond to some strategic opportunity or formidable challenge. I had dealt with a very wide variety of personalities in creating consensus on whatever the issue at hand was. And over the decades I had accumulated experience with all manner of such opportunities and challenges. There wasn't much I hadn't already encountered.

The problem – and what triggered my reflexive response to Lewis, a man for whom I had enormous respect and a resulting desire to please – was that I still had a more than full-time "day job" managing a public company with fifteen offices around the world. On top of that, my role at Penn required a dozen or more Acela trips a year to Philadelphia to attend innumerable committee meetings (budget, audit, development and so on), as well as numerous more informal chats with the president and her leadership team on the myriad and ever-changing list of issues that touch the campus of a leading university.

A couple weeks later Lewis, a man whose deliberate approach to decision-making had always been a signature characteristic, called me back: "Have you given my question any more thought?" he asked. The fact was that I had. I had by then concluded that my role at Greenhill would very likely be my last in the business world. Unlike the typical senior corporate executive, I knew I would not choose to cap off my career with a series of prestigious, moderately lucrative but time-consuming corporate board positions. I had "been there and done that," coming away with my oft-stated view that such roles typically alternate between being boring and scary. I didn't even play golf or have any similarly demanding daytime hobbies. So the bottom line was that I had concluded that I could indeed make the time for a second chair role. For me, this would be like the familiar step of taking on an interesting new transaction assignment for a client.

Somehow I had always been able to make the time to squeeze in one more intriguing opportunity.

Accordingly, I told Lewis that we were getting very close to what I saw as an extraordinarily successful conclusion to our search for Penn's next president. Further, I predicted – wrongly, it would turn out – that this would likely be the most important and time-consuming role I would ever play for Penn. With that soon behind me I felt I could take on the position he was proposing. My principal motivation in accepting this new position was that I loved the city of New York, a place that had provided me with abundant pleasure as well as great opportunity. I saw this role as my chance to play some part in what I feared would be a long and arduous post-pandemic recovery.

I knew that one of the reasons Lewis wanted me as his successor was my experience leading the search for Penn's president. Ellen Futter, the Museum's widely acclaimed president for nearly three decades, was getting ready to retire now that the Museum's long pandemic shutdown had ended and a spectacular new addition to its densely packed Upper West Side campus was nearing completion. While Penn and the Museum were each in most respects paragons of good institutional governance, both had thus ended up in a place where their two key leadership roles, chair and president, needed to be transitioned at essentially the same time. Here were further examples of the harsh reality that leadership succession is a real-life human drama, which doesn't often follow any preconceived script.

Meanwhile, back at the ranch, my day job was keeping me very busy even as I performed what were now becoming two significant non-paying roles. In the latter months of 2021 and into the new year I built my schedule around daily, often very lengthy, conference calls involving the senior management and sundry advisors of my longtime client TEGNA. That group had been working on the sale of that company, off and on in various forms, for more than two years.

For me, the long-running corporate saga we were trying to bring to conclusion encompassed nearly everything one would want to know about the world of dealmaking, starting with what motivates companies to pursue transactions. Deals happen for a wide variety of reasons – sometimes they are simply a manifestation of empire building, a natural urge since probably the beginning of human life on our planet. But the prevailing winds of M&A blow generally in the direction of two themes.

One is consolidation, simply the process of making acquisitions to eliminate competitors, increase scale and create operating efficiencies. The other primary transaction rationale is focus: the process of specializing in a fairly narrow business segment. The goal is to concentrate limited corporate resources on mastering one activity (given the intense competition in every field of endeavor, achieving just that is a sufficient challenge!) as well as help investors more easily understand and value the enterprise based on its evolving financial results. There were times like the 1960s, when the development of conglomerates – companies that own and operate assets in disparate fields with no apparent synergies between them – went against this prevailing wind, but most of the time the transactional winds blow toward focus.

The television broadcasting company TEGNA began as part of a conglomerate of sorts – the diversified media business known as Gannett. That business in turn was founded in the early 1900s as a newspaper publishing business before eventually expanding into nearly every other aspect of media. When I was first introduced to Gannett's CEO Gracia Martore in 2013 it owned, in addition to numerous local newspaper titles and the national paper *USA Today*, a collection of television stations as well as a clutch of more recently developed digital media businesses that helped consumers rent an apartment, buy a car or find a job. While having such a diversity of cash flow sources can be appealing, the stock market tends to place a discount on companies that own a portfolio of businesses with widely varying characteristics. And the businesses that Gannett had assembled over time had very widely varying characteristics.

The original business, and indeed the whole newspaper industry, was then under great pressure. Newspaper publishing was once a thriving business, with major cities each supporting multiple papers, often with both morning and afternoon editions. But over time there came to be too many papers, and there were too few advertising and subscription dollars to support them all. The initial response to that was consolidation via M&A, first within cities and then across the country. That process eliminated competitors and enabled greater efficiency in collecting and reporting news, in the use of expensive printing presses and in the purchase of newsprint paper, among other synergies.

Gannett became the dominant consolidator in the field. But as advertising dollars moved away from newspapers to television and other media outlets, the pressure on the industry increased. Gracia thus intuitively agreed with our analysis that Gannett's thriving television broadcasting business would be more favorably valued by the market, better enabling it to invest in further expanding its operations, if the newspaper business was separated out as an independent company. Indeed the outlook for newspapers was so dire by time we looked to complete that transaction in 2015 that Gracia and I first had to go to Washington to convince the Pension Benefit Guaranty Corporation, the federal government's insurer for pensions, that the stand-alone newspaper business would over time be able to make good on its pension obligations to its large, now mostly retired, unionized workforce.

At around the same time as the newspaper spin-off we worked to sell or separate out the digital media businesses. In terms of growth prospects, those were the opposite of the newspaper business. They were where advertising dollars were going when they fled the newspaper industry. The remaining company, now focused entirely on TV broadcasting and renamed TEGNA – the rejiggered letters of Gannett, sort of – then went on an acquisition spree, consolidating what was seen as a far more appealing business than newspapers.

But the saga didn't end there. When an industry is undergoing rapid consolidation a company must either continue to eat or risk being eaten. Investors are typically happy either way. In the former case the company in which they have invested benefits from continuing incremental cost synergies, and in the latter they are bought out by a buyer at a premium to where the stock market values the business on its own. So-called "activist investors," the type that often loudly voice strategic opinions rather than simply quietly picking stocks in which to invest, exist largely to help speed that process along. Two years in a row such an investor sought to take over TEGNA's board of directors. His objective was even more aggressive consolidation, likely aimed toward an outcome wherein this business with a long, proud history as an independent company would be subsumed into another company.

There are no holds barred in such fights for control. In the bitter second round of this battle the attacker even dragged the specter of racism into the contest, dredging up an incident from years earlier when Dave Lougee, the man who had succeeded Gracia as TEGNA CEO, mistook a black media executive for a hotel car valet at an industry conference.[3] Ironically, Lougee was perhaps the most politically left-leaning CEO I had ever advised – the polar opposite of the energy sector CEO who complained to me in his Southern drawl over a Houston lunch in that same period that Dr. Anthony Fauci, the ubiquitous government health expert on all things COVID, "oughta be in prison." Lougee was quick to apologize for the long-ago incident, but the allegation clearly impacted the fight for control and undoubtedly stung a man of solid character on a very personal level.

During the first round of that battle, a year before the racism card was played, we had nearly succeeded in selling TEGNA before receiving a reminder of a cardinal rule in the M&A business: never wait one minute longer than necessary to get binding transaction agreements signed. As TEGNA later publicly disclosed, in March 2020 the company was in discussions with four prospective counterparties and "engaged substantially with two of [those] parties."[4] Both made acquisition proposals just as the COVID pandemic was creeping up on financial markets. Then, given the extraordinary uncertainty of the moment and the fact that stock prices began cascading downward, both parties withdrew their proposals.

The most overused adjective bankers use in describing a situation like that is "dead," as remarkably often the glowing embers of seemingly terminated negotiations burst back into flame. Given the impact of the massive government stimulus to rejuvenate markets following the initial pandemic decline, only months later TEGNA was back in discussions relating to a possible transaction. Still, getting a deal negotiated, agreed upon and financed at that time remained very difficult. It took more than a year of dialogue with various parties before, on February 22, 2022, the sale of TEGNA for $8.6 billion was finally agreed and announced. Surprisingly, the buyer was the same fellow who had twice sought board control through the annual shareholder voting process. To underline yet again the importance of avoiding any undue delay in reaching such an important agreement, only two days after that deal announcement Russia invaded Ukraine, roiling markets yet again.

"Everyone has a plan until they get punched in the mouth."[5] Heavyweight boxing champion Mike Tyson spoke those words in response to the question whether he was concerned by an opponent's fight plan, but the wisdom inherent in his comment extends far beyond the boxing ring. While our firm's offices were all at a safe distance from the new battlefields of Eastern Europe, and none of our people would suffer anything like the agony that countless citizens of Ukraine would, the invasion was still a punch in the mouth for our firm. Until then it had seemed we were on the brink of full recovery from the pandemic. Now a war between powerful combatants – one nuclear armed – in a geopolitically strategic place would undoubtedly disrupt economic activity, impact food and energy prices, and ultimately increase general inflation. In turn, that would trigger higher interest rates, tighter credit markets and lower asset prices. All those factors, combined with a general feeling of greater uncertainty, would lead to significantly reduced transaction activity – the lifeblood of our business.

As always, my extracurricular activities provided some respite from both the steady flow of negative market news and the increasing challenges involved in leading a public company. Two weeks after the invasion of Ukraine I was elected chair of the American Museum of Natural History's board. Then in May I played the chair's role for the first time at a Penn graduation. On a scorching hot day when I practically melted under my academic robe during the outdoor ceremony at Franklin Field, my daughter Jane was among the degree recipients. The pleasure of personally handing her a diploma more than compensated for any discomfort.

In June I presided over my first AMNH board meeting. Just as had happened at Penn, the agenda for that session included disclosure that the institution's president was leaving and a search committee to find her successor was being formed. One day later I was back on the Penn campus to act as master of ceremonies for an appropriately lavish farewell dinner for Amy Gutmann. By then she was well ensconced in her role as Ambassador to Germany – an even more important post than usual given Germany's proximity to the war and historic reliance on Russia for energy supplies.

That fall, I returned to campus twice. The first time was for the "convocation" ceremony that celebrated the entry of a new class of students. That was to be the forum for Liz Magill's first major speech as president before it was rudely interrupted by more than 100 protestors, some amplified by bullhorns. The subject of the protest was a local real estate project – some wanted Penn to intervene to prevent what they saw as gentrification. Ironically, the topic of Liz's speech was the importance of engaging in productive disagreement. "Democracy cannot work unless people can live together, learn from one another and, paradoxically, disagree,"[6] she had planned to say – and did say in a later recorded version of that speech.

More happily, my second campus visit that autumn was for a whole weekend of activities relating to the formal inauguration ceremony for Liz as Penn's new president. The social events, for which we had perfect October weather, included outdoor concerts by rock and country artists Sheryl Crow and Jeff Tweedy. The inauguration itself was a much more serious event with such pomp and circumstance that it felt like a religious ceremony – even as it was held in Irvine Auditorium, a 1,000-plus seat, 1920s-era performance space where as a student I had watched the film *A Clockwork Orange* and seen comedian George Carlin perform. The only moment of levity on this occasion was when I added Harvard-educated Supreme Court Justice Elena Kagan, there for a well-attended and lively discussion of constitutional and Court matters with Liz, to the long list of those who had asked me whether I was related to Derek Bok.

Several weeks later, the search for the next leader of AMNH concluded when our committee chose Sean Decatur, an African American chemist then serving as president of Kenyon College in Ohio. Sean was selected entirely on his merits out of a strong field of candidates, but his appointment seemed doubly appropriate in that the Museum serves a local community largely of color. Surprisingly (or perhaps not), he would be the first person of color to head a major New York City museum.

Meanwhile, back at my day job, the *Financial Times* reported a "record decline" in global dealmaking during this period, explaining that this "slowdown was the result of sharp interest rate rises, in the wake of rising inflation and the war in Ukraine, hitting confidence in global markets and increasing the cost of financing."[7] Accordingly, just after the year-end, for the first time in four years our partners from across the US, Canada, Europe and Asia gathered in New York City for what had previously been an annual meeting. The stakes felt high. The ties that bind such a group had been significantly loosened as a result of prolonged physical separation over the course of the pandemic. Indeed, about a third of our managing directors had never before attended one of our partner meetings nor even shaken hands with many of their colleagues. They had either been recruited into the firm or promoted to a MD role from within since the last time we all assembled.

Given these circumstances, I put even more time than usual into preparing the remarks I would deliver to our MD group along with all of the firm's outside board members after drinks and dinner. We met at the University Club, a Civil War-era social club housed in a grand Italian Renaissance Revival building on Fifth Avenue where we had gathered for past such events. That night I spoke first of the pride I hoped people took in the history and accomplishments of our firm, reminding them that we were "a pioneer in so many ways"[8] and had built a brand "far out of proportion to our size." More quantitatively, I noted that we had earned $6 billion in fees for advising leading companies around the world on some of their most important strategic projects.

I next spoke of our firm's remarkable resilience over its twenty-seven-year history in the face of five distinct crises: the Long-Term Capital hedge fund collapse, the bursting of the dot-com bubble that was exacerbated by the September 11 terrorist attack, the global financial crisis that took down Lehman Brothers, the COVID pandemic and most recently the hard to label but particularly disorienting period of trying – in the midst of a European war – to recover from that pandemic and the myriad governmental and social responses it had prompted.

While the earlier crises felt more dramatic in nature, I warned that the ongoing attempt to bounce back from the pandemic seemed to me the greatest of the challenges that our firm, and perhaps our whole economy, had faced over these many years. Most others had somehow brought people together; the pandemic had kept them apart. Moreover, the ramifications of this current crisis went far beyond superficial economic and market matters. They impacted society's fundamental work ethic and the way people worked together, matters I believed had been central to productivity and prosperity both on Wall Street and in America at large.

I told our team that while reading John Mack's recent biography over the holidays I had been most struck not by the various dramatic events described therein but by the intensity of the Wall Street culture portrayed. That culture was far from perfect for sure – diversity had not yet emerged as a common corporate objective, misbehavior by management or staff was not uncommon, and the reckless taking of risk could in the wrong market lead to existential disaster. But equally undeniably the endless hours together, the games, pranks, constant travel and even the often-excessive drinking had together created an esprit de corps comparable to that of a wartime army.

I had lived much of the story Mack retold – so much so that initially I had no desire to read his book. Yet when I finally picked it up and allowed myself to relive some of my youth I was struck by how foreign the Wall Street life he depicted seemed relative to that of the post-pandemic era. Demonstrating just how much had changed since then, a popular *New York Times* writer I followed featured on his podcast the perspective that work is fundamentally transactional, and the notion of "family" in the context of work inherently "exploitative."[9] My experience said otherwise. Even if they were ultimately defeated, at their best the armies that Mack and his contemporary peers commanded were productive and powerful and (mostly) a pleasure to be a part of.

A principal goal of my speech to the assembled Greenhill army was to convey, as always, my sense of confidence in our team and optimism about our future. Yet at the same time I wanted to clarify, with some degree of urgency, that we remained in the market equivalent of wartime and therefore needed the intensity of commitment and the camaraderie that Mack had described. Indeed only several weeks after my speech it became clear that not everyone would survive the ongoing hostilities in the financial markets.

Market commentators, investors and regulators struggle to identify where the weaknesses in the financial system lie in each cycle. Inevitably they are someplace different than where they were when the most recent crisis arose. In the financial crisis a decade and a half earlier, big banks and complex securities were the initial source of what became the greatest economic emergency in decades. After that event, as a respected *Wall Street Journal* columnist had just put it, the "Fed [and] Congress thought smaller banks, deposits and bonds were boring and safe."[10] Yet after anxious days and weeks of markets waiting for something to break, the weakness in this new crisis turned out to lie precisely in those smaller banks, their deposits and their investments in seemingly safe government bonds.

The new crisis became real when, in mid-March, the Silicon Valley Bank (SVB) was seized by the US government, marking the largest bank failure since Washington Mutual went down just after Lehman collapsed. While SVB had only seventeen branches and many of its depositors were wealthy venture capitalists and the entities they managed, the photographs of people queued up to get their money out were reminiscent of the scene from *It's a Wonderful Life* where customers lined up to reclaim their deposits from the Bailey family's "Building & Loan." In this modern version of that story the demise of SVB happened far faster. Its technology-savvy customers were able to move their funds with nothing more than a few clicks on their phone or computer keyboard.

Personally, SVB was not a bank to which I had previously paid much attention, although in the brief moments between its collapse and rescue I would learn that several private investment funds in which I participated kept their payroll and other corporate accounts there. SVB was miniscule in comparison to America's very largest banks, but I was surprised to read that, as a result of successive decades of consolidation having eliminated many more familiar names that once ranked ahead of it, it ranked as the sixteenth largest bank in the country by assets. It was even more surprising to me that in having individual as well as corporate depositors fully protected by the US government SVB had implicitly been determined to be "too big to fail," that familiar designation from the financial crisis era.

Thus this episode provided yet another confirmation of my long-held view that governments and central banks are increasingly quick to come to the financial rescue of troubled market participants to mitigate the risk of contagion across a financial sector on which essentially all of global commerce relies.

While SVB's failure didn't seem to have much direct relevance to our own firm, its demise immediately precipitated rumors that First Republic Bank, an institution that bore similarities to SVB in terms of size as well as origin, location and strategic focus, would meet a similar fate. There are many matters one is paid to worry about as a CEO, but I had never given a minute's thought to the possibility that First Republic, where Greenhill's primary checking and payroll accounts were kept, might go under. Unless the Federal government again chose to come to the rescue of depositors, much of our working capital would be vaporized in that scenario.

First Republic, back then a relatively new player in corporate banking, became Greenhill's corporate relationship bank shortly after I joined the firm. That was around the time Bob Greenhill's personal banker at the century-and-a-half-old private bank US Trust moved there, following the sale of that prestigious old institution to brokerage firm Charles Schwab in an ill-fated diversification move that would later be unwound.

Over the years First Republic had inexorably grown in stature, gaining as customers many of our close corporate peers, as well as similar real estate, private equity and other professional services organizations of the type that populate the New York and San Francisco metropolitan areas, where both SVB and First Republic were primarily focused. Now, suddenly, after years of success, First Republic teetered on the brink of failure, bringing home to our board of directors the pithy but painful reality of my repeated quip that corporate board service can suddenly turn scary.

While we were still monitoring the First Republic situation, and only days after the government seizure of SVB, a much larger and more prominent bank than either essentially failed. The once mighty Credit Suisse – one of Greenhill's longtime large competitors – was forced by the Swiss government into a shotgun marriage at a rock-bottom price with its crosstown rival UBS.[11]

CS was already a deeply troubled institution when John Mack was recruited there from Morgan Stanley and had intermittently struggled since then. Among its recent sins was a $450-million loss on its ill-conceived investment in the now-shuttered hedge fund controlled by my friend Jamie Dinan.[12] That was a fabulous deal for Jamie, now a part-owner of the Milwaukee Bucks, the NBA champions from a year earlier. On the other side of the table, the loss on that investment for CS was obviously significant yet paled in comparison to some even larger recent missteps. Regulators, in the end, had no choice but to get comfortable with a merger of the two largest banks in Switzerland – a deal *The Wall Street Journal* called "the first megamerger of systemically important global banks since the 2008 financial crisis."[13]

CHAPTER TWENTY ONE

THERE IS A SEASON

And the seasons they go round and round[1]

– Joni Mitchell, Circle Game

S
o much had changed since Greenhill was formed. I had often spoken of how a fundamental driver of our early and extraordinary success was the fact that, at the time we launched with an almost unique business model focused solely on advising companies on large and complex deals, the global transaction advisory business was essentially owned by just nine very large banks. A survey of the damage that a quarter century of tumultuous markets had done to those institutions was sobering.

One, of course, had gone bankrupt and disappeared – Lehman Brothers in 2008. Two would have met that same fate, had they not been hurriedly forced into distressed sales to avert a similar outcome – Merrill Lynch to Bank of America just after Lehman failed, and recently Credit Suisse to UBS. Two others, Goldman Sachs and Morgan Stanley, were saved only by quick conversion to regulated bank status the same week that Lehman went under. The US government, seeking to avoid a series of major banks toppling like dominoes, engineered that move as a means of granting those firms automatic and immediate access to critically needed liquidity from the Federal Reserve. Both firms went on to perform strongly in the post financial crisis period despite that more onerous regulation.

Citicorp squeaked through that period with the help of various government programs but had continued to struggle ever since. Its stock was still down 90% from the time of our IPO. Deutsche Bank had lurched from crisis to crisis several times – in the financial crisis, in the pandemic and now in the wake of Credit Suisse's fire sale – generating chatter about a bailout from the German government. Its stock was down 80% from the time of our IPO.

UBS had done a bit better than those, as its stock fell only by around half over that long period. Consistent with its conservative Swiss banking heritage, it accomplished that better result by largely forsaking investment banking to focus on managing the investment portfolios of the world's wealthiest. That same path was somewhat circuitously taken by my alma mater Morgan Stanley after its near-death experience. That was the strategy Phil Purcell pursued until he got pushed out, and his post-crisis successors later added Smith Barney and E*TRADE to the Dean Witter brokerage business that he had brought to the table. All those prominent brands were focused on managing the capital of individual investors rather than riskier investment banking or trading activities.

J.P. Morgan stands alone among this once-elite group of nine as having prospered as an investment bank without relying on any government assistance. In fact, over time it had risen to preeminence in all aspects of US banking, creating a financial supermarket of the kind dreamed of by Bob Greenhill's one-time boss Sandy Weill, the man whose contributions to the sector included finding and training Morgan's now longtime CEO Jamie Dimon.

The remarkable proliferation of new players competing for advisory roles on major transactions contributed to the loss of dominance by this group. M&A advisors now came in all shapes and sizes. The biggest banks were, of course, still in the business, and with much expanded teams no less. Even remnants of the deceased Lehman remained active, given that the British bank Barclays had acquired its US business out of bankruptcy. In addition, a wide variety of Australian, Canadian, European and Japanese banks had also become competitors in the advisory business. Plus there were now at least a few dozen so-called independent investment banks; some were very much like our firm in structure and strategy, and others highly specialized in a particular industry sector, region or type of transaction.

To my surprise, even the erstwhile Silicon Valley Bank over time became a participant in the M&A business, first by acquiring an advisory boutique that specialized in the healthcare sector and later by recruiting from UBS a large technology-focused team. It was now hard to imagine that, back in the day, a newly minted Wharton graduate like me would not even know what an investment banker was. Now investment banks seemed almost as plentiful as Starbucks cafes and investment bankers as common as baristas.

Compounding the challenges inherent in battling such an enlarged group of competitors was the fact that the opportunities available for all those businesses to pursue had significantly diminished. Following the brief pandemic-era M&A boom that had been inadvertently engineered by US fiscal and monetary authorities as they injected copious amounts of economic stimulus into an anemic, COVID-ravaged economy, by early 2023 the number of large transactions globally was on pace to be at the second-lowest level since we became a public company. While tighter credit markets were one reason for that, another important factor was the increasing opposition of governments, particularly the heretofore largely laissez-faire US government, to large transactions.

My own hard-won TEGNA deal was one victim of that shift. A request for Federal Communications Commission (FCC) approval for that transaction languished for more than a full year after that deal was agreed and announced. Given that the TV broadcasting sector had already seen the FCC allow larger combinations to come together, we never imagined that this transaction would attract the ire of regulators. But TEGNA was only one example of a company that saw a critical strategic transaction fall prey to overzealous regulators. Indeed, in just the time since we announced that deal it felt like governmental hostility to deals of all kinds had risen to a higher level than I had experienced over the course of my entire career. It was unclear if or when that stance would soften.

There is nothing like farming, even on the very modest and decidedly amateur scale at which I practiced it, when it comes to reinforcing the words of the wise King Solomon[2] (more recently made famous by the 1960s rock band, The Byrds[3]) that for everything there is a season.

That seems especially true on a New England farm. In winter there are few signs of life. As spring arrives, hay, alfalfa and other grain crops slowly start to press up through the frozen ground. One at a time over several weeks, a cow will wander away from the herd to find a quiet place in the pasture to give birth to a calf. Those calves will initially stick close to their mother, but before long start to congregate with the other calves of their cohort. Not long thereafter they walk independently among the herd, no longer calves at all. Meanwhile, in the garden, a wide variety of crops come to life. Then, only a few months later, veritable tidal waves of diverse lettuces and tomatoes, then potatoes, peaches, apples and pumpkins, signal first the peak and then the approaching end to another growing season. Over the winter and into the next spring the whole cycle starts over again.

The Wall Street equivalent of "a time to plant, a time to reap" (to quote The Byrds' version of this bit of wisdom) is "a time to buy and a time to sell." And indeed for every asset there is a season. Given all the changes in our industry, as well as the challenging current market environment, I began to think that perhaps the time had come to sell our firm. Particularly so if it could be done in a manner that meant nothing more than a transition to a new incarnation in which our strong brand, and our talented team, could continue to flourish.

Through numerous business crises and personal tragedies I had heretofore always adhered to Bob Greenhill's mantra to "keep moving." But that need not mean always moving in the same direction. Maybe, like my ownership of the White Hart inn or like various aspects of Greenhill's business that were ultimately shed, our status as an independent public company wasn't meant to be forever. In those other instances I had shown an ability to pivot decisively, and at least initially alone, to a new path. Perhaps now I would again.

I found myself reflecting back on a comment to *The New York Times* more than a decade earlier by my fellow Penn trustee William Lauder (of the Estée Lauder founding family) that I had always found both amusing and true – "[b]eing the CEO of a public company is a [prison] sentence."[4] He added that playing such a role in a family-controlled company, to which our closely held firm had many similarities, was even worse – "a life sentence." Being a public company of any kind had indeed become increasingly less appealing over the years. And likewise leading one. I recalled the advice some time ago from my Lazard friend to "bury" the firm in some much larger financial institution. Doing so would free us from the rigors of operating a public company while allowing our team to continue to flourish as part of an organization with greater scope and scale.

The number of public companies in America had actually peaked the year our firm was founded,[5] and since then that number had fallen roughly by half. One factor in this decline was undoubtedly the evolving nature of equity markets – passive index funds now dominated markets, and Eliot Spitzer's reforms had diminished the quality of company research available to fundamental investors. As a result, there was much less room for smaller companies to thrive in today's stock market. Our own experience suggested that the increasing government regulation involved in operating a publicly owned entity was another important catalyst for this undeniable trend. It was laughable to look back and recall that only a dozen years earlier our general counsel had retired following the spin-off of our private equity business because she felt like there was not much of a role left for her in simply managing the legal affairs of a public company with personnel scattered across eleven countries around the world. Now we found ourselves weighed down by an increasing amount of what Bob Greenhill would have disdainfully called bureaucracy.

So, only four days after Credit Suisse's forced sale and while our own First Republic Bank was still teetering, I hit send on an email to follow up on a phone call I had received eight months earlier. The call had come out of the blue the previous July from a banker at Houlihan Lokey – one of our competitors – who specialized in the financial sector. I didn't know him, but I did know the founder of the small financial services specialist with which he had previously been connected.

"Are you familiar with the Japanese bank Mizuho?" he asked.

"Not really," I said. "Why?"

"They have built a substantial US investment banking business, and they're interested in expanding into M&A. Would you be open to having a conversation with their senior guy?"

"No," was my short response.

"Come on. They're in your building. Not even a cup of coffee?"

Despite realizing that, yes, I did now recall seeing the Mizuho name prominently featured in the lobby of our still relatively new headquarters building alongside that of Major League Baseball and other tenants, I repeated my negative response. In doing so I went against the advice proffered by John Mack in his about-to-be-released biography in regard to similar circumstances, that "[i]t never hurts to take a meeting. You always learn something."[6]

Several months after that brief exchange, and just three weeks after our global partners' meeting, another prospective acquirer appeared. This one was from Spain, and this time (having by then read Mack's book) I did agree to a meeting – in part because I had always enjoyed my visits to our Madrid office. The food and wine are delightful, and the people seem more vivacious and optimistic than most Europeans. Days later, over a convivial lunch in a private room at the same University Club venue where I had recently spoken to my assembled Greenhill partners, these new suitors dangled the possibility of an acquisition of our firm at a substantial premium over our current stock market valuation. They said our brand, our leadership and our team would all remain in place under their ownership.

Surprisingly that dialogue ended with just that one meeting. I later learned that the highly enthusiastic delegation that had come to woo me got instructed by its board in no uncertain terms to focus its efforts on fixing a recent unrelated US acquisition that had gone wrong before contemplating another foray into the M&A market. Yet the ideas discussed in that lunch time conversation got me thinking.

I soon concluded that I would reach out to Mizuho after all these months of silence and offer to make the short journey by elevator to hear what its management had wanted to tell me the previous summer. I wasn't a big believer in fate, but forty-three years earlier Providence had placed my future wife across the hall in my college dormitory. Perhaps it was signaling another attractive long-term marriage opportunity by installing Mizuho and our firm on contiguous floors of the beautifully refurbished former Time-Life Building on Sixth Avenue.

After some weeks of delay because Mizuho's American management was in Japan for what I now recalled was the March 31 fiscal year-end for Japanese companies, a meeting finally took place on April 12. I liked the fellow I met, an American who had built and led Mizuho's large US business for some years. And the corporate culture he described sounded like a good fit for our people. I came away from that informal chat in comfortable chairs in his corner office thinking the time was right, from our perspective as well as Mizuho's, for this particular combination.

I had just read in the *Financial Times* about Japan getting its "swagger back" after a long quiet period following the extraordinary global ascendancy that Japan was enjoying as I began my career.[7] Back then Japanese banks were the leaders of the financial world. Japanese companies were hoovering up trophy assets like Rockefeller Center and the Pebble Beach golf club at such a pace that American politicians and pundits started fretting about the Japanese "taking over the world." In retrospect that was a sure sign that this particular bubble was about to burst, which of course it soon did. For some time after, investment bankers like me would continue to solicit Japanese buyers for attractive assets we were trying to sell, but they became increasingly rare-until just recently.

While initially I knew very little about Mizuho specifically, I soon learned why that name was not so familiar to me. It resulted from a 2002 merger of three prominent Japanese banks that I had encountered at various points in my early career, particularly during my time in London – Fuji Bank, Industrial Bank of Japan and Dai-Ichi Kangyo Bank. It struck me that the Mizuho story was a Japanese version of what had evolved at America's J.P. Morgan, which over time had rolled up my original New York City checkbook provider Manufacturers Hanover, as well as Chase Manhattan, Bank One, Washington Mutual, Bear Stearns and most recently the distressed First Republic. Putting aside the huge state-owned banks in China, Mizuho was now something like the tenth biggest bank in the world – larger than Citigroup, Deutsche Bank or UBS. It also had developed a large US presence, just not in the kind of advisory businesses on which we had always focused.

Intrigued, two days after my first introductory meeting, I sat in my Palm Beach kitchen googling on my iPad to learn more about this bank while eating breakfast. At that very moment an advertisement for Mizuho popped up on the CNBC TV show I had on in the background. The tag line for that ad said Mizuho was "a name worth knowing," and I increasingly felt that indeed might be the case for me and my firm. The simple fact that this was the first Mizuho ad I had ever seen signaled to me that Mizuho must be among those Japanese institutions now regaining some of the swagger of days of old. As further evidence, I soon learned that the week after the upcoming Memorial Day holiday Mizuho would be sponsoring, for the first time, a high-profile women's professional golf tournament at the prestigious Liberty National Golf Club just outside New York.

Events moved swiftly from there. I made a full-blown presentation of what I claimed was "everything there is to know about" our business, and then I drafted a term sheet for a possible deal. That term sheet was only two pages long but covered all the issues that I cared about, from sale price to brand to our team to my personal desire to continue on as "chairman" of the group (a somewhat honorary title akin to what Bob Greenhill had once held) but give up my CEO role. I would focus my efforts on clients, along with mentoring my handpicked successors. Among many other benefits, this deal would thus facilitate the solution to my own long-running succession dilemma.

I had, of course, kept my board of directors apprised of these early discussions, but my obsession with confidentiality was such that I informed nobody else within the firm, not even my longtime assistant Maureen. The sole exception was our recently retired CFO Hal Rodriguez. From his Charlottesville, Virginia, base he played a key behind-the-scenes role gathering the necessary data, creating presentation documents and acting as my consigliere on the very wide range of issues involved in such a deal. Given that the positive response to my term sheet made clear that there remained little of real substance about which to argue, I soon involved three or four other senior colleagues to help finalize the transaction terms and documentation.

My goal quickly became to sign and announce a deal just before Mizuho's upcoming golf tournament. I had learned from experience that every deal needs a deadline, simply because the old line that "the work will expand to fill the time available" was true. The convenient excuse for this timeline would be to maximize the marketing opportunity in relation to the many important clients Mizuho would draw to such a prestigious and enjoyable event. But that schedule was extremely ambitious for any deal, let alone one with a foreign counterparty. When I first went to see my former Wachtell colleague and now co-managing partner of that firm, Ed Herlihy, to retain my alma mater as legal advisors on the transaction, he had asked me, "Have you figured who the man behind the curtain is yet? Because in every Japanese deal I've worked on it turns out there's a man behind the curtain who makes the final decisions."

I told Ed that it felt like there was no mysterious man behind the curtain, and thus I hoped I could take what I was being told at face value. And as days and weeks passed I was proven right that Mizuho's US management team had the full confidence of its Japanese parent and thus could progress swiftly toward a deal. In fact, by the time of our annual shareholders meeting and an associated board meeting on May 2 we had accomplished so much that we nudged our planned announcement date eight days earlier than the already bold day-after-Memorial Day target for which we had originally been aiming. My experience with TEGNA had reinforced my policy of never waiting even one day longer than necessary to get an important deal to signing and announcement.

Even that approach, however, had fallen short of ensuring successful completion in TEGNA's case – coincidentally the accelerated new target announcement date for our deal with Mizuho was the very same day my media client's transaction was contractually set to expire without completion. That is, unless the FCC provided a last-minute reprieve, which everyone involved knew in their heads if not their hearts would not happen.

The day after our board and shareholders meetings my counterpart and I reached agreement on the one issue that inevitably did require some debate: price. From the start, for reasons of pride as much as logic, I wanted an exceptional premium – not the typical 30–35% over current market value that public companies typically received, but something more than double our current share price.

Mizuho obviously wanted to be disciplined, but there were good grounds for them to pay such a price. For one, our stock was depressed relative to historic levels and even in comparison to its high for the previous year. In addition, there was significant potential value to be gained from the substantial "synergies" that could flow from the combination, as we performed advisory work for Mizuho's current financing clients and it provided financing and other services to our current M&A clients. Furthermore, I knew Japanese companies across all sectors had great respect for the value of a recognized brand. We had certainly built one of those – Greenhill was known to corporate executives around the world for high-quality advice and transaction execution. Plus we were not asking Mizuho to compete with others in an auction to win the Greenhill business – ours was an exclusive negotiation. Accordingly, just before heading thirty blocks north of our shared office building to a gala event to mark the opening of a major addition to the American Museum of Natural History, I gently drew a line in the sand at an even $15 per share.

Throughout that magnificent, celebratory evening I discreetly checked my phone for any messages responding to that position. Once I was startled to see an email not from my Mizuho counterpart but from a senior banker at another firm – this one Canadian – that had broached the idea of an acquisition of our firm over a long lunch more than a year earlier. Soon afterward, it had become distracted by another acquisition opportunity in a very different business segment and failed to follow up. Now we were much too far down the track with Mizuho for it to catch up. In the end, the news I was waiting for finally came early the next morning, as I traveled back to midtown from the ribbon-cutting ceremony for the Museum's grand addition, where I had stood among the mayor and other civic leaders. We were done at $15, a 121% premium over our current share price.

That sounded like a big premium in a headline sense, but Mizuho concurred that it was important that our team feel good about the deal. And the cost of that was modest relative to the strategic benefits of the transaction.

The per share price equated to a total value of $550 million for our business, including the debt on our balance sheet that Mizuho would assume. Determining whether that was a valuation for me to be proud of or embarrassed about, even for someone who had spent a career doing that kind of analysis, was not easy. I had seen our shares change hands over the years at values ranging from the fraction of a penny each that I paid when I first bought into the firm to the $60s, $70s and $80s at which we had sold shares along the way, and briefly to more than $90 in the squeeze created by the government ban on short selling of financial stocks in the wake of Lehman's bankruptcy filing. Every year of our history there had been constant gyrations – after all, on a day-to-day basis the market is a voting machine (measuring popularity), not a weighing machine (measuring value).

Stepping back to consider the $550 million figure in a fundamental sense, from a glass half-empty perspective (admittedly not my typical viewpoint) it was notable that this was not much different than the value of our firm at the time of its IPO 19 years earlier. But, in fairness, there was a fair amount of hype surrounding that IPO. We were only about a hundred human beings at the time, all but a few with little experience. So in retrospect that initial public market value was both extraordinary and unwarranted. Further, despite that high-starting point, we had in fact generated meaningful value as a public company – over time our shareholders received more than $675 million just in quarterly dividend payments. And money wasn't the only measure of success – we also had trained and well-compensated many hundreds of employees, including innumerable kids fresh out of college for whom we provided critical first full-time job experience. Plus of course we had performed valuable services for countless clients.

Back on the negative side, it was undeniable that a handful of the advisory firms that followed us into the public markets had grown to have much larger valuations than ours. None had seen their stocks take off like a rocket ship as ours did at the start, so few bankers saw the kind of windfall our early partners did. Surprisingly, over time Houlihan Lokey – the firm anyone in our industry would have viewed as the least prestigious of the independent advisory group given its focus on smaller deals – came to have the largest market value of all. The slow and steady approach they and others took ultimately paid off.

Nonetheless, I was again inclined to see the glass as at least half full. There are cycles, or seasons, in the life of every public company – moments to be a buyer and moments to be a seller. I had timed my moves in and out of our stock pretty well over the years, and as our firm's largest shareholder I was certainly aligned with other shareholders in wanting to procure for them a fair value, whatever that meant at this moment, for what we had painstakingly built over many years. Most simplistically, the vast array of buyers and sellers around the world collectively sets stock valuations every day, and we were being paid an unusually high premium over the current price of our stock. So, in conclusion, I was good with where we settled on price.

As with any M&A deal of significance, even with price settled there remained numerous details to work out and much paperwork to prepare as we hurtled toward an announcement scheduled for the morning of Monday, May 22. To a large extent those details were handled by Wachtell lawyers working the late shift as I once did, along with their counterparts on the Mizuho side. Most people in my position of chairman, CEO and largest shareholder would have likewise devoted their undivided attention in those final days to getting the deal done. But I had always found that making the time for unrelated, all-consuming diversions had a way of clearing my mind so I could make better business decisions.

Precisely a week before the planned announcement I went to Philadelphia to play my annual role in Penn's graduation. Relative to the scorching heat of my daughter's graduation the year before it was a picture-perfect day for the student march down Locust Walk to the ceremony at Franklin Field in front of thousands of parents, siblings and grandparents, which this year included President Joe Biden. My pride in all things Penn had never been greater. Adding to the uncountable "feel good" Quaker moments I had experienced over the decades, just a few weeks earlier came news that the eldest of the three girls whose father, Rakesh Chawla, died in our plane crash a dozen years earlier would be enrolling in the next freshman class at Penn – the place where her parents had met while in graduate school. The son of our office receptionist would be one of her classmates.

The time for reveling in such moments would come later. Just minutes after the graduation festivities I hustled back to Manhattan to be onsite for the last days of work on what was becoming the most important transaction in my long career of dealmaking. The next two evenings my wife and I managed to take in a show – another revival of Sondheim's *Sweeney Todd* one night and a quirky new show based on Shakespeare's *Hamlet* called *Fat Ham* the next. I spent every other waking minute, however, focused on doing whatever it took to get to the finish line on our deal. Even on the car rides home from Broadway, I found myself answering queries of lawyers still in their offices sorting through the minutiae that must be settled in the final stages of any significant deal. I was a quick decision-maker – always with a view toward reaching a tolerable compromise and keeping the process moving swiftly forward.

The weekend before the planned early Monday announcement was a blur of activity. The Greenhill board got its final briefing and approved the deal. I worked the various time zones to place individual calls to my key partners scattered around the world to personally fill them in on the news.

Included on my call list was my assistant Maureen. She too had been kept in the dark in the preceding weeks through my use of fake calendar entries and other surreptitious maneuvers. Until I knew we were going to get to the finish line, confidentiality had been of paramount importance to me. Explaining a failed attempt at a sale was unthinkable.

I also made sure that Bob Greenhill, by now long retired but still the firm's second largest shareholder, got the news early. Rather than try to speak directly for the first time since his hurried evacuation of our office and his Greenwich home a few years earlier, I conveyed our plan through his longtime financial advisor. Sunday afternoon I was thrilled to hear back from him a response via an email that was perfectly evocative of Bob's terse conversational style: "Message delivered. Great response." And with a thumbs-up emoji to boot.

Fortunately, I could handle all the calls that I needed to make from my Connecticut farm, as I also spent that weekend interviewing possible replacements for the farmer who had recently decided to leave Twin Lakes Farm after several good years. We had fifteen cows that either had just given birth or were about to calve, so time was of the essence – strangely, among the earliest spring arrivals we were experiencing a far higher rate of stillborns than ever. This heightened the urgency of our recruiting task while simultaneously proving there are startling outlier events in nature as well as in markets.

Roxanne and I had encountered all the archetypes of modern farmers in our search. There was the highly experienced fellow a bit younger than us who seemed perfect until he dropped out after being severely injured by a rambunctious steer at a livestock show that he was attending with his high school-age daughter, a regular competitor at such events. There was the aging Berkshires hippie who seemed remarkably knowledgeable about all aspects of the garden but unlikely to be able to handle delicate tasks like the annual capturing of the bull that we brought in for a few months' residence each summer to impregnate our heifers. And there was a 27-year-old local fellow reminiscent of the character on *Game of Thrones* that they called "The Mountain." He seemed to make up in youthful energy what he lacked in experience. Needless to say, we chose The Mountain and considered that weekend recruiting accomplishment almost as important as my pending sale of our firm.

With a new farmer hired and all the calls to Greenhill colleagues made, by late Sunday evening I took the time to look at my calendar and count the days since the first time I had shaken hands with a Mizuho executive. I knew we had moved faster than I had ever seen a transaction move in my nearly four decades of dealmaking. But I was shocked to calculate that only forty days had passed from our very first meeting to the announced transaction. That round number immediately conjured up childhood memories of innumerable Sundays spent in church with my parents back in Michigan. In the Christian tradition, that precise period of time – referenced in more than twenty different places in the Bible and often with the suffix "and 40 nights" – carries deep meaning and symbolizes a period of testing or trial.

Rain covered the earth for forty days while Noah and his animals drifted in the ark he had built. Moses was on a mountaintop for forty days when he received the Ten Commandments on tablets of stone. Goliath taunted the Israelites for forty days before he was slain by the future king of Israel David. After Jesus was baptized he went to the desert where he fasted for forty days and resisted the temptations of the devil. Later, following his crucifixion and resurrection, Jesus spent forty days on earth before he ascended into heaven.[8]

I hadn't slayed a Goliath, although I had often used his battle with David as a metaphor when referring to our firm's decades-long competition with banking institutions hundreds of times our size. I had brought a seventy-seven-page merger contract down from my twenty-first-floor office, not sacred stone tablets from Mount Sinai. I had endured some difficult, lonely periods as the firm faced various challenges over the years but can't quite say I ever did so in a desert. Now I was ascending from the 24/7 rigors of a CEO position into a less demanding chairman role, not into heaven.

To be clear, nothing biblical happened here. But the story of Greenhill and its competitors both large and small is as old as capitalism itself. And the metaphor struck me as having at least some relevance. Without question, I had been through a period of trial, not just for those forty days (and forty nights) of negotiations but really for the twenty-six years since my exhilarating introductory dinner in Greenwich with Bob and Gayle Greenhill. Like all those biblical figures, I emerged from my time of testing with a clear sense that one grand adventure was now over, while others were still to come.

CHAPTER TWENTY TWO

A GATHERING STORM

Come all ye loyal classmen now.[1]
– Harry E. Westervelt, The Red and Blue

S igning the agreement to sell Greenhill seemed like the perfect ending to the Wall Street adventure story I had been writing since the
early days of the pandemic. Upon completion of that sale, which I
knew was some months away given the myriad global regulatory approvals
required, I would shed the 24/7 chief executive officer title I had borne for
years and enjoy three less-demanding, supervisory "chairman" roles – of
Greenhill, the American Museum of Natural History and the University of
Pennsylvania.

I would continue to advise clients on deals, although I did not expect
to play again the kind of day-to-day transaction leadership role that I had
repeatedly undertaken over the prior quarter century or more. And especially not on a hostile takeover defense—M&A dealmakers universally
regard those as the most demanding of assignments. They had been a

particular specialty of Wachtell Lipton, the law firm I joined right out of law school, and were an important part of my work at both Morgan Stanley and Greenhill.

But my expectation was wrong. Even before the Greenhill deal closed I found myself at the center of the most unusual and high-profile takeover battle of my life – one that drew on learnings from every aspect of my career. This would not be the typical corporate contretemps played out on the pages of *The Wall Street Journal*. This was a struggle for control of the University of Pennsylvania, and it would mark the beginning of a period of nationwide campus unrest unlike anything seen since the Vietnam War era.

This harrowing saga would further illustrate how the influence of Wall Street had mushroomed since I first arrived there in the 1980s. The players in this conflict would include titans of the private equity, hedge fund and M&A worlds – here in academia just as in the more familiar corporate sphere. And as with the fiercest of contests fought in the stock market, those players would employ a wide range of weapons beyond passionate boardroom debate: money, the media, state and federal governments, the courts. The ensuing drama was such that a detailed description thereof is both gripping and illuminating, even if the ultimate outcome of the battle remains inconclusive.

It all began with a two-sentence email in early September of 2023.

"Not sure if you saw this. Not good."[2]

That email came from a longtime Penn trustee – a Wharton alum from the private equity world – one of many board members with whom I had a friendly relationship. His note was of a type that I frequently received, containing some reference to a news item that related to Penn, often accompanied by a question or suggestion as to what the University should do. The reference here was to an attached announcement that ranked colleges according to their openness to "free speech."[3] Penn had been ranked second to last by this publication, ahead only of Harvard. While the qualifications of this unfamiliar organization to make such rankings were unknown to me, this news clearly did not sit comfortably with a trustee accustomed to hearing over the years of Penn rating favorably on all sorts of comparisons.

Penn's founder Benjamin Franklin had been an advocate of free speech, once saying there is "no such thing as public liberty without freedom of speech."[4] On college campuses in recent years debate about free speech had focused almost entirely on the narrow question of whether politically conservative speakers were welcomed (or not) as members of the faculty or visiting speakers. In that sense, I knew that the fellow who wrote me wasn't the only trustee who paid attention to this issue.

Another trustee and Wharton alum, an M&A banker who had spent his career at competitors of Greenhill and many years earlier had interviewed for a spot at our firm, had been pressing me for months to have lunch with a psychologist, author and New York University professor named Jonathan Haidt. Haidt, who happened to have a PhD from Penn, had some years earlier written a seminal piece for *The Atlantic* titled "The Coddling of the American Mind." The subtitle of the piece summed up his premise: "In the name of emotional well-being, college students are increasingly demanding protection from words and ideas they don't like. Here's why that's disastrous for education – and mental health."[5]

These two trustees were in some ways representative of Penn's board, which was weighted toward Wharton grads who had made fortunes in hedge funds, private equity or elsewhere on Wall Street. Not surprisingly, that segment of the board skewed well to the right on the political spectrum. But efforts in recent years to create a more diverse board meant that not everyone shared their viewpoint, and thus it was good that for the most part board members politely kept their political views to themselves. For example, during the pandemic one trustee virulently opposed to a campus vaccine mandate – despite that being required by law in the city of Philadelphia – had expressed his concerns only to President Amy Gutmann and me rather than to the entire board.

Fortunately Penn had so far largely avoided the spotlight on the issue of free speech. In fact I knew of no cases in my many years of involvement where a student or faculty member was disciplined for speech, nor anywhere an outside speaker had been turned away. But just a short time earlier news of a Donald Trump-appointed judge being poorly treated at a Stanford University event had gone viral,[6] and similar cases had sporadically cropped up over the years, particularly at the elite universities that were Penn's peers.

Seven days later the same trustee wrote to me again, this time under the subject heading "Palestinian event." Again his message was terse: "I know there is nothing you can do but I have gotten dozens of emails on this. It's getting pretty ugly."[7]

He was referring to the Palestine Writes Literature Festival – a large gathering with more than 100 speakers scheduled to take place on Penn's campus in late September. That was the weekend just before Yom Kippur, the holiest day in the Jewish calendar, a fact that would serve to further heighten emotions around this event given the long history of conflict between Israelis and Palestinians.

In stating that there was nothing I could do my fellow trustee acknowledged the fact that academic events were not matters with which trustees got involved. All trustees knew – or should have known – that there was no centralized vetting process to determine which speakers were worthy of being allowed on Penn's campus. Each year literally hundreds of events are arranged, and innumerable speakers are invited to campus by various faculty and student groups. Any meaningful pre-approval process across numerous academic disciplines would not only entail an unwieldy bureaucracy but fly in the face of any notion of academic freedom. Trustees would not even learn of a particular event after the fact unless they happened to read about it in one of the numerous publications that Penn produced for marketing or fundraising purposes.

This particular event, however, had already crossed my radar screen. In late August an alumnus I did not know had sent me a polite note of concern: "My intention is not to advocate for cancellation; instead I am emphasizing the need for respectful discourse in line with academic integrity. I am asking that the University issue a statement raising questions about the selection of some of the speakers...."[8]

Such statements of concern or condemnation by the University president, particularly in advance of a speaker's appearance, were exceedingly rare. I couldn't recall Amy Gutmann – Liz Magill's highly regarded predecessor – issuing a single one in relation to a campus speaker in her nearly twenty-year tenure. In fact, some internal research soon determined that the last such statement by a Penn president was made some thirty-five years earlier, when Sheldon Hackney issued one in regard to an upcoming visit by Louis Farrakhan, the Black religious leader who headed the "Nation of Islam" and was known for making overtly antisemitic remarks.[9] Hackney had expressed concerns about Farrakhan, but made clear that the visit should, and would, be allowed. Now, as the flow of emails urging such a statement in regard to the Palestine Writers event grew, President Magill, after numerous discussions with me, faculty members and others across the University, decided to issue one.

The resulting two paragraph statement conceded that "many [had] raised deep concerns about several speakers" among the many to be featured who had "a documented and troubling history of engaging in antisemitism."[10] The punchline of this note was that the University "unequivocally – and emphatically – condemn[s] antisemitism as antithetical to our institutional values" but also that it "fiercely support[s] the free exchange of ideas as central to our educational mission," including "the expression of views that are controversial and even those that are incompatible with our institutional values."

That latter point was not only consistent with historic Penn policy dating back to Ben Franklin but echoed the sentiments President Magill herself had tried to convey at her first student convocation – the one where, ironically, her plea for civil discourse and debate had been shouted down by protestors.

In the lead up to issuing that proclamation, Liz had presciently warned me that, based on her experience and observation, such presidential "statements" are almost never satisfying to those who ask for them and yet at the same time typically manage to anger those on the other side of the issue at hand. Indeed, within a few days a group of thirty-six faculty members, including a prominent member of the history department who had served with me on the search committee that brought Liz to Penn, wrote a letter provided to *The Daily Pennsylvanian*, the student paper known across campus and among alumni as simply *The DP*. The professors criticized the president's statement, saying that it was "very wrong, on many levels…to suggest that Palestinian literature, culture, and aspirations be conflated with antisemitism."[11] They asked for an amendment of the statement to make it narrower in scope.

Yet at around the same time an open letter began circulating on the internet, asking for the exact opposite. That letter sought alumni signatures to "express deep concerns regarding the platforming of known antisemitic speakers."[12] This missive did not call for cancellation of the event, but rather made four specific requests: issuing a stronger condemnation, ensuring that the Penn "brand" was not associated with the event, clarifying the nature of sponsorship provided by some University departments and developing mandatory antisemitism awareness training for implementation across the University. Touching on a theme that would soon become central to the ongoing debate, the letter referenced Blacks, Asians and LGBTQ as groups the signatories believed would benefit from a stronger University reaction in comparable circumstances.

The same day the faculty letter was received, I spoke for the first time to former University Trustee Marc Rowan, who appeared to be among the leaders of the effort to gather signatures for the alumni letter. Rowan, a Wharton alumnus who graduated just a few years after me, was head of that school's advisory board, a sort of subsidiary board to the University-level board that I chaired – one without a real fiduciary or governance role. He was a highly prominent alumnus and CEO of the private equity and alternative investing giant Apollo, which he and two other refugees from the collapsed Drexel Burnham Lambert firm had founded thirty-three years earlier.

Private equity chieftains are the modern "masters of the universe" – their funds now controlled around 30,000 companies worldwide.[13] And, among what were now many hundreds of active fund managers, Apollo had been particularly successful, with each of its founders long ago achieving "billionaire" status. While Rowan had been a key senior executive in the firm from the start, he had only recently taken on the CEO role in the wake of the departure of his predecessor and co-founder Leon Black. Black, a towering Wall Street figure who was also well-known in the art world, stepped down after his close relationship to prominent sex trafficker and pedophile Jeffrey Epstein came to light but remained the firm's largest shareholder.

Our conversation was cordial. While we had never crossed paths in a business or social context, we had said a friendly hello a handful of times at Penn trustee gatherings in recent years. Our only significant conversation had taken place some months earlier. He called me to say that he needed to resign his position as a Penn trustee because he was taking on a very time-consuming leadership role at United Jewish Appeal-Federation of New York, a major nonprofit organization known by its initials UJA. I knew his attendance record had already been weak relative to most other trustees, so was not surprised by his decision. But he had been a generous benefactor of the University so I suggested, and he agreed, that I would forego bringing the typical resolution of appreciation to the next formal board meeting as we would normally do for retiring trustees – which in most cases were considerably older than him – in the hope that he might rejoin the board at a future time when his calendar was less crowded.

Notwithstanding the narrowly defined requests listed in the alumni open letter, my email inbox began to fill up with increasingly aggressive calls for the outright cancellation of the upcoming event. Many labeled the festival a "hatefest." It was not unheard of for me to receive random emails like these, written with passion by people I did not know, in regard to Penn matters. The highest volume prior to this had come a couple years earlier in regard to Lia Thomas, a transgender member of Penn's women's swimming team and classmate of my daughter who won a national championship in the 500-yard freestyle. Then President Gutmann and the Penn board – for most of the relevant period under my predecessor as chair – rode out that controversy without taking any position at all, on the grounds that it was the National Collegiate Athletics Association, not individual schools like Penn, that determined eligibility for the various sports in which Penn teams competed.

With very few exceptions, I did not respond to the flood of emails. They were too numerous, and many had a hostile tone that made me want to avoid engaging. However, President Magill and I did each speak to many Penn trustees and prominent alumni, both to hear their views and to try to chart a path out of this controversy.

As part of that effort, another trustee introduced Liz to Jonathan Greenblatt, National Director of the Anti-Defamation League (ADL), which calls itself the leading anti-hate organization in the world and has a particular focus on combatting antisemitism. A few days later that dialogue resulted in a lengthy letter from Magill to Greenblatt, which was intended to be made publicly available and both act as an expansion of her first statement and address at least some of the requests in the alumni

letter. Her letter specifically answered what seemed like the most important such request by committing to broad antisemitism awareness training
across the University. It closed with the proclamation that "[t]he University
of Pennsylvania remains unwavering in its commitment to combatting
antisemitism and supporting our Jewish community."[14]

That Jewish community had flourished at Penn for decades. Back in
the period when some Ivy League schools essentially enforced quotas in
Jewish admissions, Penn had been much more welcoming than its peers.
Thus Penn ended up with a large Jewish component to its student body
long ago. My understanding was that the Ivy quotas elsewhere were long
gone by the time I started college, but even then around a third of the kids
on my freshman floor in Warwick, a house within the huge Quadrangle
dormitory, were Jewish. A majority of my roommates in my undergraduate
years were Jewish, including one who roomed with me three years and
served as "best man" at my wedding the summer after I graduated. More
notably, three of the four Penn presidents who most recently preceded Liz
were Jewish, my predecessor as trustee chair was Jewish and many campus
buildings and programs bore the name of Jewish philanthropists who were
Penn graduates.

I knew that Jewish enrollment – along with enrollment of white Chris-
tians like me – had declined materially since my day, as room was made over
time for the many ethnic groups underrepresented back then. These included
Blacks, Latinos, people of Chinese and Indian heritage, international students
and first-generation college students of all kinds. My freshman-floor dorm
was entirely white and – apart from myself – from the Mid-Atlantic states.
Now, amid an exploding applicant pool, Penn's student body was diverse
in every sense. Yet the Jewish population among students, faculty, senior
administrators and trustees was still very substantial today.

President Magill sent the letter to the ADL on September 20, a few
days before the festival was to begin. But by the time that missive got
around, the alumni letter criticizing the event had collected thousands of

signatures. Further, many of those alumni signatories were in increasingly close communication, serving to further stoke their collective anger.

The specifics of what actually occurred at the Palestine Writes Literature Festival on the weekend of September 23 are now lost to history. The festival encompassed numerous speakers at many separate events – some large enough to fill the 1,200-seat Irvine Auditorium where President Magill's inauguration had taken place less than a year earlier, as well as smaller ones such as a poetry reading hosted by Kelly Writers House, where my wife and I had made our first reconnection to Penn as alumni.

I phoned Liz multiple times over the course of that weekend, anxious to hear news of what was happening. I knew she had some of her staff in attendance, and I knew that both *The DP* and the *Philadelphia Inquirer* had reporters on-site, undoubtedly hoping for some controversial sound bite that would create a news story for them. Indeed, an opening speaker at the conference welcomed attendees who were there to "surveil and monitor."[15] Clearly everyone knew this event was being closely watched, and not just by supporters.

From everything I heard and read that weekend and just after, all the various talks sounded fairly benign in nature. Surprisingly, no independent news organization, including *The DP* or *Inquirer*, wrote in any detail on what actually occurred at this much anticipated event until CNN, the cable news network, posted a story on its website more than a month later. That piece explained that the festival included almost eighty sessions on a wide variety of topics. It referenced dancing, poetry readings and crafts, while conceding that "[s]ome events took a more political tone."[16] Based on recordings from the event as well as interviews with both participants and critics, the CNN reporter identified no noteworthy antisemitic content.

There were, however, a couple of antisemitic acts on campus in the days leading up to the festival – the first I could recall hearing about in my tenure as a trustee. A swastika was found scrawled on a wall inside a university building, and someone whom I later heard had a history of mental illness came into the lobby of the Jewish cultural venue Hillel early one morning shouting antisemitic epithets and tipping over trash cans and tables. Both acts were appropriately and swiftly condemned by President Magill.

While we initially hoped that the passing of the conference without news of any particularly inflammatory content might cause the uproar to quiet down, it soon became clear that this would not be the case. The alumni letter had focused entirely on the festival, but its signatories were now mobilized, and there was increasing talk of a much broader agenda. Free speech, various aspects of diversity, equity and inclusion (better known by the acronym DEI), legacy admissions and declining Jewish enrollment were among the areas of grievance. In multiple conversations and emails this collection of stances was described to me as "anti-woke." "Woke" was the slang version of awake, defined by Webster's as "aware of and actively attentive to important societal facts and issues (especially issues of racial and social justice)."[17]

One surprising twist in this tale arose as we considered what to do about the fact that some trustees, including ironically the free speech advocate who had been hounding me to meet with Professor Haidt, had not only signed the open letter but had solicited support for the effort to criticize the statements and actions of the University's president. This was a so-called "governance" question and a pretty unusual one, especially for a board like Penn's that had been remarkably harmonious and free of dissent for all of my eighteen years of involvement. In the business world nearly every corporate decision I had seen made over decades had ultimately been unanimously supported – the sole exception at my old energy client Dynegy had led to disaster.

Of course, there was always room for vigorous debate around the actual or metaphorical board table as to what an organization's policies or actions should be. But in my experience, other than in cases where "activist" investors intent on forcing change had been elected to a board outside the normal nomination process, once a decision was made there were really only three alternatives for a dissenting board member. One, the most typical by far, was simply to accept and support the consensus. Indeed, the willingness to contribute to a debate but not always get one's way is a key characteristic that organizations typically look for in choosing board members. The second alternative, to force either a reversal of the decision or the exit of the decision-maker, was far less common and only possible in the rare case where at least a board majority felt strongly that the decision reached was wrongheaded. And lastly, if one is not only an outlier in the group but cannot get comfortable ultimately supporting the organization's decision, one can resign.

At two meetings our board's executive committee discussed this issue and concluded that we would not worry about the actions of our "emeritus" board members. Theirs was an honorary position that no longer held fiduciary responsibilities or voting power, and on top of that many of them were quite elderly and less connected to the University. Of Penn's nearly fifty active trustees with fiduciary obligations only three had signed the open letter, and one of those had already asked to have her name removed. She did so when she figured out that the agenda of those behind the letter was far broader than the letter itself indicated – and furthermore was misaligned with her self-described liberal political orientation.

The executive committee decided that I should ask the two remaining dissidents to reflect on whether their continuing to hold a board position was tenable given their ongoing, publicly visible dissent. The hope was that they would either realign themselves with the rest of the board or do the honorable thing and resign. Taking a more aggressive stand toward them was not possible given that the ancient and somewhat skeletal corporate charter of the University had no provision whatsoever on how to remove a trustee. Over the next weekend I then had those awkward conversations, and in both cases the individuals somewhat defiantly responded that they would remain on the board notwithstanding their outlier status.

Any lingering hope that we might over time quietly sort out our board governance issues and heal the divisions within Penn's alumni base was dashed on October 7. That was the day when members of the Hamas terrorist group crossed from Gaza into Israel, slaughtering an estimated 1,200 people and taking more than 250 hostages. The victims were almost all civilians, including many who were infants, children or elderly. For Jews worldwide it was the deadliest day since the Holocaust ended almost eighty years earlier. Most of the victims were of course Israeli, but Americans and those of other nationalities were also represented on the casualty list.

Shocking events like September 11, the murder of George Floyd and the October 7 Hamas attack are seen as horrific by thinking people everywhere. But New Yorkers who witnessed soot-covered citizens trudging northward from the World Trade Center site that day and saw smoke rising from the wreckage for weeks thereafter were more psychologically impacted by September 11 than folks where I grew up in Michigan. Black Americans painfully familiar with the long history of police bias in America were understandably more impacted than others by the viral film clip of George Floyd's life being slowly snuffed out by a police officer – in many cities they understandably took to the streets in protest. Similarly, Jewish people whose grandparents' generation was nearly obliterated by the Holocaust were undoubtedly more impacted by October 7 than others. And so this far away event and its myriad ramifications would have major implications for the already stressful situation at Penn.

CHAPTER TWENTY THREE

TWO WORLDS COLLIDE

I'll see you on the other side of the war.[1]
　　　　　　　　　　　　–Lin-Manuel Miranda, Hamilton

T
o say that the October 7 attack sent shockwaves through the Penn community would be an understatement.

It was obvious that President Magill, like most college presidents, would send out a statement condemning the perpetrators and offering sympathy and support to the victims of the attack. She did so on October 10, the Tuesday after the weekend attack, consistent with many of those presidents. Given the criticism of her recent missives on the Palestinian literature event, a great deal of thought and effort went into striking all the right notes on this one. Her statement began with a declarative statement on the heinous nature of what it called "abhorrent attacks," saying, "[w]e are devastated by the horrific assault on Israel by Hamas that targeted civilians and the taking of hostages over the weekend."[2] Much of the rest of the statement, titled "Supporting our Community," focused on those in the Penn community directly impacted by the events, such as those currently visiting or studying in the impacted region or those with personal connections there.

The very same day Liz's statement was released, Marc Rowan submitted a lengthy and highly inflammatory letter to *The Daily Pennsylvanian*. It began by drawing a direct linkage – almost as if one caused the other – between the Palestine Writes Literary Festival and the terrorist attack. He wrote, "It took less than two weeks to go from the [PWLF] on UPenn's campus to the barbaric slaughter and kidnapping of Israelis." He went on to charge that speakers at the Penn event had "advocated ethnic cleansing," "defended the necessity…of substantial violence" and "repeated various blood libels against Jews." In sum, he concluded that the conference provided "[a] tragically prescient preview" of the Hamas attack. He went on to decry a "corrupt morality" at Penn. While conceding that this "didn't begin on President Magill's and Chairman Bok's watch," he called on alumni to send the University only symbolic $1 donations until the two of us resigned.[3]

An important *DP* alum later told me that *The DP* refused to publish the letter given the lack of corroboration for its various incendiary allegations. As a former student reporter there I was proud that the paper had such standards – my assumption would have been that it would simply print any letter from a prominent alumnus. After it was already widely circulated by email, the letter eventually was made public on an online publication with no University affiliation called *PhillyVoice*. In any event, I was still unaware of the contents of this letter when I arrived at my office the next morning, four days after the Hamas attack, to find a message that Ronald Lauder wanted to speak to me.

Ronald, a tall, courtly billionaire nearing eighty years old, is the son of the late cosmetics marketer Estée Lauder. His family, which includes numerous Penn alumni, is among the wealthiest in America and had been hugely philanthropic to Penn. His older brother Leonard, a charming man with a sunny disposition, was the father of William, a current Penn trustee who years earlier made the clever quip I liked about the challenges of serving as a CEO.

Leonard had focused his energies on running the still family-controlled business after Estée's time, while Ronald had pursued more eclectic interests. As longstanding president of the World Jewish Congress, he was extremely active in world Jewish affairs. In addition, he served as the Ambassador to Austria under President Reagan, once ran for mayor of New York City and had such an extraordinary art collection that he set up his own private gallery, the fabulous Neue Galerie, on Manhattan's Upper East Side.

I had a good relationship with both Ronald and Leonard, having served for some years alongside them on the board of an international joint degree program between Wharton and Penn's school of arts and sciences that they funded. I had dined with them multiple times, often sitting next to one of the brothers, at the extraordinary art-filled home that had belonged to their mother, as well as at Ronald's nearby gallery.

Given all that history and the importance of the ongoing controversy I walked over to Ronald's office on the southeast corner of Central Park to see him in person rather than talk by phone. I was greeted warmly by Ronald when I entered his private office after surrendering my cellphone to his assistant as she requested – the first time in my life that I had been asked to do that.

"I looked at your background. I think you may be more Jewish than I am," he said with a smile, noting my undergraduate years at Penn, my first job at a predominantly Jewish law firm and the fact that my own business wasn't "so WASPy," as he put it. He expressed many concerns about what was happening in Israel and on the Penn campus but told me he was supportive of both President Magill and me. He added that he had urged Marc Rowan, when he was sitting the day before in the same chair in which I was now perched, not to publish his letter.

Still not having seen the letter, when I left Ronald's office I reached out to Rowan to propose that we have breakfast the following morning. Our recent phone conversations had been friendly enough, and my hope was that reconciliation was still possible. His assistant booked a table at The Peninsula hotel, which sat between our two offices, then twice moved the reservation earlier given he had by then arranged to appear on CNBC's *Squawk Box* later that morning.

Breakfast was cordial but serious. It didn't last long, but there was time for him to air many of his complaints, the seriousness of which surprised me given his seeming lack of interest in engaging in Penn affairs during his time as a trustee. He spoke of what he saw as the "woke" culture at Penn, said diversity efforts had gone too far, claimed that speech of those on the political right was constrained on campus and referred to what he called "the broken alumni bargain." By that, I presumed he meant the notion that by being a reasonably generous benefactor one would see one's children and grandchildren admitted.

I knew that so-called legacy admissions had represented a significant and fairly stable portion of each entering class in recent years, but given the increasingly high volume of applications that still meant that a large and growing majority of those children who applied were turned away each year. To me that was a "high class" problem – a direct result of both Penn's growing academic reputation and its increasingly generous financial aid offerings, which were funded by alumni donors like Rowan and myself.

I didn't make too many points in response to his allegations, only pointing out that faculty had always been more politically liberal than alumni, at Penn and probably everywhere, and wondering how problematic that really was. I said that it sounded like he was actually angrier at Amy Gutmann than Liz Magill – Amy had presided over nearly twenty years of what he obviously saw as a decaying culture, while Liz had arrived on campus just a year or so before. Moreover, I told him that Liz, who like me was best described as moderate in her political views, was the "least woke" of all the candidates we had seen in our recent presidential search. Finally, frustrated by what I was hearing, I said that his tactics toward our shared alma mater reminded me of that old line from the Vietnam War era: that it was necessary to destroy a village in order to save it.

With the online publication of his letter and his appearance on *Squawk Box* shortly after our breakfast, the hostilities against the leadership and policies of the University escalated to an entirely new level.

Rowan began his TV interview by expressing his "love" for Penn, and he made clear that President Magill was "not an antisemite." Yet his tone was one of righteous indignation. He spoke of "moral confusion," as well as a lack of "moral courage" and "moral clarity" at Penn. As for the degree of alumni discontent, he said there had been "a gathering storm," indicating that grievances had developed over time. And he stretched the mandate visible from the list of four specific requests in the alumni letter to claim it was "basically" telling President Magill she was "heading in the wrong direction." Sounding the alarm on "woke," he claimed "microaggressions" had been met with "extreme moral outrage." And he referred to how the University had better "found its voice" in situations affecting other, more politically favored, oppressed groups.[4]

One of the uglier aspects of the ongoing debate was that the continual envious references to "other groups" forced me and others to reflect on which groups on campus were shown the greatest sensitivity or received the best treatment. Searching for answers, I eventually looked up the University statement following the murder of George Floyd. To my surprise I discovered that it was actually two days slower to come out than the October 7-related statement. Furthermore, it had been so passive in nature that it didn't mention the police perpetrator or even that Floyd had been killed.[5] Yet I recalled no concern, let alone anger, arising in reaction to that.

A progressive publication soon skewered Rowan's moralistic tone in a story sarcastically titled, "The Moral Authority of Marc Rowan,"[6] and I confess that listening to him speak on that sort of topic was difficult for me.

While I had great respect for the business acumen of Apollo's leaders, I viewed Apollo and similar private equity funds as the most single-mindedly financially-driven of all the players in our capitalist system.

Nonetheless, Rowan's impressive business accomplishments and high profile attracted many followers. Soon after his TV appearance he began a daily series of numbered emails that purported to go to all Penn trustees, highlighting each day a supporter of his protestations. "Day 1" featured Jon Huntsman Jr, a Penn grad and former presidential candidate.[7] This was surprising given the fact that Huntsman hadn't even bothered to speak to President Magill to gain her perspective before launching his letter.

The letter was doubly surprising in that Huntsman's father, whose name adorned the main Wharton building on campus, had fought a bitter battle relating to a failed transaction with Rowan's firm some years earlier. The senior Huntsman, now deceased, wrote in a chapter in his autobiography called *The Double-Cross*, that "[I]n its effort to back out of the deal, Apollo was willing to destroy me…."[8] I remembered hearing from old-timers, when I was a new member of Penn's board, how Huntsman Senior had blackballed the Apollo partner who led that deal from ever gaining a trustee appointment.

"Day 3" featured a letter from Ronald Lauder – one that didn't call for resignations or definitively say he would cut off donations but did signal that his position on events at Penn was hardening.[9] What caught the eye of faculty members in that letter was a stunning admission that he had "two people taking photos and two more who listened" at the recent festival. Even more startling was the statement that he did "not want any of the students" in the program he and his brother funded "taught by any of the instructors who were involved in or supported" the event.

In any event, Rowan's appearance on a TV show that was probably among those most watched by Penn trustees and prominent alumni triggered a weeks' long torrent of emails, texts, phone calls and meetings for both President Magill and myself the intensity of which is hard to describe.

I later counted several thousand electronic communications, not including the innumerable robot-generated emails later sent my way as a form of harassment.

Many days consisted of an unending stream of conversations, and it seemed impossible to hold less than a forty-five-minute discussion given the overlapping and conflicting involvement of so many complex issues–among them free speech, corporate governance, Middle East history and politics, University admissions policies and antisemitism in America. In preparation for all these conversations, on many days Liz and I held the first of numerous phone calls between ourselves before 6:00 a.m.

The weekend after Rowan's TV appearance, we held two board meetings, although technically these were informal discussions and not actual "meetings" given that by Pennsylvania statute all Penn board meetings must be properly noticed and open to the public. That these meetings lasted several hours in total and were conducted virtually over Zoom with well over fifty participants explains why so many people afterward told me they found these sessions frustrating. I could have made these gatherings somewhat smaller by simply excluding emeritus trustees, but my belief was that some of those who had been around longer might have more wisdom to impart than current board members. One of the emeriti, Leonard Lauder, opened the first of the meetings on an upbeat note. I called on him because I knew he never used the mute button, had always been a supporter of mine and would have something positive to say.

In the end, these somewhat chaotic meetings served an important purpose: we ended the second session, on Sunday, with an expression of unanimous support for continuation of Liz's leadership. I sensed that a very small number of dissidents still wanted her to resign but figured nobody wanted to go on the record as being in such a small minority. Hence we were able to ultimately get to unanimity for the purposes of making a reassuring announcement to the University community. As for myself, I didn't even ask for affirmation of my position, as I did not feel like that was in real doubt. Indeed, it would have been peculiar if it were – board chairs are not decision-makers in regard to what events take place on campus, nor on what presidential statements should be issued or what those should say.

This saga took on a political dimension for the first time when I received a startling phone call from a fellow trustee just before I was to dial into Zoom for the second of the weekend board calls. Deeply involved in state politics, he was a supportive colleague with whom I had a long-ago business connection. He was calling to say that the Pennsylvania governor's office wanted my cell number.

As with so many actions we were to face, we had no specific knowledge of who was actually behind this. But we were told that people had been speaking to the governor about getting involved at Penn. And that should not have been a surprise, as political lobbying – as well as litigation, which would come later – is a tool often used alongside aggressive media efforts in activist shareholder campaigns in the corporate world.

In our situation the governor's direct involvement in board deliberations was a real possibility, as a quirk of Penn's governing statues provides that the governor can, if physically present, chair a board meeting.[10] This was something that I was told had never actually occurred. Few trustees were even aware of this provision, which seemed peculiar given that Penn is a private institution that gets little state support besides for its veterinary school. In any event, Liz and I arranged to speak with Governor Josh Shapiro – a popular Democrat in his first term – just after our board call late Sunday afternoon. The ensuing conversation was very cordial and constructive, and I came away thinking that the last thing this politician would ever want to do is to take on any responsibility for sorting out the escalating controversy at Penn.

Notwithstanding the successful outcome of the weekend calls with the board and governor, the next week was a wild one. First, having been advised not to "give more oxygen" to the dispute by appearing on CNBC or directly responding to innumerable other press inquiries, I finally succeeded in convincing our advisors that I should publish a letter to *The DP*.

Titled "Setting the Record Straight,"[11] it was a direct response to the Rowan letter that had ended up being published elsewhere.

My letter had several purposes: to reaffirm that we were horrified by the terrorist attack on Israel and that we condemned antisemitism in all its forms, to question whether the hateful comments quoted in Rowan's letter had really happened but to condemn them if they did, and finally to dispute that the open letter signed by alumni indicated a broad sense that Penn was heading in the "wrong direction" rather than narrowly focusing on the recent Palestinian cultural festival as it had on its face.

My letter led to a further escalation of communications to my inbox, including each day both some of the most complimentary, as well as some of the most hostile, emails I had received in my entire life. The volume was too great to allow response, although in a couple cases I invited to my Manhattan office for coffee a random person who was critical but seemed open to learning more about the situation.

One visitor started our meeting by pointing out that there was a trailer outside our midtown building pulling a large billboard with pictures of Israeli hostages – presumably targeted at me. I knew that on the Penn campus Liz had been enduring much worse, with such trailers picturing her and claiming that she was an antisemite who should resign constantly circumnavigating the campus. Despite the awkward start, this and my other random calls and meetings with alums I invited in were constructive. Yet the notion of winning over a few thousand people one at a time seemed impossible.

Social media, the most modern of communication forms, provided a forum to connect with people in larger numbers, but that was a realm completely unfamiliar to me. News there came in tiny fragments, moved at a lightning-fast pace and was often of uncertain origin. Thus the veracity of what appears on social media is highly questionable. Yet we were bombarded with demands to respond with urgency to short clips on Instagram – "Did this happen, and if so what are you doing about it?"

The most shocking episode related to a campus protest that took place the same day my *DP* piece was printed. That demonstration, led by pro-Palestinian protestors critical of what they saw as University policy skewed in favor of Israel, included a noisy march through campus. Soon after it ended, I was pounded by frantic emails and calls referring to Instagram posts showing Penn students calling for Jewish genocide. Even after weeks of shocking developments, I stared at my phone in disbelief. As that claim was repeated again and again my mind leaped ahead to what we could or should do in response.

What I should have done, rather than jump ahead to that question, was to listen carefully to the attached clip. Instead, like most people, I simply assumed that the headline above the video clip was true. But it turns out that headline, like some other bits of "news" with which we were presented, was false. More than a day later, after untold numbers of people had seen the inflammatory posts, it became clear that the protestors were charging Israel with genocide against Gaza, not calling for genocide against Jews.[12] The chant went: "Israel, Israel, you can't hide. We charge you with genocide." To its credit, even the ADL clarified this misunderstanding on its website. But the damage was already done.

Apart from simple questions of truth or falsehood, social media proved to be an extremely effective tool for amplifying hostile rhetoric, as well as for creating the impression for those far away that life on campus was chaotic and dangerous. In reality, based on my own direct observation on regular walks across campus, it was almost always peaceful and orderly. Unfortunately, university administrators are far less equipped than well-advised corporations to combat an activist media campaign and continually correct misinformation.

As an aside, it would be wrong to infer that the situation at Penn categorically pitted Jewish people against those like me who were not Jewish. The minority of board dissenters at that point was so small that a large majority of Jewish trustees were strongly loyal to Liz and me – and to Penn. As one of our most stalwartly supportive Jewish trustees put it in an email to a Jewish colleague regarding the debate about leadership change, "the timing of this crusade [given the need to focus on the attack on Israel and rising antisemitism] is incomprehensible to me and I will never recover from it."[13]

Having failed to gain support for the notion of removing Liz as president, in late October the small group of dissident trustees – two voting and one emeritus – wrote a lengthy appeal to the board's executive committee calling for my removal as chair. That would be both a sort of consolation prize for their efforts – a way of showing the board was "doing something" – as well as a first step toward ultimately removing Liz. It must have seemed like an opportune moment to take a run at me, as the vitriol coming my way was escalating sharply. One example:

[T]his is your legacy…This is all anyone will remember – that you stood with the haters, the violent mob, the people who called for the destruction of Israel.[14]

Or this:

[T]he only leading you are doing, is towards a second Holocaust. [T]he blood on your hands will be there for the rest of your lives, civilian blood, baby blood, innocent blood, [J]ewish blood.[15]

Somehow, I never allowed the uninformed and unchecked hate spewing from strangers who had never met me to get me down, or even distract me from the mission at hand. That mission was to keep our campus safe while protecting the values that had made Penn the great educational institution that it was. Admittedly, there were moments I felt high emotion, but those were always when kind words, often even words of admiration, came from close friends, from long-lost friends I hadn't seen in decades or even from total strangers.

Focusing on the trustee letter proposing my removal rather than the stream of hateful email from strangers, my immediate reaction was to forward it to the entire board. I asked board members to weigh in individually via the University secretary – the woman who handled governance and board relations matters – on whether the question of my leadership should be brought to the formal board meeting slated for early November. They did so, and a few days later we were set to announce that not a single one of the nearly fifty other voting trustees, nor any others from the emeritus group, had registered support for reconsidering my chairmanship.

But just at that moment yet another letter from one of the same dissidents – the M&A banker who had earlier been a free speech zealot – was circulated, calling for a second poll on the same question.[16] He immediately followed that by forwarding a private email from Marc Rowan answering some questions he had posed, presumably thinking that would help his case. Tucked within that note was a statement in bold type that caught the attention of many old timers on the board – those who had presided over remarkable advances in student applications, fundraising, endowment size, research advances and other measures indicating Penn's history of escalating success:

As Trustees we abdicated our responsibilities for the last 20 years.[17]

That email, addressed to seventy-nine current and former trustees, contained a structural mistake that I have regrettably made myself: it listed all their names in the "cc" instead of "bcc" addressee section. That meant anyone could touch "reply to all" and address the entire group. Several, starting with emeritus trustee Bob Levy, a once prominent but now retired Chicago-based fund manager, promptly did just that. One after another slapped down the restated proposal in a polite but still humiliating way. Prominent NBC News personality Andrea Mitchell was one of the respondents. For me, the highlight came from octogenarian Al Shoemaker, the former leader of First Boston who was my predecessor as board chair three chairs earlier. Despite facing significant health challenges, he replied through his son, a current trustee, with the wise words of an elder statesman:

"I am heartbroken about what is happening…." The sentiment of the first in the series of replies to all "perfectly sums up my feelings as well." He closed with, "I completely support keeping our current leadership in place."[18]

Those words from on high ended that coup attempt. Accordingly, at the public board meeting on November 3 no resolutions on leadership change were brought forward. Further, Liz delivered a rousing and very well-received speech that, for the moment at least, seemed to calm the raging storm.

But even with that meeting behind us the never-ending phone calls, texts and emails continued as we tried to move on from the crisis. At times it felt like the battle was waning – and in our favor. Yet in mid-November, another crescendo of attacks materialized. From exactly where – or from whom – these came we could not ascertain. Regardless, the *Financial Times* later summarized that those attacking Penn "waged their campaign with the same vigor – and some of the same bare-knuckle tactics – as those they have undertaken against recalcitrant corporate boards of directors."[19]

One fairly extraordinary example was the attempt to kill my still-pending $550 million deal to sell Greenhill. Given that I had intentionally negotiated an essentially unconditional deal, I knew that would not be easy. For a while there had been a bit of a "boycott Greenhill" effort ricocheting around social media – some of the random emails I received specifically threatened that. But that effort never seemed to get traction, and my work colleagues and I didn't see a single instance of a client opportunity being impacted by that initiative.

More seriously, however, one trustee wrote to Liz warning of an alumni text group that was talking about using litigation as a tool to "move things along."[20] The specific idea he pointed to was using Section 220 of the General Corporation Law of Delaware – the state in which Greenhill and indeed most public companies are incorporated – to make a so-called "books and records" request. The objective – as was the case in numerous corporate battles in which this provision has been used – would be to gain access to private corporate information for purposes of harassment and negative publicity. The trustee providing this heads up ended his email with a broader warning:

> If someone were inclined to be very belligerent, they wouldn't stop with Scott. They'd buy 1 share in every business associated with any Penn trustee and then run the same gambit at scale.

Most concerning was the effort to conjure up the notion that my work for Penn had triggered Greenhill's acquisition agreement's "material adverse change" clause, meaning that our business had been significantly and negatively impacted by the ongoing controversy. All merger contracts contained such a clause, although ours was more narrowly drafted than most. The *Financial Times* would later identify at least one of the intermediaries behind this effort, saying that a public relations firm it named had "quietly stirred a campaign to thwart the closing" of the Greenhill sale.[21] Ironically, that firm, one I had not previously heard of, was led by Steve Lipin, who in his early career as a *Wall Street Journal* reporter had been a vocal supporter of our young firm. But I did not personally know with any degree of certainty what he had done or for whom he was working.

Some of the press allowed itself to be used in this effort, particularly the *New York Post*. It used clever headlines like "His Bok's at the Wall" over reporting that was littered with untruths; one story claimed the Ronald Lauder and Jon Huntsman Jr. letters had called for me to resign (they did not).[22] An online story also included a gratuitous personal attack on my career as a dealmaker ("No one has ever said I need Scott Bok on the phone").[23] But the editor must have concluded that was going too far, as that remark was omitted from the print edition of that article. Even more reputable publications like Reuters let themselves be used in this effort to put pressure on me. Its *Breakingviews* feature called the timing of this controversy "abysmal," said private equity clients might choose to take their business to a "less polarizing" advisor and – with breathtaking hyperbole – called the risk that Mizuho was taking on with its planned acquisition "boundless."[24]

On a positive note, the flurry of news stories prompted an unexpected reunion. I was sitting at my desk one day when I saw Bob Greenhill's name flash on my phone. We hadn't spoken in more than three years, since he hastily exited our office and headed to Palm Beach.

True to form, Bob skipped the niceties and got right down to business. "Scott, Jack [Macatee, a retired Davis Polk partner whom I often ran into while walking our respective dogs in Palm Beach] just called and said he heard our name on the radio. What's going on?" Bob sounded good, unchanged despite what I had heard about some health challenges that almost inevitably come along with being his age.

"Mmm," I responded. "Do you think he might have been listening to *Fox News* on satellite radio?" Of course, typical of many older men living in "red state" Florida he was doing just that. And of course Fox, given its common ownership with the *New York Post*, was spinning tales about our deal being in jeopardy. I explained to Bob the whole situation regarding Penn and told him not to worry.

Meanwhile, back on campus, the normally quiescent Wharton board of advisors was becoming more active. My freshman floor friend, fellow trustee and Milwaukee Bucks owner Jamie Dinan, who also sat on that Wharton board, told me that group was considering passing some resolutions in regard to speech, student conduct and other matters. He told me he would recuse himself from any such vote.

The Wharton board was a who's who of Wall Street. It included Ken Moelis, who led one of Greenhill's competitors, Michael Klein, a former top M&A banker at Citibank who had pulled off several successful SPACs in the recent boom, and Dan Och, a Goldman trader who left to build a hugely successful hedge fund that later fell on hard times. Also on the board were the co-owners of the Philadelphia 76ers basketball team, David Blitzer, an affable senior Blackstone executive whom I knew and liked, and

Josh Harris, the Apollo co-founder whom I did not know. He was the one who had clashed with Jon Huntsman Sr. on a deal. More recently, he had lost out to Rowan on the top job at Apollo.

Despite the impressive accomplishments and breathtaking wealth of the Wharton board, the truth was that resolutions from that kind of subsidiary board meant nothing. Indeed, I had never heard of any such Penn board purporting to pass a resolution on anything. But I knew the optics of this would not be good, given that Wharton had seemingly always had clout within Penn – and beyond – well out of proportion to its size.

Wharton's prominence stemmed from the fact that it was the only undergraduate business school in the Ivy League. It made Penn what one witty magazine writer called an "oligarch factory."[25] Penn produced more billionaires than any other university, that author wrote, "almost wholly as a result of Wharton's magnetism to 17-year-olds seeking to become billionaires." That was the crowd, now in its 50s and 60s, with which we were now dealing.

But that was all just fun and games compared to the video that fell into Penn's hands at that moment. The slick, Hollywood-quality advertisement was reminiscent of the most memorable of presidential campaign ads. There were pictures of Liz and me, and of a recent protest on our campus, juxtaposed to clips of Adolf Hitler, marching Nazi troops and the Twin Towers in flames on September 11.

The ad finished with the narrator asking a question in solemn tones, "President Magill, Chairman Bok, how did you let antisemitism and hate flourish at Penn?"

We hastily aired the video privately to dozens of trustees and emeritus trustees, hoping someone with influence would agree this was a bridge too far and dissuade whomever the producers were from releasing it. That worked, and apart from a few close friends I shared it with the ad never saw the light of day.

Despite the wide variety of attacks, by the Thanksgiving break it felt like we, and Penn, were persevering. The trustees did receive another morning email from Rowan despite the holiday – "Day 40" in the ongoing series. But that note had a different, more conciliatory tone. I wondered, could this be signaling another divine outcome – peace – linked to the biblically significant number forty? If so, that would really give us something to be thankful for this holiday.

Unfortunately, it was not. Trustee and donor anxiety remained strong, driven in my view by continued misconceptions of what was actually happening on campus. Undeniably, a generally quiescent campus had been disrupted by a few unpleasant protests over the course of the semester. But through social media and other means the state of affairs was often wildly exaggerated. After being pelted by innumerable calls and emails about a protester "occupation" of Houston Hall, the student center in the middle of Penn's campus,[26] I looked for myself while on my way to visit President Magill the Wednesday after Thanksgiving. I was not yet as recognizable as I would soon become on campus, so I just walked into the building unnoticed. What I found was one alcove on the main floor of that large building "occupied" by a couple of signs and a few sleeping bags, while just a few feet away students not connected to the protest were quietly working on their computers the way students typically did in that space.

Just when I needed it, one bit of good news arrived. Only one day after that campus visit the Greenhill sale was finally completed. All the efforts to stop it had failed, as I had figured they would. But later that evening, after celebrating with family and friends, came a reminder that emotions in relation to this battle were continuing to escalate.

Dressed in black tie, I was sitting under the great blue whale in the Hall of Ocean Life at the American Museum of Natural History. It was the night of its fabulous gala – what had become one of my absolute favorite annual events. Both my kids were at my table as well as a Greenhill colleague and a fellow Penn trustee visiting from the West Coast, all with their spouses or significant others. Liz Magill had planned to come up from Philadelphia to join but then was summoned to testify in front of a Congressional committee the following Tuesday, so she stayed home. She planned to head to D.C. for intense preparation with lawyers already on Saturday.

Given my new notoriety, the Museum skipped the usual welcome remarks from the podium by the chair, although Senator Majority Leader Chuck Schumer, a fixture at such glittering Manhattan events, doubly reminded everyone I was there by twice – once after he lost his place in his script – thanking me among other Museum leaders and benefactors for the evening. Thereafter, *Saturday Night Live* producer Lorne Michaels delivered fabulous entertainment as he did every year – this time Seth Meyers for comedy and Mumford & Sons for music.

When the mini concert ended, the hundreds in attendance – most of whom were already on their feet – began to make their way to the exit. Just then a man made a beeline toward me. One often ran into long-ago friends or colleagues at such events, but I am bad with names, so rather than say anything I reflexively reached out my hand to shake.

"You haven't answered my emails!" With those first words I guessed the topic at hand. I missed much of what came after amid the hubbub of a large exiting crowd but avoided responding until I heard "you don't care if a Jewish kid dies on that campus!"

That I had to answer. I did so politely, offering reassurance that I deeply cared if *any* student got hurt, let alone died, on that campus. And that very possibility had indeed been weighing on my mind. So far as I knew, no Penn president, let alone board chair, had ever been blamed for a student being injured in a criminal attack or for any of the student suicides that had tragically occurred on campus.

Clearly Liz and I were more vulnerable in the current environment, and the recent shooting of three Palestinian college students in Vermont[27] demonstrated that the risk of violence in relation to the issues roiling campuses was real. Liz herself had been the target of death threats so vile that at one point I told her to have her husband quietly find alternative housing for them off campus. In an effort to minimize the risk of harm to anyone we had escalated police coverage to a level never seen before on our campus. Not wanting to be even several blocks away in a time of crisis, Liz remained in the president's house and took her chances.

The confrontation under the whale ended quickly, as a woman, presumably the fellow's wife, pulled him away. I didn't have to wait long to learn who he was. By time my wife and I got in an Uber he had emailed me, and a quick check of deleted emails confirmed that he, indeed, had sent me emails – including a somewhat scary one referring to blood on my hands. Now that I had his name, from the car I googled to find out who he was, as I was unfamiliar with the name. First thing I spotted was a blog post saying he "was a bond trader with a reputation for being bombastic, crass, and nakedly self-interested."[28] A few clicks later I learned that one of the characters portrayed in *The Big Short*, the film about the mortgage collapse that triggered the financial crisis, had been based on him.

The Congressional testimony that followed five days after that confrontation became so widely viewed and discussed that there is little need to dwell on it much further. The Republican-controlled House Education and Workforce Committee called three university presidents–of Harvard, the Massachusetts Institute of Technology and Penn–to testify. All were women. Liz, only seventeen months into her tenure at Penn, was the longest serving of the three.

We had heard that donors had been lobbying to get Congress involved in the controversy on campuses. We therefore expected something of a show trial, as it was obvious that campus unrest was an issue that could play well for Republicans – historically the "law and order" party – in the upcoming elections. And indeed the aggressive questioning made it appear that Republican Party members came to this event loaded for bear.

The Committee chair was Virginia Foxx of North Carolina, and she opened the hearing by stating that the presidents were there to "answer and atone"[29] for what was happening on their campuses. Many Committee members piled on, but it soon became clear that the primary prosecutor of the presidents would be Representative Elise Stefanik of upstate New York.

Stefanik was someone I had met years earlier in the summer of 2018. She was a Harvard classmate of one of my favorite younger Greenhill colleagues, and through that connection came to my office seeking a political contribution – which she did not get. A political prodigy in her early thirties at the time, she was in her second Congressional term. I viewed her as a political moderate, an old-fashioned Northeast Republican. Our discussion – my main area of interest – focused on where she stood in regard to America's relatively new President, Donald Trump. Her responses indicated much ambivalence and discomfort in making her stance clear. But her views changed drastically over time. In mid-2022, she tweeted "I am ultra-MAGA. And I'm proud of it."[30] Commentators were soon writing stories with titles like "What in the World Happened to Elise Stefanik?"[31] Powered by her performance at this hearing, she would soon be jockeying to be Donald Trump's presidential running mate. Later, she would land a nomination as ambassador to the United Nations.

On the Tuesday the hearing took place I stayed home from work to watch the livestream. But after a few hours I became bored by the political posturing, assumed nothing too bad would come of this and took an Uber to work.

My assumption could not have been more wrong.

As the world now knows, neither Liz nor the presidents of Harvard or the MIT would flatly state that calling for genocide – something there was no reason to believe had ever actually been done on Penn's campus – would violate their student codes of conduct. The nuanced responses of the presidents, which were instantaneously and expertly packaged for social media, quickly became the top headline of *The New York Times* and *Wall Street*

Journal, the cover story of the next day's *New York Post* and the subject of the opening skit on the following weekend's *Saturday Night Live*. I later summed up what had happened as this: "[o]ver-prepared and over-lawyered given the hostile forum and high stakes, [Liz] provided a legalistic answer to a moral question," and that "made for a dreadful 30-second sound bite in what was more than five hours of testimony."[32]

If that testimony is worth one more moment of scrutiny it would be to say that it was merely a continuation of the prior fourteen weeks of debate in relation to so-called "hate speech." Most educated people, including most of Penn's trustees, believed speech should be free and unrestrained – that is what the First Amendment of the US Constitution calls for. Penn's Code of Student Conduct – what Stefanik asked President Magill about – was rooted in that First Amendment. It said explicitly that "the content of student speech or expression is not by itself a basis for disciplinary action."[33] That's why Liz wouldn't flatly state that speech alone – any speech – would violate that code.

Understandably, many at Penn and beyond think there is an exception to free speech called "hate speech" that should not be allowed. This concept of hate speech became more familiar to many as a result of actions by social media outlets to eliminate from their realm any verbiage that marketers will not advertise alongside. Hence many came to believe that there is a fairly broadly exception to "free speech" for whatever – in their view – constitutes "hate speech."

Hate speech is not a concept found in the First Amendment. To my recollection, the phrase was never used in my Constitutional Law class at Penn Law. And so far as I know, it is not a phrase that appears in codes of student conduct. Certainly it did not appear in Penn's. And in my eighteen years as a trustee, I never heard a suggestion from anyone – trustee, faculty, administrator or student – that perhaps that code should be more restrictive.

Ironically at public universities that wasn't even a question, as the First Amendment clearly governs speech at those government-controlled institutions. How odd it would be for speech to be more constrained at Penn than at Penn State, at Columbia than on the State University of New York campuses, or at Harvard than at University of Massachusetts. But few people take the time necessary to understand that history or those nuances. Thus the three presidents got skewered when they understandably struggled to provide the "yes or no" answers demanded by Congresswoman Stefanik on the question whether some example of speech might be so heinous and hateful that it would, by itself, violate existing codes of conduct.

The few days that followed were a blur. My oft-repeated quip that serving on a board is generally either boring or scary seemed inadequate to describe the panic that infected many members of our large board after the testimony. Two days after the hearing we gathered our full board along with emeritus members for a ninety-minute Zoom discussion. That was immediately followed by an in-person meeting of our executive committee – we jettisoned the planned agenda for that regularly scheduled session and spent five full hours debating what to do to quell the firestorm of criticism. Any notion of board confidentiality now appeared to be lost, as television networks and newspapers repeatedly reached out to me looking for confirmation of what they were being told, very specifically and in real time, about our private meetings.

The range of opinions expressed during those meetings was extraordinarily broad. There were many stalwart board members who understood how universities worked and were focused on protecting the institution's long-term values. But many others raised ideas that belied a complete lack of understanding as to how universities had historically been governed. Some wanted to start disciplining students and even tenured faculty – regardless of whether existing campus rules allowed for that. Some wanted the board – separate from management – to issue a "values statement" that would speak, among other things, to the hypothetical genocide question that had been posed. A couple wanted us to formally reprimand the president for her answer at Congress, yet at the same time they – along with pretty much everyone else – wanted her to somehow continue in her role thereafter.

Adding fuel to the fire, the Pennsylvania governor – still having never appeared at a board meeting – also began weighing in publicly via statements to the press, hinting strongly at the need for board action.[34] Up until that moment his entire involvement with University leadership had consisted of a couple of brief, friendly phone conversations with Liz and myself, but now he was seeing his Republican counterparts in government make considerable political hay from the situation at Penn.

Even after the several hours of meetings I continued a never-ending series of phone calls, texts and emails with various members of Penn's board as I made my way to Philadelphia's airport. While the phone calls stopped, the electronic communications continued for my three hours in flight as well.

I called Liz as soon as I landed at Palm Beach International Airport, where I had headed for the weekend. It was 10:45 p.m., but before I even left the airport for home I wanted to convey to her my conclusion from that frenetic day: that we needed to get her out of the Penn presidency.

This was not a case of my handing down a guilty verdict. Far from it – in my view she was a new president caught in the crossfire of a culture war that was not of her making.

If there hadn't been an orchestrated attack on University leadership already in September, if the October 7 assault on Israel had not occurred, if the Congressional testimony had ended after five hours – if any one of those were true – she would have been fine. But none of those things were true, our deeply divided board was now in complete disarray and her position was no longer tenable.

Liz's longtime assistant would later lament that ours "was a partnership for the ages,"[35] and thus this was not an awkward conversation. We were simply two battle-worn colleagues trying to figure out the right next move, just as we had been innumerable times in recent months. Here, as had repeatedly been the case, we were in complete agreement. Indeed, her immediate reaction to my words suggested that she had concurrently come to the same view.

The question for me then became how to engineer her exit. Having overseen or observed many executive departures over the years I knew there was a right way and a wrong way to implement them. The right way is quietly, respectfully, following existing procedures, with appropriate legal advice and the goal of eliminating the prospect for unseemly (and costly) litigation. The wrong way is to do it sloppily, in public, in a way that angers the many in the organization who will be disappointed or even enraged at the departure, all while leaving open the prospect of litigation.

While I got to work behind the scenes, the situation on our board deteriorated further. Multiple factions developed, each groping for the right way forward. Clearly some now wanted Liz gone and had concluded that I wasn't going to make that happen. So they tried to develop a plan behind my back. But I had good visibility into all that was happening, as each subgroup seemed to have at least one person loyal enough to me that they forwarded me entire email or text chains of dialogue. A board call where I shared all my plans might have seemed the obvious next step, but that would not have been wise given the utter lack of confidentiality on our board at that point.

Friday evening, at the end of that tumultuous week, I had a glass of wine on my back patio with my fellow trustee and friend of forty-something years, Jamie Dinan. He was just off a flight from Europe en route from Miami's airport to his home a few blocks away. He had passed the time watching the World War II thriller *Darkest Hour* and was inspired to email me while still over the Atlantic that I was "one of the few Churchillian figures" he had known.[36] That was a ridiculous overstatement, but it reflected how emotional everyone was becoming and provided a welcome contrast to some of the brutally hostile communications that had come my way.

I did not fully let Jamie – or almost anyone else – in on my plans. I wanted him to help me slow the board down some so that I had time to execute those plans, but I was not hopeful he could do so.

As the board descended further into chaos I began to fear that some faction might imminently do something publicly that would heighten the uncertainty on campus and further humiliate both Liz and the University. Hence I pulled forward the planned resignation announcement date from the following Tuesday to Sunday night, then to Sunday morning, then to Saturday night, then finally to Saturday afternoon. By the time I called the first in a series of meetings to disclose that Liz was resigning, I was reminded of the scene in *To Kill a Mockingbird* where Atticus Finch (played in the film version by Gregory Peck) faced the mob that had come for the innocent Tom Robinson.

First I chaired a compensation committee meeting that, with outside advisors, thoroughly reviewed and approved the terms of Liz's exit. Then I called an executive committee meeting, at which that outcome was unanimously endorsed. Then I called a full board meeting – the fact that a huge majority of our board appeared on a weekend afternoon Zoom call on just minutes' notice makes clear where everyone's attention was focused that weekend.

The executive committee and board were simultaneously shocked and pleased at my announcement that Liz was leaving on a voluntary basis. Some, I sensed, were also a little embarrassed.

Yet I had one more surprise still to share. After noting the collapse of confidentiality and break down of the board into factions, I said that the prior few days had convinced me that now was the right time for me to resign as chairman. My parting words were these: "I wish you the best. It has been an honor to serve." I then tapped my iPad screen to drop off the call.

This wasn't my intention, but one person on that call later relayed to me with a smile that she had described my exit to her husband that night as "one of the great fuck yous of all time." Someone else later said that, if so, it was also one of the politest ones.

Of course, the story doesn't end there. Leaving the board freed me up to speak, and I did. As soon as I dropped off that call I sent a resignation statement to every news organization that had been hounding me for information. My primary purpose was to give Liz a far better send off than the board would have united behind at that fraught moment:

> The world should know that Liz Magill is a very good person and a talented leader who was beloved by her team. She is not the slightest bit antisemitic. Working with her was one of the great pleasures of my life.[37]

The next morning I woke up early and got to work on an opinion piece that I would send to the *Philadelphia Inquirer*.[38] A fundraising email that I was startled to receive from Congresswoman Stefanik further fueled my desire to again set the record straight. There was no doubt that Congressional hearing had created a wonderful fundraising opportunity for her and others.

My *Inquirer* piece in response to all that had happened served several purposes:

> To give my background "as a scholarship kid from rural Michigan"-appropriate given the increasing Google searches that presumed I was the privileged son of former Harvard President Derek Bok.
> To state my views on the terrorist attack on Israel, on antisemitism, on free expression and on the distortions of social media.
> To posit that "there are limits to what universities can do to address such matters."
> To deny that leftist faculty were attempting to brainwash students-indeed, it was undeniable that Penn each year groomed many times more Wall Street warriors than social justice warriors.
> To put recent events in perspective by stating that only a small fraction of one percent of the student body had done anything reprehensible.

To question the role of donors in university life.

To reference my all-white freshman dorm floor as a way of high-lighting the benefits of recent diversity, equity and inclusion efforts.

To describe a little bit of the craziness to which I had personally been subjected.

And to suggest that, in addressing unwanted behavior, a balance needs to be struck between avoiding chaos and violence on the one hand, and imposing McCarthyism and martial law on the other.

While many aspects of the Penn saga were familiar to me – the protagonists, the tactics and the boardroom drama were very similar to those of a typical corporate takeover contest – the stakes here seemed higher. What was at risk in my view was nothing short of the soul of the university – and perhaps by extension of all leading universities. In my view, to continue to fulfill the noble purpose that universities had historically served they needed to be independent on matters of teaching and research, to pursue knowledge even when there wasn't an immediate instrumental value in sight and to be open to hearing all perspectives. On top of such lofty ideals, universities also needed to let the undergraduate years be a time for largely unbridled intellectual and personal exploration, with a sympathetic recognition that youthful students will make mistakes.

While that was a lot of ground to cover even in a very long op-ed, my *Inquirer* piece seemed to strike a chord with many. It was widely read, in part because it was referenced in multiple *New York Times* articles in the days that followed. Numerous people from across the country reached out in support – some long-ago colleagues or classmates but many of them complete strangers. Even many Penn trustees wrote favorable responses to my piece, including one who had led a rogue faction within the executive committee. He used the word "sorry" five times and confessed that he was "sorry that in the end you could trust almost none of us."[39]

More important, my op-ed proved to be as a catalyst for others to join the ongoing debate – particularly as continuing press coverage reinforced my view that this was a political and cultural struggle, one that went far beyond questions of free speech and antisemitism. More than a thousand Penn faculty signed on to a letter to Penn trustees "oppos[ing] all attempts by trustees, donors, and other external actors to interfere with our academic policies and to undermine academic freedom."[40]

Clearly, mine was not a victory in this greatest of takeover battles. Yet neither was it defeat. Instead, the struggle would continue, likely for a long time. And I would remain part of it.

I recalled the words – "nobody gets through life unscathed"[41] – that my Broadway hero Stephen Sondheim spoke when explaining why his work focused on the inevitable challenges that all humans face. And I remembered a quote from Theodore Roosevelt, which was texted to me by a loyal friend from my freshman year at one of the more discouraging moments of this saga:

> It is not the critic who counts; not the man who points out how the strong man stumbles, or where the doer of deeds could have done them better. The credit belongs to the man who is actually in the arena, whose face is marred by dust and sweat and blood; who strives valiantly; who errs, who comes up short again and again, because there is no effort without error and shortcoming; but who does actually strive to do the deeds; who knows the great enthusiasms, the great devotions; who spends himself in a worthy cause; who at the best knows in the end the triumph of high achievement, and who at the worst, if he fails, at least fails while daring greatly, so that his place shall never be with those cold and timid souls who neither know victory nor defeat.[42]

One probably can't be chair of the American Museum of Natural History's board and not be a fan of Teddy Roosevelt. For sure, his words resonated with me. But my mantra was simpler than his. It came from the worn sign we found nailed to a rotting fence post as we were deciding to acquire our farm:

Footprints in the sands of time are not made sitting down.

In that spirit, my grand adventure traversed diverse realms. I observed – and participated in – a period of extraordinary growth and much tumult on Wall Street. I experienced both triumph and tragedy on that journey, and in the end I think it's fair to say I survived. Along the way, I also took interesting detours into inn-keeping, farming, theater, education, even – unintentionally – politics. In each arena I tried to do what was right. I leave to my readers the determination of the degree to which I succeeded.

ACKNOWLEDGEMENTS

I used numerous sources in researching and writing this book, yet inevitably had to rely extensively on my memory for the innumerable episodes described herein. While those memories are vivid, I recognize that the recollections of other participants in those events will undoubtedly vary. In some cases, there may be factual errors on my part, but the differences are likely simply a function of varying perspectives leading to different observations of a situation. For any errors on my part, I apologize in advance both to my readers and to those who were involved in the situation described.

There are many who are deserving of my gratitude for helping me live the adventure story that I have herein told. Without doubt, the person I am most grateful to in that regard is my wife, Roxanne. Our lives have been completely intertwined from the moment I walked into my junior year college dorm room one January evening and saw her, the pretty new transfer student who had just moved in across the hall, chatting with my roommate. I am thankful for all the times that Roxanne served as a sympathetic ear, sounding board, advisor or partner in relation to various aspects of my adventure.

I am also deeply grateful to Bob Greenhill for nearly 25 years of true partnership. Bob was a unique human being, with boundless energy, unflinching optimism and a love of competition. As many Morgan Stanley colleagues intimated before Bob and I became partners, we were in many ways an odd couple. But our skills, interests and personalities all turned out to be highly complementary. I enjoyed our time together. And I can't recall a single issue of importance on which we ever disagreed.

I am likewise grateful to the hundreds of people who worked at Greenhill over the years, particularly the generations of young financial analysts who spent time with us when they were fresh out of college. As for more senior team members, many whose names did not find their way into these pages, along with all of those who did, played important roles in the firm's success.

As longtime Greenhill board member Steve Goldstone often told me, it's lonely at the top. Thus it was critical to always have one particularly close consigliere within the firm when making decisions both large and small. Bob Niehaus, the late Jeff Buckalew and Hal Rodriguez each played that role at different times. John Liu and Ulrika Ekman each played many parts, first as key Greenhill colleagues, then as friends, then later as members of the firm's board of directors. And of course, Goldstone himself served as a wise counselor during his 17 years on our board.

Also among those closest to me at Greenhill, I owe a special debt of gratitude to Maureen Loughran, who has been my loyal assistant almost from day one. She typed numerous versions of this book alongside her many functions at the firm. Clients and colleagues invariably enjoyed engaging with her when they called or visited, and our team happily consumed the endless supply of treats she kept near her desk.

Lastly with respect to Greenhill, how could I forget our clients, without which the Firm would not have prospered and persevered? Collectively and over time, they paid us $6 billion in fees for our advice on important transactions. I am particularly grateful to those clients for whom I personally played the central role on our advisory team.

Apart from those connected with Greenhill, I am grateful to many valuable role models and mentors listed here who collectively deserve much of the credit for whatever I have been able to accomplish in the corporate and nonprofit worlds: Lewis Bernard, Sean Decatur, Ellen Futter, Amy Gutmann, Patricia Hayot, Aileen Hefferren, the late Paul Kelly, Marty Lipton, Liz Magill, Naneen Neubohn and Griff Sexton.

Finally, I am grateful to the many people who helped me with this book: the many family members, friends and colleagues (too many to name) who read various drafts and offered feedback, my helpful friends in the publishing world Aimee Bell and Ileene Smith, my agent Leah Spiro, Glenn Stout, my lawyer Jonathan Lyons and my editor Bill Falloon along with his many helpful colleagues at my publisher John Wiley & Sons.

NOTES

CHAPTER 1

1. Frank Loesser (lyricist), "The Company Way," *How to Succeed in Business Without Really Trying*, 1961.
2. "Where the Deals Are," *Dealmaker*, June/July 2008.
3. F. Scott Fitzgerald, notes for *The Last Tycoon* (never completed).
4. Martin Mayer, *Wall Street: Men & Money*, Harper 1959, p. 165.
5. U.S. Congress, Senate Committee on Banking and Currency, *Stock Exchange Practices*, J.P. Morgan, Jr. testimony, May 23, 1933.
6. Ron Chernow, *The House of Morgan*, Atlantic 1990, p. 597.
7. *House of Morgan*, pp. 722–723.
8. "Morgan Stanley & Co. Appoints 6 New Partners for Total of 34," *New York Times*, July 7, 1970.
9. *House of Morgan*, p. 584.
10. See Footnote 6.
11. *House of Morgan*, p. 664.
12. "S. Parker Gilbert Is Dead Here at 45," *New York Times*, February 24, 1938.
13. *New York Times*, January 25, 1986.
14. *New York Times*, March 3, 1993.
15. *New York Times*, March 23, 1995.
16. "Chairman Is Removed in an Abrupt Shake-up at Smith Barney," *New York Times*, January 11, 1996.

17. "Smith Barney's Whiz Kid," *Bloomberg*, October 20, 1996.
18. Judah Kraushaar, and Sandford I. Weill, *The Real Deal: My Life in Business and Philanthropy*, Business Plus 2006, p. 274.
19. See Footnote 16.

CHAPTER 2

1. Betty Comden and Adolph Green (lyricists), "New York, New York," *On the Town*, 1944.
2. "Derek Bok," *Wikipedia*. See also *The Americanization of Edward Bok*, Cosimo Classics, 1920.
3. *New York Times*, August 10, 1986.
4. Richard Brealey and Stewart Myers, *Principles of Corporate Finance*, McGraw-Hill 1981.
5. "Power, Greed and Glory on Wall Street," *New York Times*, February 17, 1985.
6. Michael Lewis, *Liar's Poker*, W.W. Norton 1989.
7. "Morgan Stanley, Dean Witter Are Planning Massive Merger," *Wall Street Journal*, February 5, 1997.
8. "Morgan Stanley and Dean Witter Agree to Merge," *New York Times*, February 6, 1997.

CHAPTER 3

1. Carolyn Leigh (lyricist), "I'm Flying," *Peter Pan*, 1954.
2. Alan Greenspan, speech at American Enterprise Institute, December 5, 1996.
3. "Cessna Citation X," *Wikipedia*.

CHAPTER 4

1. David Mamet, *Glengarry Glen Ross*, 1983.
2. Mark Zuckerberg, letter to potential investors, 2012.
3. "Wachtell's Fairness Opinion," *The Wall Street Journal*, October 23, 2007.
4. Unless otherwise noted, all Greenhill transactions and transaction values cited are as shown on the transaction list on Greenhill.com.
5. "Lessons of the Barings Bust," *The Wall Street Journal*, October 2, 1996.

6. All merger and acquisition market data herein sourced from Thompson Reuters Eikon.

7. All Greenhill financial data cited sourced from Greenhill Securities & Exchange Commission filings or, for the period prior to 2001, from reports provided to the author and other Members of Greenhill & Co., LLC.

8. "Greenhill Recruits Two Senior Bankers from Morgan Stanley," *Investment Dealer's Digest*, March 3, 1997.

9. "Boutiques Evercore, Greenhill Muscle in on M&A," *Corporate Financing Week*, September 22, 1997.

10. "M&A Boutique Hot Streak," *Crain's*, October 20, 1997.

11. *The Wall Street Journal*, January 28, 1998.

12. "No Room in this Town for Change Brought by an Inn," *New York Times*, November 10, 2010.

13. "Ex-Barings Executives to Head Greenhill Unit," *Financial Times*, April 24, 1998.

14. Roger Lowenstein, *When Genius Failed*, Random House, 2001, pp. 250–264.

15. Widely attributed to John Maynard Keynes, 1883–1946.

16. *Time*, February 15, 1999.

17. Original source unknown.

CHAPTER 5

1. Stephen Sondheim (lyricist), "Last Midnight," *Into the Woods*, 1986.

2. "Greenhill, in Hiring Move, Targets Merchant Banking," *The Wall Street Journal*, January 31, 2000.

3. Greenhill Capital Partners, L.P. Confidential Offering Memorandum, March 2000.

4. All references to Greenhill Capital Partners fund sizes, transactions and investment returns are sourced from reports to limited partner investors in the relevant funds.

5. "At a Wall Street Firm, Juniors' Voices Roar," *New York Times*, April 8, 2000.

6. "Boutique Greenhill Snatches Veteran Restructuring Banker," *The Wall Street Journal*, January 18, 2001.

7. "Greenhill Climbs," *The Daily Deal*, June 14, 2001.

8. Bruce Springsteen, "My City of Ruins," *The Rising*, 2002.

9. *House of Morgan*, p. 582.

10. "The World's Most Admired Companies," *Fortune*, October 2, 2000.

11. "Enron's Many Strands," *New York Times*, February 16, 2002.
12. "Justices Unanimously Overturn Conviction of Arthur Andersen," *New York Times*, May 31, 2005.
13. "Leading Class-Action Lawyer Is Sentenced to Two Years in Kickback Scheme," *New York Times,* February 12, 2008.
14. "Well-Known Bankruptcy Lawyer to Leave His Firm, Weil Gotshal," *The Wall Street Journal*, July 10, 2002.

CHAPTER 6

1. Stephen Sondheim (lyricist), "The Road You Didn't Take," *Follies*, 1971.
2. "Credit Suisse Unit Confirms Agreement to Acquire DLJ in a $11.5 Billion Deal," *The Wall Street Journal*, August 30, 2000.
3. "DLJ Takeover Triggers Clause Accelerating Access to Bonuses," *The Wall Street Journal*, November 14, 2000.
4. "Credit Suisse Pays Price for 16-Year-Old Misstep," *The Wall Street Journal*, February 4, 2016.
5. "Credit Suisse Reports $2.2 Billion Loss from Charges, Lower Revenue," *The Wall Street Journal*, February 10, 2022.
6. "Wasserstein and Perella, Stars and Profit Centers, Plan a New Merchant Bank—Can They Do It Alone?" *The Wall Street Journal*, February 3, 1988.
7. William D. Cohan, *The Last Tycoons: The Secret History of Lazard Freres & Co.*, Doubleday 2007, p. 540.
8. "Wasserstein Stake Sold," *New York Times*, July 27, 1988.
9. "Partners, at Meeting, Revolt Against Wasserstein Deal," *The Wall Street Journal*, May 2, 1997.
10. "Dresdner Bank Is Negotiating to Acquire Wasserstein, Perella," *The Wall Street Journal*, September 12, 2000.
11. "Merrill, Others Given Credit on AOL-Time Warner Deal," *The Wall Street Journal*, May 8, 2000.
12. *Tycoons*, p. 532.
13. *Tycoons*, pp. 532–533.
14. "Wasserstein to Join Lazard in Bid to Revive the Firm," *The Wall Street Journal*, November 16, 2001.
15. "Michel David-Weill and the Succession Drama at Lazard Freres," *Vanity Fair*, March 1, 1997.

16. See Footnote 9.
17. *Tycoons*, p. 440.
18. "Investment Group Buys the National Enquirer and Star Magazine," *New York Times*, February 17, 1999.

CHAPTER 7

1. Jerry Herman, "Open a New Window." *Mame*, 1966.
2. "Spitzer Guns for Merrill," *New York Post*, April 9, 2002.
3. "Wall Street Firms Settle Charges over Research in $1.4 Billion Pact," *The Wall Street Journal*, April 29, 2003.
4. "Banker Files to Take Firm Public, Putting His Pay Package on View," *New York Times*, March 12, 2004.
5. "What's His Deal," *Barron's*, May 3, 2004.

CHAPTER 8

1. Stephen Sondheim (lyricist), "Our Time," *Merrily We Roll Along*, 1981.
2. Attributed to Humphrey B. Neill, author of *The Art of Contrary Thinking*, The Caxton Printers Ltd., 1971.
3. "Knickerbocker Club," *Wikipedia*.
4. "Greenhill, Dealmaker for Redstone, Tilts at Giants," *Bloomberg*, March 23, 2005.
5. *Investment Dealers' Digest*, January 16, 2006.
6. "Red Light for Greenhill," *Barron's*, February 25, 2006.
7. *The Deal*, February 26, 2006.
8. *Institutional Investor*, March 2006.
9. Attributed to Benjamin Graham, in *Security Analysis*, McGraw-Hill, 1934. Paraphrased by Warren Buffett, in 1987 annual letter to Berkshire Hathaway shareholders.
10. Roxanne Bok, *Horsekeeping: One Woman's Tale of Barn and Country Life*, Prospecta Press, 2011.
11. "Chapin School," *Wikipedia*.
12. *New York Times*, August 22, 2008.

CHAPTER 9

1. Sheldon Harnick (lyricist), "Tradition," *Fiddler on the Roof,* 1964.
2. Patricia Beard, *Blue Blood and Mutiny*, Morrow 2007, p. 347.
3. "Morgan Stanley Timeline," *The Wall Street Journal,* June 13, 2005.
4. *Blue Blood,* pp. 182–187.
5. "Schilling Is Out to Silence Mystique, Aura and Fans," *New York Times*, October 12, 2004.
6. See Chapter 1, Footnote 5.
7. "Director to Step Down at Morgan Stanley," *New York Times*, July 23, 1991.
8. *Blue Blood,* pp. 199–201.
9. "Ex-Morgan Stanley Executives Gilbert, Fogg, Greenhill Comment," *Bloomberg*, Mar. 29, 2005.
10. *The Wall Street Journal*, Apr. 4, 2005.
11. *Newsweek*, May 1, 2005.
12. See Chapter 4, Footnote 1.
13. *CNN Money*, June 13, 2005.
14. Morgan Stanley press release, June 30, 2005.
15. *Blue Blood,* pp. 338–339.
16. John Mack, *Up Close and All In*, Simon & Schuster 2022, p. 241.

CHAPTER 10

1. Oscar Hammerstein II (lyricist), "A Cockeyed Optimist," *South Pacific*, 1949.
2. "Animal Spirits (Keynes)," *Wikipedia.*
3. Francis Coppola and Mario Puzo, *The Godfather Part II*, 1974.
4. "United Airline Deal: A Costly Fiasco," *New York Times*, October 25, 1989.
5. Greenhill quarterly earnings release, Apr. 26, 2007.
6. Greenhill quarterly earnings release, Oct. 25, 2007.
7. "Endeavor and the Troubling Pursuit of SPACs," *M&A Law Prof Blog*, June 11, 2007.
8. "The Unseen Merger Boom: SPACs," *New York Times*, January 6, 2008.

CHAPTER 11

1. Stephen Schwartz, "Defying Gravity," *Wicked*, 2003.
2. "JC Flowers Team Drops Sallie Mae Bid," *Financial Times*, September 26, 2007.

3. AIG investor conference call, August 9, 2010.

4. AIG quarterly report on 10-Q, November 7, 2008.

5. AIG investor conference call, December 5, 2008.

6. "Key Dates in the Saga of the Failed BCE Buyout," *Reuters*, December 11, 2008.

7. "When the Shoeshine Boys Talk Stocks," *CNN Money*, April 15, 1996.

8. AIG annual report on Form 10-K, February 28, 2008.

9. J.P. Morgan/Bear Stearns press release, March 16, 2008.

10. "Bear Stearns Neared Collapse Twice in Frenzied Last Days," *The Wall Street Journal*, May 29, 2008.

11. "JPMorgan Acts to Buy Ailing Bear Stearns at Huge Discount," *New York Times*, March 16, 2008.

12. Stephen Sondheim, "Move On," *Sunday in the Park with George*, 1984.

13. "All songs considered," *NPR*, September 21, 2017.

14. "Video: Stephen Sondheim Sings 'Move on,'" Broadwayworld.com.

15. See Chapter 1, Footnote 2.

16. *Up Close*, p. 250.

17. *Up Close*, p. 283.

18. "SEC Halts Short Selling of Financial Stocks," Securities and Exchange Commission press release, September 19, 2008.

19. Frequent comment, believed to have been first stated in 1992.

20. "The Greening of Palm Beach: Palm Beach Country Club," *New York Social Diary*, September 22, 2020; "Everglades Club," *Wikipedia*.

21. *Vanity Fair*, October 2002.

22. "Widow of Madoff Victim Sells NYC home for Massive loss," *New York Post*, April 13, 2018.

23. "Every Man for himself," *New York Times*, January 23, 2009.

24. "The Heartland Breach: A Cautionary Tale for e-Commerce," *Comodo Cybersecurity*, October 15, 2013.

25. U.S. Department of Justice press release, February 15, 2018.

26. Fred Schwed Jr., *Where Are the Customers' Yachts?* Wiley 2006.

CHAPTER 12

1. Fred Ebb (lyricist), "Money Makes the World Go Around," *Cabaret*, 1966.

2. "Half a Century Later, Economist's 'Creative Destruction' Theory Is Apt for the Internet Age," *New York Times*, June 10, 2000.

3. "The King of Wall Street," *Business Week*, December 22, 1985.

4. See Chapter 8, Footnote 5.
5. "One Bluff Too Many," *Newsweek*, August 25, 1991.
6. *Tycoons*, p. 606.
7. *Tycoons*, p. 613.
8. *Tycoons*, p. 643.
9. *Tycoons*, p. 628.
10. "Stifel Financial Expected to Acquire Thomas Weisel Partners," *The Wall Street Journal*, April 26, 2010.
11. "Altman's Double Life as a Politician Brings Him to the Edge of Scandal," *New York Times*, August 2, 1994.
12. "Evercore and Fleming Form Venture to Advise on Cross-Border Mergers," *The Wall Street Journal*, October 6, 1998.
13. Evercore Partners Inc. S-1 registration statement, filed with Securities and Exchange Commission Apr. 20, 2007.
14. "The Pressure of Great Expectations," *New York Times*, April 27, 2007.
15. "Boutique Bank that's Riding Out the Storm," *New York Times*, February 29, 2008.
16. "How a Thousand Quick Decisions Helped This Founder Survive the Financial Crisis," *Inc.,* June 2018.
17. "Moelis's Raid of UBS for New Firm Begins," *The Wall Street Journal*, May 2, 2007.

CHAPTER 13

1. Peter Benchley, *Jaws*, 1971.
2. "Clients Worried about Goldman's Many Hats," *New York Times*, May 18, 2010.
3. "Carl Icahn Relishes His Raider Role," *Los Angeles Times*, June 9, 1985.
4. Oliver Stone and Stanley Weiser, *Wall Street*, 1987.
5. Greenhill quarterly earnings announcement, January 26, 2010.
6. Greenhill quarterly earnings announcement, April 21, 2010.
7. Greenhill press release, March 16, 2010.
8. *The Lakeville Journal*, May 20, 2010.
9. "No Room in this Town for Change Brought by an Inn," *New York Times*, November 10, 2010.
10. "A Yellow Light for Greenhill Shares," *Barron's*, May 15, 2010.
11. "Growing Greenhill Faces Pay Puzzle," *The Wall Street Journal*, April 26, 2011.

12. "Greenhill's George Said to Leave as Departures Quicken," *Bloomberg*, July 15, 2011.
13. *The Wall Street Journal*, July 15, 2011.
14. *Financial Times*, July 17, 2011.
15. "Finance Firm Is Still Too Pricey," *Barron's*, July 23, 2011.

CHAPTER 14

1. Bruce Springsteen "One Minute You're Here," *Letter to You*, 2020.
2. *Bloomberg*, December 20, 2011.
3. *New York Post*, December 21, 2011.
4. "Pilot in Fatal I-287 Plane Crash Tried to Declare Emergency," *CBS News New York*, December 24, 2011.
5. National Transportation Safety Board report, January 25, 2013.
6. Frank Capra, *It's a Wonderful Life*, 1947.

CHAPTER 15

1. Oscar Hammerstein II (lyricist), "You'll Never Walk Alone," *Carousel*, 1945.
2. Fred Ebb, "New York, New York," 1977.
3. "Post Party, Banker Killed on AC Road Trip," *New York Post*, August 2, 2012.
4. Believed to be paraphrased from Woody Hayes, *Football at Ohio State*, 1957.
5. "Cut His Dividend? Good Luck with That," *Crain's New York Business*, November 26, 2011.
6. Greenhill earnings Q2 2012 earnings call teleconference, July 19, 2011.
7. Author speech script.

CHAPTER 16

1. Oscar Hammerstein II (lyricist), "Many a New Day," *Oklahoma*, 1943.
2. Warren Buffett, 1986 annual letter to Berkshire Hathaway shareholders.
3. *Financial Times*, October 27, 2015.
4. "Review: 'Dry Powder,' A High-Finance Comedy Drama," *New York Times*, March 22, 2016.
5. *Financial Times*, January 23, 2017.

6. "Wall Street Made Charles Murphy Successful and Rich, but Happiness Eluded Him," *The Wall Street Journal*, April 9, 2017.
7. *The Wall Street Journal*, September 26, 2017.

CHAPTER 17

1. Fred Ebb (lyricist), "Sunrise, Sunset," *Fiddler on the Roof*, 1964.
2. *Bloomberg*, March 26, 2018.
3. Emails dated February 1 and February 12, 2018. Unless otherwise noted (as is the case here), all emails referenced were addressed either to or from the author.
4. William D. Cohan, *Power Failure*, Portfolio, 2022.
5. "Succession," HBO Television series, 2018–2023.
6. *Up Close*, p. 299.

CHAPTER 18

1. See Chapter 10, Footnote 2.
2. The Museum of Modern Art announcement, July 14, 2020.
3. Apr. 3, 2015.
4. Governor Cuomo statement, March 1, 2020.
5. "Merkel Gives Germans a Hard Truth about the Coronavirus," *New York Times*, March 12, 2020.
6. February 29, 2020, email from author.
7. March 11, 2020, email from author.
8. "NY Declares State of Emergency," *CNBC*, March 12, 2020.
9. Martin Seligman, *Learned Optimism*, Vintage 2006.
10. Martin Seligman, "A Simple Exercise to Stay Calm," *Penn Today*, March 13, 2020.
11. March 16, 2020, email from author.
12. "During George Floyd Protests, 2 lawyers' Futures Went Up in flames," *New York Times*, January 26, 2023.
13. June 4, 2020, email from author.
14. "In Biggs, Wall Street Loses the Voice of a Bygone Era," *The Wall Street Journal*, July 16, 2012.
15. "Fed Sticks to Whatever It Takes with No Sign of Virus Easing," *Bloomberg*, July 29, 2020.

16. "Jamie Dinan's York Capital Management to Largely wind Down Hedge Fund Operations," *The Wall Street Journal*, November 24, 2020.
17. "Coronavirus Deals a Blow to M&A Boom," *Financial Times*, June 30, 2020.

CHAPTER 19

1. Alain Boublil and Jean-Marc Natel (lyricists, original French) and Herbert Kretzmer (lyricist, English-language libretto), "One Day More," *Les Miserables*, 1978.
2. "1271 Avenue of the Americas," *Wikipedia*.
3. "How 'Hamilton' Got $30 million in Federal Aid," *New York Times*, June 29, 2021.
4. Attributed to Mark Twain.
5. *Bloomberg*, December 19, 2020.
6. "From Crypto Art to Trading Cards, Investment Manias Abound," *New York Times*, March 13, 2021.
7. "Franklin Templeton to Acquire Lexington Partners," Franklin Templeton press release, November 1, 2021.
8. "Goldman's Junior Bankers Complain of Crushing Workload amid SPAC-fueled Boom in Wall Street Deals," *CNBC*, March 18, 2021.
9. "Great Resignation," *Wikipedia*.
10. "Feeling Blah During the Pandemic? It's Called Languishing," *New York Times*, December 3, 2021.
11. "Covid-19 Pandemic Triggers 25% Increase in Prevalence of Anxiety and Depression Worldwide," World Health Organization press release, March 2, 2022.
12. "Columbia University Student Dies in Stabbing Near Campus," *New York Times*, December 3, 2021.
13. "The Schuyler Sisters," *Hamilton*, 2015.

CHAPTER 20

1. Julie Taymor (lyricist), "Endless Night," *Lion King*, 1996.
2. *RBG*, Storyville Films and CNN Films, 2018, and *On the Basis of Sex*, Focus Features et al., 2018.
3. "TEGNA CEO Apologizes for Racial Incident," *Deadline*, March 9, 2021.
4. TEGNA proxy statement filed with Securities and Exchange Commission, April 13, 2022.

5. Mike Tyson, 1987.
6. "Protesters Crash Convocation, Cutting Liz Magill's First Speech Short," *The Daily Pennsylvanian,* August 29, 2022.
7. "Sharp Decline in Deal Making Brings Pandemic-Era Frenzy to a Halt," *Financial Times,* December 29, 2022.
8. Author speech script.
9. "Ezra Klein: On the Topic of Working at Home," *New York Times,* September 17, 2022.
10. "SVB-fueled Turmoil Junks Lessons of the Global Financial Crisis," *The Wall Street Journal,* May 21, 2023.
11. "UBS to Acquire Credit Suisse," UBS press release, March 19, 2023.
12. "Credit Suisse Flags $450 Million Impairment on York Capital Management Stake," *Reuters,* November 24, 2020.
13. "UBS Agrees to Buy Credit Suisse for More Than $3 Billion," *The Wall Street Journal,* March 19, 2023.

CHAPTER 21

1. Joni Mitchell, "Circle Game," *Ladies of the Canyon,* 1966.
2. Ecclesiastes 3:1.
3. Pete Seeger, "Turn! Turn! Turn!" 1959.
4. "Estée Lauder's Beauty Empire, Aiming at New Markets," *New York Times,* March 26, 2011.
5. "Number of Listed Companies for United States," Federal Reserve Bank of St. Louis, updated March 23, 2022.
6. *Up Close,* p. 257.
7. "How Japan Got its Swagger Back," *Financial Times,* May 19, 2023.
8. Genesis 7:4; Exodus 34:28; 1 Samuel 17:4–7, 15; Matthew 4:1–11; Acts 1:3.

CHAPTER 22

1. Harry E. Westervelt, *The Red and Blue,* 1898.
2. September 6, 2023, email received by author.
3. "Harvard Gets Worst Ever in FIRE's Free Speech Rankings," Foundation for Individual Rights and Expression (FIRE), September 6, 2023.

4. Benjamin Franklin, "Silence Dogood, No. 8," printed in *The New-England Courant*, July 9, 1722.
5. *The Atlantic*, Sept. 2015.
6. "Behind the Story: Free Speech Controversy at Stanford," *New York Times*, April 12, 2023.
7. September 13, 2023, email received by author.
8. August 25, 2023, email received by author.
9. "In Tense Times at Penn, Enter Farrakhan," *New York Times*, April 11, 1988.
10. "Statement on Palestine Writes Literature Festival," University of Pennsylvania, September 12, 2023.
11. *Daily Pennsylvanian*, October 16, 2023.
12. "Top UPenn Supporters Protest Their Alma Mater's Antisemitic Festival," *Jewish Insider*, September 22, 2023 (alumni letter attached).
13. "Global Private Equity Report 2024," Bain & Co., March 11, 2024.
14. "Penn's Message to Anti-Defamation League CEO Jonathan Greenblatt," September 20, 2023.
15. "UPenn Donors Were Furious about the Palestine Writes Literature Festival. What about It Made Them Pull Their Funds?" *CNN*, October 25, 2023.
16. Ibid.
17. Merriam-Webster.com.

CHAPTER 23

1. Lin-Manuel Miranda. "Story of Tonight," *Hamilton*, 2015.
2. "A Message from Liz Magill on the Terrorist Attacks in Israel," University of Pennsylvania, October 10, 2023.
3. "Marc Rowan: The Opinion Piece the University of Pennsylvania Didn't Want You to Read," *PhillyVoice*, October 14, 2023.
4. Marc Rowan, *CNBC.com*, October 12, 2023.
5. "Statement on the Death of George Floyd," University of Pennsylvania, May 30, 2020.
6. *American Prospect*, October 21, 2023.
7. October 15, 2023, email received by author.
8. Jon M. Huntsman Sr., *Barefoot to Billionaire*, Overlook Duckworth, Peter Mayer Publishers 2014, p. 507.
9. October 17, 2023, email received by author.
10. "Statutes of the Trustees, as Amended on March 3, 2023," secretary.upenn.edu.

11. *Daily Pennsylvanian*, October 16, 2023.
12. "A Chant Used at Anti-Israel Protests on Two College Campuses Does Not Call for 'Jewish Genocide,'" *Associated Press*, October 31, 2023.
13. October 16, 2023, email received by author.
14. October 30, 2023, email received by author.
15. October 27, 2023, email received by author.
16. October 30, 2023, email received by author.
17. October 30, 2023, email received by author.
18. October 30, 2023, email received by author.
19. "The Ivy League, Wall St Donors and the Furor over Antisemitism," *Financial Times*, December 10, 2023.
20. November 12, 2023, email received by author.
21. See Footnote 19.
22. *New York Post*, November 16, 2023.
23. Ibid.
24. "Greenhill Starts Mizuho with Costly Culture Clash," *Reuters Breakingviews*, October 27, 2023.
25. See Footnote 6.
26. "Penn Community Members occupy Part of Houston Hall in teach-in," *Daily Pennsylvanian*, November 14, 2023.
27. "For Palestinian Students Shot in Vermont, a Collision of Two Worlds," *New York Times*, December 3, 2023.
28. Shortform.com summary of Michael Lewis, *The Big Short*.
29. "Transcript: What Harvard, MIT and Penn Presidents Said at Antisemitism Hearing," rollcall.com.
30. Rep. Elise Stefanik (@RepStefanik), X, May 12, 2022.
31. *New York Times*, July 26, 2022.
32. "Resignation of Board of Trustees Chair Scott Bok," *University of Pennsylvania Almanac*, December 9, 2023.
33. "Code of Student Conduct," catalog.upenn.edu.
34. "Penn President Liz Magill's Antisemitism Testimony Brings Resignation Pressures," *Philadelphia Inquirer*, December 9, 2023.
35. December 11, 2023, email received by author.
36. December 8, 2023, email received by author.
37. See Footnote 32.
38. "Donors Should Not Decide Campus Policies," *Philadelphia Inquirer*, December 12, 2023.

39. December 12, 2023, email received by author.
40. "Penn Faculty Letter to Trustees," December 2023.
41. *Six by Sondheim*, HBO, 2013.
42. Theodore Roosevelt, speech at the Sorbonne in Paris, April 23, 1910.

ABOUT THE AUTHOR

Scott L. Bok built a career on Wall Street as a corporate advisor and deal-maker during a period of extraordinary expansion that was punctuated by intermittent crises. His work has encompassed mergers and acquisitions, private equity, IPOs, SPACs, debt restructurings, activist shareholders and assorted boardroom dramas.

After a brief stint as a mergers and acquisitions (M&A) lawyer, he spent more than a decade in Morgan Stanley's New York and London offices before joining the M&A specialist Greenhill & Co. in its start-up phase. He served twenty-eight years at Greenhill, including sixteen years as CEO.

During his time at Greenhill the firm undertook a major global expansion and engineered a wildly successful first-of-its-kind IPO, much later a leveraged recapitalization, and ultimately a sale to a major global bank.

He has played a boardroom role at numerous nonprofits, rising to board chairman at the University of Pennsylvania, the American Museum of Natural History and Prep for Prep. In the Penn role he was at the center of a controversy that marked the start of a period of nationwide campus protests unlike anything since the Vietnam War period.

Born in Grand Rapids, Michigan, today he and his wife of forty-three years divide their time between Manhattan, a farm in Connecticut's Litchfield hills and south Florida. They have two adult children.

INDEX

Sinatra, Frank, 282

Singapore, 42

Sipprelle, Scott, 159–161, 165, 166

Smartphones, 82

Smith Barney, xii, 11–13, 25, 27, 28,
30, 35, 38, 40, 45, 69, 70, 73,
81, 109, 110, 231, 262, 334,
374, 402

Socata (plane), 270–271

Social media, 441, 442, 445, 449,
452, 453

Sofitel Hotel (New York City),
312

Solomon, David, 135

Solotar, Joan, 125–127

Sondheim, Stephen, 59, 93,
139, 179, 201–202,
377–378, 414

Sound Point, 319

South Dakota, 153–154, 344

South Pacific (musical), 171

SPACs (special purpose acquisition
companies), 186–189, 196–198,
204, 208, 221, 241–243,
247–248, 267, 288, 303, 372,
373–374, 447

Spain, 407

Spanish flu pandemic, 378

Spitzer, Eliot, 118–120, 181,
327–328, 405

Spring Awakening (musical), 179

Springsteen, Bruce, 80, 265

Squawk Box (television program),
436, 437

SSAB (Swedish steel company),
174, 178, 180, 186

Stagflation, 6

Standard & Poor's (S&P),
63, 317, 320

Stanford Law School, 381

Stanford University, 385–386, 422

Stanley, Harold, 7

State Street Bank, 318

State University of New York, 454

Stefanik, Elise, 452, 454, 458

Steichen, Alfred, 75, 347

Steinbeck, John, 16

Stern, Edouard, 110

Stewart, Jimmy, 277

Stifel Financial, 230

Stock market crash (1929), 196

Stock market crash (1987),
57–58, 172

Stone, Oliver, 23, 25, 246

Streep, Meryl, 258

Succession (television show), 335

Sullivan, Martin, 194–195

Summers, Lawrence, 56

Sunday in the Park with George
(musical), 201, 377

Sunday Times Magazine,
22, 23, 308

Supreme Court, 86, 384, 386, 395

Sweeney Todd (musical), 414

Swiss Bank, 50

Swiss Banking Corporation
(SBC), 236

Switzerland, 5, 400